Special Education Assessment

Issues and Strategies Affecting Today's Classrooms

Effie P. Kritikos
Northeastern Illinois University

Merrill
Upper Saddle River, New Jersey
Columbus, Ohio

Library of Congress Cataloging-in-Publication Data

Kritikos, Effie P.
  Special education assessment : issues and strategies affecting today's classrooms / Effie P. Kritikos.
    p. cm.
  ISBN-13: 978-0-13-170064-2
  ISBN-10: 0-13-170064-2
  1. Special education—Evaluation—Textbooks.   2. Children with disabilities—Education—Evaluation—Textbooks.
  I. Title.
  LC4015.K73 2010
  371.9'043—dc22   2008053922

Vice President and Editor in Chief: Jeffery W. Johnston
Executive Editor: Ann Castel Davis
Editorial Assistant: Penny Burleson
Senior Managing Editor: Pamela D. Bennett
Senior Project Manager: Sheryl Glicker Langner
Project Coordination: Rebecca K. Giusti, GGS Higher Education Resources
Art Director: Candace Rowley
Photo Coordinator: Valerie Schultz
Cover Image: SuperStock
Cover Design: Rachel Hirschi
Senior Operations Supervisor: Matthew Ottenweller
Operations Specialist: Laura Messerly
Vice President, Director of Sales & Marketing: Quinn Perkson
Marketing Manager: Erica DeLuca
Marketing Coordinator: Brian Mounts

This book was set in Galliard by GGS Higher Education Resources. It was printed and bound by Edwards Brothers, Inc. The cover was printed by Edwards Brothers, Inc.

Chapter Opening Photo Credits: David Mager/Pearson Learning Photo Studio, p. 2; Pearson Scott Foresman, p. 18; Anthony Magnacca/Merrill, pp. 36, 82, 122, 230; Scott Cunningham/Merrill, p. 58; Rubber Ball Productions, p. 142; Ken Karp/Prentice Hall School Division, p. 162; Lori Whitley/Merrill, p. 184; Frank Siteman, p. 206; T. Lindfors/Lindfors Photography, p. 266; Laima Druskis/PH College, p. 288.

Pearson® is a registered trademark of Pearson plc
Merrill® is a registered trademark of Pearson Education, Inc.

Pearson Education Ltd., London
Pearson Education Singapore, Pte. Ltd.
Pearson Education Canada, Inc.
Pearson Education—Japan
Pearson Education Australia PTY, Limited

Pearson Education North Asia, Ltd., Hong Kong
Pearson Educación de Mexico, S.A. de C.V.
Pearson Education Malaysia, Pte. Ltd.
Pearson Education Upper Saddle River, New Jersey

Merrill
is an imprint of

www.pearsonhighered.com

10 9 8 7 6 5 4 3 2 1

ISBN 13: 978-0-13-170064-2
ISBN 10:   0-13-170064-2

Providing appropriate assessment services for students requires an authentic standards- and performance-based approach provided by someone with expertise in diversity, technology, and legal issues. The ultimate goal in assessment is to provide a link from assessment to instruction. *Special Education Assessment: Issues and Strategies Affecting Today's Classrooms* was written to ground future teachers' learning in research-based and practical information so they can better serve their students.

This book includes current legal changes, as well as the latest revisions of formal and informal assessments. Different types of assessments are discussed in relation to the decision-making process. Information regarding response to intervention (RTI) is integrated in the text. Accommodations and modifications are explained in the discussion and context of various disabilities.

Field-based case studies present real-life scenarios and are included in each chapter. Breakpoint practices, end-of-chapter activities, discussion of case study applications, illustrations of assessment tools, and lists of websites provide resources for self-assessment and higher-level analysis.

This text is organized into four parts. Part 1, "Foundations of Special Education Assessment," facilitates students' learning in the areas of understanding special education assessment and its legal requirements, reliability and validity, norms and test scores, and curriculum-based assessments. The reauthorization of Individuals with Disabilities Education Act (IDEA), No Child Left Behind, and Section 504 are discussed in this part. Technical information related to formal testing, curriculum-based measurement and informal assessment, and multicultural considerations are explained.

Part 2, "Assessing Performance Skills," includes behavioral, cognitive, and adaptive skills; achievement; and receptive and expressive language assessment. Definitions, formal and informal assessment measures, and multicultural considerations are analyzed in this part. Technical information is discussed, and examples are provided to facilitate the understanding of these content areas.

Part 3, "Additional Considerations," addresses early childhood assessment; assessing students with visual, motor, and/or hearing disabilities; and transition assessment. Definitions, formal and informal assessment measures, and multicultural considerations are discussed in the context of family involvement and assistive technologies.

Part 4, "Interpreting and Linking Assessment to Instruction," includes interpreting tests and reports. Components of an evaluation report, student comparisons, communicating results, linking assessment to instruction, and multicultural considerations are described in this part.

FEATURES OF THE TEXT

Each chapter includes the following features to support the comprehension, reflection, and application of subject matter:

- **Case study:** A case study grounds each chapter in a real-life, context-based scenario, allowing students to assess their skills at the beginning and end of the chapter.
- **Breakpoint practice:** Self-assessment follows each main section of the chapter to utilize higher-level applications, thus creating a more robust understanding of the material and at the same time making the material more relevant.
- **Multicultural considerations:** Current research-based, appropriate material is discussed in its own section regarding the content of each chapter, giving students opportunity for reflection on the subject areas as they relate to students who are linguistically and culturally diverse.
- **Review of current assessments:** Technical and practical information regarding the most utilized formal and informal assessments in each content area is analyzed and discussed.

ACKNOWLEDGMENTS

I would like to express my deepest appreciation to students and colleagues at Northeastern Illinois University who supported me in the development of this project. In particular, I would like to thank Barry Birnbaum, Sandra Beyda-Lorie, and Phyllis Le Dosquet for contributing chapters in this book. I would also like to thank the experts who reviewed this manuscript: Jeffrey Bakken, Illinois State University; Susan Bruce, Boston College; Marlaine Chase, University of Southern Indiana; Katherine Cook, Missouri Western State College; Lee Cross, University of Central Florida; Ronald Drossman, Northern Arizona University; Preston Feden, La Salle University; Dan Fennerty, Central Washington University; Barbara Fulk, Illinois State University; Kim Goodfellow, State of South Dakota Schools; Bob Ives, University of Nevada at Reno; Margaret McLane, The College of St. Rose; Jamey Nystrom, Frostburg State University; A. Sandy Parsons, California State University—San Marcos; Paul Riccomini, Clemson University; Roberta Strosnider, Towson University; and Cheryl Wissick, University of South Carolina.

I would like to thank the many students who provided valuable input that enhanced this book.

I would also like to thank my family, including Harry, Anton, Lia, my parents, Aglaia and Tom, and my sister, Vicky, for their immeasurable encouragement.

BRIEF CONTENTS

CONTENTS

NOTE: Every effort has been made to provide accurate and current Internet information in this book. However, the Internet and information posted on it are constantly changing, so it is inevitable that some of the Internet addresses listed in this textbook will change.

Foundations of Special Education Assessment

The Law and Special Education

Barry W. Birnbaum

due process: Guarantees that the parents will be equal participants in the development of the IEP and there will be safeguards in the administration of the child's program.

equal protection: Guaranteed by the U.S. Constitution.

free appropriate public education (FAPE): All students can and will learn when given the opportunity to do so, which includes educational and related services.

nondiscriminatory assessment: The evaluation must be administered in the student's native language or other appropriate form of communication. The instruments used must be standardized for the purpose for which they are being used and must be administered by properly trained administrators.

parental participation: The parents are responsible for giving written permission for testing and evaluation, participating in the decision to place the child, participating in the development of the IEP, providing feedback during the triennial evaluation, and advocating for the child.

least restrictive environment (LRE): A range of placements, from self-contained to full inclusion, for delivery of special education and related services.

individual education plan (IEP): The educational plan designed to meet the individual needs of each student. The IEP is a legal document and is based on the data generated through assessment of the child by the child study team.

individual transition plan (ITP): Must be included in a student's IEP by the time he or she reaches age 16. The transition plan is developed around meeting the needs of the child once she or he leaves high school.

individual family service plan (IFSP): The IFSP is similar to an IEP, however, it is written for children from birth to 3 years of age and includes a stronger family component.

prereferral: Includes screening and interventions that are attempted before a full referral is made.

referral: A referral is completed only after a prereferral has been made and interventions have been attempted. The referral includes an extensive and comprehensive evaluation of the child's abilities, including achievement and intellectual functioning.

response to intervention: A technique that evaluates the child based on academically proven research strategies that are effective in the remediation process.

Assessing Sandy: A Case Study

Sandy is a student who is 10 years old and in the fifth grade. She was referred for special education because of poor academic performance throughout her school years. Sandy is in your classroom and you have identified that she has problems processing information and paying attention to directions. You have attempted prereferral strategies in the classroom and she still exhibits difficulties. Sandy's mother has left you a message with questions regarding the evaluation process, including the paperwork and her legal rights. Sandy is also bilingual. Her mother has requested involvement of an interpreter or bilingual professional in Spanish.

What information do you provide Sandy's mother?

What other individuals should be involved in the discussion?

What are Sandy's rights?

You will be able to answer all of these questions after reading this chapter. You will also be able to identify what laws would benefit Sandy in the long run. You will have a better understanding of cases that have shaped the history of special education and service delivery. You will be able to understand the aspects of your legal responsibility to utilize assessments related to initial placement and continuous assessment linked to instruction, and you will be able to explain the rules governing assessment of students receiving special education services. You will understand the placement process and its continuum of services. You will learn about the IEP, ITP, and IFSP.

The Council for Exceptional Children (CEC), Content Standard 1, specifically addresses the use of legal and judicial systems that deal with special education (http://www.cec.sped.org/ps/perf_bases_stds/standards.html). These standards are endorsed by the National Council for Accreditation of Teacher Education (NCATE) (http://www.ncate.org). Colleges and universities have been responsible for providing teacher-training courses that prepare candidates to work with students with disabilities while entitling them to a free, appropriate public education (FAPE).

HISTORY OF FEDERAL LEGISLATION

Since the 1970s, federal law has dictated the role special education takes with regard to students, their placement in classrooms, their individual needs, and their education. These laws have evolved and improved through the years to bring a clearer picture of how services in special education are delivered to students. Some of these laws have been taken to the courts, where interpretations of them abound (Birnbaum, 2006).

Since the passage of Public Law 94-142 (P.L. 94-142) in 1975, also known as the Education for All Handicapped Children Act (EAHCA), the federal government has outlined a series of steps that protect the rights of children with disabilities. It did not take a simple law, however, to motivate the Congress of the United States. Their actions were based on previous cases that involved the decisions of lower courts within local, state, and federal jurisdictions.

The civil rights of individuals with disabilities were not protected to this point. Those who advocated for people with disabilities sought relief through the court and sometimes fought a difficult battle. Some of the court decisions provided civil rights to persons with disabilities that had not previously existed and ensured these guarantees and promises. As the twentieth century progressed, more laws were passed that provided more legislation that favored persons with disabilities. Most of these laws, including P.L. 94-142, were based on previous court decisions that ruled in favor of individuals with disabilities. A few key court decisions are examined next.

Brown v. Board of Education of Topeka, Kansas, was ruled on by the U.S. Supreme Court in 1954. This law ended the "separate but equal" manner in which Caucasian children and African American children were treated. No longer could white children and black children be taught in different classrooms and schools. All children were given the right to attend the same school, and it was determined that African American children were being denied their constitutional rights under the Fourteenth Amendment to the U.S. Constitution. This landmark legislation overturned *Plessy v. Ferguson* 1896, which upheld that separate schools were permissible because they were seen as equal.

The *Brown v. Board of Education* ruling ended segregation in schools that had existed for years. The ruling had an impact on special education some twenty years later because it became the basis of court rulings that determined that students with disabilities were being taught in separate environments from their nondisabled peers.

This law was the basis for determining that similar discrimination occurred when it came to teaching children with disabilities.

In *Hobson v. Hansen* (1967), it was determined that African American children were being placed in lower educational tracks in the Washington, DC, public schools. While all students were placed in public schools, the problem was that students from lower socioeconomic status or from minority groups were being discriminated against. Most of the tests used were normed on white, middle-class children, which discriminated against other racial groups. Some students from minority groups were erroneously labeled and placed in segregated classrooms, such as those that provided services to children with special needs, particularly mental retardation.

This resulted in African American students being taught a curriculum that was significantly different than the one being taught to other students. The court ruled that this was discriminatory and that it forced students to receive an inferior education. It was determined that the practices of using standardized tests that were normed on only one population must cease and that compensatory education must be provided.

The Pennsylvania Association for Retarded Children (PARC) sued the Commonwealth of Pennsylvania in 1972. This case, *PARC v. Commonwealth of Pennsylvania*, became one of the more important ones dealing with provision of services in special education. The suit was brought by a group of parents with children with mental retardation who felt that their children were being taught in separate schools because of their disability. This case was based on due process and equal protection as guaranteed by the U.S. Constitution.

The ruling determined that the schools could not serve children with mental retardation by segregating them from the public schools. Those students who resided in Pennsylvania were given the right to attend public schools and interact with their peers who were nondisabled. This was considered a landmark decision because it stopped segregation of children with disabilities. It became the foundation for the least restrictive environment (LRE) portion of the law.

The next case, *Mills v. Board of Education of the District of Columbia* (1972), was a class action suit that stated that the plaintiffs (children with behavioral disorders, hyperactivity, emotional problems, and mental retardation) had been suspended, transferred, expelled, and reassigned without due process. They were denied an equal opportunity to a free and appropriate public education. The decision of the court reinforced the rights of the children with disabilities to a free and appropriate public education (FAPE).

In *Diana v. Board of Education*, the courts ruled again about standardized tests. This case, which took place in 1970, was filed on behalf of nine Mexican American students. These students were placed in classrooms for special education in California based on the administration of intelligence tests in English that were once again normed on a white population, with items that were considered culturally biased. The court stated that students should be compared to their peers rather than to nonminority groups of children. This case ensured that nonbiased testing was considered for all children.

Larry P. v. Riles was a case that was similar to *Diana v. Board of Education*, with the only difference being that the plaintiff was African American. The case determined that the assessments used were biased and that the educational placement was discriminatory, because in both situations, IQ tests were used as the basis of ability. The issue in this case was that the tests had not been standardized on an appropriate population that included minority students. Because of the testing, a significantly large population of minority students was placed in classes for special education. The ruling also addressed the issue that no students, particularly minorities, could be placed in classes for students with disabilities until nonbiased tests were developed and administered. States were forced to retest all students in programs assigned for children with exceptional needs and to provide them with compensatory education.

Advocacy groups continued to pursue legislation that would provide due process and civil rights to children with disabilities. Congress was impressed with the amount of advocacy on behalf of persons with disabilities and by the number of laws passed to support these individuals. This motivated the U.S. Congress to pursue federal legislation that would forever change the way people with disabilities were treated.

SECTION 504

The Rehabilitation Act of 1973 was considered the first law to guarantee civil rights to persons with disabilities. This law, known as Section 504, stated:

> No otherwise qualified individual with a disability in the United States . . . shall, solely by reason of her or his disability, be excluded from the participation in, denied the benefits of, or be subjected to discrimination under any program or activity receiving federal financial assistance or under any program or activity receiving federal assistance or under any program or activity conducted by any Executive agency or by the United States Postal Service. (29 U.S.C. § 794).

This law clearly made it mandatory that federal programs could not discriminate against persons with disabilities, and it extended the rights previously granted to minorities. This act does not promise funding for persons with disabilities, but it does afford rights previously not granted to a segment of society. The act allows individuals to file a complaint with the U.S. Department of Education (DOE) if discrimination occurs. The DOE can investigate and determine whether discrimination against a child with a disability has taken place. If it is so determined, the DOE has the power, with judicial oversight, to terminate federal funds to the school in question. It has done so in the past. A person with a disability may also sue school districts directly and, as the claimant, can collect damages and attorney's fees if his or her case is successful.

Breakpoint Practice

1. How did Section 504 come about?
2. What are the requirements of Section 504?
3. How do these laws affect you in the classroom?

P.L. 94-142

Public Law 94-142, the Education of All Handicapped Children Act of 1975 (EAHCA), was the major law Congress passed that provided equal rights for children with disabilities and protected them under the Fourteenth Amendment of the U.S. Constitution. This law is required reading for anyone in special education and has a great deal to do with educating persons with disabilities (Crowell, 1989). Everyone who deals with children in special education has to understand not only the spirit of the law, but its content as well. A working knowledge and practical application of the law must be understood as a basis for understanding special education law. Those laws that followed or superseded P.L. 94-142 are based on the premise of it.

P.L. 94-142 was a basic bill of rights for children with disabilities that included federal funding for the increased financial responsibilities placed on the states to educate these children (Murdick, Gartin, & Crabtree, 2002). The basic premise of the law was to (a) provide a free appropriate public education (FAPE) to students with disabilities in the public schools while providing necessary related services that these children would need, (b) protect children with disabilities and their parents from discrimination, (c) help the state education agencies (SEAs) and local education agencies (LEAs) grant a free appropriate public education to students with disabilities, and (d) evaluate and guarantee the efficacy of educating these students.

This act was developed for the purpose of providing educational services to a group of students otherwise excluded from the public schools (Murdick et al., 2002). According to the law, students must first demonstrate that they have mental retardation, visual impairments, auditory impairments, learning disabilities, behavior or emotional disorders, orthopedic impairments, traumatic brain injury, autism, deaf-blindness, or multiple handicaps. Second, students must demonstrate that because of these impairments, they have unique needs for special services to be able to benefit from their educational experiences [34 C.F.R. § 300.7(a)(1)]. The law covered children between the ages of 3 and 21. Those students between the ages of 3 and 5 may receive special services if they are experiencing developmental delays in certain areas. The law has eight parts that are important to understand when working with children with special needs.

The first part, zero reject, implies that all children, regardless of the severity of the disability, are provided services for a free and appropriate public education (FAPE). This part of the law assumes that all students can and will learn when given the opportunity to do so. This is known in the law as a free, appropriate public education (FAPE), which includes educational and related services. Among related services, physical therapy, occupational therapy, and speech therapy are included.

These services are to be provided at the expense of the public and free of charge to the parent and student. It is also important that the SEA include services in preschool, elementary school, and high school. These services are to be provided in conjunction with an individual education plan (IEP) that meets the individual needs of the child.

Nondiscriminatory assessment is the second part of P.L. 94-142. Once children with special needs are placed in the public school, they are to be appropriately evaluated and assessed. This is accomplished by designing and conducting a nondiscriminatory evaluation. The evaluation must be administered in the student's native language or other appropriate form of communication. The instruments used must be standardized for the purpose for which they are being used. Properly trained administrators must be utilized to administer such diagnostic tools. No single measurement or device may be used to determine whether a child is eligible for services (Murdick et al., 2002).

The evaluation must include a multidisciplinary approach where several professionals from various disciplines take part in the decision-making process. The parent is also to be included because she or he has expert status by review of the background knowledge she or he possesses about the child and his or her development. This parent is to be fully informed and to actively participate.

The third part, procedural due process, is one of the most important components of the law. Procedural due process guarantees that the parents will be equal participants in the development of the IEP and that there will be safeguards in the administration of the youngster's program. These safeguards include the protection of parents if they disagree with the decision of the school. Procedural due process also gives the parents the opportunity to refuse placement, as well as the right to refuse to make a written referral for evaluation, if they feel it is wrong. This refusal would then involve due process litigation, which brings in an impartial due process hearing officer to decide whether the school or parent has the best interest of the child in mind.

Parental participation, the fourth part of P.L. 94-142, guarantees that the parents are pivotal components of the multidisciplinary team (MDT). The parents are responsible for giving written permission for testing and evaluation, actively participating in the decision to place the child in LRE, participating in the development of the IEP, providing feedback in the triennial evaluation (an evaluation that occurs every third year) to determine whether there is continued need for special education and related services, and advocating for the child. Parents may also participate at the state level by advocating for all children who are disabled (Murdick et al., 2002).

The fifth part, the least restrictive environment (LRE), states that the best placement for a child with disabilities is in the regular classroom: ideally, in the same classroom she would attend and in the same school she would attend if she did not have a disability. Within the continuum of services, ranging from self-contained classrooms to inclusion, students are to be placed where they will be most successful. The basic tenet of LRE allows for children with disabilities, including those in public and private schools or other care facilities, to be educated with children who are not disabled and that any placement outside the regular classroom occurs only when the nature or severity of the disability is such that the student cannot be taught in regular classes (34 C.F.R. § 300.500).

The IEP, the sixth part of P.L. 94-142, is essential to the provision of a free, appropriate public education of children with disabilities. An IEP is a legally binding document written for a child who is disabled; it is developed according to the requirements of the law. It is the means by which an appropriate educational program is developed for the child with exceptionalities. It also directs how the child will be taught and how services will be provided.

The IEP must include a statement of (1) the child's current level of educational performance; (2) annual goals, including short-term objectives; (3) specific special education and related services that will be provided; (4) the degree to which a child is able to participate in the general curriculum; (5) the dates for the beginning of services and the anticipated length the services will be in effect; and (6) appropriate objective criteria and evaluation procedures and schedules for determining how well the short-term objectives are being attained (Murdick et al., 2002).

A transition plan must also be included. Discussion involving school-to-adult transition issues begins by age 14. No later than age 16 and earlier if deemed appropriate, the student's IEP must contain a statement of the transition services needed before the child leaves school. The transition plan must also include a statement indicating that transition services may not be needed if it has been so determined.

The IEP is developed collaboratively between the school personnel and the parents. The document itself states that parental input is paramount in the process of its development. The IEP holds schools accountable to the parents for delivery of instruction to students with special needs.

There have been several reauthorizations and amendments to EAHCA. Public Law 99-457, the Education of the Handicapped Act Amendments of 1986, expanded the original legislation to cover children with disabilities between the ages of 3 and 5. Funding for early intervention programs for young children with exceptionalities was addressed. This law expanded Part B of EAHCA. Part B deals with procedural safeguards guaranteed to children and parents as well as the funds that regulate special education.

IDEA (P.L. 101-476)

In 1990 the Individuals with Disabilities Education Act (IDEA), also known as P.L. 101-476, encouraged the use of "person first" language when describing disabilities. Part B was also amended so that services to children between the ages of 18 and

21 years could be described more properly. Transition services were more clearly defined and the role of assistive technology (AT) was added. Assistive technologies were included in the law so that students in need of such devices would be able to obtain them. Children with diagnostic categories of traumatic brain injury (TBI) and autism were also included as part of those considered disabled, thereby increasing the number of federally approved categories of disabilities by two.

In 1991, IDEA was reauthorized and was known as P.L. 102-119. The gist of these amendments was to reauthorize Part H, the section that deals with young children and funding for their services. Federal funds were allocated to help states educate infants, toddlers, preschoolers, children, and youth with disabilities (Murdick et al., 2002). Rather than require an IEP for children between birth and 3 years of age, an individual family service plan (IFSP) was required. The emphasis is on assisting the family to begin to understand the child and how the developmental delay/disability affects the family as well as the child. The process of early intervention is "family-focused" or "family-centered." Professionals are to support the family in determining its needs and deciding how those needs can best be met. The IFSP includes information about the child's status, family information, outcomes, early intervention services, dates, duration of services, service coordinator(s), and transition information from Part H (Murdick et al., 2002).

P.L. 105-17, the IDEA Amendments of 1997, changed the basic structure of the antagonistic relationship between parents and schools (Gorn, 1997). The legislation protected the educational rights of students who were disabled but were violent or dangerous, while giving educators opportunities to remove such children from their current educational placement. This amendment also mandated that schools include students with exceptionalities in local, district, and statewide assessments. These amendments also required mediation as an option so that parents and schools would have an additional outlet for settling disputes that might otherwise be given due process.

P.L. 105-17 also changed the way schools receive federal funds. The amendments permit local districts to seek assistance when paying for assistive technology (AT), related services, and supplementary devices so that the cost is spread across different agencies. The districts had to pay for many of these services out of tax funds and received little, if any, relief from other sources.

Other laws support those provided under IDEA. P.L. 93-112, the Rehabilitation Act of 1973, and P.L. 101-336, the Americans with Disabilities Act (ADA) of 1990, provide antidiscrimination legislation at the federal level (Murdick et al., 2002). First and Curcio (1993) stated that the ADA was probably the most sweeping legislation since the passage of EAHCA in 1975 and that it provided a comprehensive national mandate that eliminated discrimination against individuals with disabilities.

Yell (1998) defines the different parts of the laws that govern special education and provides a historical perspective of how these laws came to be. For many years, children with disabilities were excluded from schools and received little or no services. It took many years for the legislation to come about, so there are many stories of abuse of children with disabilities in the years preceding the enactment of the current legislation.

For example, in the 1800s, students with disabilities were excluded from schools under court order. In 1893, the Massachusetts Supreme Judicial Court ruled that a child who was "weak in mind" could be expelled from public school (Yell, 1998; *Watson v. City of Cambridge*, 1893). Similar cases occurred through the early 1900s, and these cases, when challenged, were upheld by the courts. In one situation in 1919, a student was removed from school because he had a disability, even though he had attended school through the fifth grade (Yell, 1998).

NO CHILD LEFT BEHIND (NCLB)

The purpose of NCLB is to ensure that all students, including those with disabilities, are included in the monitoring process in order to provide appropriate instruction. The law is tied into standards-based assessment and instruction. Each state must monitor the schools for compliance, which translates into accountability issues at all levels, including the teachers and the schools (see Chapter 8 for more discussion). This law has caused the reshaping and rethinking of the educational school system paradigm.

Breakpoint Practice

1. How is IDEA 2004 different from P.L. 94-142?
2. How has NCLB affected the schools?
3. Why are IEPs, ITPs, and IFSPs such important documents?

PARENTAL ADVOCACY

Parental advocacy remains an important component of legal decisions affecting children and persons with disabilities. Parents began to form groups to discuss what they could do about the exclusion of their children from public schools and how they could best address their concerns. Yell (1998) states that the first such group formed in Ohio in 1933. The group, known as the Cuyahoga County Ohio Council for the Retarded Child consisted of five mothers who got together to protest the deplorable treatment their children received in being excluded from school. This protest helped to create a special classroom for these children, backed by the parents themselves. Without such past advocacy, the services provided to children with disabilities today would be a great deal less effective (Yell, 1998).

The parental advocacy movement was a large part of why the U.S. Congress enacted laws that supported children with disabilities. The parents were part of the process of writing the laws and advising Congress in making their decisions concerning the rights of persons with disabilities. While many think that the laws strongly favor the children, without these laws persons with disabilities would still be excluded from schools and the greater society.

Several organizations, such as the Council for Exceptional Children (CEC) (http://www.cec.sped.org), have spoken for persons with disabilities. Today, the CEC takes political stands on issues concerning disabilities. Through legal action, these organizations ensure that the rights of persons with disabilities are not infringed upon and that these individuals are treated equally and with respect.

Table 1.1   Legislation Concerning Special Education

1954	*Brown v. Board of Education*
1972	*PARC v. Commonwealth of Pennsylvania*
1973	Section 504 of the Rehabilitation Act of 1973
1974	P.L. 93-380, Education Amendments of 1974
1975	P.L. 94-142, Education for All Handicapped Children Act
1986	P.L. 99-457, Education of the Handicapped Amendments
1990	P.L. 101-476, IDEA
1990	P.L. 101-336, ADA
1997	P.L. 105-17, IDEA Amendments
2004	Reauthorization of IDEA

Breakpoint Practice

1. What are some of the important issues involving parental advocacy?
2. How are professional organizations connected to parental advocacy?
3. To which organizations in your area would you refer parents for advocacy issues?

ASSESSMENT AND THE LAW

Assessment serves many purposes. It is used for screening, placement, and evaluation of student progress. It is a cyclical process in special education because it never ends. A student is initially tested or assessed to determine whether he or she is eligible for services in special education when parents submit a written request for evaluation. When eligibility has been determined (the student has a disability and needs special education and/or related services), an IEP is collaboratively written and followed. The teacher frequently checks the student's progress against the IEP and reports data to the student and the parents, making changes as needed. If the student is not making progress on the IEP, the Multidisciplinary committee (MDC). schedules another meeting, reviews the most current data, and makes whatever modifications are required in order for the child to be more successful. Assessment is used to determine whether a child is eligible for special education. The team determines whether a disability exists and to what extent the disability is interfering with the child's school progress.

While standardized tests are used for the purpose of special education assessment, children have often been misdiagnosed because of language differences or cultural factors. Testing can be harmful if it is not administered by a trained professional and includes any aspects that discriminate against students. The test administrator must be highly skilled in administering, interpreting, and scoring the tests so that no errors in diagnosis are made. Too many students are still misdiagnosed or placed in programs that are inappropriate for meeting their needs.

Scott Cunningham/Merrill

PREREFERRAL

Screening is a process that usually helps to filter out any gross problem areas. Most students have a vision and hearing screening completed before a full assessment of tests is ordered. It helps to establish whether a potential difficulty exists. The vision and hearing screening is usually completed by the school nurse or the nursing assistant; however, it checks only acuity aspects, and these screenings are not highly reliable. Children may pass these because they are based on acuity elements and are assessed with limited training. Yet difficulties exist and require more in-depth investigation. A speech screening is completed by a speech therapist, while a health screening is conducted by the school nurse or assistant.

Screening instruments for specific disabilities are relatively inexpensive to purchase and use. For example, screening checklists for attention-deficit hyperactivity disorder (ADHD) are available in bulk. The parent and the teacher each complete ratings on their forms; one and a member of the MDC, usually the psychologist, determines if further assessment is needed. The same holds true for gathering initial evidence on the possible diagnoses of autism, learning disabilities, mental retardation, and behavior disorders. Some schools create their own screening instruments that are used to gather specific data before a formal recommendation for assessment may occur.

Podemski, Marshall, Smith, and Price (1995) state that teacher-made tests, checklists, rating devices, interviews, inventories, record reviews, socioeconomic ratings, anecdotal records, and observations are also some examples of some good screening instruments. The screening device must be dependable and meet federal and state requirements. The goal is to use as few screening instruments as possible.

In some instances, analysis and follow-up on the results of these devices may be all that is needed to determine whether a disability exists. For example, a child may be having trouble in the classroom, and a vision screening determines that the child has problems seeing. A simple referral to an optometrist or vision specialist may solve the problem. Glasses or prescription lenses may allow the student to function successfully. The same holds true for the hearing screening. A referral to an audiologist may be all that is required. Removal of ear wax or reduction of fluid in the middle ear may help improve the child's performance.

Screening does not provide enough information to qualify or determine eligibility for special services. The law states that a full assessment must be completed for this purpose. Placement is contingent on assessment results, as is the IEP. All are parts of the due process system that is in place under IDEA. Collaboration efforts of parents and members of the MDC construct the assessment process.

It is the responsibility of several qualified test administrators to administer the assessments that are needed to determine whether the child is eligible for special education services. Different instruments are used to determine eligibility. Some are formal; some are informal. The use of assessment is not a direct science because it does not always deal with specific symptoms of a disability.

REFERRAL

It is sometimes difficult to assess that a disability exists because no test can accurately measure symptoms or characteristics. In medicine, a physician can sometimes view the problems that exist and pinpoint their causes. It is not so easy in special education. Different disabilities may have the same characteristics, and it is easier to misdiagnose a problem. For example, a student may be acting out in class and the resulting assessment concludes the student has a learning disability. This diagnosis is made based on test scores and may overlook the behavior problem. The key is asking the right questions that lead the team to construct the best assessment plan to answer those questions accurately.

The definitions of the different disabilities in special education also vary. Intelligence is often used as a determining factor in placement, yet it is not always possible to measure intelligence in all children. With mental retardation, it is difficult to measure intelligence, especially if the student's disability is considered severe or profound. In the case of ADHD, the diagnosis is usually made on the basis of data completed from checklists from the teacher and the parent. The diagnosis is made by a child psychiatrist or pediatrician. The symptoms may not appear in the doctor's office and the physician has to rely on what the teachers and the parents say.

Assessment is not always accurate. The time of day or week when the instrument was administered can affect the results. The child may not perform as well first thing in the morning and may do better in afternoon testing sessions. The child may perform less well for unfamiliar staff in unfamiliar settings. Or the child may perform much better than typical daily performance. The tests do not always measure all characteristics of a child and may favor certain areas over others. In other words, a child's score may be inflated or deflated based on statistical regression found in the test (see Chapter 2).

Sometimes, students have medical conditions that may be overlooked during a school-based assessment. It is rare for a physician to administer tests to a child unless there is a concern about a medical condition. Emotional disturbances (ED) and mental retardation (MR) sometimes have underlying causes. Many students with MR may have digestive or seizure disorders that may go undetected because they are not serious enough to be detected during screening or testing in the school.

States set their own guidelines that concern specific disabilities (Podemski et al., 1995). They have the right to set the definitions for categories as long as they agree with the federal interpretations. Sometimes, these rules may vary greatly from state to state. The states may also determine what tests are going to be used to determine if a given disability exists.

Breakpoint Practice

1. What is the process of prereferral?
2. What is the process of referral?

TYPES OF ASSESSMENTS

The types of assessment used depend on the suspected disability and the state guidelines that go along with it. This is why it is so critical that students, parents, and the MDC ask the right questions so that the assessment provides good data for good decisions. An ecological assessment is usually conducted with children who are suspected of having a behavior disorder or a learning disability. This type of assessment requires that the student be observed in the natural environment. Valuable information can be gathered from these types of assessments that cannot be gleaned from standardized tests (Podemski et al., 1995). The direct observation can be structured or nonstructured. It can include checklists, rating forms, and sociometric techniques, or it can be a lengthy running record transcript of all that occurs during the observation. The ecological assessment determines how the child fits into the environment and can include the observation of specific behaviors that are counted each time they occur. This helps measure how well the child functions in the environment and helps to determine what types of behavior problems may exist.

Podemski et al. (1995) discuss perceptual assessment that measures visual perception, perceptual-motor functioning, auditory perception, memory for information presented both verbally and visually, and motor function. Standardized tests are used for this purpose, as are checklists and rating scales that can be developed by the school. This type of assessment is usually utilized when it is suspected that the child has a learning disability.

Spoken-language assessments are used to determine whether a learning disability, mental retardation, speech disorders, or hearing disorders exist. Many of these assessments are standardized. Because language is important to learning, these assessments provide a wealth of information about the student's ability to use it both receptively and expressively in the process of learning.

When a learning disability is suspected, a written language assessment is also usually conducted. These are usually standardized tests, but very few effective ones are available. They usually are subjective in nature and do not always yield sufficient information about the written language process.

One purpose of assessing students is to determine educational functioning (Podemski et al., 1995). The test administrator tries to establish educational functioning by assessing subject areas, learning styles, and the strengths and weaknesses of the student. Social/emotional functioning is also assessed. A physical/sensory assessment is often conducted as well. Cognitive functioning, including intelligence tests, are also used widely for the purpose of determining functional levels. In the case of MR, adaptive behavior scales must be completed. A language assessment is also important because language is an important part of learning.

Certain personnel are in charge of assessing students with special needs. These individuals are either hired by or work for the district. The psychometrist is responsible for assessing IQ and personality profiles, the speech and language pathologist assesses speech and language, the school nurse screens for health issues and performs the vision and hearing screening, and the social worker does the home assessment. Teachers also collaborate on assessment practices. They provide informal assessment results from the classroom. Furthermore, some formal adaptive behavior and language skills are assessed by teachers. Each has an important role in the assessment of the individual with disabilities and is responsible for service provision in some instances.

The student with a potential disability is assessed using a variety of instruments (Podemski et al., 1995). These instruments cover intelligence, achievement, written expression, language, perceptual and sensory abilities, and behavior/personality. These tests are administered by a clinician who is an expert in the field of the assessment.

Norm-referenced tests, although controversial, are the most common type of assessment used in special education. They have objective scoring techniques, are standardized on a population throughout the country, and detail how well a child does compared to his or her peers. One of the drawbacks of this type of assessment is that it might test items that the student has not yet learned. These tests also compare children against those who may not receive special education services. The results provide only an overall assessment of the child's abilities and do not pinpoint specific areas of strengths and weaknesses.

Criterion-referenced tests are based on a sequence of skills within a particular area of the curriculum (Podemski et al., 1995). Criterion-referenced tests are based on a criterion rather than a norm and evaluate the child's ability to accomplish certain tasks. They are limited because they measure only individual tasks that the child may or may not be able to complete. They also do not provide a standardized score or measure that provides specific data compared to how others in the student's peer range are doing.

Outcomes-based assessment or curriculum-based assessment is another type of testing used. These tests are based on the local curriculum and measure specific things the student should have learned, based on the curriculum. Areas where the student is weak can be identified and remediated. This information can be recorded and written into the IEP.

Portfolio assessment is another type of evaluation that can be used. Portfolios are becoming more and more popular for evaluating teachers as well as students. The portfolio contains the student's written artifacts that demonstrate how well the student is doing in a particular subject over time. This is a more authentic way to document proficiency in an area.

Testing can be harmful if it is misused or abused. The tests are quite expensive to use, and standardized tests are usually re-normed every five to ten years. The test administrator is responsible for using the most recent edition of the test and must keep current with the changes that appear in the revised editions. Some of these tests are not clinically sound, and great care must be taken in evaluating the results. Misdiagnosis is a potential problem that can lead to parental litigation and due process. That is one reason why it is so important for the individual administering the assessment to keep current in test administration.

As mentioned earlier, many diagnoses are made on the basis of norm-referenced tests that contain cultural and language biases. Even though the student must be tested in his or her native language, something in the translation may be lost, providing a biased result. Test administrators must be careful in interpreting any test results before labeling a child. Too many children are actually placed in special education because there appears to be no other reason for their failure. This does not serve the best interest of the student and can lead to future problems.

IDEA protects the parent and child more than it protects the school. If a misdiagnosis is made, problems can result in the child's failure to thrive. When this occurs, it leads to potential behavior problems and the potential for dropping out of school. The only one who loses is the student.

Breakpoint Practice

1. What are some types of assessments?
2. What is the purpose of assessing students who are being evaluated for special education?
3. Who is responsible for the assessment of students in special education?

Multicultural Considerations

Multicultural considerations and discriminatory practices have shaped the field of special education in relation to changes in the law. Cases have changed the rules regarding special education services. Specific aspects of assessment are addressed within these laws. Students should be tested in their native and primary language. The parents should also be informed of their rights and are provided interpretation of test results in their native language. This is only one consideration of the multicultural approach to the assessment process in special education.

(continued)

Cultural rules are provided in the laws so that students are given every opportunity to succeed. These considerations include bias-free testing and placement. This is another example of how the laws address the individual needs of students.

Researchers have supported the use of prereferral of students in need of special education services to reduce overidentification and underidentification of students who are culturally or linguistically diverse (Nelson, Smith, Taylor, Dodd, & Reavis, 1991). Important considerations during the prereferral process include carefully choosing the individuals on the prereferral team and addressing proactively differences in language that can affect communication and collaboration. Also, learning styles must be considered, as well as concepts of time (importance of being exactly on time) and cooperation (working in groups versus competition) during the process (Dodd, Nelson, & Spint, 1995).

Standardized tests are also flawed when evaluating students who are culturally and linguistically diverse. Many of these tests do not provide fair opportunities for the students who speak a language other than English. Using performance-based, curriculum-based, and dynamic assessment could increase the validity of the assessment process (Salend, Garrick, Duhaney, & Montgomery, 2002).

REASSESSING SANDY

Sandy's family should be informed of their rights in writing and in their native language. Sandy's mother should be informed about safeguards that will be used during the evaluation process. Furthermore, all participants in the evaluation of Sandy should be actively involved in the process. Participants include the psychologist, the social worker, occupational and speech therapists, as well as special education and inclusion teachers. Teachers should list prereferral strategies used in the classroom. More input should also be obtained from Sandy.

Sandy has the right to a free, appropriate public education in the least restrictive environment based on a nondiscriminatory assessment. The informal and formal assessment tools should be written in her native language. They should be administered by properly trained administrators, and the instruments should be standardized for the purpose for which they are being used. Any variation in the standardization procedures should be noted and described in the evaluation report. Her family members should have a voice in the decision-making process. She is entitled to due process and to protections under the law that will provide her an individualized education based on her needs.

ACTIVITIES

1. Identify three websites that deal with legal issues, parent rights, and self-advocacy in special education.
2. Create a visual display of special education law from *Brown v. Board of Education* through IDEA.
3. Name and describe three parental rights in relation to the evaluation process.
4. Name and describe three critical elements of nondiscriminatory assessment.

WEB RESOURCES

http://www.wrightslaw.com

http://www.ed.gov/parents/needs/speced/edpicks.jhml

http://www.specialchild.com/legal/html

http://www.nichcy.org

http://www.abspedpac.org/specialeducationlaw.htm

http://www.napas.org

http://idea.ed.gov

http://www.disabilityrights.org/glossary.htm

http://www.edjj.org

http://www.ncmhjj.com

REFERENCES

Birnbaum, B. W. (2006). *Foundations of special education leadership: Administration, assessment, placement and the law.* Lewiston, NY: Edwin Mellen Press.

Crowell, A. R. (1989). *Organization and procedures for special education.* Lewiston, NY: Edwin Mellen Press.

Curcio, J. L., & First, P. F. (1993). *Violence in the schools: How to proactively prevent and defuse it.* Newbury Park, CA: Corwin Press.

Dodd, J. M., Nelson, R., & Spint, W. (1995). Prereferral activities: One way to avoid biased testing procedures and possible inappropriate special education placement for American Indian students. *Journal of Educational Issues of Language Minority Students, 15,* 1–10.

Gorn, S. (Ed.). (1997). *1997 IDEA amendments: An overview of key changes.* Horsham, PA: LRP.

Murdick, N., Gartin, B., & Crabtree, T. (2002). *Special education law.* Upper Saddle River, NJ: Merrill/Pearson Education.

Nelson, J. R., Smith, D. J., Taylor, L., Dodd, J. M., & Reavis, K. (1991). Prereferral intervention: A review of research. *Education and Treatment of Children, 14,* 243–253.

Podemski, R. S., Marsh, G. E., II, Smith, T. E. C., & Price, B. J. (1995). *Comprehensive administration of special education* (2nd ed.). Upper Saddle River, NJ: Merrill/Pearson Education.

Salend, S. J., Garrick Duhaney, L. M., & Montgomery, W. (2002). A comprehensive approach to identifying and addressing issues of disproportionate representation. *Remedial and Special Education, 23*(5), 1–15.

Yell, M. L. (1998). *The law and special education.* Upper Saddle River, NJ: Merrill/Pearson Education.

Reliability and Validity

Reliability: Consistency of scores.

Validity: Quality of test; test measures what it says it measures.

Norm-referenced test: Test compares student's score to other students of the same age or grade level through the use of a norm group.

Standardized test: Test given and scored the same way each time.

Assessment battery: Compilation of assessment instruments.

Correlation Coefficients (r): Measure the relationship between two or more sets of scores.

Direction of r: Positive (variables increase), negative (one variable increases as the other decreases), no relationship (no pattern).

Strength of r: Power of r.

Interpretation of r: Usefulness of the test judged via strength of correlation coefficient.

Test-retest reliability: Stability of a score over time.

Alternate forms reliability: Stability over item samples.

Interrater reliability: Stability over raters.

Internal Consistency: Stability over items.

Split-half Reliability: Half of the test items compared to the other half in order to determine internal consistency.

Kuder-Richardson Formulas: Formulas comparing the average correlation of all possible split halves (right or wrong answers) to determine internal consistency.

Coefficient alpha: Method of comparing the average correlation of all possible split halves (varying credit).

Standard error of measurement: Difference between a true and an observed score.

True score: Observed score without error.

Obtained score: Observed score.

Confidence intervals: Range of possible scores.

Validity coefficients: Measure of the relationship between two or more sets of scores.

Content validity: How well learning area is measured.

Construct validity: How well psychological theory is measured.

Criterion-related validity: How well an instrument's scores relate to another criterion or measure.

Concurrent validity: Comparison of two different measures.

Predictive validity: Comparison of measures of a person's performance based on a criterion from one time to a later time.

Accommodations: Changes to a way a person is tested in order to eliminate barriers.

Case Study: Akis

Akis is a student currently enrolled in a public school kindergarten class. His teacher has concerns regarding his performance in class. He is barely keeping up with the other students. His difficulties include using phonics skills, following directions, and being unkind to students. Furthermore, he performed marginally on his state assessment test in the areas of language and cognition. His school district is known for doing very well on standardized tests (it is rewarded financially for good results).

Akis was born in the United States. He is of Greek descent, and he and his parents appear to speak English fluently. Akis attended preschool for a couple of years before starting kindergarten. His mother reports developmental milestones well within normal limits. She also reports that he learned to speak English a year and a half prior to entering kindergarten. He is simultaneously learning literacy skills in Greek and English at home and at Greek school. He speaks and hears English 50 percent of the time and Greek 50 percent of the time. The family notes that his strengths are in language and gross motor skills and that his areas of need are social and emotional. He has had several ear infections each year. Overall, they report that he appears to be within normal limits.

What do the characteristics of this child tell us about the validity of his standardized test score results?

How does this information influence our decision-making process regarding test results?

What information do we need to help us determine the next steps for assessment and instruction, if any?

Would we refer this student for further evaluation? Explain your answer.

What should the parents do to make sure their child is provided for in the best way possible?

What are the social implications of Akis's assessment interpretation?

Based on the case study of Akis, by the end of the chapter you should be able to discuss the questions posed. You should also be able to explain the process by which test makers establish the reliability and validity of tests. You should be able to name, explain, and interpret reliability and validity types measured through correlation coefficients. In addition, you should be able to utilize these concepts when choosing appropriate tests for evaluation purposes.

This chapter addresses CEC Content Standard 8 (http://www.cec.sped.org/ps/perf_bases_stds/standards.html), which specifically addresses assessment. Reliability, validity, bias, and interpretation aspects of assessment as they relate to special education are clearly articulated within this content standard.

Educational decisions made with support and guidance from professionals shape the lives of students. Society counts on educators to make consistent, accurate, and fair educational decisions. To do so, educators rely on the concepts of reliability and validity to choose appropriate norm-referenced, standardized tests for their assessment batteries. They also consider these factors when interpreting test results and making placement and service decisions. It is the responsibility of educators to understand and apply these terms in the work setting.

Reliability and validity are constructs that are strongly related. For a test to be valid, it must be reliable. In other words, reliability is a prerequisite of validity (Salvia & Ysseldyke, 2007). Reliability deals with the consistency of test results (Kaplan & Saccuzzo, 2005). If a test is consistent, it is reliable. Validity deals with the notion of the quality of the test; that is, does the test measure what it is designed to measure (Overton, 2006). If one is testing the understanding of vocabulary, is that what the test is measuring? It makes sense that if a test is not consistent, the quality of that test is jeopardized.

CORRELATION COEFFICIENTS

Before discussing the types of reliability, it is important to have a firm understanding of correlation coefficients (Best & Kahn, 2005). Educators depend on correlation coefficients when judging the quality or reliability of an instrument. For that reason, meaning, direction, strength, and interpretation of correlation coefficients will be discussed as a precursor to reliability.

MEANING

Correlation or reliability coefficients measure the relationship between two or more sets of scores (Cohen, Cohen, West, & Aiken, 2003). Reliability coefficients are often indicated by the letter r or the Greek letter rho (p). Note that a relationship between two or more variables does not indicate causality. For example, in general, language and intelligence have been positively correlated. But intelligence is not necessarily the cause of poor language skills, or vice versa.

DIRECTION

Comparison of variables could result in a positive or a negative relationship, or a finding of no relationship could be determined. When a set of scores increases as another set of scores increases, the relationship is positive (see Figure 2.1). That is, both sets of scores are increasing (Abdhi, 2007). A plus sign or no sign preceding a number indicates a positive relationship. For instance, a positive direction can be indicated by a +.75 or .75. An example of a positive direction could be the number of classes a college student participates in and class activity scores. As the number of classes a college student participates in during the semester increases, assignment scores in those classes would increase. Intelligence and academic achievement have also shown a positive relationship in past studies (Atkinson, Atkinson, Smith, & Bem, 1993). If both sets of scores are decreasing, this is also a positive relationship because they are going in the same direction (i.e., .8). For example, as intelligence scores decrease, academic achievement scores would decrease. It all depends on the perspective one takes.

When a set of scores increases as another set of scores decreases, the relationship is negative (see Figure 2.2). A minus sign preceding a number indicates a negative

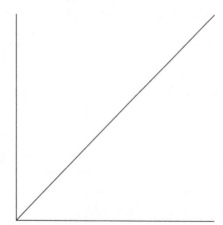

Figure 2.1 Visual representation of a positive relationship, correlation coefficient *r*

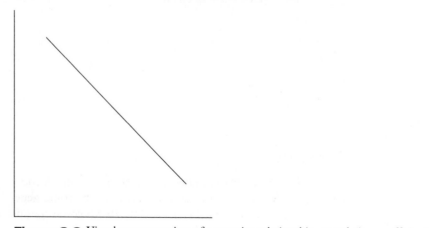
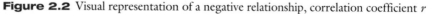

Figure 2.2 Visual representation of a negative relationship, correlation coefficient *r*

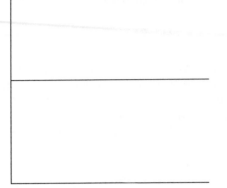

Figure 2.3 Visual representation of no relationship, correlation coefficient *r*

relationship. A correlation of −.8 indicates a negative direction. An example of a negative relationship could be the number of parties a college student attends and test scores. As the number of parties a college student attends during the semester increases, test scores in classes would decrease. Time spent practicing multiplication facts and errors in multiplication have shown a negative relationship in past studies (Koshmider & Ashcraft, 1991). The sets of scores in this case are going in the opposite direction.

When two or more sets of scores are not associated with each other, the relationship is zero (0), indicating a lack of any relationship (see Figure 2.3). In a scatter plot, the scores do not vary with each other. An example of no relationship would be hair length and test score results. The scores in this case are not related at all.

Breakpoint Practice

1. Name two variables that have a positive relationship.
2. Name two variables that have a negative relationship.
3. Name two variables that have no relationship.
4. Would the following coefficients indicate a positive relationship, a negative relationship, or no relationship?
   a. .6
   b. .4
   c. −.3
   d. 0
   e. +.5

STRENGTH

The direction of a coefficient does not affect its strength. A coefficient of .95 is equally as strong as −.95. One way of viewing strength is by some general criterion of strength (Best & Kahn, 2005). A coefficient of .00–.20 would be considered negligible; .20–.40,

Table 2.1 Coefficient Chart

Coefficient (*r*)	Relationship
.00 to .20	Negligible
.20 to .40	Low
.40 to .60	Moderate
.60 to .80	Substantial
.80 to 1.00	High to very high

Source: Coefficient Chart, *Research in Education*, 10e, Best & Kahn, 2005.

low; .40–.60, moderate; .60–.80, substantial; and .80–1.0, high to very high (see Table 2.1).

The value of a coefficient is always between -1.0 and $+1.0$. The closer the coefficient is to -1.0 or $+1.0$, the stronger it is (Chen & Popovich, 2002). For example, $-.40$ is a stronger coefficient than $-.20$ or $.20$. In addition, $.85$ is a stronger coefficient than $.6$ or $-.6$. The coefficients of -1.0 and $+1.0$ indicate a perfect relationship. This is a very rare outcome of the data.

Breakpoint Practice

Indicate the strength of the following coefficients using the relationship criteria:

a. .65

b. −.30

c. −.75

d. .95

e. −.95

Reorder the list from weakest to strongest.

INTERPRETATION

Educators utilize coefficients when choosing and interpreting the value of specific tests. When making placement decisions, researchers have supported a cutoff of .90 for reliability (Nitko & Brookhart, 2006). That is, the reliability coefficient of a testing tool should be at least .90 if it is to be used to make special education placement decisions for students. Any coefficient under that cutoff would be considered inadequate. It is important that the meaning of this technical information (validity) is shared with families.

Breakpoint Practice

1. If the strength of at least one coefficient of a test in the assessment battery is under .90, how could Akis's parents work this topic into the conversation regarding Akis's test results?

2. If a test had coefficients that ranged from .8 to .9, would that be acceptable? Explain your answer.

RELIABILITY TYPES

Examiners look at test manuals to find reliability coefficients reported by test makers. In general, the following types of reliability can be found: test-retest reliability, alternate forms reliability, interrater reliability, internal consistency, and measurement error. Often information is not included on all of these types of reliability. However, clearly the more types of reliability that are reported, the better. It is also important to note that composite scores usually include higher reliability coefficients than individual subtests. This is because more test items are utilized in calculating coefficients for composite scores. Furthermore, because the results for each grade level and age level have different and sometimes variable coefficient scores associated with them, it is important to look at each level as well as the average coefficient results for full subtests. If a score falls below the desirable cutoff for the age or grade level of the student(s) you are testing, it is important to note that in the decision making about the tool you will choose or in the discussion of the results as a caution.

TEST-RETEST RELIABILITY

Test-retest reliability is a measure of stability of a score over time (Litwin, 2002). The same test is administered to the same students on two different days. The first and second test administrations are then compared to produce a reliability coefficient (r). The coefficient describes the consistency or reliability between the two sets of test scores. As previously mentioned, a score of .90 or higher is an acceptable score when using tests to make educational decisions. It is important that the test makers report the length of time that elapsed between the two testing dates. The most optimal time frame is two to four weeks. Anything less than two weeks time will inflate the correlation coefficient r due to learning from the first testing experience. On the other hand, retesting more than four weeks after the first testing will deflate the correlation coefficient r. This deflation can be due to developmental changes or events.

Breakpoint Practice

1. You read through a test manual and see that the retesting was done after eight weeks. How do you address this issue?

2. You read through a test manual and see that the coefficient of test-retest reliability is .80. What do you do?

3. You read through a test manual and see that the coefficient of test-retest reliability is .85. What do you do?

ALTERNATE FORMS RELIABILITY

Alternate forms reliability is a measure of stability over item samples. It is also known as equivalent forms reliability or parallel forms reliability (McMillan, 2002). When a test has more than one form, this type of reliability should be used. In this case, the items from different forms of the test are given to the same students. The items are matched for level of difficulty. For example, if three multiplication problems are included on one form of the test, three multiplication problems are included on the other form of the test. The students' scores from both forms are paired and a positive correlation is expected. A high positive correlation indicates equivalence of the forms.

As in the previous example, a score of .90 or higher is an acceptable score when using tests to make educational decisions. Establishing two different equivalent forms of a test can be challenging. In terms of time, sometimes items from both forms are given in the same testing period and then separated afterward. If the two forms are given more than four weeks apart, maturation could negatively affect the correlation coefficient.

Breakpoint Practice

1. Would you expect to see this reliability type mentioned for tests that have only one form?
2. How would you interpret an alternative forms reliability coefficient of .92?

INTERRATER RELIABILITY

Interrater reliability indicates stability over raters. It is otherwise known as interscorer reliability or interobserver reliability. Two or more different raters independently score the same test (Litwin, 2002). Errors or differences in judgment negatively influence this type of reliability. The more structure a test has, the less error is expected. In tests where examiners have to exercise more judgment about behavior, it is especially important to examine this area of reliability. A score of .90 or higher is an acceptable score for interrater reliability when using tests to make educational decisions.

Breakpoint Practice

1. How would you interpret a coefficient of .88?
2. How would interrater reliability be influenced on a measure of behavior of a child who is culturally diverse? Could the cultural background of the examiner play a part in this evaluation? Could this have played a part in Akis's assessment? What part could it play?

INTERNAL CONSISTENCY

Internal consistency is a measure of stability over items. In this type of reliability, the items within a test are compared. Only one administration of the test takes place. Three different methods are generally used: split-half reliability, Kuder-Richardson formulas, and coefficient alpha (McMillan, 2002). In the split-half method, half of the test items are compared to the other half of the test items. The most common procedure is comparing the odd and even items of the test. The items of each half are then correlated to establish the relationship of one half of the test with the other half. Coefficients from this type of reliability could sometimes be lower than the types previously mentioned due to the splitting of the items.

Kuder-Richardson formulas involve comparing the average correlation of all possible split halves. In this case, all items within a test are compared. This method can be used only if a test consists of right or wrong answers. When varying credit is given or when items are scored pass/fail, coefficient alpha could be utilized. This type of reliability yields slightly lower numbers in terms of reliability coefficients. Therefore, a coefficient of .85 would be acceptable for educational decisions, and it is a bit lower than the other reliability types.

Breakpoint Practice

1. Which type of internal consistency would be used for a test involving student preferences or likes and dislikes?
2. Which type of internal consistency would be used for a test involving vocabulary?

STANDARD ERROR OF MEASUREMENT

Standard error of measurement (SEM) considers the difference between an individual's true score and the observed score. In other words, the observed score includes measurement error. The true score is never actually known. Theoretically, it exists in a range of scores. This range is smaller or larger based on confidence level and amount of error. All test scores contain some measurement error, but some contain more than others. The more error within a score, the less reliable and desirable that score is. Error can result from the testing environment, the examiner, the examinee, or the test itself (Cohen & Spenciner, 2007).

The SEM provided in a testing instrument is the average measurement error. The SEM gives us information on how certain or confident we can be regarding the score. The SEM takes standard deviation of a norm group and a reliability coefficient into consideration. The formula is as follows:

$$SEM = SD \sqrt{1 - r}$$

Knowing the quantity of this error allows the educator to recognize a range of scores in which the true score lies. Adding the SEM to and subtracting it from the obtained score produces a range of possible true scores. This is known as calculating a band of confidence. For example, Erin's actual (raw) score on a test is 82. The SEM is calculated as 7.5. If Erin were to take this test several times, we could be confident that her scores would usually fall between ±7.5 of her raw score of 82, or between the scores of 74.5 (82 − 7.5) and 89.5 (82 + 7.5).

In this case, we can be 68 percent sure that the true score lies in the range produced. Chances of the true score falling out of the range would be 32 percent. To be more confident, we must extend the band of confidence. For example, to be 95 percent confident, we would add two standard errors of measurement to the obtained score. Now 85 + 2(7.5) = 70 to 100 at the 95 percent confidence interval. Here, the chances of the true score falling outside the range would be 5 percent.

Breakpoint Practice

1. If the SD is 1.5 and the *r* is .7, calculate the SEM.
2. If the score is 8, report the 68 percent confidence interval. Report the 95 percent confidence interval.

FACTORS THAT INFLUENCE RELIABILITY

Test length: In terms of test items, the longer the test, the more reliable it is.

Group homogeneity: The more heterogeneous the group of examinees, the more reliable the measure.

Item difficulty: Because this concept refers to narrowing the range of performance, there is little variability and reliability will be low.

Variation within the testing situation: As the amount of error in the testing situation increases, reliability is negatively affected. Errors could include test error (e.g., unclear test directions), error associated with examinees (e.g., hunger), and/or error associated with the environment (e.g., uncomfortable temperature level) (Mehrens & Lehmann, 1991; Sattler, 2001).

VALIDITY TYPES

Validity is a primary consideration in choosing and utilizing tests appropriately. Test makers, examiners, and decision makers determine the extent to which a test is valid for the individual or individuals it is used to assess. Appropriate use and fairness associated with validity will be discussed after definitions of types of validity are explored later in this chapter. Educators look at test manuals to find validity coefficients and discussion of how validity was established as reported by test makers. In general, the following types of validity can be found: content validity, construct validity, and criterion-related validity (concurrent validity and predictive validity). Often not all of these forms are included. However, clearly the more types of validity that are reported, the better (see Table 2.2).

CONTENT VALIDITY

Content validity measures how well the content domain or learning area is reflected within the test or subtest (Cronbach & Meehl, 1955). For example, if oral expressive language is assessed, then the full area would be included and another domain (i.e., writing) would not. Therefore, it is not surprising that content validity is the most important validity type. For a test to have good content validity, the items must be appropriate for and represent the area of study. For example, if a test has only questions involving receptive vocabulary skills and the test makers claim that it is a test of receptive and expressive vocabulary, it does not represent the domain measured. Therefore, it does not have good content validity. Several items from each level and skill being measured should be included.

In addition, the way the items assess the content is critical. The presentation and response format should match the content area. In terms of presentation format, if a student is asked to read items to show expressive language, the reading domain is tested. This may affect the results. Therefore, validity is jeopardized. Also, if a test is measuring oral expressive language and the student is asked to supply a written response, the different response format invalidates the results.

Table 2.2 A Checklist of Reliability and Validity Types

Reliability	Appropriate (Y/N)	Validity	Appropriate (Y/N)
Test-retest		Content	
Alternate forms		Construct	
Internal consistency		Concurrent	
Interrater		Predictive	
Standard error of measurement			

Experts in the field judge the quality of items on a test. These experts can include teachers, professors, curriculum experts, and test specialists. Test makers should indicate the composition of the expert panel evaluating the test.

> ### Breakpoint Practice
> 1. If you were making up a test on driving a vehicle, how would you establish content validity?
> 2. If you were constructing a test on the quality of food, how would you establish content validity?

CONSTRUCT VALIDITY

Construct validity deals with how well an instrument measures a psychological theory or construct. A construct refers to a theoretical trait or characteristic that cannot be observed (Cronbach & Meehl, 1955). Examples include intelligence, happiness, and love. One can see why this type of validity is the most difficult to establish. There is indirect evidence linked to the theory. A test maker should define a construct and develop the instrument to measure that construct. The test maker should include a connection and rationalization of how the items relate to the theory. Not all tests will have all types of validity. One must consider the nature of the test. For example, if the purpose of assessment is to measure intelligence, and because it is based on a psychological construct, one would look for evidence of construct validity.

> ### Breakpoint Practice
> 1. If you were making up a test on driving, how would you establish construct validity?
> 2. If you were constructing a test on the quality of food, how would you establish construct validity?

CRITERION-RELATED VALIDITY

Criterion-related validity measures the extent to which an instrument's scores relate to another criterion or measure. These measures can include another test, observations, or grades. Two types of criterion-related validity exist: concurrent and predictive validity. The timing of these validity types distinguishes them from each other. Concurrent validity deals with current temporal relationships of the criterion (i.e., comparing two tests at the same time), whereas predictive validity involves a comparison of a present and a future timing regarding the criterion (i.e., using a measure to predict future grade point average).

Concurrent Validity

Concurrent validity involves a comparison of two different measures. If two tests are compared, tests should be administered at about the same time or in short succession (Overton, 2006). The time difference should not be more than two weeks or it may not be an accurate measure of the current temporal relationship. Test makers compare the two test scores and calculate the correlation between the scores. The closer the

Scott Cunningham/Merrill

validity coefficient is to 1.00, the stronger the relationship between the two numbers and the higher the concurrent validity. It makes sense that a new test in an area would be more valid if it is compared to an already existing valid and respected test. If the same results were found on both tests, the two tests would be related and measure the same objectives. If the new test is related to an invalid test, a high correlation coefficient does not have much meaning.

Predictive Validity

On the other hand, predictive validity is a comparison that measures a person's performance or a specific criterion from one point in time to a later time (Kaplan & Saccuzzo, 2005). Predictive validity predicts future student behavior from a test score. The student behavior can be measured by grades or teacher ratings. One can look at school success by comparing entry test scores to grade point average at graduation. If school success and grade point average at graduation have a high predictive validity, then we can make an accurate estimation of that student's grade point average in the future based on a test score (i.e., college entrance test scores).

Breakpoint Practice

1. If you were making up a test on driving, how would you establish criterion-related validity?
2. If you were constructing a test on the quality of food, how would you establish criterion-related validity?

FACTORS THAT INFLUENCE VALIDITY

Reliability: If the reliability is low, then validity is low, because if a test is not consistent, then it is not an effective test.

Examinee factors: Life experiences of the examinee, such as a death, divorce, a fight, lack of sleep, and hunger. Furthermore, physical problems such as respiratory, endocrine, vision, auditory, social/emotional, attention deficit/hyperactivity, substance abuse, and home/personal issues can negatively affect testing (Spinelli, 2005).

Test factors: Unclear test instructions, unfamiliarity with test items, inappropriate test pictures, unfair test items, and language fluency.

Examiner factors: Scoring errors, biased testing.

Norms: Individuals in the norm group should be representative of the test taker.

Multicultural Considerations

A major challenge facing the field of special education is the appropriate assessment of differences and disorders of individuals who are culturally and linguistically diverse. The United States is a racially and culturally diverse nation. U.S. census data (2000) reveal that more than 60,000,000 individuals are from racial/ethnic/minority groups. Approximately 30,000,000 of these individuals report that they speak a language other than English. Furthermore, in the United States, the population is white, 81 percent; African American, 12.7 percent; Asian, 3.8 percent; other, 2.5 percent; Hispanic, 12.6 percent. Of the 81 percent white population, white/not Hispanic currently equals 69.4 percent. The percentage of the white/not Hispanic group is projected to decrease to 50.1 percent by 2050.

In the United States, 19.3 percent of the general population has a disability. When looking at the racial composition of this group, nearly 18.5 percent reported being white alone (or about 1 in every 5 persons); 24.3 percent reported being African American alone; 24.3 percent, American Indian and Alaska Native alone; 16.6 percent, Asian alone; 19 percent, Native Hawaiian and other Pacific Islander alone; 19.9 percent, some other race alone; 21.7 percent, two or more races; and 20.9 percent, Hispanic or Latino (of any race). As the number of minority group members increases, we can expect the numbers of students who are linguistically and/or culturally diverse and needing special education diagnostic evaluations to increase.

Based on the data (2000), it is clear that there is an overrepresentation of minorities placed in special education services. Some reasons for the disproportionate numbers include declining numbers of culturally and linguistically diverse educators (Campbell-Whatley, 2003; Kea, Penny, & Bowman, 2003; Patton, Williams, Floyd, & Cobb, 2003), lack of professionals who speak the student's language, inappropriate interpreters, content and linguistic bias in tests (Laing & Kamhi, 2003), and the number of tests available in languages other than English. In addressing this challenge, special educators must differentiate true disabilities from language and/or cultural differences when providing assessment services to individuals who are culturally and/or linguistically diverse. In fact, special educators who do not recognize linguistic and/or cultural differences affecting performance may be violating legal mandates.

Students who are culturally and/or linguistically diverse should be compared to other individuals who are culturally and/or linguistically diverse so that the interpretation of results is valid. These students are not represented or underrepresented in the sample group from many tests, rendering the test results invalid. In addition, even when individuals from diverse backgrounds are included in the sample, typically developing students may still perform below the mean (Laing & Kamhi, 2003). Furthermore, test content and measures may represent the dominant culture (Rivera & Vincent, 1997).

Unfortunately, inappropriate practices exist and students are placed in special education classrooms. Many times, expectations for these students are lowered. These errors do severe injustice to individuals who are culturally and/or linguistically diverse and to society in general. It is our responsibility and ethical duty to be educated and effective assessors of all of our students.

Some best practices regarding English as a second language include the following considerations. Students and families should be asked if they speak a language other than English. This question should always be asked, regardless of perceived fluency in English. Research indicates that, although students may appear fluent in social language, (which takes two to three years to develop), they may not be fluent in academic language until seven years of exposure and practice (Cummins, 1979). When the information leads to the fact that more than one language is spoken within the home, a language proficiency test should be administered. A professional speaking the language other than English should be utilized. If one cannot be found, the use of an interpreter should be closely scrutinized.

During assessment and as a member of a team, one must also consider the following issues in order to choose the most appropriate interpreter. When family members are used to interpret, their task may upset family dynamics. Furthermore, they may change information due to feeling embarrassed or a lack of understanding, or maybe nothing in the native language is equivalent. They may give away answers to help the student. When members from the community are utilized, confidentiality issues may be present. Also, differences in socioeconomic status, country, or nationality, or political, religious, gender, and/or age differences may affect the results of interviews, test answers, and/or observations. In addition, translations of professional language may be compromised (Cheng & Hammer, 1992). Increasing awareness of these issues and addressing these concerns can increase the validity of the evaluation.

The translation of tests brings in other validity issues. Languages differ in elements such as semantics, structure, and dialectal variations, to name just a few. Translation of the gender of language, word order, developmental levels of vocabulary in different languages, and words often not having a direct translation all can influence students' performance on tests. Translations often deal with the surface issues and fail to look at these deeper variables. Abedi, Hofstetter, and Lord (2004) note that translating test items does not appear to be a successful strategy. However, using the students' primary language of instruction in the assessment process can increase the validity of the assessment process. This would provide an appropriate linguistic context for the student.

The test items themselves may be an issue. If the student has not been exposed to certain terms and concepts, he or she will probably not do well if tested on those terms. If the student will not use those terms in everyday life, then they are not authentic or culturally appropriate items. If students from certain cultural backgrounds have poorer results on specific items, than those items are biased and negatively influence validity. Qualitatively addressing these items in the report would further increase the validity of the evaluation.

Also, when a student is not represented in the sample group, this information should be indicated in the results and discussion. Results can be discussed

(*continued*)

only qualitatively because the instrument cannot be interpreted using statistical information. Any discussion of these numbers statistically would be unjust and invalid. Informal assessment is extremely important in these situations. Dynamic assessment, which concentrates on responses to learning situations, has been investigated and found to be a less biased method for assessing students who are culturally and/or linguistically diverse (Gutierrez-Clellen, Brown, Conboy, & Robinson-Zanartu, 1998; Quinn, Goldstein, & Pena, 1996; Ukrainetz, Harpell, Walsh, & Coyle, 2000).

Students should be compared to members of their own community to indicate whether a disability is present. Behavior is learned through the family/community context. Also, the understanding of what is and what is not within normal limits is culturally determined (Kayser, 1995). Teachers' decision making influences the results of evaluations. The lens of the teacher may affect a decision of whether or not to refer a child for special education services. Teachers may lack the information necessary to determine whether a student has a disability, when considering the cultural context. On the other hand, being aware of the issues at hand and gaining the information needed to assess an activity appropriately could be empowering to the teacher, the student, and the school community.

REASSESSING AKIS

Based on the previous discussion, it is clear that the validity of Akis's assessment could easily have been negatively affected by his cultural and linguistic diversity. Phonics, which was a concern of his teacher, could be difficult for Akis due to the newness of English language learning because phonics differ in the two languages. Furthermore, the same may be true of semantics, syntax, and pragmatics. Pragmatics (social language) would certainly be affected by his cultural diversity. It could also affect the way his behavior is perceived. Different rules for behavior may exist within the Greek culture or his family's rule system, which would indicate a cultural and language difference instead of a language delay or disorder.

In addition, information regarding a history of repeated ear infections over time also points to validity difficulties in testing receptive language. Investigating the results of a hearing screening and then exploring a need for further investigation would give clarity to whether or not Akis can identify what he hears. Therefore, the validity of the standardized test results is in question, and the assessment team's decision making must be influenced by this information. More informal types of assessments could be incorporated. For instance, observations of Akis in various settings (i.e., classes, recreational activities, home), work-sample analysis of projects completed in class (i.e., writing, homework assignments), and interviews (i.e. student, teachers, parents) could be utilized to incorporate information regarding Greek language and culture into the comparison of appropriate language behavior.

Also, test information should be qualitatively described and the results of the statistics not used in this situation. In addition, a hearing screening should be recommended for Akis. Parents could request that assessment be done in Greek. They could also request a parent advocate. If Akis is incorrectly diagnosed, academic as well as social consequences could result.

ACTIVITIES

1. Give an example of two factors that would be positively correlated.
2. Give an example of two factors that would be negatively correlated.
3. Give an example of two factors that would have no relationship.
4. Which of the following has the strongest correlation? Why?

   a. .57
   b. −.7
   c. 0
   d. 1.2

5. A test has the following reliability coefficients:

   Test-retest = .91
   Equivalent forms = .92
   Kuder-Richardson = .83
   Interrater = .90

   How would you interpret these results?

6. Choose the appropriate reliability type for the situation described:

   1. An examiner wants to look at the consistency of a score over time.
   2. An examiner wants to investigate the consistency of a score over scorers.
   3. An examiner is interested in whether two forms of the same test are consistent.
   4. An examiner is interested in item consistency; items have right or wrong answers.

7. Apply the reliability types to a real-life situation and give examples of how you would show each type.
8. Apply the validity types to a real-life situation and give examples of how you would show each type. Give a visual representation of the situation. You can draw a picture or act out a situation (For examples, car performance, hair cut results, food tasting).
9. Calculate the standard error of measurement from the items provided.

SD = 7	r = .85	SEM =
SD = 5	r = .90	SEM =
SD = 10	r = .92	SEM =

10. If the student's score is 87, calculate the following confidence range for each of the three previous examples.

    68 percent confidence interval
    95 percent confidence interval

    What do the ranges indicate?

11. Evaluate a test manual in cooperation with two other students. Discuss the types of reliability and validity types used. Judge the adequacy of the results. Would you use this test? Explain your answer. Discuss in a large group.

12. If test reliability ranges from .75 to .95 on a particular test, what does that tell you? Would you use the test? Explain your answer.

13. If the mean reliability coefficient is .9 for the same test, would you use the test? Explain your answer.

WEB RESOURCES

http://allpsych.com/researchmethods/validityreliability.html

http://changingminds.org/disciplines/hr/selection/validity.htm

REFERENCES

Abdi, H. (2007). Coefficients of correlation, alienation and determination. In N. J. Salkind (Ed.), *Encyclopedia of measurment and statistics.* Thousand Oaks, CA: Sage.

Abedi, J., Hofstetter, C. H., & Lord, C. (2004). Assessment accommodations for English Language Learners: Implications for policy-based empirical research. *Review of Educational Research, 74,* 1–28.

Atkinson, R. L., Atkinson, R. C., Smith, E. E., & Bem, D. J. (1992). *Introduction to psychology* (11th ed.). Fort Worth, TX: Harcourt Brace Jovanovich.

Best, J. W., & Kahn, J. V. (2005). *Research in education* (10th ed.). Boston, MA: Allyn & Bacon.

Campbell-Whatley, G. D. (2003). Recruiting and retaining of culturally and linguistically diverse groups in special education: Defining the problem. *Teacher Education and Special Education, 26*(4), 255–263.

Chen, P. Y., & Popovich, P. M. (2002). *Correlation: Parametric and nonparametric measures.* Thousand Oaks, CA: Sage Publications.

Cheng, L. L., & Hammer, C. S. (1992). *The use of an interpreter/translator.* San Diego, CA: Los Amigos Research Associates.

Cohen, J., Cohen, P., West, S. G., & Aiken, L. S. (2003). *Applied multiple regression/correlation analysis for the behavioral sciences* (3rd ed.). Hillsdale, NJ: Lawrence Erlbaum Associates.

Cohen, L. G., & Spenciner, L. J. (2007). *Assessment of children and youth: With special needs* (3rd ed.). New York: Longman.

Cronbach, L. J., & Meehl, P. E. (1955). Construct validity in psychological tests. *Psychological Bulletin, 52,* 281–302.

Cummins, J. (1979). Cognitive/academic language proficiency, linguistic interdependence, the optimum age question and some other matters. *Working Papers on Bilingualism, 19,* 121–129.

Gutierrez-Clellen, V. F., Brown, S., Conboy, B., Robinson-Zanartu, C. (1998). Modifiability: A dynamic approach to assessing immediate language change. *Journal of Children's Communication Development, 19*(2), 31–42.

Kaplan, R. M., & Saccuzzo, D. P. (2005). *Psychological testing: Principles, applications, and issues* (5th ed.). Belmont, CA: Wadsworth.

Kayser, H. (1995). *Bilingual speech-language pathology.* San Diego, CA: Singular Publishing Group.

Kea, C. D., Penny, J. M., & Bowman, L. J. (2003). The experiences of African American students in special education master's programs at traditionally white institutions. *Teacher Education and Special Education, 26*(4), 273–287.

Koshmider, J. W., & Ashcraft, M. H. (1991). The development of children's mental multiplication skills. *Journal of Experimental Child Psychology, 51,* 53–89.

Laing, S. P., & Kamhi, A. (2003). Alternative assessment of language and literacy in culturally and linguistically diverse populations. *Language, Speech, and Hearing Services in Schools, 34*(1), 44–55.

Litwin, M. S. (2002). *How to assess and interpret survey psychometrics. The Survey Kit Series* (Vol. 8). Thousand Oaks, CA: Sage Publications.

McMillan, J. H. (2002). *Essential assessment concepts for teachers and administrators* (3rd ed.). Thousand Oaks, CA: Corwin Publishing Company.

Mehrens, W. A., & Lehmann, I. J. (1991). *Measurement and evaluation in education and psychology.* Fort Worth, TX: Holt, Rinehart & Winston.

Nitko, A. J., & Brookhart, S. (2006). *Educational assessment of students* (5th ed). Upper Saddle River, NJ: Merrill/Pearson Education.

Overton, T. (2006). *Assessing learners with special needs: An applied approach* (5th ed.). Upper Saddle River, NJ: Merrill/Pearson Education.

Patton, J. M., Williams, B. T., Floyd, L. O., & Cobb, T. R. (2003). Recruiting and retaining culturally and linguistically diverse teachers in special education: Models for successful personnel preparation. *Teacher Education and Special Education, 26*(4), 288–303.

Quinn, R., Goldstein, B., & Pena, E. D. (1996). Cultural linguistic variation in the United States and its implications for assessment and intervention in speech-language pathology: An introduction. *Language, Speech, and Hearing Services in Schools, 27*, 345–346.

Rivera, C., & Vincent, C. (1997). High school graduation testing: Policies and practices in the assessment of English language learners. *Educational Assessment, 4*(4), 335–355.

Salvia, J., & Ysseldyke, J. E. (2007). *Assessment* (10th ed.). Boston, MA: Houghton Mifflin.

Sattler, J. M. (2001). *Assessment of children: Cognitive applications.* San Diego, CA: Author.

Spinelli, C. G. (2005). *Classroom assessment for students with special needs in inclusive settings.* Upper Saddle River, NJ: Merrill/Pearson Education.

Ukrainetz, T. A., Harpell, S., Walsh, C., & Coyle, C. (2000). A preliminary investigation of dynamic assessment with Native American kindergarteners. *Language, Speech, and Hearing Services in Schools, 31*(2), 142–154.

U.S. Census Data. (2000). Retrieved from http://factfinder.census.gov/servlet/DatasetMainPageServlet on October 20, 2008.

Norms and Test Scores

KEY TERMS

Domain: An area of study or testing area.

Item pool: Items collected representing an area of study.

Field testing: Testing of an initial version occurs with a small sample.

Normative group: Test administration, data collection, and data analysis occur on a final version with a larger sample.

Stratified sample: Sample represents subdivisions of the population.

Basal: Starting point of a test; specific rules in the test manual.

Ceiling: Ending point of a test; specific rules in the test manual.

Nominal scale: Numerical naming tool; weakest measurement scale.

Ordinal scale: Numerical naming; ranking tool.

Interval scale: Numerical scale used for naming, ranking, and determining equidistant points.

Ratio scale: Numerical scale used for naming, ranking, and determining equidistant points and absolute zero.

Inferential statistics: Measurements that allow assessors to interpret information about test results.

Raw scores: Total items correct.

Derived scores: Obtained using raw scores.

Standard scores: Represent equal units of measurement.

z-scores or sigma scores: Derived standard deviation scores.

Percentile ranks: Percentage of scores at or lower than a student's score.

Stanines: Derived scores divided in nine parts.

Age equivalents: Obtained score equated to an average age score.

Grade equivalents: Obtained score equated to an average grade score.

Measures of central tendency: How scores cluster together.

Mean: Average score.

Median: Middlemost score.

Mode: Most common score.

Measures of dispersion: How scores are spread out.

Range: Highest minus lowest score.

Deviation from the mean: How far away scores are from the mean of a distribution.

Variance: How scores differ from the mean.

Standard deviation: Square root of variance.

Measures of relative position: How scores relate to other scores.

Central limit theorem: Allows assessors to interpret sample scores of individual students.

Normal curve: A representation of scores based on the population.

Culture: Shared rules of a group.

Sociocultural theory: Vygotsky's theory that social environment shapes learning.

Case Study: Keisha and Judy

Keisha and Judy are two students in your fifth-grade class. Both have been evaluated in the areas of intelligence, achievement, language, and behavior. Keisha tested in the mild mental retardation range, whereas Judy tested in the low average range. However, Keisha does well in your class in informal assessment, whereas Judy struggles.

What are some of the possible reasons for this scenario?

What would be some follow-up actions?

If we know that Keisha is African American and Judy is Caucasian, how does this information influence the interpretation of the results in light of multicultural considerations?

How could this situation be addressed in the future?

By the end of this chapter, you should be able to answer the questions based on the case study involving Keisha and Judy. Furthermore, you should be able to explain the basics of test design and test administration of standardized, norm-referenced tests. You should be able to utilize basals and ceilings. You should also be able to use the scales of measurement and to calculate central tendency measures (mean, median, and mode), measures of dispersion (range, deviation from the mean, variance and standard deviation), and measures of relative position (z-scores and percentile rank). In addition, you should be able to interpret standard scores. You should also be able to discuss how culture affects the interpretation of scores.

This chapter addresses CEC Standards 8 (assessment) and 9 (professional and ethical practice). Information regarding knowledge and application of technical assessment information and assessment decisions based on multicultural information will facilitate learning about these standards.

STANDARDIZED ASSESSMENT

A significant component of an evaluation process involves utilizing norm-referenced, standardized tests. Norm-referenced tests involve comparing students to other students of the same age or grade level. Professionals use comparisons to determine whether the student is at the level at which they would expect him or her to be functioning or is performing significantly below that level. Evaluators use basic statistics to make this decision. Means and standard deviations allow comparisons of the student to the norm group and thus the general population using the normal curve. Depending on the content area and type of test (i.e., language testing), different cutoff levels are used within the distribution. These cutoffs will be shared during later chapters, which involve specific content areas.

TEST DEVELOPMENT

According to Overton (2006), the following steps take place in test development: A domain of a test is defined, experts in the field collect items for an item pool, a developmental version is put into place, field-testing is conducted, and data is analyzed. Changes are then made to the original version. Afterward, sampling procedures occur in the area of recruitment of sample participants and testing coordinators. Next, test administration, data collection, and data analysis are conducted to establish norms, reliability, and validity. Finally, the test is prepared for use.

One of the most critical pieces of test development is establishing a normative group. According to Bailey (2004), the sample should be stratified and represent cultures, regions, gender, income levels, and urban-rural distributions proportionately. Furthermore, in terms of representativeness, age, grade in school, acculturation of parents, and intelligence (although controversial) are also factors (Salvia & Ysseldyke, 2007). If any of these items are not represented, validity issues are raised. The year of testing should also be recent. If it is not, the results are not necessarily representative of the content and culture of today's society. Furthermore, at least 100 participants for each grade or age level should be included (Sattler, 2001).

TEST ADMINISTRATION

Chronological Age

To administer a standardized test, some basic building blocks of the testing procedure should be mastered. The first is filling out the protocol or answer sheet. On the protocol, usually the name of the student, grade level, date of birth, and date of exam, along with other identifying information, is listed. Usually, after filling out the name and grade level, one must first determine the examinee's chronological age. This is found by subtracting the student's age from the testing date. It is helpful to start with days, months, and then years in the subtraction process (Pierangelo & Giuliani, 2005). For example, if the student was born on 04/14/98 and the test date was 04/14/04 the following computations would be made:

Year	Month	Day
2004	04	14
− 1998	04	14
6	0	0

The calculations reveal that the examinee is 6-0, that is, six years, zero months. A dash is used to show years and a period is used to show grade levels. So, 6.0 would indicate the sixth grade. Grade equivalents are articulated in grades and tenths of grades. It is important to note this distinction. Another issue to keep in mind is that when years, months, and days are subtracted, 30 days are used for months and 12 months for the year. The days do not fluctuate with the number of days in that particular month. For example, if this same examinee was tested on 06/04/04 the following computations would be made:

Year	Month	Day
2004	05	34
− 1998	04	14
6	01	20

One month was borrowed to increase the day column (30 + 4 = 34). A month was subtracted from the month column (6 − 1 = 5) to balance the equation. The age of the examinee is 6-1-20. When the days are 15 or more, the months' column is rounded up by one. In this case, the solution is 6-2.

When the number of months of the birth date exceeds the number of months in the testing date, months are borrowed from the year column. For example, if the examinee in the previous examples was tested on 03/03/04, the following computations would be made:

Year	Month	Day
2003	14	33
− 1998	04	14
5	10	19

In this case, 30 days were borrowed from the month column (30 + 3 = 33), 12 months were borrowed from the year column (12 + 2 = 14), and subtraction took place (14 − 4 = 10). It is important not to forget to subtract the month and year that were borrowed from each column. The solution to this problem is 5-10-19. Rounding takes place (month up) because the days are 19 (greater than the 15-day cutoff). Therefore, this examinee is 5 years 11 months, or 5-11.

> ### Breakpoint Practice
> Determine the chronological age of the following students using the test date of 06/16/04:
> 1. Date of birth: 05/14/00.
> 2. Date of birth: 07/20/98.

Basals and Ceilings

After the examiner determines the age of the examinee, he or she checks with the test manual to determine which item number to use to start testing the examinee. For some tests, this will be the first item. For other tests, it will be a certain section or item number. The next step is to check the basal and ceiling rules for the test. Basals and ceilings serve as the parameters of the test items that are to be administered. To proceed with the test, one must establish a basal. It would be assumed that any item number less than this basal point would be correct, even though we may not actually test those items. For example, if the basal was three consecutive items correct and one started with item 17, 17, 18, and 19 would have to be correct (basal level) before one proceeded with the rest of the test.

Item Number	Correct or Incorrect
17	Correct
18	Correct
19	Correct (basal achieved)

If this was not the case, one would check the test manual to see how to proceed. Generally, the rule is to go backward until a basal is achieved. So 16, 15, 14, and so on, would be administered until three correct answers were established.

Item Number	Correct or Incorrect
17	Correct
18	Correct
19	Incorrect (in this case, go backward on items before 17 until basal is achieved).
16	Correct (16, 17, and 18 are correct, so basal is achieved).

Sometimes, students will not achieve a basal at all (scattered items correct and incorrect).

Item Number	Correct or Incorrect
1	Correct
2	Correct
3	Incorrect
4	Correct
5	Incorrect
6	Correct
7	Correct
8	Incorrect
9	Incorrect
10	Incorrect

This happens with students with disabilities. In this case, the score could not be compared to the norm group because this would cause validity violations; that is, a standard score should not be calculated. However, the results must be looked at informally. They could be discussed qualitatively in terms of items missed and items correct, which could make an important link from assessment to instruction. In some cases, going back to establish a basal may give two basals. In this case, the second basal would be used.

Item Number	Correct or Incorrect
1	
2	
3	
4	
5	Correct (going backward)
6	Correct (starting point)
7	Correct (first basal)
8	Incorrect
9	Correct
10	Correct
11	Correct (second basal)

In looking at the ceiling of a test, one should again consult the manual for rules regarding when the testing should stop. It is important to comply with these rules for the sake of validity and to avoid frustrating the examinee. If the basal is three in a row incorrect, testing takes place until the student gets three consecutive items incorrect.

Item Number	Correct or Incorrect
6	Correct
7	Correct
8	Correct
9	Correct
10	Incorrect
11	Correct
12	Incorrect
13	Incorrect
14	Incorrect (ceiling—stop testing)

This is the ceiling level. The examiner assumes item numbers higher than this point are incorrect, even though he or she has not administered these items. As with the basal, a ceiling sometimes may not be achieved. This should also be noted in the discussion of the results. The results should be explained qualitatively in terms of the student performing in at least the age or grade level indicated. A test or at least a subtest utilizing higher ages or grades is generally administered to see at what level the student is actually performing.

Breakpoint Practice

If a student does not achieve a basal, what is your next step?

If a student does not achieve a ceiling, what is your next step?

STATISTICS

Statistics give educators the tools to interpret information or the test results of a student by allowing us to compare a student to other students of the same age or grade level. These inferential statistics allow professionals to interpret large sets of data. After obtaining raw scores and chronological age, one can use this information to understand and locate derived scores from the norm tables in manuals of tests.

Derived scores may include standard scores; z-scores; percentile ranks; stanines; age equivalents (i.e., examinee's raw score is the average performance for that age group); grade equivalents (i.e., examinee's raw score is the average performance for that grade-level group); and other standardized scores, such as W-scores. To use these derived scores, we must first have mastery of measures of central tendency, dispersion, and relative position to help us organize and understand data or test scores.

SCALES OF MEASUREMENT

Four scales of measurement will be discussed. Those scales include the nominal, ordinal, interval, and ratio scales.

Nominal Scale

The least powerful or meaningful scale is the nominal scale. It can be thought of as a naming or identification tool. Numbers used to identify players on a basketball team can be used as an example of this type of scale. A player with a higher number does not indicate that he or she has more value. The number simply substitutes for his or her name.

Team Blue	Team Red	Team Green
Eddie (#21)	Joseph (#55)	Lucy (#17)
Judie (#42)	Vicki (#7)	Carrie (#99)
Suzie (#3)	Stephen (#88)	Eleni (#28)

Ordinal Scale

The next level of the scales of measurement is the ordinal scale. This scale serves as a ranking tool. For instance, players on a basketball team can be ranked in order of points earned on the court. Player 55 could have earned 22 points, first rank; player 23 could have earned 20 points, second rank; and player 90 could have earned 5 points, third rank. We know that player 55 earned more than player 23, who earned more than player 90. However, we do not know how many more points player 55 earned than player 23 based solely on the ranking. Furthermore, the points are not equidistant.

Player	Points	Rank
Player 23	22	1
Player 90	20	2
Player 55	5	3

When two players have equal points, those ranks are averaged, For example:

Player	Points	Initial Rank	Final Rank
Player 23	22	1	1
Player 90	20	2	2
Player 55	5	3	3.5
Player 36	5	4	3.5
Player 20	3	5	5

Clearly, if two players have equal points, one cannot have a higher rank than the other, nor could they take up the same spot. The other players are not affected by the equal rank of the two players.

Interval Scale

In the interval scale, numbers are equidistant. For instance, in the assessment of intelligence or cognitive ability, one can add and subtract numbers. A score of 60 is 15 more than 45 (score of 60 = 15 + score of 45). However, we cannot multiply or divide scores. A person who scored a 45 does not have three-fourths the intelligence of a person who scored a 60 on a test of cognitive abilities. Furthermore, a score of 0 does not indicate that a person has no cognitive abilities. Therefore, there is no absolute zero in this type of a scale.

Ratio Scale

The fourth level of measurement, ratio scale, possesses all of the qualities indicated in the previous three scales and an absolute zero. When looking at time or seconds, one can identify, rank, add, subtract, multiply, divide, and have an absolute zero. A score of 0 seconds means no time. One second is half of two seconds, and two less than three seconds. Therefore, it is the most robust and powerful scale in terms of interpreting data.

Day	Length of Temper Tantrum in Seconds
Monday	120
Tuesday	123
Wednesday	96
Thursday	34
Friday	0

Monday's tantrum lasted 24 seconds longer than Wednesday's tantrum and 3 seconds less than Tuesday's tantrum. In order from most to least time, the tantrums are ranked in the following order:

Day	Rank
Tuesday	1
Monday	2
Wednesday	3
Thursday	4
Friday	5

Breakpoint Practice

1. How would you utilize each of the scales in an educational assessment?
2. Which would be the most useful? Why?
3. Which scale(s) could be used in informal assessment?
4. Rank the following measures:

   5

   7

   5

   6

   3

MEASURES OF CENTRAL TENDENCY

Measures of central tendency involve the concept of how data cluster around the mean. Three measures of central tendency include the mean, median, and mode (see Figure 3.1).

Mean

The mean is otherwise known as the average. These methods are often used in informal assessment. For example, when teachers calculate grades for scores on teacher-made tests, they incorporate these methods. One simply adds up the scores in a distribution and divides by the number of scores. For example, if a distribution included the following scores:

Score (x)
99
93
92
90
86

the total or sum ($99 + 93 + 92 + 90 + 86$) would be 460. Dividing by the number of scores, or 5, produces a result of 92. Therefore, the mean or average of this distribution is 92.

Median

The median or middlemost score of this distribution is 92. Half of the scores are above this score and half of the scores are below this score. In this case, the set of scores is odd: It has five scores. The median is simply the score in the middle. If a set of scores were even, then the two numbers in the middle would be averaged. For example, if a distribution included the following scores:

Score (x)
99
92
90
86

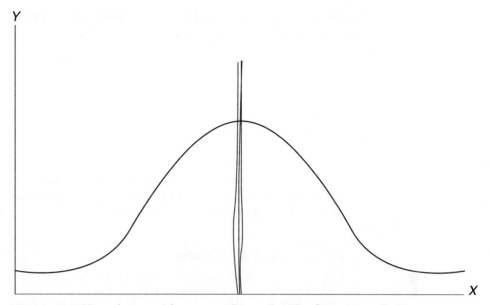

Figure 3.1 Normal curve with mean, median, and mode of population distribution

92 and 90 would be averaged. So 92 + 90/2 = 182/2 = 91. Therefore, 91 is the median. Remember that to determine the median correctly, it is helpful to rank the numbers from largest to smallest and thus minimize error.

Mode

The mode is simply the most commonly occurring number. If a distribution included the following scores:

Score (x)
100
92
92
90

the most commonly occurring score is 92. In the previous example (99, 92, 90, 86), no number occurred more than once. Therefore, there is no mode. Note that the mode is not 0. In the following distribution of scores:

Score (x)
100
100
92
92
90
90
90

the most commonly occurring number or score is 90. The mode in this example is 90. If the distribution were as follows:

Score (x)
100
100
92
92
90

then there would be two modes, or a bimodal distribution, as shown in Figure 3.2. Those modes would include 100 and 92. It is important to note that when outliers exist, the median would most likely be less affected by those scores than the mean and mode.

Breakpoint Practice

Indicate the mean, median, and mode for the following distribution:

Scores on Math Test

90

95

100

80

85

MEASURES OF DISPERSION

Measures of dispersion involve the concept of how data are diffused or spread about the mean. Four measures of dispersion include the range, deviation from the mean, variance, and standard deviation.

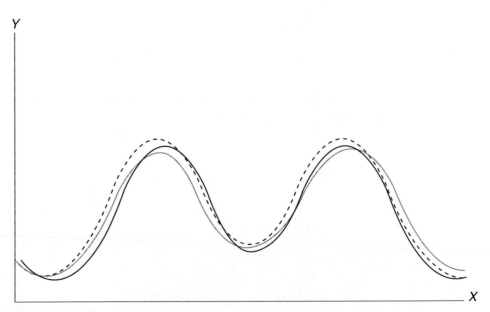

Figure 3.2 Bimodal distribution

Range

The range is the difference, spread, or distance between the highest score and the lowest score. Range is calculated by subtracting the lowest from the highest score. In the previous example, it would be $100 - 90 = 10$. In the following example:

Scores (x)
100
92
90
85
83

the range would be $100 - 83 = 17$. Because the range is larger in the second set of data scores, we know that more variability exists.

Deviation from the Mean

The deviation from the mean measures how far each score is from the mean of the distribution. The mean must be subtracted from each of the scores in a distribution. Let's take the previous example a step further:

Scores (x)	Deviation from the mean ($x - \bar{x}$)
100	$100 - 90 = 10$
92	$92 - 90 = 2$
90	$90 - 90 = 0$
85	$85 - 90 = -5$
83	$83 - 90 = -7$

Sum = 450

Mean = 450/5 = 90

Because there are five scores in this distribution, there are five deviations from the mean $(10, 2, 0, -5, -7)$. Negative numbers must be kept intact. It is interesting to note that when adding all of the deviations from the mean, a sum of zero is the result. This is a good way to check your work, unless rounding takes place. If rounding occurs, it will throw off the number a bit.

Variance and Standard Deviation

The values of standard deviation are most commonly used as descriptors of how the scores are spread about the mean. Calculating variance is a precursor to determining standard deviation. Variance is the square of the standard deviation. Therefore, the standard deviation is the square root of the variance. If the standard deviation is 2, the variance is 4. Variance is otherwise known as s^2 or Greek s^2. It makes sense then that standard deviation is commonly referred to as s or Greek s.

The variance is calculated by summing the squared deviations from the mean, then dividing by the number of scores. The formula for variance is:

$$s^2 = s(x - x)^2/n$$

$$s^2 = \sum(x - \bar{x})^2/N$$

When using the previous example, we have the following results:

Scores (x)	Deviation from the mean ($x - x$)	$(x - x)^2$
100	$100 - 90 = 10$	100
92	$92 - 90 = 2$	4
90	$90 - 90 = 0$	0
85	$85 - 90 = -5$	25
83	$83 - 90 = -7$	49
Sum = 450	Sum = 0	Sum = 178

Mean = 450/5 = 90

Variance = 178/N = 178/5 = 35.6

Standard deviation = square root of 35.6 = 5.97 rounded = 6

Breakpoint Practice

Indicate the range, deviation from the mean, standard deviation, and variance for the following distribution:

Scores on Math Test

90

95

100

80

85

MEASURES OF RELATIVE POSITION

Measures of relative position involve the concept of how the scores relate to the other scores. Two measures of relative position include sigma or z-scores and percentile rank scores. These measures give us much quantitative information (see Figure 3.3).

For example, if you simply look at a score (50), you do not know how a student performed on a test. Was it out of 50 or 100 points? How did everyone else do? We have very little information to go by. However, if you know a z-score or percentile rank, you know exactly how well a student has performed.

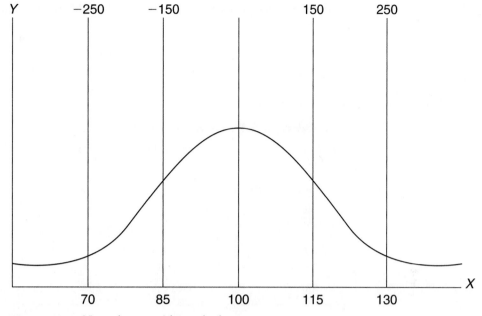

Figure 3.3 Normal curve with standard score

Sigma Score

A z-score or sigma score reveals how many standard deviations (SDs) a score is above or below the mean. A positive z-score indicates that the student did better than the mean. A negative z-score indicates that the student did worse than the mean. Anything above +1 indicates that the student did significantly better than the mean. Anything below −1 indicates that the student did significantly below the mean. The formula for calculating z-scores is as follows:

$$\text{Score} - \text{mean/standard deviation}$$

If the previous example is used and if a score (x) of 90 is examined, we have:

Scores (x)	Deviation from the mean ($x - x$)
100	$100 - 90 = 10$
92	$92 - 90 = 2$
90	$90 - 90 = 0$
85	$85 - 90 = -5$
83	$83 - 90 = -7$

Sum = 450

Mean = 450/5 = 90

90 (score) − 90 (mean)/ ... (SD) = 0

Percentile Rank

Another method for determining relative position is the percentile rank. It reveals the percentage of scores that occur at or below an obtained score. Therefore, the range of percentiles is between below 1 and over 99. A percentile does not reach 0 or 100. If a student has a percentile rank of 82, then he or she scored as well or better than 82 percent of the individuals who took the exam. A percentile rank of 20 indicates that he or she did the same or better than 20 percent of the students who took the same test. This method is often used when sharing the results of standardized tests. It is significant that the difference in the middle of the curve could be less than the difference at the ends of the curve (Venn, 2000).

The equation for determining the percentile rank is as follows: $100 - (100RK - 50)/n$. This formula has some constants. The numbers that vary depending on the distribution include RK (the rank) (see the section on scales of measurement) and n (the number of scores).

Breakpoint Practice

Indicate the z-score and percentile ranks for each of the scores in the following distribution:

Scores on Math Test
90
95
100
80
85

DISTRIBUTION OF SCORES

The reason that educators can take a student's score and apply statistics to it is the notion that a normal distribution exists. A normal distribution represents scores from a population for whom the test was designed. So educators are assuming the distribution reflects every person of the same age or grade level. They can make this assumption due to the existence of the central limit theorem. The central limit theorem states that, given a distribution with a mean and a variance, the mean of a sample approaches a normal distribution. This allows the test makers to chart averages from different age and grade levels. An examiner can take a score and calculate or convert that single score into standard scores, percentile ranks, age scores, and other standardized scores. The process is incredible.

Many test makers offer software that helps in the scoring of tests. In this case, the examiner could compute the raw scores for subtests. After inputting this data, the software would facilitate the calculation of derived scores. In many cases, this software helps save at least 15 minutes per test.

Normal Curve

The normal curve has certain characteristics associated with its definition. It is frequently referred to as the bell curve (see Figure 3.3). The most frequently occurring score is in the middle of the curve, the mean equals the median, symmetry exists across the vertical axis, and the tails of the curve never touch the x-axis. It is important to note that, in a normal distribution, the standard deviations can be used as a ruler. They are consistent in their units of measurement. More than 68 percent of the scores fall within 1 standard deviation above (to the right) and below (to the left) of the mean. Furthermore, about 95 percent of the scores fall within 2 standard deviations of the mean. In addition, standard scores typically have a mean of 100 and a standard deviation of 15. Therefore, if a standardized score (i.e., standard score, percentile rank, z-score) is known, one can locate its position on the normal curve and determine whether a student's score falls within normal limits. This will vary and depend on the type of test given. For example, in intelligence tests, 2 standard deviations below the mean is the cutoff for mental retardation. The student must also meet requirements in age and adaptive skills. More detail will be given in this area in Chapter 6.

Skewed Distributions

When the scores do not fall along the pattern indicated for normal curves, the curve is known as a non-normal curve or a skewed distribution. In this case, there may be more than one mode, and the curve may be bimodal (two modes) or multimodal (more than two; see Figure 3.4). When the curve has more scores on the negative portion of the curve, it is referred to as positively skewed because it is skewed to the right (see Figure 3.5). Conversely, when the curve has more scores on the positive portion of the curve, it is referred to as negatively skewed because it is skewed to the left (see Figure 3.6).

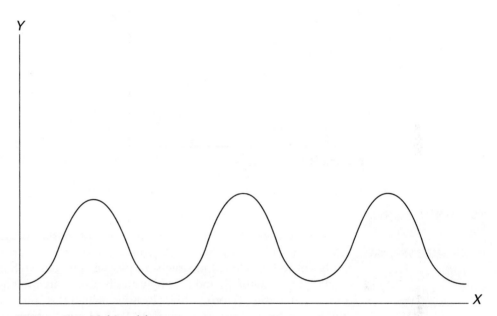

Figure 3.4 Multimodal curve

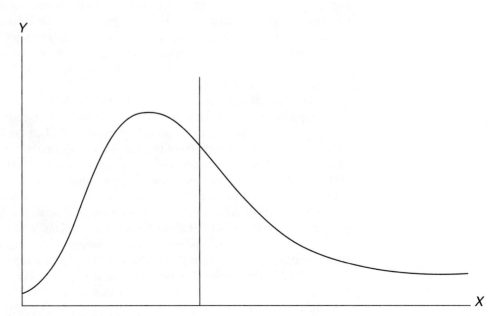

Figure 3.5 Positive skew

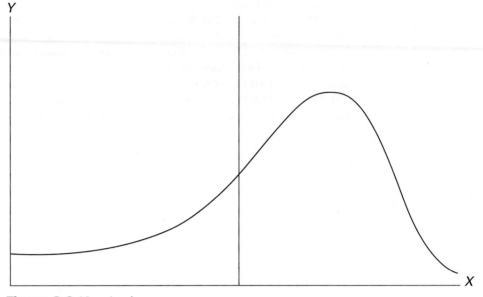

Figure 3.6 Negative skew

Multicultural Considerations

Large-scale assessments are based on the concepts of statistics and normal curve. The No Child Left Behind Act requires students who are limited-English-proficient to be included in large-scale assessments. Research indicates that students who are culturally and/or linguistically diverse are most acutely affected by this type of testing (Horn, 2003). Reasons behind this issue include inappropriate testing and interpretation practices. Lack of norm sample representativeness, accommodations, teachers' decision making, and family involvement have an important impact on the outcome of these assessments. See the discussion in Chapter 2 regarding representation of linguistic and/or culturally diverse individuals in normative samples. For examiners to even consider giving, let alone interpreting, norm-referenced standardized testing, the examinee must be represented in the norm group. If he or she is not, the rules of statistics are defied and the results are meaningless.

Accommodations on assessments are another factor in adequately administering and interpreting tests. For more general information regarding accommodations, see Chapter 11. Accommodations are noted within No Child Left Behind. Furthermore, although IDEA and Section 504 of the Americans with Disabilities Act also allow for assessment accommodations, sometimes they are not used (Gagnon & McLaughlin, 2004). Hollenbeck, Tindal, and Almond (1998) found that only 21 percent of the general education and special education teachers they surveyed reported using accommodations specified in the statewide testing manual. Furthermore, only 55 percent reported knowledge of allowable accommodations on statewide tests.

Those accommodations may include longer testing time, small-group administration, individual administration, and testing in a separate location with more breaks. Furthermore, the use of modified English and a customized dictionary have been reported in addressing an increase in the validity of test results (Abedi, Hofstetter, & Lord, 2004) for students who are linguistically diverse.

Abedi et al. (2004) also noted that examiners should be aware that a valid accommodation should assist the target students yet not affect the scores of the other students. Examiners should also be aware that certain accommodations may be effective with certain students due to student characteristics (Abedi, Lord, Hofstetter, and Baker, 2000).

In looking at students with possible disabilities and considering the assessment-to-instruction connection, it is important to see if adaptations to the testing materials in presentation and response modes will affect student performance. For example, if a student has reading difficulties and one is assessing the student in math, his or her reading may be interfering with the information the examiner is receiving regarding math. Clearly there is a validity issue regarding the content area. The evaluator may consider reading the problem to the student. This would allow him or her to get more information regarding the area of math. The results could not be used to compare the individual to the norm group. However, the results could be looked at qualitatively and used by the teacher in the area of instruction. Other changes could include paraphrasing instructions, demonstrating tasks, extending time, using accommodations (i.e., calculators), and prompting the student (Elliot & Marquart, 2004; McLoughlin & Lewis, 2005).

Examiners' decisions regarding linguistically and culturally diverse students have been reported to be affected by linguistic and cultural factors (Kritikos, 2003). An examiner's decision-making process must be as bias-free as possible to come to a fair and valid conclusion regarding the results. Social environment shapes learning (Smagorinsky, 1995). Furthermore, the use and participation in exchange shapes humans' cultural learning (Das, 1995).

Professionals' learning processes take place over a long period of time with interaction with adults and/or more knowledgeable peers in various contexts (Vygotsky, 1978). During the process of discussion, new ideas and understanding become part of a person's way of seeing the world. Individuals' learning is part of their experiences in various contexts, which shape their beliefs (Rios, 1996).

Culture affects beliefs, which influence knowledge (Pajares, 1992). Sociocultural theory justifies the importance of considering the factors and relationships in beliefs, knowledge, and decision making. Examining the cultural and linguistic background of students, referral (Hosp, 2003; Hosp & Reschley, 2004), test development, normative group selection, and examiners' cultural and linguistic background is important.

Research has indicated that recommended assessment practices regarding students who are culturally and/or linguistically diverse are not reflected in actual practice (Banks, 1997). In the investigation of young Native American students, Banks found that norm-referenced instruments were used 100 percent of the time; checklists and observations, 91 percent of the time; and interviews and criterion-based instruments, 37 percent of the time. Only 54 percent of the respondents reported that the assessments were conducted in the child's primary language.

Lack of involvement of the families may contribute to less-than-perfect assessment practices. Even though the law and research studies have stressed the importance of active participation, sometimes parents are not involved in decisions made about their children (Garriott, Wandry, & Snyder, 2000).

(continued)

Furthermore, research findings have indicated that parents report that they are often not heard during the assessment process (Banks, 1997). It is important that families be guided to professional and parent organizations (i.e., Council for Exceptional Children, Wright's Law) in order to understand terms in reports and be informed consumers and partners. Also, linguistic and cultural information regarding families' expectations for future grade levels and post–high school would frame stages of discussion about assessment and instruction. In addition, students should be key partners in learning about assessment data so they can describe performance and expectations, contribute to decision making, and self-monitor skills.

Researchers have also reported that information valued by some cultures is often disregarded (Alexander & Parsons, 1991). Increasing the effectiveness of collaboration between educators and family members could lead to a more robust understanding of the students' strengths and needs (Lowenthal, 2003). Blue-Banning, Summers, Frankland, Nelson, and Beegle (2004) found six indicators of professional behavior that assisted collaborative partnerships: communication, commitment, equality, skills, trust, and respect. Positive team building among family members and educators could improve practices because of the bridge between school and home (Dabkowski, 2004).

Breakpoint Practice

After reading and thinking about the information and ideas mentioned in the section above, it would seem reasonable to say that assessment in the chapter-opening case study is not an accurate indicator of student performance. Therefore, we should question the assessment that was performed for both Keisha and Judy. Some of the work samples should be used as performance-based assessment for both students. Both students' families should be encouraged to share information and be involved.

Keisha needs to function at her potential in the classroom. Learning behavior involves connections between the student and his or her environment (Kroeger, Burton, Comarata, Combs, Hamm, Hopkins, & Kouche, 2004). These could include error analysis, checklists, and self-evaluation components. Therefore, Keisha's work samples should be used as performance-based assessments. She should also be reevaluated to make sure the material is challenging enough for her to grow to the maximum. This information may have implications regarding her school setting. Her family should be brought into the evaluation to determine how she is functioning at home and in social settings. If it is determined that Keisha is functioning well in these settings (school, home, and social), her family should push for the removal of the label given to her.

Judy appears to need more support in the classroom. The support should be given in the classroom to see that she functions to the best of her potential. If it appears that Judy still needs additional assistance, she should be reevaluated. The informal assessments within the classroom should be used in the assessment battery. Furthermore, the family should be brought into the evaluation to determine how she is functioning at home and in social settings.

ACTIVITIES

1. Calculate the chronological age of the following students:

   a. Date of birth: 5/20/96
      Exam date: 10/25/04
   b. Date of birth: 08/15/00
      Exam date: 09/22/03
   c. Date of birth: 11/27/97
      Exam date: 9/03/04

2. Consider the following list of responses. The basal rules are four consecutive correct responses; the ceiling rules are four consecutive incorrect responses.

14+	20+
15+	21+
16+	22−
17+	23−
18−	24−
19+	25−

   What is the basal? What is the ceiling? What is the raw score?

3. Calculate the final rank for the following students:

Student	Math Test
Joe	95
Martha	88
Julie	88
Bobbie	70
Steve	50
Lloyd	50
Fay	50

4. Calculate the mean, median, and mode for the following distribution:

Reading Test	
Vicky	100
George	94
Marcus	92
Kathy	87
Ben	81
Elaine	65

5. Calculate the range, deviation from the mean, variance, and standard deviation for the example in Activity 3.

6. Calculate the z-score and percentile rank for Kathy in Activity 3.

WEB RESOURCES

http://www.wrightslaw.com/advoc/articles/tests_measurements.html
http://www.ldaamerica.us/about/position/print_state-wide-testing.asp
http://www.aamr.org/Policies/mental_retardation.shtm

REFERENCES

Alexander, P. A., & Parsons, J. L. (1991). Confronting the misconceptions of testing and assessment. *Contemporary Education, 62*(4), 243–249.

Bailey, D. B. (2004). Tests and test development. In *Assessing infants and preschoolers with special needs* (3rd ed.). Upper Saddle River, NJ: Merrill/Pearson Education.

Banks, S. R. (1997). Caregiver and professional perceptions of assessment practices and validity for American Indian/Alaska Native families. *Journal of American Indian Education, 37*(1), 16–44.

Blue-Banning, M., Summers, J. A., Frankland, H. C., Nelson, L. L., & Beegle, G. (2004). Dimensions of family and professional partnerships: Constructive guidelines for collaboration. *Exceptional Children, 70*(2), 167–184.

Dabkowski, D. M. (2004). Encouraging active parent participation in IEP team meetings. *Teaching Exceptional Children, 36*(3), 34–39.

Das, J. P. (1995). Some thoughts on two aspects of Vygotsky's work. *Educational Psychologist, 30,* 93–97.

Elliot, S. N., & Marquart, A. M. (2004). Extended time as a testing accommodation: Its effects and perceived consequences. *Exceptional Children, 70*(3), 349–367.

Gagnon, J. C., & McLaughlin, M. J. (2004). Curriculum, assessment, and accountability in day treatment and residential schools. *Exceptional Children, 70*(3), 263–283.

Garriot, P. P., Wandry, D., & Snyder, L. (2000). Teachers as parents, parents as children: What's wrong with this picture? *Preventing School Failure, 45,* 37–43.

Hollenbeck, K., Tindal, G., & Almond, P. (1998). Teachers' knowledge of accommodations as a validity issue in high-stakes testing. *The Journal of Special Education, 32*(3), 175–183.

Horn, C. (2003). High stakes testing and students: Stopping or perpetuating a cycle of failure? *Theory into Practice, 42*(1), 30–41.

Hosp, J. L. (2003). Referral rates for intervention or assessment: A meta-analysis of racial differences. The *Journal of Special Education, 37*(2), 67–80.

Hosp, J. L., & Reschly, D. J. (2004). Disproportionate representation of minority students in special education: Academic, demographic, and economic predictors. *Exceptional Children, 70*(2), 185–199.

Kritikos, E. P. (2003). Speech-language pathologists' beliefs about language services for bilingual/bicultural individuals. *American Journal of Speech-Language Pathology: A Journal of Clinical Practice, 12,* 73–91.

Kroeger, S., Burton, C., Comarata, A., Combs, C., Hamm, C., Hopkins, R., & Kouche, B. (2004). *Student voice and critical reflection: Helping students at risk, 36*(3), 50–57.

Lowenthal, B. (2003). Cultural competencies for American early interventionists. *Learning Disabilities: A Multidisciplinary Journal, 12*(3), 125–130.

McLoughlin, J. A., & Lewis, R. B. (2005). *Assessing students with special needs* (5th ed.). Upper Saddle River, NJ: Merrill/Pearson Education.

Overton, T. (2006). *Assessing learners with special needs: An applied approach* (5th ed.). Upper Saddle River, NJ: Merrill/Pearson Education.

Pajares, M. F. (1992). Teachers' beliefs and educational research: Cleaning up a messy construct. *Review of Educational Research, 62,* 307–332.

Pierangelo, R., & Giuliani, G. A. (2006). *Assessment in special education: A practical approach* (2nd ed.). Boston, MA: Allyn & Bacon.

Rios, F. (1996). *Teacher thinking in cultural contexts.* Albany, NY: State University of New York Press.

Salvia, J., & Ysseldyke, J. E. (2007). *Assessment* (10th ed.). Boston, MA: Houghton Mifflin.

Sattler, J. M. (2001). *Assessment of children: Cognitive applications* (4th ed.). San Diego: Author.

Smagorinsky, P. (1995). The social construction of data: Methodological problems of investigating learning the zone of proximal development. *Review of Educational Research, 65,* 191–212.

Venn, J. (2000). *Assessing students with special needs* (2nd ed.). Upper Saddle River, NJ: Merrill/Pearson Education.

Vygotsky, L. S. (1978). *Mind in society.* Cambridge, MA: Harvard University Press.

Curriculum-Based Assessment and Informal Assessment

Summative assessment: Assessment that documents performance at the end of a specified time period and is usually quantitative.

Formative assessment: Ongoing assessment as skills are learned; used to aid learning.

Formal assessment: Norm-referenced, standardized testing.

Curriculum-based measurement: A measurement tool used for assessing students' academic growth repeatedly over time, providing additional strategies to support students' needs, and ascertaining the need for additional diagnostic testing.

Curriculum-based assessment: Assessment based on curriculum content used.

Authentic assessment: Assessment in a real-life application.

Performance-based assessment: The student is constructing and demonstrating his or her knowledge.

Portfolio: An organized collection of work indicating learning.

Product portfolio: Project-oriented portfolio.

Process portfolio: A collection of artifacts that show the development and growth of a person's knowledge.

Task analysis: Separating a task into its subcomponents.

Error analysis: A technique used to investigate patterns of errors, looking at the process of producing product.

Rubrics: Includes categories, scores, and descriptions that are used as a guide to evaluate projects or products.

Analytic scoring: Each aspect of a task gets an individual rating.

Holistic scoring: Rating of aspects as a product.

Criterion-referenced assessment: Student is assessed by level of mastery instead of being compared to other students.

Case Study: Paul

Paul is a student in your second-grade class. He is having a difficult time with math tasks such as adding and subtracting math facts, money, time, and organizing items. He has not performed well on statewide assessment measures, as well as classroom measures. He is having a harder and harder time catching up with classroom tasks. You have followed current curriculum, state standards, methods, and materials used. You have collected response to intervention data and have tried various instructional interventions. You have attempted the use of manipulatives, peer tutors, and additional resources for home use prior to lessons (i.e., outlines, notes, and additional manipulatives). Paul's parents also reported difficulties with quantitative concepts. After several levels of support and meetings, the parents asked for an evaluation to determine eligibility for special education and related services. The team will conduct an evaluation consisting of formal achievement, intelligence, adaptive behavior, and language measures. It is your task to collect informal assessment information regarding Paul's math skills and student preferences.

How many measures will you select to contribute to the evaluation process?

What measures will you select to contribute to the evaluation process?

How will you report these measures?

What information do you want to tap into?

How will you show that the skills are authentic?

How will they tie into instruction?

By the end of this chapter you should be able to discuss answers regarding the questions from the case study about Paul. Furthermore, you should be able to discuss the meaning and use of curriculum-based measurement, curriculum-based assessment, and other informal measures. You should be able to discuss authentic and performance-based measures, including the use of a portfolio. Also, you should be able to identify and discuss the difference between product and process portfolios. Furthermore, you should be able to identify different types of teacher-made tests. You should be able to explain criterion-based tests (teacher-made and commercial). You should be able to identify issues related to validity in assessing achievement using informal measures in individuals who are culturally and/or linguistically diverse. You should be able to discuss how results are connected with planning and how planning is connected with instruction.

This chapter addresses CEC Standards 3 (individual learning differences) and 8 (assessment). These correspond to INTASC standards about learner diversity (3) and assessment (8) (www.cec.sped). Information regarding definition, identification, assessment instruments, formal and informal assessments, influence of diversity, and assessment decision information will facilitate learning related to these standards.

The more diversified the assessment techniques, the more robust the information that will be received by the evaluators, the school, the student, and the student's family members. Traditional formal tests give us useful information. However, concerns such as technical inadequacy, insensitivity to slight changes in student progress, infrequent summative assessment (Chatterji, 2003), using tests to compare students to others when that is not the purpose of the test, and not having the detail needed to make instructional changes (Madelaine & Wheldall, 1999) cause us to turn to alternative types of assessment to help our students.

DEFINING CURRICULUM-BASED ASSESSMENT

Curriculum-based assessment (CBA) (Gickling & Havertape, 1981) was developed as an assessment of a student's performance on the implemented curriculum. In this approach, teachers develop instruction based on the curriculum and a student's skills related to that curriculum. Tucker (1987) reported that CBA has three elements: test items taken directly from the curriculum used, repeated measurement over time, and utilization of information for instruction.

Research supports the use of the CBA approach as an effective tool for student performance (Shapiro, 1992; Shapiro & Ager, 1992) as well as student behavior (Roberts, Marshall, Nelson, & Albers, 2001). However, less validation data exist regarding CBA as compared to curriculum-based measurement (CBM) (Hosp & Hosp, 2003).

Jones (2001) reported on mathematics vocabulary and comprehension curriculum-based measures of assessment. She noted using word lists and word problems representing math operations and reasoning as an alternate way of instructing and assessing math understanding. She provided word lists for grades 1 through 6. Furthermore, she provided an example of a math-monitoring chart. Steps for preparing and administering math CBAs included gathering materials, creating lists and word problems, administering lists (oral reading by student) and/or completing problems (answering questions), determining accuracy, and determining levels.

Roberts et al (2001) also provide an example of validation data regarding CBA. They studied CBA combined with functional behavior analysis as related to escape behaviors from difficult academic tasks. They found that CBA was an effective alternative measure of investigating off-task behaviors related to curriculum material.

CBA has been investigated by researchers and is utilized in training programs for preservice professionals (Shapiro, Angello, & Eckert, 2004). However, teachers often do not use CBA (Arthaud, Vasa, & Steckelberg, 2000). Shapiro et al. found that teachers reported not using CBA due to a perception of difficulty, time demands, efficacy with CBA, and state or district guidelines with regard to performance objectives (perception of not needing CBA type of assessment).

Researchers have discussed the distinction between CBA and CBM. Hosp and Hosp (2003) note that CBA and CBM differ based on mastery measurement and general outcome measurement. They report that CBA measures mastery (tests like task analysis, developed for each skill taught) and CBM measures general outcome measurement (continuous measurement of more global skills). They add that CBM is a standardized process.

Breakpoint Practice

1. Define CBA.
2. Describe the similarities between CBA and CBM.
3. When would you use CBA?

DEFINING CURRICULUM-BASED MEASUREMENT

Curriculum-based measurement (CBM) is a measurement tool used for assessing students' academic growth repeatedly over time, providing additional strategies to support students' needs, and ascertaining the need for additional diagnostic testing (Howell & Nolet, 1999). Curriculum-based measurement was developed to utilize formative measurement information in evaluating and improving instructional efficacy (Deno, 1985). This avenue of repeated measures provides teachers with the data as tools to monitor and adjust their instruction (Deno & Mirkin, 1977).

Deno (2003) studied the literature and offered general characteristics and uses of CBM. General characteristics include reliability and validity, standard tasks, specific instructional materials, specifics in terms of administration and scoring, sampling through direct observation, repeated sampling, time efficiency, and ease of teaching. General uses include improving instructional programs, predicting performance, developing normative samples, increasing collaboration, identification of high-risk students, appraising prereferral interventions, decreasing bias, finding different identification systems, investigating inclusion placements, predicting performance on high-stakes tests, looking at content area growth, evaluating English language learners (ELLs), and predicting performance in the early grade levels.

Fuchs and Fuchs (1999) offered criteria for successful measurement structures, which include meeting standards for reliability and validity; modeling growth over time; being affected by instructional adaptations quickly; not involving just one specific instructional program; and being quick, inexpensive, and efficient.

PROGRESS MONITORING

CBM is progress monitoring rather than mastery measurement (Fuchs, 2006b). Safer and Fleischman (2005) also tap into the concept of monitoring instruction through continuous assessment. They discuss a rate of progress through the use of probes and their connection to improved instruction. That is, the teacher looks at samples of skills the student is expected to learn by the end of the year. The teacher examines the probes

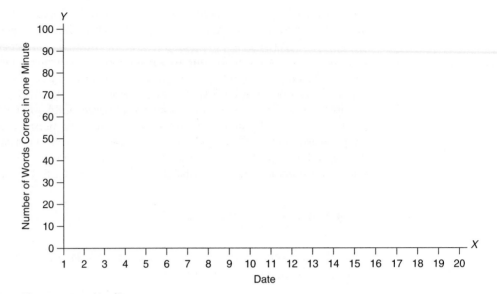

Figure 4.1 Aim line

on a weekly, biweekly, or monthly basis. Teachers can then graph the students' progress to see if instruction must be altered. Altered instruction would then yield better student outcomes. Students could also be involved in graphing and self-monitoring. Students can take responsibility for meeting with the teacher if the aim line is not reached three days in a row (see Figure 4.1). Data would be shared with family members.

Swain (2005) tapped into the students' self monitoring, that is, the self-determination aspect of CBM. She studied goal-setting awareness, knowledge, and setting daily reading goals in students with learning disabilities. Students in the goal-setting treatment group increased knowledge but had difficulty setting realistic goals.

Progress monitoring has been tied into standards-based assessment and connected positively to accountability, expectations, and outcomes (Quenemoen, Thurlow, Moen, Thompson, & Morse, 2003). Monitoring of the student's progress provides a continuous feedback loop to the teacher and student, which improves assessment and instruction outcomes (Fuchs & Fuchs, 1986a, 1986b). Furthermore, this method provides graphic displays of each individual's data and qualitative accounts of student demonstrations of skills (Fuchs & Fuchs, 2002). More specifically, this method can be used for designing effective individualized programs, including setting goals and monitoring progress toward goals (Fuchs, 2006a).

Response to Intervention

In concentrating on the instructional or intervention aspect of this CBM process, response to intervention (RTI) (Gresham, 1991) is a concept that is critical to the discussion of students with and without disabilities (Fuchs, 2006b). Gresham (1991) referred to RTI as a "change in performance as a function of an intervention." He also described resistance to intervention as academic performance that does not change in response to research-based intervention.

RTI has also been discussed as a possible alternative to using a questioned discrepancy model (VanDerHeyden & Jimerson, 2005; Vellutino, Scanlon, & Lyon, 2000) when identifying learning disabilities (Massanari, 2004). Issues included by researchers were variability in the number of standard deviations used in this model, differentiation and difficulties with reliability, and waiting until student failure occurs (Vaughn &

Fuchs, 2003). Mellard (2004) notes the following as strengths of RTI: high-quality instruction, instruction grounded in research, students' assessment in the classroom curriculum, universal screening, progress monitoring, interventions grounded in research, progress monitoring during interventions, and technical adequacy.

RTI looks at student performance after educational interventions. Instruction is changed based on what the data reveal regarding the effectiveness of those interventions. Different methods work for different students. Several tiers of this method reveal useful information regarding the student. As we progress in the three-tier continuum of interventions, intensity increases (Barnett, Daly, Jones, & Lentz, 2004), and identification of difficulties becomes more evident (Fuchs, 2006b). Those tiers include tier one, where the student fails to show improvement (even with research-based interventions) in the general education classroom. In tier two, a multidisciplinary team attempts to problem-solve different and more intense interventions regarding the student in question. In tier three, an eligibility evaluation for special education services takes place (CASP Board of Directors, 2003).

Therefore, CBM not only provides us with tools for monitoring and enhancing student growth and reflecting and changing our instructional practices, but also with information in the area of diagnostic evaluation. Fuchs and Fuchs (2002) described identifying students with disabilities and the notion of nonresponders. In their dual discrepancy approach, they refer to this notion as students who are nonresponsive to otherwise effective instruction. Traditionally, special educators have looked at a discrepancy between achievement and intelligence measures. However, we can look at learning disabilities from a different perspective. We are providing specialized instruction to students who perform below expectations and show a significantly lower learning rate. Utilizing CBM, we can identify and enhance learning in nonresponders.

In terms of showing a need for special education services, a CBM must show that discrepancies exist in performance and growth rate between the student and his or her peers, the student's learning rate with adaptations is below level, and special education services result in enhanced progress (Fuchs & Fuchs, 1997).

ASSESSMENT PROCEDURES

Alternative assessment tools use problem solving through formative assessment (Deno, 2002). That is, practical information ties assessment and instruction on a day-to-day basis in a constant decision-making loop. Students' understanding of how they learn certain tasks best supports metacognition. This collaboration with teachers, parents, and students (Gable, Arllen, Evans, & Whinnery, 1997) and self-directed learning process could aid in the improvement of students' achievement (Stiggins & Chappuis, 2005).

Reading

Madelaine and Wheldall (1999) conducted a critical review of the literature regarding CBM and reading. They noted that oral reading fluency (accuracy and rate) is an area that has been noted in the literature as a popular and much-studied area of reading. They note that it is measured by a passage reading test, in which the student usually reads a passage for one minute. The assessor marks the errors on a copy of the passage and then calculates how many words per minute were read correctly.

Scott and Weishaar (2003) discussed these steps in detail when utilizing CBM with middle and high school students with disabilities in the area of reading. They noted that the first step included dissecting the language arts curriculum. Approximately 21 one-minute samples (included three baseline measures) should consist of one to three passages from each story read. The samples should be at the student's instructional level (age-appropriate material with a possibly different reading level). Next, to be in tune with the curriculum and the passage, calculate the readability level for each passage. Input the passages (student copy and your copy). The student copy will be the passage only. Your copy will include student information and space for the score. Then develop a chart from graph paper to chart progress, which will include the number of probes/weeks and the number of words that were read accurately during that minute target. The authors then note that you should set your schedule (as free from distractions as possible). Then discuss CBM with your students and review procedures with students just before beginning. When the student is reading, record errors and score the number of words correct (with errors having a line through them). The three probes will reveal a baseline score. Determine an aim line for each student's graph. Based on the data, draw a development line. When the data is below or above the aim line for three consecutive times, reassess instruction. The student can be a partner in designing a new instructional plan. As previously mentioned, the student could take responsibility in charting data. Communicate with parents regarding progress in writing.

Hargrove, Church, Yssel, and Koch (2002) remind their readers that the length of the passages, including pictures and color coding text, may improve the students' skills as they are progressing through the process. Furthermore, they report that selecting entries from a number of sources will improve the process. Authentic expository and narrative text should be utilized.

In addition, Hintze and Christ (2004) investigated controlling the curriculum content material difficulty level and CBM outcome. Results revealed significantly less measurement error in controlled grade-level material compared with uncontrolled grade-level material in CBM. These data show that assessors should be sensitive to content difficulty when utilizing CBM. It is important to consider passages that are related to students' interests and are reflective of culture. The teacher may also have to rewrite content area information at a lower readability level.

Written Expression

Espin, Shin, Deno, Skare, Robinson, and Benner (2000) investigated CBM scoring in written expression for students in the sixth, seventh, and eighth grades. Researchers specifically explored reliability and validity of growth indicators. They also studied type and duration of writing of growth indicators. Data demonstrated that correct minus incorrect word sequences were the most reliable and valid predictors of writing proficiency. However, type or duration of writing revealed no differences.

For examples of CBM and technology programs in the measures of math, reading, and written language, see http://www.jimwrightonline.com and http://www.aimsweb.com. See also Figures 4.2 and 4.3.

Figure 4.2 Oral reading fluency probes

Administration of CBM reading probes
The examiner and the student sit across the table from each other. The examiner hands the student the unnumbered copy of the CBM reading passage. The examiner takes the numbered copy of the passage, shielding it from the student's view.

The examiner says to the student:

When I say "Start," begin reading aloud at the top of this page. Read across the page **[demonstrate by pointing]**. *Try to read each word. If you come to a word you don't know. I'll tell it to you. Be sure to do your best reading. Are there any questions?*

[Pause] *Start.*

The examiner begins the stopwatch when the student says the first word. If the student does not say the initial word within 3 seconds, the examiner says the word and starts the stopwatch. As the student reads along in the text, the examiner records any errors by marking a slash (/) through the incorrectly read word. If the student hesitates for 3 seconds on any word, the examiner says the word and marks it as an error. At the end of 1 minute, the examiner says "*Stop*" and marks the student's concluding place in the text with a bracket (]).

Scoring

Reading fluency is calculated by first determining the total words attempted within the timed reading probe and then deducting from that total the number of incorrectly read words.

The following scoring rules will aid the instructor in marking the reading probe:

➤ Words read correctly are scored as correct:
   —Self-corrected words are counted as correct.
   —Repetitions are counted as correct.
   —Examples of dialectical speech are counted as correct.
   —Inserted words are ignored.

➤ Mispronunciations are counted as errors.

> ### Example
>
> Text: The small gray fox ran to the cover of the trees.
> Student: "The *smill* gray fox ran to the cover of the trees."

➤ Substitutions are counted as errors.

> ### Example
>
> Text: When she returned to the house, Grandmother called for Franchesca.
> Student: "When she returned to the *home*, Grandmother called for Franchesca."

➤ Omissions are counted as errors.

> ### Example
>
> Text: Anna could not complete in the late race.
> Student: "Anna could not in the late race."

➤ Transpositions of word-pairs are counted as 1 error.

> ### Example
>
> Text: She looked at the bright, shining face of the sun.
> Student: "She looked at the *shining bright* face of the sun."

➤ Words read to the student by the examiner after 3 seconds have gone by are counted as errors.

Source: Wright, J. (date unknown). Excerpts regarding probes in oral reading fluency from "Curriculum-Based Measurement: A Manual for Teachers." From www.interventioncentral.org

Figure 4.3 Mathematics probes

Administration of CBM math probes

The examiner distributes copies of one or more math probes to all the students in the group. (Note: These probes may also be administered individually.) The examiner says to the students:

The sheets on your desk are math facts.

If the students are to complete a single-skill probe, the examiner then says: *All the problems are [addition or subtraction or multiplication or division] facts.*

If the students are to complete a multiple-skill probe, the examiner then says: *There are several types of problems on the sheet. Some are addition, some are subtraction, some are multiplication, and some are division* **[as appropriate]**. *Look at each problem carefully before you answer it.*

When I say, "Start," turn them over and begin answering the problems. Start on the first problem on the left on the top row **[point]**. *Work across and then go to the next row. If you can't answer the problem, make an 'X' on it and go to the next one. If you finish one side, go to the back. Are there any question?*

Say "*Start*". The examiner starts the stopwatch.

While the students are completing worksheets, the examiner and any other adults assisting in the assessment circulate around the room to ensure that students are working on the correct sheet, that they are completing problems in the correct order (rather than picking out only the easy items), and that they have pencils, etc.

After 2 minutes have passed, the examiner says "*Stop*". CBM math probes are collected for scoring.

Scoring

The following scoring rules will aid the instructor in marking single- and multiple-skill math probes:

→ Individual correct digits are counted as correct.
  —Reversed or rotated digits are not counted as errors unless their change in position makes them appear to be another digit (e.g., *9* and *6*).

→ Incorrect digits are counted as errors.
  —Digits that appear in the wrong place value, even if otherwise correct, are scored as errors.

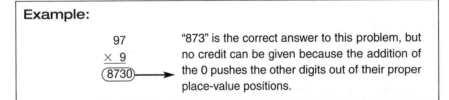

Example:

"873" is the correct answer to this problem, but no credit can be given because the addition of the 0 pushes the other digits out of their proper place-value positions.

→ The student is given credit for "place-holder" numerals that are included simply to correctly align the problem. As long as the student includes the correct space, credit is given whether or not a "0" has actually been inserted.

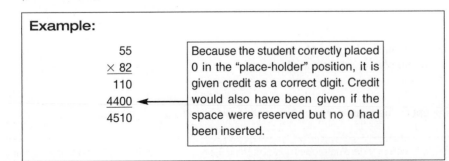

Example:

Because the student correctly placed 0 in the "place-holder" position, it is given credit as a correct digit. Credit would also have been given if the space were reserved but no 0 had been inserted.

➤ In more complex problems such as advanced multiplication, the student is given credit for all correct numbers that appear below the line.

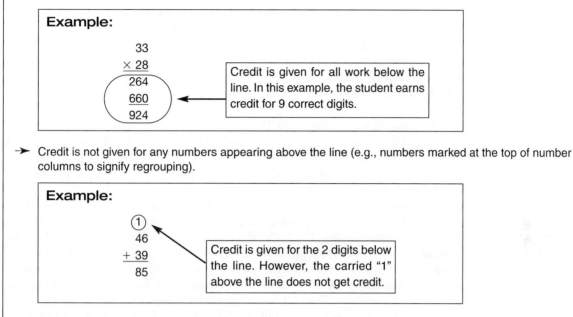

Example:

33
× 28
264
660
924

Credit is given for all work below the line. In this example, the student earns credit for 9 correct digits.

➤ Credit is not given for any numbers appearing above the line (e.g., numbers marked at the top of number columns to signify regrouping).

Example:

①
46
+ 39
85

Credit is given for the 2 digits below the line. However, the carried "1" above the line does not get credit.

Source: Wright, J. (date unknown). Excerpts regarding probes in math computation from "Curriculum-Based Measurement: A Manual for Teachers." From www.interventioncentral.org

---

Breakpoint Practice
1. Discuss the procedure of response to intervention.
2. What are examples of probes in the areas of reading, writing, and mathematics?
3. What are positive and negative aspects of response to intervention?

TECHNICAL ADEQUACY

CBM and Other Informal Assessments
Researchers have compared CBM with performance assessment. Elliott and Fuchs (1997) reviewed applied research literature regarding the usefulness of curriculum-based measurement and performance assessment. They suggested combining curriculum-based measurement and performance assessment as a means to link curriculum, instruction, and assessment with a focus on useful teaching data. They noted that curriculum-based measurement was a more useful tool and that performance-based assessment could be utilized as an enhancement to the assessment process. That is, asking for the development of a product that supports the curriculum links the instruction to assessment in a meaningful way. In addition, they reported that these alternative approaches to assessment are more closely tied to the classroom curriculum than are standardized tests and can therefore guide instruction in a significant and authentic manner.

A Comparison of CBM Systems
Researchers have compared CBM systems for technical adequacy. Fuchs and Fuchs (1999) explored three reading progress-monitoring systems: mastery measurement, curriculum-based measurement, and Dynamic Indicators of Basic Early Literacy Skills

(DIBELS). They found that mastery measurement had several limitations. For example, it restricts a teacher's teaching options due to a tight link between what is instructed and what is measured. Furthermore, questions exist regarding validity and reliability. Also, growth cannot be readily assessed. In CBM, they found questions regarding feasibility of such a program and noted that for younger students, additional measures should be used. For DIBELS, questions regarding a lack of data for growth, technical information, and use of data to guide instruction were noted. It is important to note that many preschool and primary students are being routinely assessed using DIBELS. Research data provide important implications.

CBMs Compared to Standardized Tests

Researchers have compared CBMs with standardized assessments. Helwig, Anderson, and Tindal (2002) examined the correlation of a math CBM and an achievement test. They found high positive correlations. Helwig and Tindal (2002) also found no differences between general outcome measures and state achievement tests.

Clarke and Shinn (2004) also examined the technical adequacy of four math measures. Their focus was on investigating the usefulness of these tools in terms of early identification of math issues. The Early Mathematics–CBM (EM-CBM) included one-minute measures in oral counting, number identification, quantity discrimination, and missing number measure. Experimental measures were compared to Math Curriculum Based Measurement (M-CBM), Woodcock Johnson—R Applied Problems subtest, and Number Knowledge Test. All four experimental measures were found to be of acceptable technical adequacy, and students showed growth on all measures over time.

McGlinchey and Hixson (2004) also investigated the correlation and prediction of CBM with a state standardized test in the area of reading. They found that the two measures were positively correlated. Crawford, Tindal, and Stieber (2001) also found a positive correlation between a reading CBM and statewide achievement tests. Furthermore, Espin, Shin, and Busch (2005) investigated CBM, student grades, and a social studies subtest of the Iowa Test of Basic Skills (ITBS). Results revealed validity for utilizing vocabulary-matching tasks in content areas. This adds to the data supporting the validity of CBM for assessing student learning.

Previous research studies have also indicated good reliability and validity (Shinn, Good, Knutson, Tilly, & Collins, 1992; Shinn & Habedank, 1992). When the issue of teaching to the test is raised (Bradshaw, Craft-Tripp, & Glatthorn, 2003; Popham, 2001; Posner, 2004) because of high-stakes testing, this information has hopeful implications. A CBM approach might provide a positive alternative to current testing trends.

INCLUSION

Studies regarding CBM and inclusion have provided interesting results. For example, Paulsen (1997) reported on a study where students with and without disabilities in an inclusive setting participated in CBM, which benefited all students.

Fuchs, Roberts, Fuchs, and Bowers (1996) investigated three students in their journey from resource to general education classrooms for math instruction via use of CBM. Results revealed that after one year, students either were back in the special education classroom or were never successfully placed in the inclusive setting.

Mathes, Fuchs, Roberts, and Fuchs (1998) investigated the effects of CBM and transenvironmental programming (TP) on reintegration. TP consists of appraisal and development, preparation, translation across environments, and evaluation. Findings revealed that the combination of CBM and TP increased academic interventions (in an effort by teachers to attempt an increase in preparation before placing students into general education) when compared to those teachers who did not receive CBM information. These findings have important implications in the area of reintegration.

TEACHERS' BELIEFS

Results involving teachers' beliefs and CBM provide useful implications for the field. Allinder and Oats (1997) investigated CBM, teachers' beliefs ("treatment acceptability"), and math gain in their students. Teachers were placed in groups of high and low acceptability of CBM based on their responses to a questionnaire. Implementation and student math growth were compared. Researchers found a significant difference in some implementation measures and students' rate of math growth. Teachers with high acceptability of CBM scored higher than the low acceptability group in the implementation measures of the number of probes and set more ambitious goals. Furthermore, the slopes in the graphs representing their students's scores were greater, showing greater progress for their students over the school year. Results have significant implications in the beliefs regarding CBM, use of CBM, and student progress.

Shapiro, Angello, and Eckert (2004) found a significant increase in the use of CBA by psychologists over a ten-year period (1990–2000). However, just over half (54 percent) reported using this valid method of assessment. The psychologists most often noted insufficient training for CBA as the reason they were not using this method. Clearly, more training needs to be done for evaluators during preservice and in-service.

Breakpoint Practice

1. How do CBM measures compare to other types of measures?
2. Discuss the connections among progress monitoring, RTI, and instructional links.
3. How can CBMs influence your instruction?

DEFINING INFORMAL ASSESSMENT

Informal assessment is any assessment that is not formal, so informal assessment is any type of assessment that is not a standardized, norm-referenced test. It may take the form of many types of assessments. Some examples include authentic assessment, performance-based assessment, criterion-referenced assessment, checklists, rubrics, task-and-error analysis, and teacher-made quizzes (i.e., multiple-choice, true/false, matching, fill-in-the-blank, and essay).

Teachers use these methods on a day-to-day basis in the classroom to support instruction. Furthermore, these methods can be used for an annual individualized education program (IEP) report to determine progress toward goals. In addition, teachers' reports regarding informal methods should contribute toward initial diagnostic evaluations of students. Information regarding student performance in the context of the classroom gives examiners critical authentic assessment data. Detail regarding content, format of the assignment, and behavioral responses provide diagnosticians with application of tasks within the classroom.

Informal behavior techniques such as functional behavioral assessment and observation recordings are discussed in Chapter 5. Dynamic assessments (involving samples) are discussed in Chapter 9. Curriculum-based assessments were explored in this chapter.

AUTHENTIC ASSESSMENT

Authentic assessment is a term that has been widely used in the field of education for decades. Simply put, the term means that one is assessing student skills and/or behavior in the real world. The student is demonstrating those skills in a true environment.

For example, instead of a student filling out worksheets involving money, the student provides the appropriate amount of money to a store clerk to pay for a sandwich. This type of instruction/assessment allows the teacher to better prepare the student to use money skills. The exercise provides the student with a real-life context and cuts out the many steps involved in generalizing the skill from the classroom. Furthermore, the experience gives the student the opportunity to practice the skills to produce mastery. In the traditional classroom approach, the question of whether the student could use money skills in a real-life setting would still exist. Other examples include reading a menu, balancing a checkbook, cooking a meal, and taking public transportation.

PERFORMANCE-BASED ASSESSMENT

In performance-based assessment, the student constructs and demonstrates her or his knowledge. Thus, the student takes an active instead of a passive role in his or her learning. This could be done via portfolios, exhibitions, projects, and more. Checklists and rubrics could measure the performance of these performance-based tasks. Putting together a project involving photosynthesis could be a performance-based task. The student could do an Internet search to gather information for a presentation using a visual (an actual plant). To make this task a more authentic one, the student could grow tomatoes in a garden. Ideally, tasks should be authentic and performance-based.

In this type of assessment, instruction and assessment become one. That is, if one is constantly assessing skills in a real-life setting, instruction of those skills in a real-life setting would be optimal. Furthermore, the fact that these skills are assessed and taught in a student's real-life setting makes those skills culturally appropriate. Because the skills would be culturally appropriate and useful, we can expect the student's motivation to learn those skills to increase.

Breakpoint Practice

1. Give an example of authentic assessment.
2. Give an example of performance-based assessment.
3. Contrast authentic and performance-based assessment.

Portfolios

One type of performance-based assessment is a portfolio. There are many different types of portfolios (Bullock & Hawk, 2001). Product portfolios simply show the end product (for example, a PowerPoint presentation). A table of contents can include the PowerPoint slides, a personal narrative on the subject, Internet sites related to the topic, and a reflection regarding the learning experience. On the other hand, a process portfolio shows the development and growth of a person's knowledge. For instance, in a process portfolio, a student can show the development of a literature review of the topic of fetal alcohol syndrome. A table of contents can include outlines, searches, annotated bibliography, and drafts of the paper, including the final paper and a reflection. Dated artifacts with grades and comments leading up to the final paper would show how much the student has learned and not just the literature review. In an effort to integrate technology into education to foster learning (Banister & Vannata, 2006; Jeffs & Banister, 2006), electronic portfolios are an option to consider. Products can be scanned or electronic files can be saved and uploaded to various Web programs (Stansberry & Kymes, 2007).

Other questions to consider are: Is the portfolio schoolwide or teacher-based? Is it a semester-long project or a four-year project? Is it teacher-generated, student-generated, and/or family-generated? Does everything stay in the portfolio or are elements taken out and added in during the process? Who does that? Who evaluates the portfolio? Is there self-assessment? How is the portfolio graded? By a rubric? What are the categories?

Checklists and Rubrics

Work samples must be scrutinized to be useful. Checklists and rubrics are a critical component of those assessment practices. They allow us to measure skills examined in authentic and/or performance-based assessments. Good checklists and rubrics involve a strong knowledge of the skills a teacher is expecting the student to master. That is, what are we assessing and why are we assessing those skills? In developing measurements, those questions are at the forefront of the thought process.

When we are looking for specific skills that require a yes or no answer, a checklist can guide us toward measurement outcomes. Let us look back at the example of giving the appropriate amount of money for a sandwich. What are the skills we are looking for? Knowledge of dollars, quarters, dimes, nickels, and pennies and how to add those together are at the center of that measurement. If a sandwich is $6.67 and we want the student to pay with exact change, then we would look at what was given to the store clerk. For example, from the pile of money given to the student, did he or she provide the correct number of dollars, quarters, dimes, nickels, and pennies?

In the example of evaluating the tomato-growing procedures of our student's garden, a rubric would be appropriate. For example, how far apart were the tomatoes? How often did he or she water the tomatoes? Fertilize the tomatoes? Weed the tomatoes? And what was the general quality of the tomatoes? Each of these five skills can go in a separate line within an analytic rubric, or they can be combined with different criteria in a holistic rubric.

Figure 4.4 Analytic scoring rubric

	Excellent (4)	Good (3)	Fair (2)	Poor (1)
General Quality: red, juicy, tasty tomatoes	3/3	2/3	1/3	0/3

Figure 4.5 Holistic rubric example

Excellent (4)	Good (3)	Fair (2)	Poor (1)
Tomatoes no less than one foot apart; watered daily; fertilized weekly; weeded daily; and they were red, juicy, and tasty			Tomatoes were spaced less than one foot apart; not watered daily, fertilized weekly, or weeded daily; and they were pale, not juicy or too juicy, and did not taste good.

In an analytic rubric, each line (skill) can receive a score of excellent (4), good (3), fair (2), or poor (1). So there would be 20 boxes (see Figure 4.4). An example could be how the general quality line (one out of the five lines, or four boxes) would receive a score. For example, in general quality, for the excellent category, one could expect that red, juicy, and tasty tomatoes would receive an excellent. Two out of three of those descriptors would receive a good. One out of three of those descriptors would receive a fair. Zero out of three of those descriptors would receive a poor.

In a holistic approach, a narrative of what is expected for each level of all five skill items combined is included in four boxes (see Figure 4.5). Each box consists of what would be necessary to receive a rating of excellent, good, fair, or poor. In the excellent box, one would expect that the tomatoes were no less than one foot apart; watered daily; fertilized weekly; weeded daily; and they were red, juicy, and tasty.

In analytic scoring, each skill gets its own box with a rating; in the holistic approach, the skills are combined for each rating. One could have a rating scale of three categories (0–2 or 1–3; good, fair, poor), four categories (excellent, good, fair, poor) or five categories (excellent, good, fair, poor, attempted), or more. The more detail in the description of what constitutes a certain score, the better the assessment tool. For example, including qualitative areas like level of description, examples, details, and accuracy will give you a more detailed expectation and project than will including description alone. When students have detailed rubrics to work from, they will produce more robust products more often.

Breakpoint Practice

1. Define portfolio assessment.
2. Contrast product and process portfolio assessment.
3. How do you measure portfolio assessment?

OTHER INFORMAL MEASURES

Teacher-made assessments are used for day-to-day assessment involved in continuous assessment of skills incorporated into lesson plans. A strength of informal assessment is that it can tap into the subskills of a curriculum. Looking at smaller pieces of the curriculum in depth can provide useful instructional information to the teacher. These assessments are generally meant to test students quickly and thus make sure they are grasping the concepts taught. Some of these quizzes, tests, and exercises involve rating scales (Likert scale), questionnaires, interviews, true/false, matching, multiple-choice tests, problem exercises (including analysis of work samples), fill-in-the-blank, short essay, long essay, application, and interpretation problems. These may be timed or not timed, in class or take home, and individual or group based.

A criterion for mastery is usually attached to these types of assessments. Vital in the concept of criterion-based assessment is that the student is not compared to others of the same age or grade level, but to him- or herself. That is, how is the student doing with regard to mastering the skill? What is the percentage correct? Some examples include 90 percent or 9 out of 10 for an A grade or 85 percent needed to move on to the next level. Many times, these criteria are tied to students' IEP goals.

In analyzing work samples, a teacher can examine the responses given. A teacher analyzes the tasks (task analysis); that is, he or she looks at the pieces needed to complete an academic task (Cegelka, 1995). Error analysis is a technique used to investigate patterns of errors. Information regarding where in the process a student is having difficulty (i.e., addition of two-digit numbers) gives much more useful information to the teacher than a simple percentage correct.

Breakpoint Practice

1. List three types of informal assessments.
2. Which types would you most probably use? Why?
3. Which type would you most probably not use? Why?

STANDARDIZED CRITERION-REFERENCED ASSESSMENTS

As shown above, teacher-made criterion-referenced assessments can be useful on a day-to-day basis. Standardized criterion-referenced assessments also exist. The most common example of this type of assessment is the Brigance inventories (Brigance, 1981, 1994, 1995, 1999, 2004): the Brigance Diagnostic Inventory of Early Development—Second Edition (Brigance IED-II) (Brigance, 2004), the Brigance Diagnostic Comprehensive Inventory of Basic Skills—Revised (Brigance, 1999), and the Brigance Diagnostic Inventory of Essential Skills (Brigance, 1981). More specialized Brigance inventories include the Life Skills Inventory (Brigance, 1994) and Employability Skills Inventory (Brigance, 1995).

For example, the Brigance IED-II includes sections in perambulatory motor skills, gross-motor skills, fine-motor skills, self-help, speech and language, general knowledge, and social-emotional development. Early academic areas include readiness, basic reading, manuscript writing, and basic math.

In general the inventories provide many subtests, which include objectives that can be connected to IEP development. The Brigance Diagnostic Inventory of Early Development—Second Edition is aimed toward children at birth through 7 years of age. The Brigance Comprehensive Inventory of Basic Skills—Revised is for children in pre-K through grade 9. English and Spanish versions of the Basic Skills Inventory exist. The Brigance Inventory of Essential Skills is for grade 6 through adult. The Brigance Life Skills Inventory is for grades 2 through 8, and the Brigance Employability Skills Inventory is for students and adults who will be entering jobs.

Multicultural Considerations

Researchers have discussed the difficulties related to ethnicity, race, and SES status as they relate to the measurement of academic achievement (Goldenberg, 1996; Bentz & Pavri, 2000) and strategies (Plasencia-Peinado & Alvarado, 2001).

Measurement of Academic Achievement

McCloskey and Schicke Athanasiou (2000) investigated the assessment practices of school psychologists related to individuals who were linguistically diverse. They found that some school psychologists used curriculum-based, dynamic, and portfolio assessment. However, most used traditional norm-referenced tests.

Researchers have investigated whether biases related to individuals who are culturally and/or linguistically diverse exist within informal tools used by professionals. VanDerHeyden and Witt (2005) investigated the relationship among the components of teacher referral, race, gender, high and low student achievement, and assessment. More specifically, they examined the efficacy of teacher referral and assessment problem solving. They used the Problem Validation Screening (PVS), a universal screening tool, in the examination of these aspects. Results revealed that PVS was a more accurate instrument than teacher referral in the identification of students at risk for learning difficulties. Teachers were 61 percent accurate compared to a PVS accuracy of 86 percent in referring Caucasian students. Teachers were 78 percent accurate compared to a PVS accuracy of 90 percent in referring minority students for evaluations. Furthermore, teachers were 63 percent accurate compared to a PVS accuracy of 87 percent in referring males, and they were 69 percent accurate compared to a PVS accuracy of 85 percent in identifying females. These results reveal important information regarding teacher referral efficacy and curriculum-based assessment related to race and gender. This tool can benefit teachers in increasing appropriate assessment and instruction to students.

In addition, Kranzler, Miller, and Jordan (1999) researched racial/ethnic and gender bias involving reading CBM in African American and Caucasian students. Results revealed no significant differences in grades 2 and 3. However, racial/ethnicity bias was revealed in grades 4 and 5, and gender bias was found in grade 5. Results revealed overestimates for African American students and the opposite effect for Caucasian students. Furthermore, overestimates for girls and underestimates for boys were noted.

MacMillan (2000) also explored the area of reading and CBM related to gender. The researcher found growth in reading for all students. However, small gender differences were found. Girls outperformed boys.

Evans-Hampton, Skinner, Henington, Sims, and McDaniel (2002) investigated cultural bias and CBM. They focused on math performance and timing in African American and Caucasian students. Specifically, data involving digits correct per minute and percentage of digits correct were evaluated. No difference was found between the two groups in terms of timing groups. Therefore, CBM shows positive results in the area of culture.

Seaman, Guggisberg, Malyn, Payne, and Scheibe (2001) investigated the validity of a copying curriculum-based fluency measure. They found that females performed significantly better than boys at the fifth- and sixth-grade levels. Malecki and Jewell (2003) also investigated writing CBM as it relates to gender. They found that girls performed significantly better than boys did at all grade levels. Teachers should increase their awareness regarding these outcomes and consider this information while assessing students.

Supovitz and Brennan (1997) investigated fairness in the use of portfolio assessment. They compared standardized test results and performance utilizing portfolio assessment in a large sample of students. The researchers looked at gender, socioeconomic status, and race within the context of their sample. Results indicated that differences in gender, socioeconomic status, and race bias existed even with the alternative measures. Portfolio assessment showed a smaller difference between African American and Caucasian students, but a larger difference between males and females, than did standard test scores. Results indicate that more work needs to be conducted in this area of study. Teachers should be aware of these results and consider this data when using portfolio assessment.

Strategies

Researchers have discussed using computer programs to support teachers in the assessment and instruction of students in the areas of reading, spelling, and math (Fuchs, Fuchs, & Hamlett, 1994). Teelucksingh, Ysseldyke, Spicuzza, and Ginsburg-Block (2001) examined the use of Accelerated Math (a computer based CBM) in relation to math outcomes for English language learning (ELL). Two groups of ELL students were compared with regard to math performance. Students who received Accelerated Math in addition to a math curriculum performed significantly better than ELL students who received instruction in math curriculum alone. Therefore, data support the use of Accelerated Math with ELL students.

Al Otaiba (2005) conducted a study investigating the effects of a reading tutorial in English for ELL students and their preservice teachers. She found significant increases in word attack, passage comprehension, and sound identification areas. Preservice teachers also showed improvement in the areas of teacher knowledge and language structure. Results reveal important instructional implications. A reading tutorial in English can provide an increase in reading skills and benefit ELL students.

Prereferral supports are important in the implementation of response to intervention supports and students who are culturally and/or linguistically diverse (Ortiz, 2002). Garcia and Ortiz (2004) discussed responsive prereferral interventions as a possible remedy to decreasing disproportionate representation for students who are culturally and/or linguistically diverse. They noted that providing a range of general and special education service options, forming collaborative partnerships with families, and increasing professional development dealing with effective practices for students who are culturally and/or linguistically diverse can help in the area of achievement and with students who are culturally and/or linguistically diverse. Furthermore, they offered suggestions involving early intervention for students who were beginning to experience difficulties, diagnostic teaching, and general education support systems.

Breakpoint Practice

1. Name and discuss three issues related to diversity and informal assessment.
2. Which informal assessment technique do you favor for students who are culturally and/or linguistically diverse? Why?

REVISITING PAUL

Taking at least five authentic, performance-based informal assessment results from various contexts will add to the usefulness of your data input to the team who is working with Paul from the chapter-opening case study. Providing information from interviews with Paul and his parents, classroom projects with analytic rubrics, error analysis, and a process portfolio would add qualitative information to the evaluation. Classroom projects can include the handling of money, telling time, and manipulating objects in addition and subtraction tasks. These tasks can include individual and group work (with various group partners).

Information can be given without support and with varying levels of support. Paul's comments, as well as products with associated rubrics and teacher-made tests (essay, multiple-choice, checklists, fill-in-the-blank, and percentages of mastery), can be given as data. A portfolio of one of Paul's projects involving a subtraction unit can be included with the other sources of information. The data would show specific information that is not accessed by standardized, norm-referenced tests.

ACTIVITIES

1. What are some advantages to using informal assessment?
2. What are some disadvantages to using informal assessment?
3. Compare and contrast curriculum-based, portfolio, and teacher-made tests related to students who are culturally and/or linguistically diverse.
4. What information have researchers revealed regarding gender differences in informal assessments? How would that information affect you as a teacher?

WEB RESOURCES

http://www.progressmonitoring.org/chart/chart.asp

http://www.progressmonitoring.org/library/articles.asp

http://www.ncld.org

http://www.nichcy.org/toolkit/pdf/ProgressMonitoring-InclusiveStandard.pdf

http://rubistar.4teachers.org/index.php

http://www.teach-nology.com/web_tools/rubrics

http://intranet.cps.k12.il.us/Assessments/Ideas_and_Rubrics/Rubric_Bank/rubric_bank.html

REFERENCES

Abedi, J., Hofstetter, C. H., & Lord, C. (2004). Assessment accommodations for English language learners: Implications for policy-based empirical research. *Review of Educational Research, 74,* 1–28.

Abedi, J., Hofstetter, C. H., Lord, C., & Baker, E. (2000). Impact of accommodation strategies on English language learners' test performance. *Educational Measurement: Issues and Practice, 19*(3), 16–26.

Allinder, R. M., & Oats, R. G. (1997). Effects of acceptability on teachers' implementation of curriculum-based measurement and student achievement in mathematics computation. *Remedial and Special Education, 18*, 113–120.

Al Otaiba, S. (2005). How effective is code-based reading tutoring in English for English learners and preservice teacher-tutors? *Remedial and Special Education, 26*(4), 245–254.

Arthaud, T. J., Vasa, S. F., & Steckelberg, A. L. (2000). Reading assessment and instructional practices in special education. *Diagnostique, 25*(3), 205–227.

Banister, S., & Vannatta, R. (2006). Beginning with a baseline: Insuring productive technology integration in teacher education. *Journal of Technology and Teacher Education, 14*(1), 209–235.

Barnett, D. W., Daly, E. J. III, Jones, K. M., & Lentz, F. E. Jr. (2004). Response to intervention: Empirically based special service decisions from single-case designs of increasing and decreasing intensity. *The Journal of Special Education, 38*(2), 66–79.

Bentz, J., & Pavri, S. (2000). Curriculum-based measurement in assessing bilingual students: A promising new direction. *Diagnostique, 25*(3), 229–248.

Bradshaw, L. K., Craft-Tripp, M., & Glatthorn, A. (2003). Taking the offensive. *Principal Leadership, 4*, 55–59.

Brigance, A. H. (1981). *Brigance Diagnostic Inventory of Essential Skills.* N. Billerica, MA: Curriculum Associates.

Brigance, A. H. (1994). *Brigance Life Skills Inventory.* N. Billerica, MA: Curriculum Associates.

Brigance, A. H. (1995). *Brigance Employability Skills Inventory.* N. Billerica, MA: Curriculum Associates.

Brigance, A. H. (1999). *Brigance Diagnostic Comprehensive Inventory of Basic Skills.* N. Billerica, MA: Curriculum Associates.

Brigance, A. H. (2004). *Brigance Diagnostic Inventory of Early Development—Second Edition.* N. Billerica, MA: Curriculum Associates.

Bullock, A. A., & Hawk, P. P. (2001). *Developing a Teaching Portfolio: A Guide for Preservice and Practicing Teachers.* Upper Saddle River, NJ: Prentice-Hall.

CASP Board of Directors. (2003). *Critical constructs and principles regarding the reauthorization of IDEA: Position paper of the California Association of School Psychologists.* Retrieved April 14, 2008, from http://www.casponline.org/.

Cegelka, P. T. (1995). Identifying and measuring behavior. In P. T. Cegelka & W. H. Berdine (Eds.), *Effective instruction for students with learning difficulties.* Boston: Allyn & Bacon.

Chatterji, M. (2003). *Designing and using tools for educational assessment.* Boston, MA: Allyn & Bacon.

Clarke, B., & Shinn, M. R. (2004). A preliminary investigation into the identification and development of early mathematics curriculum-based measurement. *School Psychology Review, 33*(2), 234–248.

Crawford, L., Tindal, G., & Stieber, S. (2001). Using oral reading rate to predict student performance on statewide achievement tests. *Educational Assessment, 7*(4), 303–323.

Deno, S., & Mirkin, P. (1977). Data-based program modification. Minneapolis, MN: Leadership Training Institute for Special Education.

Deno, S. L. (1985). Curriculum-based measurement: The emerging alternative. *Exceptional Children, 52*, 219–232.

Deno, S. L. (2002). Problem solving as "best practice." In A. Thomas & J. Grimes (Eds.), *Best practices in school psychology IV* (pp. 37–56). Bethesda, MD: National Association of School Psychologists.

Deno, S. L. (2003). Developments in curriculum-based measurement. *Journal of Special Education, 37*(3), 184–192.

Elliot, S. N., & Fuchs, L. S. (1997). The utility of curriculum-based measurement and performance assessment as alternatives to traditional intelligence and achievement tests. *The School Psychology Review, 26*(2), 224–233.

Espin, C. A., Shin, J., & Busch, T. W. (2005). Curriculum-based measurement in content areas: Vocabulary matching as an indicator of progress in social studies learning. *Journal of Learning Disabilities, 38*(4), 353–363.

Espin, C. A., Shin, J., Deno, S., Skare, S., Robinson, S., & Benner, B. (2000). Identifying indicators of written expression proficiency for middle school students. *The Journal of Special Education, 34*(3), 140–153.

Evans-Hampton, T. N., Skinner, C. H., Henington, C., Sims, S., & McDaniel, C. E. (2002). An investigation of situational bias: Conspicuous and covert timing during curriculum-based measurement of mathematics across African American and Caucasian students. *School Psychology Review, 31*(4), 529–540.

Fuchs, D. (2006a). Monitoring student progress in the classroom to enhance teaching and planning and student learning. *International Conference on Special Education 2006*, Hong Kong.

Fuchs, D. (2006b). On the changing definitions of learning disabilities and what it means for special education: A cautionary tale. *International Conference on Special Education 2006*, Hong Kong.

Fuchs, L. S., & Fuchs, D. (1997). Use of curriculum-based measurement in identifying students with disabilities. *Focus on Exceptional Children, 30*, 1–14.

Fuchs, L. S., & Fuchs, D. (1999). Monitoring student progress toward the development of reading competence: A review of three forms of classroom-based assessment. *School Psychology Review, 28*, 659–671.

Fuchs, L. S., & Fuchs, D. (1986a). Curriculum-based assessment of reading progress toward long-term and short-term goals. *The Journal of Special Education, 20*, 69–82.

Fuchs, L. S., & Fuchs, D. (1986b). Effects of systematic formative evaluation: A meta-analysis. *Exceptional Children, 53*, 199–208.

Fuchs, L. S., & Fuchs, D. (2002). Curriculum-based measurement: Describing competence, enhancing outcomes, evaluating treatment effects, and identifying treatment non-responders. *Peabody Journal of Education, 77*(2), 64–84.

Fuchs, L. S., Fuchs, D., & Hamlett, C. L. (1994). Strengthening the connection between assessment and instructional planning with expert systems. *Exceptional Children, 61*(2), 138–146.

Fuchs, D., Roberts, P. H., Fuchs, L. S., & Bowers, J. (1996). Reintegrating students with learning disabilities into the mainstream: A two-year study. *Learning Disabilities Research and Practice, 11*, 214–229.

Gable, R. A., Arllen, N. L., Evans, W. H., & Whinnery, K. M. (1997). Strategies for evaluating collaborative mainstream instruction: "Let the data be our guide." *Preventing School Failure, 41*, 153–158.

Garcia, S. B., & Ortiz, A. A. (2004). *Preventing disproportionate representation: Culturally and linguistically responsive prereferral interventions*. National Center for Culturally Responsive Educational Systems: Practitioner Brief Series. Retrieved April 14, 2008, from www.ncccrest.org.

Gickling, E. E., & Havertape, S. (1981). *Curriculum-based Assessment*. Minneapolis, MN: School Psychology Inservice Training Network.

Goldenberg, C. (1996). The education of language-minority students: Where are we, and where do we need to go? *The Elementary School Journal, 96*(3), 353–361.

Gresham, F. M. (1991). Conceptualizing behavior disorders in terms of resistance to intervention. *School Psychology Review, 20*, 20–36.

Groves, S. V., Weishaar, M. K. (2003). Curriculum-based measurement for reading progress. *Interventions in School and Clinic, 38*(3), 153–159.

Hargrove, L. J., Church, K. L., Yssel, N., & Koch, K. (2002). Curriculum-based assessment: Reading and state academic standards. *Preventing School Failure, 46*(4), 148–151.

Helwig, R., Anderson, L., & Tindal, G. (2002). Using a concept-grounded, curriculum-based measure in mathematics to predict statewide test scores for middle school students with LD. *The Journal of Special Education, 36*(2), 102–212.

Helwig, R., & Tindal, G. (2002). Using general outcome measures in mathematics to measure adequate yearly progress as mandated by Title I. *Assessment for Effective Intervention, 28*(1), 9–18.

Hintze, J. M., & Christ, T. J. (2004). An examination of variability as a function of passage variance in CBM progress monitoring. *School Psychology Review, 33*(2), 204–217.

Hosp, M. K., & Hosp, J. L. (2003). Curriculum-based measurement for reading, spelling, and math: How to do it and why. *Preventing School Failure, 48*(1), 10–17.

Howell, K. W., & Nolet, V. (1999). *Curriculum-based evaluation: Teaching and decision making* (3rd ed.). Belmont, CA: Wadsworth.

Jeffs, T., & Banister, S. (2006). Enhancing collaboration and skill acquisition through the use of technology. *Journal of Technology and Teacher Education, 14*(2), 407–433.

Jones, C. J. (2001). CBA's that work: Assessing students' math content-reading levels. *Teaching Exceptional Children, 34*(1), 24–28.

Kranzler, J. H., Miller, M., & Jordan, L. (1999). An examination of racial/ethnic and gender bias of curriculum-based measurement of reading. *School Psychology Quarterly, 14*(3), 327–342.

MacMillan, P. (2000). Simultaneous measurement of reading growth, gender, and relative age many-faceted Rasch applied to CBM reading scores. *Journal of Applied Measurement, 1*(4), 393–408.

Madelaine, A., & Wheldall, K. (1999). Curriculum-based measurement of reading: A critical review. *International Journal of Disability, Development, and Education, 46*(1), 71–85.

Malecki, C. K., & Jewel, J. (2003). Developmental, gender, and practical considerations in scoring curriculum-based measurement writing probes. *Psychology in the Schools, 40*(4), 379–390.

Massanari, C. (2004). Responsiveness to intervention LD identifier or schoolwide improvement. *MPRRC Today, 6*(3), 4–5.

Mathes, P. G., Fuchs, D., Roberts, P. H., & Fuchs, L. S. (1998). Preparing students with special needs for reintegration: Curriculum-based measurement's impact on transenvironmental programming. *Journal of Learning Disabilities, 31*(6), 615–624.

McCloskey, D., & Schicke Athanasiou, M. (2000). Assessment and intervention practices with second-language learners among school psychologists. *Psychology in the Schools, 37*(3), 209–225.

McGlinchey, M. T., & Hixson, M. D. (2004). Using curriculum-based measurement to predict performance on state assessments in reading. *School Psychology Review, 33*(2), 193–203.

Mellard, D. (2004). Understanding responsiveness to intervention in learning disabilities determination. *MPRRC Today, 6*(3), 6–8.

Ortiz, A. A. (2002). Prevention of school failure and early intervention for English language learners. In A. J. Artiles & A. A. Ortiz (Eds.), *English language learners with special education needs: Identification, assessment, and instruction* (pp. 31–63). Washington, DC: Center for Applied Linguistics and Delta Systems.

Paulsen, K. J. (1997). Curriculum-based measurement: Translating research into school-based practice. *Intervention in School and Clinic, 32*, 162–167.

Plasencia-Peinado, J., & Alvarado, J. L. (2001). Assessing students with emotional and behavioral disorders using curriculum-based measurement. *Assessment for Effective Intervention, 26*(1), 59–66.

Popham, W. J. (2001). Teaching to the test? *Educational Leadership, 58*(6), 16–20.

Posner, D. (2004). What's wrong with teaching to the test? *Phi Delta Kappan, 85*(10), 749–751.

Quenemoen, R., Thurlow, M., Moen, R., Thompson, S., & Morse, A. B. (2003). *Progress monitoring in an inclusive standards-based assessment and accountability system (Synthesis Report 53)*. Minneapolis, MN: University of Minnesota, National Center on Educational Outcomes. Retrieved June 29, 2006, from http://education.umn.edu/NCEO/OnlinePubs/Synthesis53.html

Roberts, M. L., Marshall, J., Nelson, J. R., & Albers, C. A. (2001). Curriculum-based assessment procedures embedded within FBA's: Identifying escape-motivated behaviors in a general education classroom. *School Psychology Review, 30*(2), 264–277.

Scott, V. G., & Weishaar, M. K. (2003). Curriculum-based measurement for reading progress. *Intervention in School and Clinic, 38*(3), 153–159.

Seaman, J., Guggisberg, K., Malyn, D., Payne, J., & Scheibe, R. (2001). Validation of a procedure to measure copying fluency. *NASP Communique, 30*(2), 1–8.

Shapiro, E. S. (1992). Use of Gickling's model of curriculum-based assessment to improve reading in elementary age students. *School Psychology Review, 21*, 168–176.

Shapiro, E. S., & Ager, C. (1992). Assessment of special education students in regular education programs: Linking assessment to instruction. *Elementary School Journal, 92*, 283–196.

Shapiro, E. S., Angello, L. M., & Eckert, T. L. (2004). Has curriculum-based assessment become a staple of school psychology practice? An update and extension of knowledge, use, and attitudes from 1990 to 2000. *School Psychology Review, 33*(2), 249–257.

Shinn, M. R., Good, R. H., Knutson, N., Tilly, W. D., & Collins, V. L. (1992). Curriculum-based measurement reading fluency: A confirmatory analysis of its relation to reading. *School Psychology Review, 21*, 459–479.

Shinn, M. R., & Habedank, L. (1992). Curriculum-based measurement in special education problem identification and certification decisions. *Preventing School Failure, 36,* 11–15.

Stansberry, S. L., & Kymes, A. D. (2007). Transformative learning through "Teaching With Technology" electronic portfolios. *Journal of Adolescent & Adult Literacy, 50*(6), 488–496.

Stiggins, R., & Chappuis, S. (2005). Putting testing in perspective: It's for learning. *Principal Leadership, 6*(2), 16–20.

Supovitz, J. A., & Brennan, R. T. (1997). Mirror, mirror on the wall, which is the fairest test of all? An examination of the equitability of portfolio assessment relative to standardized tests. *Harvard Educational Review, 67*(3), 472–506.

Swain, K. D. (2005). CBM with goal setting: Impacting students' understanding of reading goals. *Journal of Instructional Psychology, 32*(3), 259–265.

Teelucksingh, E., Ysseldyke, J., Spicuzza, R., Ginsburg-Block, M. (2001). *Enhancing the learning of English language learners: Consultation and a curriculum based monitoring system.* Minneapolis, MN: University of Minnesota, National Center on Educational Outcomes.

Tucker, J. (1987). Curriculum-based assessments is no fad. *Collaborative Educator, 1*(4), 4–10.

VanDerHeyden, A. M., & Jimerson, S. R. (2005). Using response-to-intervention to enhance outcomes for children. *The California School Psychologist, 10,* 21–32.

VanDerHeyden, A. M., & Witt, J. C. (2005). Quantifying context in assessment: Capturing the effect of base rates on teacher referral and a problem-solving model of identification. *School Psychology Review, 34*(2), 161–183.

Vaughn, S., & Fuchs, L. S. (2003). Redefining learning disabilities as inadequate response to instruction: The promise and potential problems. *Learning Disabilities Research & Practice, 18,* 137–146.

Vellutino, F. R., Scanlon, D. M., & Lyon, G. R. (2000). Differentiating between difficult-to-remediate and readily remediated poor readers: More evidence against the IQ-achievement discrepancy definition of reading disability. *Journal of Learning Disabilities, 33,* 223–238.

Wright, J. (date unknown). Curriculum-Based Measurement: A Manual for Teachers. Retrieved January 15, 2006, from www.interventioncentral.org.

Assessing Performance Skills

Behavioral Assessment

Sandra Beyda Lorie

Functional behavioral assessment: A systematic process for describing problem behavior and identifying the environmental factors and events associated with it.

Functional analysis: An attempt to test one's hypothesis about the function a problem behavior serves by manipulating antecedents or consequences.

Target behavior: Any observable and measurable act.

Antecedents: Triggering events.

Setting events: Physiological, environmental, or social factors that set the occasion for problem behavior.

Consequences: Events that follow some target behavior.

Event recording: Recording a frequency count of behavior.

Interval recording: Dividing an observation period into a number of short time spans and recording some target behavior.

Time sampling: Dividing an observation period into equal time spans and observing the target behavior at the end of each time span.

Duration recording: Recording that focuses on the length of time some behavior lasts.

Latency recording: Recording how long it takes for an individual to initiate some target behavior.

Baseline: A measure of the level of some target behavior prior to intervention.

Case Study: Assessing Dion

Dion is an African American student in your fourth-grade class who has been diagnosed as having an emotional/behavioral disorder since the end of first grade. During his toddler years he seemed to have a great deal of energy and slept very little. He was alert and his motor development was normal. At age 4, he attended a preschool located in his urban neighborhood. However, in the first few weeks of the program, he began having trouble following directions and sitting still in class. He became physically aggressive with the other children, and three months later his mother was asked to remove him from the program. His parents moved at this time to a nearby suburb.

Dion attended an all-day kindergarten class. Again he had problems sitting still and attending to the teacher. When he became aggressive with the other children, his teacher attempted some behavioral interventions with no success. For example, at the universal (Tier 1) level of response to intervention (RTI), the teacher reviewed the classwide expectations for appropriate behavior (e.g., reminded students of the classroom rules, such as being respectful and listening to others, and provided examples of each rule), developed lessons to teach these behaviors, and reinforced students who exhibited these behaviors.

Dion was evaluated by his pediatrician for attention deficit hyperactivity disorder (ADHD) and put on Ritalin. Although medication improved Dion's ability to focus during teacher-led instruction, he remained aggressive with peers during unstructured situations like recess and at times during group work.

By the fall of first grade, it was clear that Dion was performing below his peers in reading and writing. He had few friends and continued to get into physical fights with his peers. At this time, he was referred for evaluation for special education services and was later placed in a self-contained classroom for students with emotional disturbance (ED). He continued to receive services in self-contained settings throughout the third grade.

Although Dion still receives the majority of his services in a self-contained classroom, he has recently been included in a general education classroom for math and science, where both the general educator and the special educator are present. His special education teacher has implemented a behavior program involving immediate incentives for work completion and responding appropriately to peers during group work. However, there are days when he refuses to work and exhibits angry outbursts during instruction, particularly when he is asked to read or write. At these times, Dion has been known to rip papers, throw books on the floor, and swear. The general education teacher has begun to question whether Dion is ready for even part-time inclusion.

By the end of this chapter you should be able to discuss answers regarding the following questions: Does Dion qualify for services under the category of ED? Why or why not? How might Dion's cultural diversity affect the evaluation process? What assessment data would you recommend including so that you can reach a diagnosis of ED? What assessment information would be valuable in designing an appropriate program for Dion? What behavior might you target first for intervention? What data would be helpful to collect for conducting a functional analysis of this target behavior? How might you set up a direct observational recording system to assess this behavior?

This chapter addresses CEC Content Standard 8 (assessment) and CEC Content 4 (instructional strategies). Different methods of formal and informal assessment and designing behavioral interventions based on those findings are clearly articulated within these content standards as they relate to special education (http://www.cec.sped.org/ps/perf_bases_stds/standards.html).

DEFINING BEHAVIOR

What is behavior? Alberto and Troutman (1995) define behavior as any observable and measurable act of an individual. The process of behavioral assessment is low inference. That is, the practitioner is concerned with responses that can be seen, rather than inferences one might make about the inner states of the individual (e.g., aggressiveness, fear). Kazdin (1982) suggests that "the definition should be so unambiguous that it could be read, repeated, and paraphrased by others" (p. 24). In other words, a behavior should be described so completely that many different observers of that behavior would agree on what it was they were observing. For instance, although many people might understand what the word *aggressiveness* means, we cannot easily collect data on this behavior unless it is described with enough specificity that a stranger could observe an aggressive act and record its occurrence or nonoccurrence. Does aggressiveness mean hitting another person? If so, what about hitting someone in jest? Perhaps a better description of aggressiveness might be to hit, poke, or in any way strike another person in such a way that this results in a negative response from that person (e.g., crying, swearing, yelling, giving a mean look). Defining behavior is not as easy as it seems. Focusing on what we can observe and measure helps us remain objective about the behavior in question rather than imbue it with value judgments we may consciously or unconsciously hold.

DETERMINING ELIGIBILITY

There are two reasons to conduct an assessment of behavior. One purpose is to determine whether a student is eligible for special education services under the classification of Emotional and/or Behavioral Disorders, referred to as emotional disturbance (ED) under the 1997 reauthorization of the Individuals with Disabilities Education Act (IDEA). The federal definition of ED is as follows:

(i) The term means a condition exhibiting one or more of the following characteristics over a long period of time and to a marked degree, which adversely affects educational performance:

   a. An inability to learn which cannot be explained by intellectual, sensory, or health factors;

   b. An inability to build or maintain satisfactory interpersonal relationships with peers and teachers;

   c. Inappropriate types of behavior or feelings under normal circumstances;

   d. A general pervasive mood of unhappiness or depression; or

   e. A tendency to develop physical symptoms or fears associated with personal or school problems.

(ii) The term includes children who are schizophrenic. The term does not include children who are socially maladjusted, unless it is determined that they are seriously emotionally disturbed. [34 C. F. R. 300.5 (b) (8)]

The criteria listed above apply to children and youth who have externalizing and/or internalizing behavioral problems. Externalizing behavior typically refers to a broad array of undercontrolled or acting-out behaviors, including aggression, arguing, defiance, oppositionality, and impulsivity. Support for the construct of an externalizing dimension of behavior problems has been studied extensively (Achenbach, 1985; Coie, Belding, & Underwood, 1988; Quay, 1986; Sroufe & Rutter, 1984). According to the Diagnostics and Statistical Manual—Fourth Edition (DSM-IV, 1994), the three most prevalent types of disorders within the externalizing domain are conduct disorder, oppositional defiant disorder, and attention deficit hyperactivity disorder (ADHD). Although ADHD falls under the federal definition of Other Health Impairment (OHI), students who exhibit externalizing behavior are most often referred for services under the ED classification (Gresham, Lane, MacMillan, & Bocian, 1999). On the other hand, internalizers who exhibit overcontrolled behavioral problems such as social withdrawal, loneliness, depression, and anxiety are rarely referred (Kauffman, 1993).

It is important to note, however, that many of the above terms (e.g., *externalizing, oppositional defiant disorder*) are recognized by psychiatrists and psychologists but not necessarily by persons who work in the educational setting. The psychiatric-based DSM system is a classification system that views emotional and behavioral problems as mental diseases that reside in the individual (Merrell, 1994). In addition, many of the disorders found in the DSM have little utility in guiding intervention as far as school professionals are concerned. Nevertheless, researchers from psychiatry and clinical psychology professionals developed many of the assessment instruments used in the ED area.

The classification system that professionals in the educational community use (i.e., the federal definition) likewise has its flaws (for a review, see Kauffman, 1993). One of the issues surrounds the exclusionary clause of "social maladjustment." Although the term *social maladjustment* was added to the original federal definition of emotional disturbance, it was never defined, nor were procedures delineated that could differentiate it from the other characteristics of ED (Merrell & Walker, 2004). In fact, it has been suggested that attempting to apply the social maladjustment exclusionary clause does nothing to correct the problems of significant underidentification of students who might otherwise benefit from services for ED (Merrell & Walker, 2004; Olympia, Farley, Christiansen, Pettersson, Jenson, & Clark, 2004).

A related problem is that few behavioral rating scales include a social maladjustment scale. One exception is the Scale for Assessing Emotional Disturbance (SAED;

Epstein & Cullinan, 1998). Even here, however, the authors of the scale admit that students could score high on the Socially Maladjusted Scale and also on one or more characteristics of ED (Epstein, Cullinan, Harniss, & Ryser, 1999; Epstein, Cullinan, Ryser, & Pearson, 2002).

In addition, a critical aspect of the federal definition of ED involves the adverse affect on educational performance. That is, it is assumed that unless a student's behavioral problems interfere with his or her academic performance, practitioners are not obligated to refer that student for services under the label ED. However, several researchers have criticized the educational performance clause as confusing at best (Forness & Knitzer, 1992; Kauffman, 1993).

There is no single assessment instrument sufficient for identifying a student with ED. States and local education agencies vary in the specific assessment procedures they use in determining eligibility for ED (Merrell, 1994). Instead, it is crucial that practitioners use a multimodal approach to identifying those students who require services. Typically, the following types of data are collected and integrated to determine eligibility for ED.

(a) An individual standardized multifactored test of learning capability

(b) An assessment of academic strengths and weaknesses and present levels of academic functioning

(c) A behavior/emotional evaluation that documents coping skills and emotional functioning

(d) A social and developmental history

(e) Systematic observation of the student in the general education classroom and at least one other appropriate setting

(f) Behavioral rating scales, at least one of which is a standardized behavior measurement instrument

(g) Documentation of interventions attempted to make behavioral and academic achievement possible in the general education setting and the effects of such interventions (This aspect of data collection is critical for conducting Tier 1 [universal] and Tier 2 [targeted group] interventions of RTI models.)

(h) Documentation of conferences with the parent and appropriate school personnel concerning the student's specific problems

(i) Evidence that the student, after receiving supportive general education assistance, still exhibits a disability consistent with the definition

(j) Evidence that the disability is not the result of a physical, sensory, or intellectual deficit

(k) Evidence that the student's learning process is consistently and significantly disrupted

An explanation of a variety of rating scales, interview formats, and direct observational methods useful for determining eligibility will be given later in this chapter.

In addition, evaluation for ED should include assessment of language. This recommendation is made based on more and more research suggesting a strong relationship between language problems and behavioral difficulties (Getty & Summy, 2006; Rogers-Adkinson & Hooper, 2003). For instance, in adolescents, rates of co-occurrence between speech and/or language disorders and behavioral problems have been reported to range from 60 percent (Giddan, Milling, & Campbell, 1996) to 80 percent (Warr-Leper, Wright, & Mack, 1994). In younger children, percentages are reported between

55 percent and 83 percent for pragmatic language problems combined with severe behavioral disorders (Griffith, Rogers-Adkinson, & Cusick, 1997). Pragmatic skills include turn taking, conveying communicative intent, rules of politeness, and other verbal and non-verbal behaviors that contribute to using language in a social context. Difficulties with pragmatic language can show up in problematic behaviors such as interrupting peers, not being able to negotiate with others, or an inability to request rather than grab a desired item.

Stevenson and Richman (1978) report rates of behavior problems in preschoolers with language delays as high as 60 percent. Language problems may be an early risk factor for behavioral difficulties. In fact, receptive and expressive language problems at kindergarten predicted conduct problems and behavioral dysfunction at grade 3 (Hooper, Roberts, Zeisel, Poe, & Graham, 2003). If language deficits are not considered in the evaluation process, students may be incorrectly identified for ED services in place of speech and/or language services. Additionally, understanding the possible co-occurrence of language deficits and ED would assist in designing educational programs that include speech and/or language intervention plans.

Breakpoint Practice

1. What are some criticisms of the current federal definition of ED?

2. Why are students with externalizing disorders more likely to be referred for evaluation for ED than students with internalizing disorders?

3. What possible outcomes might there be for failing to identify students with internalizing disorders?

4. Why might the lack of uniform procedures and assessment instruments for identifying students with ED be problematic?

5. How might language deficits explain the "inability to build or maintain satisfactory interpersonal relationships with peers and teachers" for a student with ED?

DESIGNING BEHAVIORAL INTERVENTIONS

A second purpose for behavioral assessment is to design appropriate interventions and evaluate their effectiveness. A functional behavioral assessment is conducted for this purpose. A functional behavioral assessment is "a systematic process for describing problem behavior, and identifying the environmental factors and surrounding events associated with problem behavior" (Office of Special Education Programs, 2001, p. 1). A functional behavioral assessment (FBA) is also a legal requirement according to the reauthorization of IDEA, 1997 and 2004. The law indicates that a school must conduct an FBA if a student has been suspended for more than 10 school days in a year, regardless of whether the behavior is determined to be a manifestation of the child's disability or whether he or she is removed from his or her current placement. In addition, FBAs are useful for: (1) identifying a student's behavioral problems, (2) targeting an appropriate replacement behavior, and (3) designing an intervention.

The FBA consists of two parts: a functional analysis and behavior intervention plan (BIP). Functional analysis is the process of collecting data about some problem behavior and attempting to determine the function it serves. Here the practitioners attempt to bring together all the available information gathered about the child. Information gleaned from interviews, rating scales, and direct observations would be used to more clearly and fully describe the target behavior. (Information on each of these instruments will be described later in this chapter.) In addition, the practitioner would attempt to identify the function that this behavior is serving based on any patterns that may be discerned between the problematic behavior and associated setting events, antecedents, and consequences. Simply put, the teacher forms a hypothesis about why the student is behaving in a certain way.

To verify whether this hypothesis is accurate, the practitioner attempts to test it by manipulating antecedents or consequences before designing and deciding on an appropriate intervention. For instance, a teacher might hypothesize that a student is exhibiting problematic behavior to avoid working with peers. The teacher would test this hypothesis by setting up a situation in which the student is required to complete a task alone and another one that requires him or her to complete a highly similar task with two other peers.

If the teacher is correct, then a formal BIP would be established for that child. The BIP is part of the FBA mandated by IDEA, and it is a way to delineate a strategy for helping the student with his or her problematic behavior. It is intended to be understood easily by others and is included as part of a student's individualized education program (IEP), when appropriate.

As was previously stated, the teacher forms a hypothesis about the function a behavior might be serving. Zentall and Javorsky (1995) use the term *payoffs* to refer to the possible function of a behavior. That is, behavior always serves a purpose for the child or youth, even when it is inappropriate as far as adults are concerned. Behavior serves to get us something or help us to avoid something. Table 5.1 lists the possible functions of inappropriate student behavior.

Behavior may serve more than one function for a particular individual. Also, the same behavior may serve different functions for different students. The reader who is interested in learning more about the functions of problematic behavior is referred to Umbreit, Ferro, Liaupsin, and Lane (2007) and Zentall (2006).

The next section will describe direct observational procedures that are useful for conducting an FBA or that are used as one of the required types of data before determining eligibility for ED.

Table 5.1 Payoffs for Misbehavior

	Types	Examples
The Student Gets:	Attention or relatedness from adults or peers	Social interaction with friends, praise from an adult
	Access to tangibles or activities	Gaining access to a favorite toy, being able to continue using the computer
	Stimulation	Physiological excitement that accompanies anger or fear, physical pleasure of cigarette smoking, cognitive stimulation generated from daydreaming
	Sense of competence or mastery	Demonstrating one's personal or scholarly accomplishments, showing off one's abilities
The Student avoids:	Social punishment or failure	Feeling of shame when asked to read when one cannot
	Attention from others	Rejection from peers, anxiety produced from being around too many people
	Stimulation	Being bored or experiencing a sensory-related discomfort like loud noises
	Physical pain or harm	Being slapped by a peer

MEASURES OF BEHAVIOR

DIRECT OBSERVATION

Perhaps the most valuable method of obtaining data about a student's problem behavior is to directly observe the student as he or she exhibits it. Observations, when used along with interviews and rating scales, are useful for forming a hypothesis about what function a particular behavior serves. They are used, therefore, in developing appropriate interventions (BIPs).

ABC Procedure

A commonly used direct observation approach is called the critical incident log or ABC procedure. In this approach, the classroom teacher makes brief written entries regarding both appropriate and inappropriate behavior exhibited by a student in a particular setting. Data is collected on (a) the target behavior observed, or any observable and measurable act of an individual; (b) antecedents or triggering events for the problematic behavior; and (c) consequences, or what follows the target behavior. Antecedents are environmental events that occur prior to or are concurrent with problematic as well as appropriate behaviors. Chandler and Dahlquist (2006) provide an extensive list of common antecedent stimuli. Examples include giving a student an instruction or task demand, providing a difficult or boring activity, offering choices, the type of materials or tasks presented, and peer or adult attention that occurred prior to the behavior in question.

Consequences refer to events that follow the target behavior and serve to strengthen or maintain the target behavior. They may include the results of some behavior and reactions to it. Examples of consequences are praise, reprimands, change in activity, stimulation, and tangibles such as acquiring a desired incentive. However, the same consequence does not have the same effect on all students. Therefore, it is crucial to record exactly what follows some target behavior, rather than attempt to interpret it.

In addition, setting events (e.g., time of day, subject area, hunger, medication, health) are noted because these might also affect how a student responds to antecedents and consequences. Setting events are of three types: physiological/biological, physical/environmental, and social/situational (Chandler & Dahlquist, 2006). See Table 5.2.

Observational Recording System

Another direct observation method, which is far more systematic, is referred to as an observational recording system (ORS). Whereas the ABC procedure is less structured, an ORS requires a little more advanced planning before recording behavior as it

Table 5.2 Types of Setting Events

Types of Setting Events	Examples
Physiological/biological	Fatigue, medication, time of day, health
Physical/environmental	The lighting in the room, seating arrangements, size of the area, noise level
Social/situational	Changes in routine, presence or absence of particular individuals, home-related issues that occurred prior to the observational session

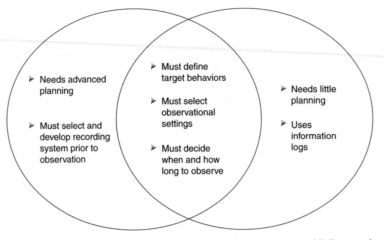

Needs advanced planning

Must select and develop recording system prior to observation

Must define target behaviors

Must select observational settings

Must decide when and how long to observe

Needs little planning

Uses information logs

Figure 5.1 Comparing observational recording systems to ABC procedures

occurs. Like the ABC procedure, the observer must define the target behavior, select the observational settings (at least three settings have been recommended; see Yssledyke, 1998), and decide when and for how long to observe. In an ORS, the observer also must select and develop a recording system prior to the observation. These procedures can fit appropriately with a functional behavior assessment. See Figures 5.1 and 5.2.

There are five types of recording systems: event recording, interval recording, time sampling, duration recording, and latency recording (see Table 5.3). Each of these will be described next.

Event recording is used to document the frequency or rate of occurrence of some target behavior (see Figure 5.3). According to Alberto and Troutman (1995), event recording is typically used when a teacher wants to decrease the number of times a student engages in a problematic behavior (e.g., use of profanity) or increase the incidence of positive behaviors (e.g., raising hands, number of math problems completed). To use event recording effectively, behaviors must be discrete; that is, the behavior must have an obvious beginning and ending. To record the frequency of a behavior, a tally mark is made every time a student exhibits the discrete behavior in a given period of time (e.g., 14 talkouts in 20 minutes). When the time periods of observation vary (e.g., 20 minutes one day, 30 minutes another day), frequencies are converted to rates; that is, the observer divides the frequency of responses by the number of minutes observed each day. This measure yields a frequency per minute, or rate of response. For example, a student who, over 3 daily class activities of different durations, was out of his seat 3 times in 20 minutes, 4 times in 30 minutes, and 5 times in 18 minutes, was out of his seat at a rate of 0.15, 0.13, and 0.28 per minute. Event recording is not appropriate if (a) the behavior occurs at such a high frequency that the number cannot be counted accurately, and/or (b) when the behavior occurs for extended time periods (Alberto & Troutman, 1995).

Sometimes an observer is interested in recording continuous behaviors and/or high-frequency behaviors (e.g., hand flapping, playing) for which event recording is not useful. In such cases, two other types of recording systems, interval recording and time sampling procedures, are recommended. Interval recording consists of partial-interval or whole-interval recording. In partial interval recording, a target behavior is observed for a block of time (e.g., 30 minutes), which is divided into short, equal

Figure 5.2 Functional behavioral assessment form

Complete when gathering information about a student's behavior to determine the need for a Behavioral Intervention Plan. If used in developing a Behavioral Intervention Plan, the Functional Behavioral Assessment must be reviewed at an IEP meeting and may be attached to the IEP.

This page was developed using the criteria established in the Illinois State Board of Education's *Behavioral Interventions in Schools: Guidelines for Development of District Policies for Students with Disabilities.* For further clarification regarding the Functional Behavioral Assessment page, reference the most recent *Behavioral Interventions in Schools: Guidelines for Development of District Policies for Students with Disabilities.*

STUDENT	GRADE	DATE

Participants/Titles   **Participants/Titles**

_____   _____

_____   _____

TARGET BEHAVIOR - Include a description of the intensity, frequency, and duration of the behavior.

SETTING - Include a description of the setting in which the behavior occurs (e.g., physical setting, time of day, person involved).

ANTECEDENTS - Include a description of the relevant events that preceded the target behavior.

CONSEQUENCES - Include a description of the consequences that resulted from the target behavior.

ENVIRONMENTAL VARIABLES - Include a description of any environmental variables that may affect the behavior (e.g., medication, medical conditions, sleep, diet, schedule, social factors).

STUDENT STRENGTHS - Include a description of behavioral strengths (e.g., ignores inappropriate behavior of peers, positive interactions with staff, ability to redirect, accepts responsibility, etc.).

FUNCTIONAL ALTERNATIVES - Include a description of appropriate behaviors that could serve as functional alternatives to the target behavior.

ISBE 37-45 (10/00)

Figure 5.2 (Continued)

BEHAVIORAL INTERVENTION PLAN

Complete when the team has determined a Behavioral Intervention Plan is needed.

STUDENT	GRADE	DATE

SUMMARY OF FUNCTIONAL BEHAVIORAL ANALYSIS (may attach completed form)

STUDENT'S STRENGTHS

SUMMARY OF PREVIOUS INTERVENTIONS ATTEMPTED

COMPLETE PAGE 2 PRIOR TO THESE SECTIONS:
DATA COLLECTION PROCEDURES AND METHODS FOR MONITORING INTERVENTIONS

PROVISIONS FOR COORDINATING WITH THE HOME

ISBE 37-441 (10/00)

Figure 5.2 (Continued)

TARGETED BEHAVIOR	POSITIVE BEHAVIORAL INTERVENTIONS	SUPPORTS **(if needed)**	RESTRICTIVE INTERVENTIONS **(if needed)**

ISBE 37-441 (10/00) PAGE 2 OF 2

Source: Illinois State Board of Education. (2005). Functional Behavior Assessment Form from http://isbe.net. Copyright © 2005; Illinois State Board of Education, reprinted by permission. All rights reserved.

Table 5.3 Types of Recording Systems

Recording System	Definition	Examples	Guidelines for Use
Event recording	Used to document the frequency or rate of a target behavior.	Raising hands. Use of profanity. Number of math problems completed.	Behavior must be discrete. Not appropriate for high-frequency behavior or for behavior that occurs for extended time periods.
Interval recording	Used to document continuous behaviors and/or high-frequency behaviors: A block of time is divided into short, equal intervals. In partial interval recording, the target behavior is recorded if it occurs at any time during that interval. In whole-interval recording, the target behavior is recorded only if it occurred for the entire interval.	Hand flapping. Playing.	Used to provide an estimate of frequency and duration of behavior.
Time sampling	Used to document continuous behaviors and/or high-frequency behaviors: A block of time is divided into long, equal intervals (e.g., minutes of time), and a target behavior is recorded only if it was occurring at the end of the interval.	Engaging in positive interaction. Engaging in negative interaction. Off-task behavior.	Does not require an observer's undivided attention, as does interval recording, but can underestimate the frequency of a target behavior.
Duration recording	Used to document the length of time a target behavior lasts.	Amount of time student interacts with peers. Time spent writing. How long a tantrum lasts.	Appropriate for continuous behaviors. Practitioner should note the time the target behavior began and the time when it ended.
Latency recording	Used to document how long it takes for an individual to initiate a target behavior.	How long it takes to sit down once the bell has rung. How long it takes to comply with a teacher's direction.	Practitioner should note the time the cue was given and the time the student actually responded.

intervals (e.g., 30 seconds). The observer makes a tally mark if the behavior occurred at any time during that interval. If the behavior occurred more than once during an interval, only one tally mark is recorded. Generally the observer wears a headphone and listens for a beep indicating when 30 seconds have passed. Whole-interval recording is set up the same way; however, the tally mark is made only if the behavior occurred for the entire interval (see Figure 5.4). Interval recording is useful because it provides an estimate of frequency and duration of behavior.

Momentary time sampling is similar to interval recording except that the intervals are usually broken down into minutes rather than seconds (see Figure 5.5). In addition, the tally mark is made only if the student is observed engaging in the target behavior

Figure 5.3 Sample data collection record for event recording

Student: Tobias
Observer: Ms. Richardson
Target behavior: VR and NR

Observation Time	Subject	Number of VR	Number of NR
Mon: 10:00–10:25	Reading	+ + + +	
Tues: 10:15–10:50	Reading	+ + +	
Thurs: 1:05–1:25	Math		+ +

VR: verbal refusal; recorded when the student makes a verbal statement of refusal regarding the completion of a task and/or complying with the request of an adult (e.g., "I'm not doing this").

NR: negative verbal; recorded when the student makes a negative verbal statement but is still complying with adult's request and/or instructions (e.g., "This is dumb," "I hate this").

(e.g., engaging in positive or negative social interactions, off-task behavior) at the end of the interval. Because the observer has to watch the student only at the end of each interval, momentary time sampling does not require one's undivided attention, as does interval recording. Observations resulting from either interval recording or time sampling procedures can be converted into a percentage (e.g., talkouts that occurred during four out of five intervals = 80 percent of the observation time). That is, the observer divides the number of intervals during which the behavior occurred by the total number of intervals observed. This ratio is multiplied by 100 to yield a percentage. Time sampling can provide an estimate of the proportion of time a particular behavior occurs. However, it can underestimate the frequency of behavior because a behavior might occur immediately before or after the moment of recording, yet that instance would not be recorded.

Duration recording is used when the focus of the observation is on the length of time some behavior lasts (see Figure 5.6). This procedure is appropriate for continuous behaviors rather than discrete behaviors or behaviors of short duration (e.g., the amount of time the student interacts with peers, time spent writing, how long tantrums last).

Figure 5.4 Sample data collection record for whole-interval recording

Date: October 14, 2009
Student: Krystal
Observer: Ms. Danion
Subject: Social studies independent seatwork time
Start time: 1:50
Target behavior: Talking with peers unrelated to class work; 10-second intervals

1	2	3	4	5	6
X	X	X	X	0	0

Number of intervals of occurrence: 4
Percentage of intervals of occurrence: 67%
X = Occurrence
0 = Nonoccurrence

Figure 5.5 Sample data collection record for partial interval recording

Date: February 25, 2009
Student: Bobby
Observer: Mr. Juarez
Subject: Mathematics
Start time: 9:45   End time: 10:05
Target behavior: Negative social (NS)
1-minute intervals over 20-minute time span

1	2	3	4	5	6	7	8	9	10	11	12	13	14	15	16	17	18	19	20
		✓		✓			✓	✓		✓	✓		✓	✓		✓	✓	✓	✓

Intervals in which at least one instance of NS occurred = 12
Percentage of intervals in which NS occurred = 60%
Negative social behavior (NS): Defined as any time student is interacting verbally or nonverbally with another student or adult in an inappropriate manner.

Like event recording, duration recording is suitable for recording discrete behaviors. The observer uses a stopwatch, audiotape, or videotape of the target behavior. Three methods of determining the duration of some target behavior include total duration, average duration, and duration per occurrence.

Total duration is the entire time a student engages in a target behavior during a period of time (e.g., how long a child continues working on an independent seatwork assignment). For example, a teacher might want to find out how much time a student is off task (e.g., looking away from the teacher or book, looking at or playing with materials other than materials peers are using) during a 30-minute reading instruction session. The teacher adds the separate time periods of off-task behavior (e.g., 3 minutes, 7 minutes, 2 minutes per 30-minute time period = 12 minutes total duration). The total duration of 12 minutes would be recorded and graphed. That is, the student is off task during reading instruction for a total of 12 minutes out of 30 minutes. Duration per occurrence is the length of time per episode that a student engages in a target behavior.

Figure 5.6 Sample data collection record for duration recording

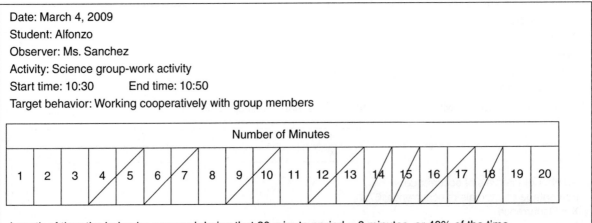

Date: March 4, 2009
Student: Alfonzo
Observer: Ms. Sanchez
Activity: Science group-work activity
Start time: 10:30   End time: 10:50
Target behavior: Working cooperatively with group members

Number of Minutes																			
1	2	3	4	5	6	7	8	9	10	11	12	13	14	15	16	17	18	19	20

Length of time the behavior occurred during that 20-minute period = 8 minutes, or 40% of the time.

Figure 5.7 Sample data collection record for latency recording

Date: January 20, 2009
Student: Tifany
Observer: Mr. Polster
Activity: Paying for groceries at the checkout counter
Start time: End time:
Target behavior: The amount of time it takes to pay the cashier once the cashier has stated the amount.

Date	Time of Stimulus Cue	Time of Response	Latency
2/12	11:03:00	11:04:00	60 seconds
12/13	11:23:05	11:23:55	55 seconds
12/14	11:11:07	11:11:25	18 seconds
12/15	11:21:15	11:21:31	16 seconds
12/16	10:54:01	10:54:12	11 seconds

In the previous example, the teacher records and graphs each separate episode of off-task behavior (3, 7, and 2). Average duration is when the observer finds the average length of time across several episodes of duration recording. The observer calculates average duration by adding the lengths of time of each episode of the target behavior and dividing by the total number of episodes (e.g., [3 + 7 + 2]/3 = 4). That is, the student is off task during reading instruction an average of 4 minutes out of 30 minutes.

Latency recording refers to how long it takes a student to initiate a target behavior once some signal has been given (see Figure 5.7). For example, how long does it take a student to sit down in her or his seat once the bell rings? Once the target behavior is carefully defined, the observer uses a stopwatch or records the time when the behavior begins and ends.

The teacher also uses a recording system to collect data during baseline. Baseline is a time period where a teacher gathers data on what is naturally occurring (current status). Therefore, baseline data are measures of the level of behavior as it occurs prior to intervention. The teacher graphs the data to provide a visual depiction of the behavior. Alberto and Troutman (2006) recommend collecting and plotting at least five baseline data points to obtain a realistic description of the behavior and rule out unusual occurrences, such as a student's illness. In the case of a busy teacher, a paraprofessional can be trained to collect baseline data.

Teachers can also look at data and (1) decide that what appeared to be a concern really is not, (2) recognize that the student's behavior is their own pet peeve, or 3) choose to address teaching factors that they have more control over versus student behavior.

The next step would be to implement some intervention and collect data immediately following that intervention. Postintervention data is analyzed to determine whether the intervention has succeeded. The teacher hopes that a problem behavior will decrease (e.g., frequency of talkouts during whole-class instruction, latency of response to teacher direction) or that appropriate behaviors will increase (e.g., number of math problems completed during independent seatwork, use of appropriate comments during cooperative groups) depending on what behavior has been targeted for change. Monitoring the progress of students receiving interventions is a critical practice for RTI models, particularly at the Tier 2 (group) and Tier 3 (individual student) levels. A description of each of these intervention designs is beyond the scope of this chapter. The reader is referred to Alberto and Troutman (1995) for a more detailed explanation of these interventions.

Other direct observation procedures that have been standardized are available. The Behavior Assessment Scale for Children—2 (BASC-2; Reynolds & Kamphaus, 2004) and the Achenbach System of Empirically Based Assessment (ASEBA; Achenbach & Reescorla, 2001) both include a direct observation protocol in their assessment systems. The BASC-2 and ASEBA will be described later in this chapter.

Breakpoint Practice

1. What is a functional behavior assessment (FBA)?

2. How is the FBA conducted?

3. Why is it important to conduct direct observations of student behavior?

4. What are the differences between using a critical incident log or ABC procedure versus an observational recording system?

5. Why would event recording be an unsatisfactory way to measure a behavior such as hand flapping?

6. What other recording system would be better to use for a behavior like hand flapping?

7. Explain the difference between time sampling and interval recording.

8. What recording system might an educator use to track the incidence of swearing in the classroom?

9. How will the educator know if there has been an improvement in a target behavior?

10. What is the importance of collecting baseline data?

Interviews

Interview protocols are part of the eligibility determination process for ED and are necessary for conducting an FBA. It is difficult to gain a complete understanding of a student's behavioral problems without talking to those who are familiar with the student. Therefore, assessment of behavior must include information gleaned from interviews with parents, teachers, and the child, who is the best source of information when age and language skills permit. The practitioner should remember that interviews are used as one component of a multiassessment process. The multiassessment approach is especially important due to the low to moderate agreement found between parent and child interview responses (Hodges, 1993; Hughes & Baker, 1990). One purpose of an interview is to help define a student's problematic behavior and the environmental and other factors associated with it. When children are interviewed, their responses can provide information about how they perceive their problems and what strategies they currently possess to address these challenges. Information can also be obtained about how responsive the child may be to treatment.

Parents and/or guardians are interviewed to obtain descriptive information not limited to a child's behavior. Parents' view of the problematic behavior, the quality of the parent-child relationship, and other family circumstances affecting the child may be revealed (Barkley, 1990; Busse & Beaver, 2000). The data obtained from parent interviews can also help with the development of interventions that are both useful and feasible. McConaughy (2005) recommends having parents complete rating scales prior to the parent interview. Results from the rating scales can then be used to formulate additional questions about a child for clarification.

Interviews may be structured, semistructured, or unstructured. Most of the structured interviews in the area of ED derive from the mental health field. These diagnostic interviews collect data on childhood disorders (e.g., anxiety disorders, attention deficit hyperactivity disorders, depressive disorders) identified in the DSM-IV (American Psychological Association, 2000). McConaughy (2003) has delineated many advantages of using diagnostic interviews, including their ability to provide systematic comparisons of child and parent reports for the same symptoms and diagnoses, and the fact that they are systematic to use. However, there is no clear alignment between having a psychiatric diagnosis and qualifying for special education services (Gresham & Gansle, 1992). Nevertheless, teachers may find results from diagnostic interviews included in certain students' files. Therefore, it is worthwhile to mention them here in addition to other interview protocols.

Two structured diagnostic interview protocols are the Diagnostic Interview for Children and Adolescents (DICA; Herjanic & Reich, 1982; Reich & Welner, 1992; DICA-IV; Reich, Welner, Herjanic, & MHS Staff, 1997) and the Diagnostic Interview Schedule for Children (DISC; Costello, Edelbrock, Dulcan, Kalas, & Klaric, 1984; DISC-R; Shaffer, et al., 1993; DISC-2.3; Shaffer, 1992; NIMH DISC-IV; Shaffer, Fisher, Lucas, Dulcan, & Schwab-Stone, 2000). Both are highly structured diagnostic interviews that were developed primarily for research and clinical assessment. Both include protocols for interviewing children and youth as well as parents. Structured interviews have the advantage of collecting data in a systematic and comprehensive manner. In addition, the DICA has demonstrated adequate reliability (Herjanic & Reich, 1982; Herjanic, Herjanic, Brown, & Wheatt, 1975) and discriminant validity (Herjanic & Campbell, 1977). However, further validity testing of the DICA is needed. Additionally, the DISC has yielded lower test-retest reliabilities for younger children versus older children (Edelbrock, Costello, Dulcan, Kalas, & Conover, 1985; Jensen et al., 1995).

A semistructured diagnostic interview is the Schedule for Affective Disorders and Schizophrenia for School-age Children (K-SADS) (Puig-Antich & Chambers, 1978). It was designed for children ages 6 to 18 years. It has a protocol for parents and for children. There are two versions of the K-SADS: The Present Episode version is designed for use in assessing current or present episodes of psychopathology, and the Epidemiologic version is used to assess psychopathology that has occurred over the course of the individual's entire life. The K-SADS consists of over 800 questions, including open-ended and structured questions. The trained interviewer obtains information on a wide range of emotional and behavior problems and then classifies these problems according to the DSM-IV diagnostic criteria. The K-SADS takes approximately 90 minutes to three hours to administer. Both versions have yielded adequate test-retest reliability (Chambers et al., 1985) and validity (Orvaschel, Puig-Antich, Chambers, Tabrizi, & Johnson, 1982).

The Autism Diagnostic Interview-Revised (ADI-R) (Lord, Rutter, & Le Couteur, 1994) is a standardized, semistructured interview focusing on the criteria of the DSM-IV-TR (American Psychological Association [APA], 2000). Trained clinicians use the ADI-R to interview parents and caregivers of children as early as 18 months. Its primary focus is on developmental abnormalities in the areas of communication, social development, play, repetitive and restricted behaviors, and general behavior problems for children between the ages of 48 months and 60 months.

The interviews discussed next are more common to school-related assessment procedures. These include semistructured interview protocols. The Semistructured

Clinical Interview for Children and Adolescents (SCICA; McConaughy & Achenbach, 2001) is a semistructured interview protocol designed for use with children age 6 to 18 years. Assessment developers of the Achenbach System of Empirically Based Assessment (ASEBA; Achenbach & Reescorla, 2001) designed the instrument to be used in combination with the rating scale's other components (see Rating Scales). The protocol covers nine areas: activities, school, and job; friends; family relations; fantasies; self-perceptions and feelings; parent- or teacher-reported problems; achievement tests for ages 6 through 11; screening for fine- and gross-motor abnormalities for ages 6 through 11; and adolescent issues for ages 12 through 18. Along with asking open-ended questions, the interview also requests a Kinetic Family Drawing (KFD) (Burns, 1992) for children age 6 to 12. The KFD is a personality testing technique, that involves asking children to draw a picture of themselves with their family doing something. The examiner gathers information by asking the child questions about the drawing and noting certain characteristics about it (e.g., family members not included, size of the child in the picture compared to others, etc.). The entire protocol, including the KFD, takes approximately 90 minutes to complete. Reliability and validity of the SCICA are adequate.

A semistructured parent interview protocol is the Structured Developmental History of the BASC (Reynolds & Kamphaus, 1992). It was designed to obtain information about a child's developmental history from parents or primary caregivers. Questions address the areas of the mother's pregnancy and birth, family history, family health, the child's developmental milestones, medical history, friendships, interests, behavior, adaptive skills, and educational history.

Interviews have also been designed as part of a functional analysis. One of these is the Functional Analysis Interview Form (FAI) (O'Neill et al., 1997). The FAI consists of questions addressing:

(a) the topography, frequency, duration, and intensity of problematic behaviors;

(b) environmental conditions related to behavior;

(c) contextual variables that may be related to the behavior;

(d) functional alternative behaviors and communication skills exhibited by the student; and

(e) potential reinforcers and interventions.

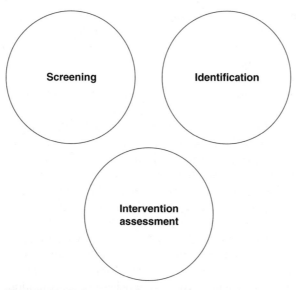

Figure 5.8 Purposes of rating scales

It takes 45 to 90 minutes to complete. Information obtained during this interview can lead to hypotheses about the function of problematic behavior that can then be verified or refuted using the Functional Analysis Observation Form (O'Neill et al., 1997).

Rating Scales
Rating scales represent one method of collecting information relative to an individual's behavior or emotional status. Typically they allow for multiple informants (i.e., parent, teacher, student). These instruments may be used as a screening device in the prereferral process before a child is officially evaluated for special education services. This process takes place at the Tier 1 (universal) level and the Tier 2 (targeted group) level of RTI models and may lead to special education services. Rating scales are also included as one means of assessing students who meet the criteria for ED. When used for identification purposes, rating scales should always be supplemented by other data-collection methods due to issues of rater reliability. Finally, rating scales are often useful as a means for evaluating the effectiveness of a particular intervention (see Figure 5.8).

Behavior rating scales that assess a wide variety of behavior, also called broadband measures, are typically most useful as general screening and diagnostic instruments (Breen, Eckert, & DuPaul, 2003). After using a broadband instrument, the practitioner might find that using a narrow-band rating scale will provide more detail about one particular behavior problem (e.g., attention deficit hyperactivity disorder [ADHD], social skills deficits). However, both broadband and narrow-band rating scales can be used to screen, diagnose, or treat children with ED. A description of some of the more commonly used rating scales follows.

Breakpoint Practice
1. What is the difference between broadband and narrow-band rating scales?
2. Why might the practitioner want to include rating scales of both types when identifying students for ED?

Rating Scales Across Problem Behavior. The Achenbach System of Empirically Based Assessment (ASEBA; Achenbach & Reescorla, 2001) is the updated version of the Child Behavior Checklist (Achenbach, 1991), the most frequently used assessment of child and youth behavior. It is also available in 58 languages. The current version consists of a preschool form for 18 months through 5 years, the Teacher-Completed Form (TRF/6-18) and Parent-Completed Form (CBCL/6-18) both for ages 6 through 18, and the Youth Self-Report (YSR) for students ages 11 through 18. The system includes a Direct Observation Form and Profile to allow for the systematic observation of children's behavior in a classroom or other group setting as well as a semistructured protocol for conducting child and youth interviews (see Interviews). It is by far the most detailed and well-researched behavioral evaluation system available.

The Teacher-Completed Form consists of 113 items (e.g., "can't sit still, restless, or hyperactive"; "destroys property belonging to others") including a section related to adaptive behaviors (e.g., "How hard is he/she working?"). The items are rated as 0 (not true), 1 (somewhat or sometimes true), or 2 (very true or often true). The form takes 15 to 20 minutes to complete. Items are scored across eight syndrome scales: Withdrawn/ Depressed, Anxious/Depressed, Somatic Complaints, Rule-Breaking Behavior, Social Problems, Thought Problems, Aggressive Behavior, and Attention Problems. The last scale is subdivided into two factors: Inattention and Hyperactivity-Impulsivity. In addition, all forms have DSM-oriented scales. The TRF has six DSM-oriented scales: Affective Problems, Anxiety Problems, Somatic Problems, Attention Deficit/Hyperactivity Problems, Oppositional Defiant Problems, and Conduct Problems.

Raw scores may be converted to normalized T-scores and percentile ranks for each syndrome and DSM-oriented scale. These scores are provided separately for each gender for ages 6 through 11 and 12 through 18.

Normative samples are current (February 1999 through January 2000) and were cross-sectioned on the basis of socioeconomic status; ethnicity; region; and urban, suburban, or rural residence. Normative data for the CBCL/6-18, TRF/6-18, and YSR were based on a large, nationally representative sample. Reliability is excellent and includes test-retest, interrater, and internal consistency. Content, construct, concurrent, and discriminative validity information is available in the manual.

The Behavior Assessment System for Children–2 (BASC-2; Reynolds & Kamphaus, 2004) is a "multi-method, multidimensional approach to evaluate the behavior and self-perception of children 4 to 18 years of age" (p. 1). It was designed to measure observable adaptive (positive) and maladaptive behavior using a comprehensive system of assessment. According to the authors, the BASC was developed to:

(a) facilitate the identification of certain clinical disorders or emotion and behavior,

(b) assist in the educational classification of severe emotional/behavioral disorders,

(c) assist in distinguishing between students with ED and those with social maladjustment or conduct disorder,

(d) foster the development of IEPs,

(e) monitor the efficacy of student progress and treatment effects, and

(f) support research efforts centering on varying aspects of child and adolescent psychopathology.

The system includes teacher-, parent-, and child-completed rating scales. It also includes forms for conducting a student observation, a general measure of personality, and structured developmental history inventory (see Interviews).

The Teacher Rating Scale (TRS) includes three different forms: preschool, child, and adolescent (109, 148, and 138 items, respectively). Informants rate students using a 4-point rating scale (N = never occurs, S = sometimes occurs, O = often occurs, A = almost always occurs). The TRS takes approximately 10 to 20 minutes to complete. Sample adaptive behavior items include "makes decisions easily," "is well organized," "offers help to other children." Sample problem behavior items include "blames others," "bullies others," "uses foul language," "sleeps during class." The TRS produces three composite scores of clinical problems: externalizing problems (i.e., aggression, hyperactivity, conduct problems), internalizing problems (i.e., anxiety, depression, somatization), and school problems (i.e., attentional and learning deficits). In addition, positive behaviors are presented on an adaptive skills profile scale (i.e., leadership, social skills, study skills). Raw scores may be converted to a standard T-score and percentile rank.

Most recent normative data were gathered from August 2002 and May 2004 from over 375 sites. The manual details the sample's age, gender, ethnicity, geographic region, residence, and parent education characteristics. Norms are more than adequate. General and clinical norm data are provided. The manual reports adequate internal consistency, test-retest, and interrater reliability. Content, criterion-related, and construct validity are more than adequate. The amount of information reported on concurrent validity is also impressive.

Behavior Evaluation Scale–2 (McCarney & Leigh, 1990) has been designed to screen for behavioral problems, assess the behavior of students referred for behavioral disorders, and assist in the diagnosis of emotional/behavior disorders. It can also be used to develop interventions and document subsequent student progress. The scale includes 76 items, developed and validated by classroom teachers and professionals in special education. It is appropriate for use with children in kindergarten through grade 12 and takes 15 to 20 minutes to complete. Items are scored on a 7-point rating system (1 = never or not observed, 2 = less than once a month, 3 = approximately once a month, 4 = approximately once a week, 5 = more than once a week, 6 = daily at various times, 7 = continuously throughout the day). Each of the items falls under one of five subscales: Learning Problems (e.g., "does not grasp basic concepts or information related to academic tasks"), Interpersonal Difficulties (e.g., "verbally or physically threatens other students or teachers"), Inappropriate Behavior (e.g., "does not obey teachers' directives or classroom rules"), Unhappiness/Depression (e.g., "cries in response to personal or school situations"), and Physical Symptoms/Fears (e.g., "exhibits excessive fatigue").

The BES-2 has a School Version, which consists of three protocols: (1) Student Record Form, completed by the informant; (2) the Data Collection Form, used for observing and recording behaviors on a daily basis over a one-month interval; and (3) the Pre-Referral Behavior Evaluation Checklist—2. There is also a Home Version of the BES-2 written in English and in Spanish.

The normative sample included 2,272 students from 31 states to represent four geographic regions of the United States. Five hundred sixty-eight regular education teachers administered the BES-2 to randomly selected students from their classes during the fall of 1988 and the spring of 1989. Internal consistency and test-retest reliability are adequate. Construct, discriminant, and concurrent validity are available. However, researchers have recommended the need for further studies to establish concurrent validity of the BES-2 (Breen & Fiedler, 2003).

The Scale for Assessing Emotional Disturbance (SAED; Epstein & Cullinan, 1998) is a standardized, norm-referenced rating scale that operationalizes the federal definition of ED. It is comprised of 52 statements that are grouped into six subscales. This corresponds to the five characteristics of the definition, plus the exclusionary clause: (1) Inability to Learn, (2) Relationship Problems, (3) Inappropriate Behavior, (4) Unhappiness or Depression, (5) Physical Symptoms or Fears, and (6) Social

Maladjustment. The scale takes approximately 10 minutes to complete by teachers or others who have worked with the student for at least 2 months. The norm sample included 1,371 students with ED and 2,266 students without ED, ranging in age from 5 to 18 years. Students were selected from 34 states. Test-retest reliability, inter-rater, and internal consistency reliability are adequate. The SAED has also been found to discriminate between students with and without ED. Further information on validity needs to be collected because the scale is still quite new.

See Table 5.4 for an overview of the rating scales for identifying problem behavior.

Table 5.4 Rating Scales for Identifying Problem Behavior

Name	Publisher	Content	Age or Grade Level	Time to Administer
Achenbach System of Empirically Based Assessment (ASEBA)	Thomas Achenbach, University of Vermont	Broadband, comprehensive assessment system includes: teacher-completed form (TRF), parent-completed form (CBCL), youth-completed form (YSR), preschool forms (CBCL/P), direct observation form, and semistructured interview protocol.	Teacher completed form (TRF) = 6–18 years. CBCL = 6–18. YSR = 11–18. CBCL/P = 18 months– 5 years.	15–20 minutes
Behavior Assessment System for Children (BASC-2)	American Guidance Service	Broadband, comprehensive assessment system includes teacher rating scale (TRS), parent rating scale (PRS), and Self Report of Personality (SRP) completed by the child, a direct observation and interview protocol.	TRS = 4–5, 6–11, and 12–18 years. PRS = 4–5, 6–11, and 12–18 years. SRP = 8–11 and 12–18 years.	15–20 minutes
Behavior Evaluation Scale-2 (BES-2)	Hawthorne Educational Services	A behavior questionnaire consisting of a school version and a home version. The school version includes a rating scale, a data collection form for direct observation of behavior, and a prereferral checklist.	School version = grades K–12. Home version = ages 5–18	15–20 minutes
Scale for Assessing Emotional Disturbance (SAED)	PRO-ED	A behavior rating scale designed to align with the federal definition of ED.	5–18 years.	10 minutes

> **Breakpoint Practice**
>
> Name two popular multi-method assessment systems.

Functional Behavior Assessment Rating Scales. Less time-consuming functional analysis protocols have also been developed. Some of these include the Functional Analysis Screening Tool (FAST, Iwata, 1995), the Motivation Assessment Scale, (MAS; Durand & Crimmins, 1988), and the Problem Behavior Questionnaire (PBQ; Lewis, Scott, & Sugai, 1994). These consist of 18 items, 16 items, and 15 items, respectively.

The MAS was designed for self-injurious behavior, although it has been used for other behaviors such as aggression (Sigafoos, Kerr, & Roberts, 1994). This scale was intended to help practitioners identify the possible function of problem behavior. Several limitations must be considered before you use the MAS. Unfortunately, reliability estimates have varied across studies, leaving the technical adequacy of this scale questionable (Barton-Arwood, Wehby, Gunter, & Lane, 2003). Furthermore, the scale has been recommended for individuals with severe developmental disabilities rather than for use with students with ED (Fox, Conroy, & Hechaman, 1998).

In contrast, the PBQ was designed for use with students with mild behavioral challenges in general education settings. Yet the PBQ lacks information about its technical adequacy. Easy-to-use, empirically validated FBA rating scales remain a crucial area of need (Barton-Arwood, et al., 2003).

> **Breakpoint Practice**
>
> Explain some problems associated with existing functional behavior assessment rating scales.

Rating Scales for Attention Disorder Hyperactivity. The diagnosis of attention deficit hyperactivity disorder (ADHD) is determined by a set of criteria of the DSM-IV (American Psychological Association, 2000). Accordingly, the disorder has three subtypes: (1) hyperactive-impulsive, (2) inattentive, and (3) combined. The third type (combined) has the highest rates of co-occurrence with externalizing behavior (aggression) (Banaschewski, Brandeis, Heinrich, Albrecht, Brunner, & Rothenberger, 2003). Individuals with ADHD may qualify for special education services under the IDEA under (a) a co-occurring category of disability (e.g., learning disabilities and emotional and behavioral disorders) or (b) under the category of other health impairment. Behavior rating scales are the most widely employed measures of ADHD for classification purposes (Zentall, 2006).

The ADD-H: Comprehensive Teacher Rating Scale (ACTeRS; Ullmann, Sleator, & Sprague, 1984, 1991) was developed for identifying children (grades K–5) with ADHD and measuring response to intervention. It consists of 24 items relevant to classroom behavior; these items are rated on a 1 (almost never) to 5 (almost always) Likert scale. Factor analysis of the ACTeRS has yielded four dimensions: attention, hyperactivity, social problems, and oppositional behavior. Internal consistency, test-retest, and interrater reliability are reported in the manual (subscales range from .51 to .97, with the median being .87). The profile sheet used with the ACTeRS converts raw scores to percentiles. The ACTeRS subscales have been found to differentiate between children with ADD and without ADD and those with learning disabilities (Ullmann et al., 1984, 1991). The authors claim that it can be used to differentiate hyperactive from nonhyperactive subtypes of ADHD (Ullmann, Sleator, & Sprague, 1985). Currently, information on criterion-related and predictive validity is lacking.

The Attention Deficit Disorders Evaluation Scale—2 (ADDES; McCarney, 1995) was designed as a screening, diagnostic, and intervention tool for students age 4 to 18. It consists of 60 items on the school version rating form and 46 items on the home version rating form (e.g., "Does not appear to listen to what others are saying," "runs in the house."). Items are divided into two subscales: Inattentive and Hyperactive-Impulsive. It was designed to measure the three constructs of ADHD posited in *The Diagnostic and Statistical Manual of Mental Disorders*, Fourth Edition: ADHD-combined type, ADHD-inattentive type, and ADHD-hyperactive type. Each item is scored on a 5-point scale (0 = "does not engage in the behavior," 1 = "one to several times per month," 2 = "one to several times per week," 3 = "one to several times per day," 4 = "one to several times per hour."). Raw scores are converted to standard scores. Subscale standard scores can be converted to percentile ranks. Norms are representative of the United States, although information about the representativeness of individual age-gender norms is not reported. Test-retest, interrater, and internal consistency is reported in the manual. Content and criterion-related validity appears strong.

The ADHD Rating Scale (ADHD-IV; DuPaul, Power, Anastopoulos, & Reid, 1998) is an 18-item questionnaire composed of the DSM-IV criteria for attention deficit hyperactivity disorder (ADHD). Each item is scored on a 3-point Likert-type scale, ranging from 0 (never or rarely) to 3 (very often), on symptoms indicative of ADHD (e.g., "has difficulty paying attention," "often blurts out answers to questions"). Both Home (parent) and School (teacher) versions are available. Reliability of the ADHD-IV is adequate. Normative data for each version of the ADHD-IV include children and adolescents between the ages of 4 and 20 years from over 20 school districts in the United States. Normative data are reported separately for gender and age. Concurrent, predictive, discriminative, and validity data are available. The ADHD-IV also appears to be treatment sensitive (Barkley, Connor, & Kwasnik, 2000; Bostic et al., 2000; Rugino & Copley, 2001).

The Conners Teacher Rating Scale—39 (CTRS-39) (Connors, 1989, 1997) was the first standardized rating scale designed to assess teacher perceptions of hyperactivity and other learning and behavioral problems in children age 3 through 17 years. It was originally developed to document changes in behavior for children being treated with medication. It consists of 39 items and takes about 15 minutes to administer. Each item is scored on a 4-point rating scale (0 = not at all, 1 = just a little, 2 = pretty much, 3 = very much). The CTRS-39 contains five factors: daydreaming/inattentive, hyperactivity, conduct problems, anxious/fearful, and sociable/cooperative. The CTRS-39 has been used in numerous studies over the past 30 years. There is also a shorter version of the scale, called the CTRS-28, which contains four factors: conduct problem, hyperactivity, inattention/passive, and hyperactivity index. Two parent versions of the scale, the Connors Parent Rating Scale—48 and 39 (Connors, 1989) take 20 minutes and 30 minutes, respectively, to administer. The scales were recently revised (CRS-R; Connors, 1997). A self-report version was added for use with adolescents age 12 through 17. Norms for the parent scales overrepresent Caucasian parents, although the teacher scales are racially proportional.

See Table 5.5 for an overview of the rating scales for ADHD.

Table 5.5 Rating Scales for Attention Deficit Hyperactivity Disorder

Name	Publisher	Content	Age or Grade Level	Time to Administer
ADD-H: Comprehensive Teacher Rating Scale (ACTeRS)	Psychological Assessment Resources	Teacher rating scale for identifying children with ADHD and measuring response to intervention.	Grades K–5	5–10 minutes
Attention Deficit Disorders Evaluation Scale—2 (ADDES)	Hawthorne Educational Services	A rating scale designed to address the three major symptom areas of ADHD: inattention, impulsivity, and hyper-activity. It consists of a teacher and a parent version.	4–18 years	12–15 minutes
ADHD Rating Scale (ADHD-IV)	By author: Guilford Publications	A rating scale designed to assess symptoms of ADHD in line with the DSM-IV. It includes a parent and a teacher version.	5–17 years	5 minutes
Connors Rating Scale—39 (CTRS-39)	Multi-Health Systems	Rating scale for evaluating ADHD symptomatology. It includes a teacher and a parent version in a long and a short version and a self-report version.	Teacher = 3–17 years. Parent = 3–17 years. Adolescent = 12–17 years.	Long form = 15–20 minutes. Short form = 5–10 minutes. Adolescent form = 5–10 minutes.

Rating Scales for Autism. According to IDEA of 1997, autism is considered a separate category of disability. However, it is referred to as a developmental disability that affects communication and social interaction. According to the *Diagnostics Statistical Manual, Fourth Edition, Text Revised* (DSM-IV-TR; APA, 2000), autism is considered a pervasive developmental disorder with five subtypes: autistic disorder, Asperger's disorder, Rett's disorder, childhood disintegrative disorder, and PDD—not otherwise specified. Some behavioral manifestations include engagement in repetitive activities and stereotyped movements, resistance to environmental change or change in daily routines, and unusual responses to sensory experiences. Currently, few diagnostic rating scales are available in this area. In addition to those listed below, the reader might also want to review the more general behavioral rating scales previously described. In fact, assessment of the behavioral problems often exhibited by children and youth with autism may be best accomplished with a combination of direct observation and interviews.

The Childhood Autism Rating Scale (CARS; Schopler, Reichler, & Renner, 1988) is a combination structured interview and observation screening device for youngsters ages 2 and above who may have autism. Fifteen areas are addressed, each scored on a 7-point Likert scale to indicate degrees of autism-related symptoms: relating to people; imitation; emotional response; body use; object use; adaptation to change; visual response; listening response; taste, smell, and touch response and use; fear or nervousness; verbal communication; nonverbal communication; activity level; level and consistency of intellectual response; and general impressions.

The Gilliam Autism Rating Scale (GARS; Gilliam, 1995) consists of a behavioral checklist designed to diagnose autism spectrum disorder in accordance with the diagnostic criteria of the DSM-IV-TR (APA, 2000). It can also be used to measure severity of symptoms. There are four subtests: Stereotyped Behaviors, Communication, Social Interaction, and Developmental Disturbance. Completion of the GARS takes approximately 10 minutes.

The Gilliam Asperger's Disorder Scale (GADS; Gilliam, 2001) is a rating scale for individuals age 3 to 22 with suspected Asperger's syndrome. It consists of 32 items completed by someone familiar with the individual. The items are scored on a 4-point scale (0 = never observed, 1 = seldom observed, 2 = sometimes observed, 3 = frequently observed). Four subtests include Social Interaction, Restricted Patterns of Behavior, Cognitive Patterns, and Pragmatic Skills. Like the GARS, it takes about 10 minutes to complete. Scores are summed and converted to standard scores and percentile ranks. The norm sample for the GADS included 371 individuals with diagnosed Asperger's syndrome from 46 states and 4 foreign countries. The GADS has adequate reliability, content, and discriminant validity.

Asperger Syndrome Diagnostic Scale (ASDS; Myles, Bock, & Simpson, 2001) was designed to diagnose individuals age 5 to 18 with suspected Asperger's syndrome. Persons familiar with the individual use this checklist consisting of five subtests: Language, Social Skills, Maladaptive Behavior, Cognition, and Sensorimotor Development. Raw scores may be converted to standard scores and percentiles. The norm sample included 115 individuals (age 5 to 18) with diagnosed Asperger's syndrome from 21 states. Interrater consistency is excellent. However, internal consistency is weak. Content and discriminative validity data are also available.

See Table 5.6 for a summary of the rating scales for autism.

Table 5.6   Rating Scales for Autism

Name	Publisher	Content	Age or Grade Level	Time to Administer
Childhood Autism Rating Scale (CARS)	Western Psychological Services	A rating scale designed to identify children with autism. It may be based on a direct observation of the child.	2 years and above	5 minutes, unless a direct observation is needed.
Gilliam Autism Rating Scale (GARS)	PRO-ED	A checklist to diagnose autism spectrum disorder and measure symptom severity.	3 through 22 years	5–10 minutes
Gilliam Asperger's Disorder Scale (GADS)	American Guidance Service	A checklist to diagnose Asperger's syndrome.	3–22 years	5–10 minutes
Asperger Syndrome Diagnostic Scale (ASDS)	PRO-ED	A checklist to diagnose Asperger's syndrome.	5–18 years	5–10 minutes

Rating Scales for Social Skills. Social skills rating scales yield information useful for identifying deficits inherent in the definition of ED (i.e., an inability to build or maintain satisfactory interpersonal relationships). They can be useful for prioritizing instruction in the area of social skills training and for assessing progress. A description of some of the more well-known social skills rating scales follows.

The Social Skills Rating System (SSRS; Gresham & Elliot, 1990) was designed for use with children considered to be at risk for serious interpersonal difficulties, including ED, LD, conduct problems, and developmental disabilities. The SSRS can be used with children age 3 through 17. It has a form for the teacher, parent, and student. Three domains of behavior addressed by the SSRS include social skills, problem behaviors, and academic competence. Each domain yields a standard score and percentile rank. The SSRS consists of 55 items (for each form) that are rated on a 3-point Likert scale. In terms of social behavior, respondents rate how often a social behavior occurs (0 = never, 1 = sometimes, 2 = very often) and also how important a behavior is perceived for social development (0 = not important, 1 = important, 2 = critical). Examples of items include: "argues with others," "initiates conversations with peers," "compared with other children in my classroom, the overall academic performance of this child is . . ." In this way, professionals may target for intervention any problematic social behavior that was both important and that occurs frequently.

Normative data for the SSRS are based on a national sample of 5,000 children with and without disabilities, age 3 to 18 years. Reliability information is adequate and reported in the manual. Validity information is also reported.

The Walker-McConnell Scale of Social Competence and School Adjustment (Walker & McConnell, 1988) was developed to screen and identify social skills deficits in elementary age children age 5 through 11. It measures two areas of social skills: school-related interpersonal competence and adaptive behavior. The content examines three subscales: Teacher-Preferred Social Behavior, Peer-Preferred Social Behavior, and School Adjustment Behavior. The scale consists of 43 positively worded descriptions of social skills (e.g., "accepts constructive criticism from peers without becoming angry," "invites peers to play or share activities," "listens carefully to teacher directions"). Items are rated on a 5-point Likert scale from 1 (never occurs) to 5 (frequently occurs). Raw scores are converted to standard scores for the subscales and for the total scale and then are converted to percentile rankings.

Normative data are based on a sample of 1,812 students from grades K–6, with and without disabilities, from 15 states. Although adequate, norms do tend to overrepresent western states. Three kinds of reliability data are provided: test-retest, interrater, and internal consistency. The manual includes extensive validity information as well. However, further research is needed about predictive validity and treatment sensitivity of the scale.

Rating Scales for Self-Concept. Students with problems in school performance may have poor self-concepts, which affect their "ability to build or maintain satisfactory interpersonal relationships with peers and teacher" or explain "inappropriate behavior or feelings under normal circumstances," as addressed in the federal definition of ED. Therefore, administering a self-concept assessment may be useful in both the diagnosis and treatment of a behavioral disorder. Several devices are available for measuring self-concept and self-esteem.

The Multidimensional Self-Concept Scale (MSCS; Bracken, 1992) is a self-report scale for students in grades 5 through 12. It consists of 150 items, such as "A lot of people make fun of me," "I enjoy life," I often feel dumb." Respondents rate each statement according to how well it applies to them (strongly agree = 4, agree = 3, disagree = 2, strongly disagree = 1). Six self-concept subscales developed on a conceptual basis address the following areas: social, competence, affect, academic, family, and physical. Raw scores are converted to standard scores and percentile ranks for each of these areas and for the total test score.

Normative data are based on a sample of 2,501 students from 9 states from all regions of the United States and are representative of the 1990 U.S. Bureau of the Census. Test-retest reliability coefficients range from .73 to .90. Internal consistency reliability coefficients fall at or above .86 for both genders and all grade levels on the subscales and total scale. Information on construct, discriminant, and concurrent validity is available. Information on the appropriateness of the MSCS as a treatment outcome measure is limited, however.

The Piers-Harris Children's Self-Concept Scale (PHCSCS; Piers, 1984) is one of the most popular assessment instruments in this area. It is comprised of 80 declarative statements such as "My classmates make fun of me," "I am smart," and "It is hard for me to make friends." Items are scored as yes (0) or no (1). Originally designed as a research tool, it has been used by schools as a screening device to identify students who struggle with self-concept. The PHCSCS is appropriate for children in grades 4 through 12. Raw scores can be converted to percentile ranks and stanine scores. Six factor or cluster scores are obtained that correspond to six dimensions of self-concept: behavior, intellectual and school status, physical appearance and attributes, anxiety, popularity, and happiness and satisfaction. However, use of the total scale score may be of greatest use to practitioners because of mixed support for the clusters across diverse samples.

Normative information on the PHCSCS is from a single school district in Pennsylvania from the late 1960s. Therefore, when interpreting total and cluster scores, Piers (1984) has recommended that practitioners develop local norms to ensure generalizability to similar populations.

Test-retest reliability (median = .73, range = .42 to .96) and internal consistency reliability (total score = .90; cluster scales range = .73 to .81) are adequate. With respect to validity, correlations between the PHCSCS and other measures of self-concept range from .40 to .85. The PHCSCS has been found to discriminate between clinic-referred and normal control children (Guiton & Zachary, 1984; Moller & Schnurr, 1995). There is empirical support for using the PHCSCS to assess the effectiveness of a variety of therapeutic interventions (e.g., group psychotherapy [Stevens, 1975], cognitive-behavioral therapy [Jackson, 1974]), and specialized reading training (Jackson, 1974). In sum, the PHCSCS is best used as an informal measure of self-concept unless local norms are developed.

The Self-Perception Profile for Children (SPPC; Harter, 1985) is one of the most widely used scales to assess multidimensional self-concept in children age 8 to 15. There is also an adolescent version (Harter, 1988). The scale consists of 36 pairs of statements that reflect opposing views of various areas of self-concept. Children select the statement that is most like them. Then they rate their response on a 4-point scale. The SPPC assesses six dimensions of self-concept: perceptions of academic competence, social relations, physical appearance, athletic competence, behavioral conduct, and global self-worth. The SPPC also includes two additional instruments: a teacher rating scale and an importance rating scale for children. For instance, a low score on a particular dimension may not be cause for concern if the child did not also rate that area as important. The psychometric properties of the SPPC are good. However, the norm sample of both the SPPC and its adolescent version was limited to children from the state of Colorado.

Rating Scales for Depression and Anxiety. According to the federal definition of ED, some identified students may exhibit "a general pervasive mood of unhappiness or depression" or "a tendency to develop physical symptoms or fears associated with personal or school problems." There are several useful rating scales to address depression and/or anxiety. Diagnosis of depression and other mood disorders is generally left to psychologists or psychiatrists. However, educators might still want to be familiar with some of the most commonly used rating scales in this area (see Table 5.7).

The Children's Depression Inventory (CDI; Kovacs, 1981, 1992) and its short form (CDI-S; Kovacs, 1992) were adapted from the Beck Depression Inventory (Beck, Ward, Mendelson, Mock, & Erbaugh, 1961). The CDI was designed to measure depression in children and adolescents age 7 to 17. It represents the most thoroughly researched self-report measure of childhood depression (Finch, Saylor, & Edwards, 1985). Its 27 items (10 for the short form) measure the five factors of (1) negative mood, (2) interpersonal problems, (3) ineffectiveness, (4) anhedonia, and (5) negative self-esteem. Sample items include "I hate myself" and "I like myself." Both the long and short forms were standardized on a sample of 1,266 boys and girls (primarily Caucasian, middle socioeconomic status). Internal consistency is above .80. However,

Table 5.7 Rating Scales for Depression and Anxiety

Name	Publisher	Content	Age or Grade Level	Time to Administer
Children's Depression Inventory (CDI)	Multi-Health Systems	A self-report rating scale to measure depression in children and adolescents.	7–17 years	10 minutes
Revised Children's Manifest Anxiety Scale (RCMAS)	Western Psychological Services	A self-report rating scale to measure general distress in children.	6–19 years	10–15 minutes
Reynolds Child Depression Scale (RCDS)	Psychological Assessment Resources	A self-report rating scale to assess depressive symptoms according to the DSM-III-R criteria.	8–13 years	10 minutes
Reynolds Adolescent Depression Scale (RADS)	Western Psychological Services	A self-report rating scale to measure depressive symptoms in adolescents.	13–18 years	10 minutes
Social Anxiety Scale for Children—Revised (SASC-R)	La Greca, A. M. Department of Psychology, University of Miami, Coral Gables, FL	A self-report measure of anxiety, with a focus on anxiety in social interactions.	Grades 4–6	5 minutes
State-Trait Anxiety Inventory for Children (STAIC)	Consulting Psychologists Press	A self-report measure of state anxiety at a specific point in time and trait (anxiety in general) in two separate scales.	9–12 years	10 minutes per scale

test-retest reliability has been reported to be in the moderate range (Saylor, Finch, Spirito, & Bennett, 1984). Concurrent validity is adequate. Discriminative validity and construct validity are available. The CDI has also been judged to be a good index of response to intervention (Garvin, Leber, & Kalter, 1991).

The Revised Children's Manifest Anxiety Scale (RCMAS; Reynolds & Richmond, 1985) is a self-report measure for children and youth age 6 to 19. It consists of 37 items that yield yes/no responses (e.g., "I worry a lot of the time," "I often feel sick to my stomach"). The scale takes between 10 and 15 minutes to complete. The RCMAS was standardized on a sample of 4,972 children between the ages of 6 and 19 from across all major geographical regions of the United States (Reynolds & Paget, 1981). The scale has adequate test-test reliability and internal consistency over time. Construct, discriminant, and concurrent validity information is also available. Although the RCMAS has been found to discriminate children with and without anxiety disorders, it has not been found to differentiate children with anxiety disorders from children with other disorders (e.g., ADHD; Perrin & Last, 1992). Therefore, it is best used as (1) one part of a battery for assessing internalizing problems in children or (2) as a measure of general distress. There is also no information about the sensitivity of the RCMAS to treatment.

Reynolds Child Depression Scale (RCDS; Reynolds, 1989) was designed for children age 8 to 13. It was developed to assess depressive symptoms according to the earlier DSM-III-R criteria, so it must be used with caution. Thirty items are rated on a 4-point rating scale for frequency of occurrence over the past 2-week period (e.g., "I feel that no one cares about me," "I feel like playing with other kids"). One of these items includes a global rating of one's dysphoric mood state (an emotional state characterized by anxiety, depression, or unease) by asking the child to place an X on one of five smiley-type faces that depicts various feelings. The items are administered orally to children in grades 3 and 4 and to children with reading problems. Otherwise, the scale is written at a second-grade level. The standardization sample of the RCDS included over 1,600 students from a wide variety of ages, ethnicities, and socioeconomic status. Test-retest reliability is adequate, and the manual includes validity data.

The Reynolds Adolescent Depression Scale (RADS; Reynolds, 1987) is appropriate for youth age 13 to 18. It also consists of 30 items (e.g., "I feel sad," I feel happy," "I feel like talking to other students"). These items are rated on a 4-point rating scale, asking how the youth felt during the past week or so. If the student indicates either "somewhat depressed" or "depressed," then he or she must provide a reason. One caution with the RADS is that the time when the scale is administered may affect the results. The RADS can be administered individually or with groups. The reading level is low enough for an adolescent with reading problems to understand the items. The scale takes approximately 10 minutes to complete. The RADS was normed on a sample of 2,460 adolescents from one geographical region, and included a heterogeneous sample. Similar to the RCDS, several types of validity have been examined and reliability has been adequate.

The Social Anxiety Scale for Children—Revised (SASC-R; La Greca & Stone, 1993) is the most recent self-report measure of anxiety with a focus on elementary-age children's anxiety in social interactions. It consists of 22 items (e.g., "I get nervous when I talk to new kids") and takes 5 minutes to complete. Children indicate on a 5-point Likert scale how much each statement is true for them (1 = not at all, 2 = hardly ever, 3 = sometimes, 4 = most of the time, 5 = all of the time). The SASC-R has three subscales: Fear of Negative Evaluation, Social Avoidance and Distress—Specific to New Peers or Situations, and Social Avoidance and Distress—General. The scale was normed on 459 students in grades 4 through 6 from schools in one southeastern metropolitan area. Additional research is needed to ensure a more representative sample. Currently, there is no information regarding test-retest reliability for each of the subscales. However, overall test-retest reliability is adequate. Internal consistency is sound. Validity information is available and appears adequate.

The State-Trait Anxiety Inventory for Children (STAIC; Speilberger, 1973) was developed as a downward extension of the State-Trait Anxiety Inventory (Speilberger, Gorsuch, & Lushene, 1970) for adolescents and adults. The STAIC is a self-report instrument for trait anxiety and state anxiety for children age 9 to 12. It consists of two separate scales, which can be administered separately or together to individuals or groups. The state anxiety scale asks the child how anxious he or she feels at the time. The trait anxiety scale asks the child how anxious he or she feels in general. Each scale has 20 items and each takes about 10 minutes to complete. Each item requires the child to choose one of three statements that best describes how he or she feels. These items are scored 1, 2, or 3, with the higher number reflecting stronger symptoms of anxiety. The STAIC was normed on 1,554 children in grades 4 through 6 in the state of Florida. Approximately 35 percent of the sample was African American children. Raw scores may be converted to T-scores and percentiles. Reliability and validity information are reported. A caution is that further research has been recommended to update the normative data using a nationally representative sample (Merrell, 1994).

Breakpoint Practice

Name the most common rating scales in the area of depression and anxiety.

Multicultural Considerations

As in all areas of assessment, understanding a student's cultural values and customs is necessary before assuming that the student's behavioral differences are indicative of ED. As Kauffman (1993) states, "nearly all behavioral standards and expectations—and therefore nearly all judgments regarding behavioral deviance—are culture-bound" (p. 260). Differences in the expectations of cultural groups can contribute to the problem behavior of students who belong to different cultural groups.

Cultural bias may be one reason why students from certain ethnic groups are overrepresented in the ED category. Coutinho and Oswald (1998) found that students who were African American were one-and-a-half times as likely as students who were not African American to be identified as having ED. It is possible that the disproportionate representation of individuals who are African American in these programs occurs because practitioners who refer and identify these students do not understand the culture-specific behaviors of these individuals. According to Harry (1994), in the case of ED placement, there is no single standardized assessment instrument or procedure, so teacher perception is crucial in whether or not a student is referred. Teachers in the United States are predominantly white and female. They may not understand the behavioral differences exhibited by their students who are male and African American.

For instance, students who are African American may be more expressive with their feelings than students from European American backgrounds. Their high physical activity levels may be particularly problematic for the average white female teacher (Harry, 1994). Similarly, teachers often consider students who are

(*continued*)

African American to be inattentive, restless, lacking in self-control, and disruptive (Gay, 1975; McIntyre, 1993, 1995). In fact, Coutinho, Oswald, Best, and Forness (2002) found that the rate of ED identification was higher for students who are African American and live in a largely white community than it was for those who live in a community with a greater culturally and linguistically diverse (CLD) population. This study supports the hypothesis that students who appear and act differently from the mainstream may be susceptible to referral or identification for ED.

In contrast, at least one study (Cullinan & Kauffman, 2005) failed to support a racial bias theory in teacher perceptions of emotional and behavioral problems for the overrepresentation of students who are African American versus students who are European American. That is, teacher raters who were African American or European American did not significantly differ in their ratings of behavioral problems in students who were African American or European American. Yet one study limitation included a possible selection bias in teachers willing to participate. Studies are still needed to examine the possibility of racial bias in the separate areas of referral, evaluation for identification, and assessment instruments used specifically with regard to overrepresented and underrepresented groups in the category of ED (i.e., students who are Hispanic, Asian, or Pacific Islander; National Center for Education Statistics, 2003).

Another consideration in the assessment of behavior is the complex interrelationship of ethnicity and poverty. Increased poverty has been associated with increased ED identification rates (Coutinho et al. 2002). Poverty has also been found to be a significant predictor of aggressive and disruptive behavior among boys in the first grade and in a six-year follow-up (Kellam, 1999). It is not clear whether it is poverty itself that poses a risk factor for ED placement or associated factors such as living in an impoverished neighborhood. For instance, Kalff et al. (2001) found that living in an economically deprived neighborhood was associated with increased levels of problem behavior. Clearly, it is important to consider a variety of sociodemographic risk factors when assessing CLD students for behavior problems.

Bias in evaluation instruments is another area of concern when assessing students' behavioral problems. For example, interviews are only as useful as the respondents queried (Breen & Fiedler, 2003). If key informants, such as extended family members in the case of students from Hispanic backgrounds, are never included, crucial information may be missing related to the function of a particular target behavior.

In the case of direct observations, interpretations about problematic behavior must always be viewed in a cultural context. As Coutinho and Oswald (1998) suggest, cultural and ethnic factors may influence what behavior one targets for observation and how it is defined. Similarly, the rate of student misbehavior may be associated with factors such as teaching style, types of instructional formats used (e.g., cooperative learning, whole-class instruction), types of reinforcers used, and teacher proximity. A teacher's ethnic and cultural background may influence each of these decisions (e.g., to use or not to use cooperative learning, to allow or not to allow unstructured student discussion). Likewise, different ethnic groups interpret these factors in different ways, thus influencing student behavior.

In the case of rating scales, it is crucial that practitioners examine the groups for which the scale was normed. Currently, only a limited number of rating scales are available for use with students from minority cultural and linguistic backgrounds (Breen & Fiedler, 2003). Also, as is the case with interviews, rating scales are typically completed by the teacher, parent, or student. However, family members other than the parent may be in a better position to rate adaptive and maladaptive behavior.

Breakpoint Practice

1. How might cultural expectations influence the referral or identification process of a student for services under the category of ED?

2. How might a teacher's culture perspective influence the direct observational process?

3. What beliefs or values do you hold about students who exhibit maladaptive behavior such as aggression?

REVISITING DION

In the case of Dion, new contextual aspects and requirements could be influencing behavior in a negative way. It appears that reading and writing tasks are triggering negative behavior. The teacher could assess the level of performance at which he or she is presenting and requiring work for Dion. While the work may be age or grade appropriate, it may be at too low or too high a level for Dion to achieve at least 80 percent success. Also, an analysis of the group environment could be examined. Perhaps a different group, setup of the assignment, or demands of the assignment could be arranged. A conversation with Dion and his family could supply critical information that would resolve the issue. Furthermore, the special educator could provide collaboration and consultation to the general educator.

ACTIVITIES

1. What are some issues that arise in diagnosing a student as ED?

2. How might the exclusionary clause of "social maladjustment" contribute to the underidentification of students eligible to receive services under ED?

3. Why might it be difficult to attribute a student's problematic behavior to ED if that student also has difficulties with language?

4. Identify and observe a student who is exhibiting behavioral problems. Describe (a) the target behavior you intend to observe, (b) the direct observation system you will use, and (c) how you intend to collect data. Collect baseline data on this target behavior by implementing this direct observation procedure, and (d) develop a hypothesis for the function this problematic behavior is serving Finally, (e) use your findings to design an appropriate intervention. Indicate where in this chapter there is support for each of your choices.

5. Why is it important to use a variety of approaches to assessment in the area of ED?

6. Discuss the extent to which one's personal values and expectations might exert positive and negative influences in the assessment of behavior.

WEB RESOURCES

http://cecp.air.org/fba

http://www.pbis.org/main.htm

http://www.ccbd.net

http://www.proteacher.com/030001.shtml

http://www.focusas.com/BehavioralDisorders.html

http://www.nasponline.org/publications/cq/cq352pbs_ho.aspx

http://www.autismspeaks.org

REFERENCES

Achenbach, T. M. (1985). *Assessment and taxonomy of child and adolescent psychopathology.* Newbury Park, CA: Sage.

Achenbach, T. M. (1991). *Manual for the Child Behavior Checklist/4-18 and 1991 Profile.* Burlington: University of Vermont, Department of Psychiatry.

Achenbach, T. M., & Reescorla, L. A. (2001). *Manual for the ASEBA school-ages forms and profiles.* Burlington: University of Vermont, Research Center for Children, Youth, & Families.

Alberto, P. A., & Troutman, A. C. (2006). *Applied behavior analysis for teachers* (7th ed.). Upper Saddle River, NJ: Merrill/Pearson Education.

American Psychological Association. (2000). *Diagnostic and statistical manual of mental disorders* (4th ed., text rev.). Washington, DC: Author.

Banaschewski, T., Brandeis, D., Heinrich, H., Albrecht, B., Brunner, E., & Rothenberger, A. (2003). Association of ADHD and conduct disorder—Brain electrical evidence for the existence of a distinct subtype. *Journal of Child Psychology and Psychiatry, 44,* 356–376.

Barkley, R. A. (1990). *Attention deficit hyperactivity disorder: A handbook for diagnosis and treatment.* New York: Guilford Press.

Barkley, R. A., Connor, D. F., & Kwasnik, D. (2000). Challenges to determining adolescent medication response in an outpatient clinical setting: Adderall and methylphenidate for ADHD. *Journal of Attention Disorders, 4,* 102–113.

Barton-Arwood, S. M., Wehby, J. H., Gunter, P. L., & Lane, K. L. (2003). Functional behavior assessment rating scales: Intrarater reliability with students with emotional or behavioral disorders. *Behavioral Disorders, 28,* 386–400.

Beck, A. T., Ward, C. H., Mendelson, M., Mock, J. E., & Erbaugh, J. K. (1961). An inventory for measuring depression. *Archives of General Psychiatry, 4,* 561–571.

Bostic, J. Q., Biederman, J., Spencer, T. J., Wilens, T. E., Prince, J. B., Monuteaux, M. C., Sienna, M., Polisner, D. A., & Hatch, M. (2000). Pemoline treatment of adolescents with attention deficit hyperactivity disorder: A short-term controlled trial. *Journal of Child & Adolescent Psychopharmacology, 10,* 205–216.

Bracken, B. A. (1992). *Multidimensional Self Concept Scale.* Austin, TX: PRO-ED.

Breen, M. J., Eckert, T. L., & DuPaul, G. J. (2003). Interpreting child-behavior questionnaires. In M. J. Breen & C. R. Fiedler (Eds.), *Behavioral approach to assessment of youth with emotional/behavioral disorders* (pp. 171–188). Austin, TX: PRO-ED.

Breen, M. J., & Fiedler, C. R. (2003). *Behavioral approach to assessment of youth with emotional/behavioral disorders* (2nd ed.). Austin, TX: PRO-ED.

Burns, R. C. (1992). *Self-growth in families: Kinetic family drawings (K-F-D) research and application.* New York: Brunner/Mazel.

Busse, R. T., & Beaver, B. R. (2000). Informant report: Parent and teacher interviews. In E. S. Shapiro & T. R. Kratochwill (Eds.), *Conducting school-based assessments of child and adolescent behavior* (pp. 235–273). New York: Guilford Press.

Chambers, W., Puig-Antich, J., Hersche, M., Paey, P., Ambrosini, P. J., Tabrizi, M. A., & Davies, M. (1985). The assessment of affective disorders in children and adolescents by semi-structured interview: Test-retest reliability of the K-SADS-P. *Archives of General Psychiatry, 42,* 696–702.

Chandler, L. K., & Dahlquist, C. M. (2006). *Functional assessment: Strategies to prevent and remediate challenging behavior in school settings* (2nd ed.). Upper Saddle River, NJ: Merrill/Pearson Education.

Code of Federal Regulations, 34 C. F. R. 300.5.

Coie, J. D., Belding, M., & Underwood, M. (1988). Aggression and peer rejection in childhood. In B. B. Lahey & A. Kazdin (Eds.), *Advances in clinical child psychology* (vol. 2, pp. 125–158). New York: Plenum Press.

Connors, C. K. (1989). *Connors Rating Scales Manual.* North Tonawanda, NY: Multi-Health Systems.

Connors, C. K. (1997). *Connors Rating Scales—Revised; technical manual.* North Tonawanda, NY: Multi-Health Systems.

Costello, A. J., Edelbrock, C., Dulcan, M. K., Kalas, R., & Klaric, S. H. (1984). *Report on the Diagnostic Interview Schedule for Children (DISC).* Pittsburgh: University of Pittsburgh, Department of Psychiatry.

Coutinho, M. J., & Oswald, D. P. (1998). Ethnicity and special education research: Identifying questions and methods. *Behavioral Disorders, 24,* 66–73.

Coutinho, M. J., Oswald, D. P., Best, A. M., & Forness, S. R. (2002). Gender and sociodemographic factors and the disproportionate identification of culturally and linguistically diverse students with emotional disturbance. *Behavioral Disorders, 27,* 109–125.

Cullinan, D., & Kauffman, J. M. (2005). Do race of student and race of teacher influence ratings of emotional and behavioral problem characteristics of students with emotional disturbance? *Behavioral Disorders, 30,* 393–402.

DuPaul, G. J., Power, T. J., Anastopoulos, A. D., & Reid, R. (1998). *Manual for the AD/HD Rating Scale IV.* New York: Guilford Press.

Durand, V. M., & Crimmins, D. B. (1988). Identifying the variables maintaining self-injurious behavior. *Journal of Autism and Developmental Disabilities, 18,* 99–117.

Edelbrock, C., Costello, A. J., Dulcan, M., Kalas, R., & Conover, N. C. (1985). Age differences in the reliability of the psychiatric interview of the child. *Journal of Abnormal Child Psychology, 16,* 219–275.

Epstein, M. H., & Cullinan, D. (1998). *Scale for Assessing Emotional Disturbance.* Austin, TX: PRO-ED.

Epstein, M. H., Cullinan, D., Harniss, M. K., & Ryser, G. (1999). The Scale for Assessing Emotional Disturbance: Test-retest and interrater reliability. *Behavioral Disorders, 24,* 222–230.

Epstein, M. H., Cullinan, D., Ryser, G., & Pearson, N. (2002). Development of a scale to assess emotional disturbance. *Behavioral Disorders, 28,* 5–22.

Finch, A., Saylor, C., & Edwards, G. (1985). Children's Depression Inventory: Sex and grade norms for normal children. *Journal of Consulting and Clinical Psychology, 53,* 424–425.

Forness, S. R., & Knitzer, J. (1992). A new proposed definition and terminology to replace "serious emotional disturbance" in Individuals with Disabilities Education Act. *School Psychology Review, 21*(1), 12–20.

Fox, J. J., Conroy, M. A., & Hechaman, K., (1998). Research issues in functional assessment of the challenging behavior of students with emotional and behavioral disorders. *Behavioral Disorders, 24,* 26–33.

Garvin, V., Leber, D., & Kalter, N. (1991). Children of divorce: Predictors of change following preventive intervention. *American Journal of Orthopsychiatry, 61,* 438–447.

Gay, G. (1975, October). Cultural differences important in the education of Black children. *Momentum,* 30–33.

Getty, L. A., & Summy, S. E. (2006). Language deficits in students with emotional and behavioral disorders: Practical applications for teachers. *Beyond Behavior, 15*(3), 15–22.

Giddan, J. J., Milling, L., & Campbell, N. B. (1996). Unrecognized language and speech deficits in preadolescent psychiatric inpatients. *American Journal of Orthopsychiatry, 66,* 85–92.

Gilliam, J. E. (1995). *Gilliam Autism Rating Scale.* Austin, TX: PRO-ED.

Gilliam, J. E. (2001). *Manual for the Gilliam Asperger Disorder Scale.* Circle Pines, MN: American Guidance Service.

Gresham, F. M., & Elliot, S. N. (1990). *Social Skills Rating System manual.* Circle Pines, MN: American Guidance Service.

Gresham, F. M., & Gansle, K. A. (1992). Misguided assumptions of the DSM-III-R: Implications for school psychological practice. *School Psychology Quarterly, 7,* 79–95.

Gresham, F. M., Lane, K. L., MacMillan, D. L., & Bocian, K. M. (1999). Social and academic profiles of externalizing and internalizing groups: Risk factors for emotional and behavioral disorders. *Behavioral Disorders, 24,* 231–245.

Griffith, P. L., Rogers-Adkinson, D. L., & Cusick, G. M. (1997). Comparing language disorders in two groups of students with severe behavioral disorders. *Behavioral Disorders, 22,* 160–166.

Guiton, G., & Zachary, R. A. (1984, August). *Criterion validity of the Piers-Harris Children's Self-Concept Scale.* Paper presented at the annual meeting of the American Psychological Association, Toronto, Canada.

Harry, B. (1994). The disproportionate placement of African American males in special education programs: A critique of the process. *The Journal of Negro Education, 63,* 602–619.

Harter, S. (1985). *Self-Perception Profile for Children.* Denver, CO: University of Denver, Department of Psychology.

Harter, S. (1988). *Self-Perception Profile for Adolescents.* Denver, CO: University of Denver, Department of Psychology.

Herjanic, B., & Campbell, W. (1977). Differentiating psychiatrically disturbed children on the basis of a structured interview. *Journal of Abnormal Child Psychology, 5,* 127–134.

Herjanic, B., Herjanic, M., Brown, F., & Wheatt, T. (1975). Are children reliable reporters? *Journal of Abnormal Child Psychology, 3,* 41–48.

Herjanic, B., & Reich. W. (1982). Development of a structured psychiatric interview for children: Agreement between child and parent on individual symptoms. *Journal of Abnormal Child Psychology, 10,* 307–324.

Hodges, K. (1993). Structured interviews for assessing children. *Journal of Child Psychology and Psychiatry, 34,* 49–68.

Hooper, S. R., Roberts, J. E., Zeisel, S. A., Poe, M., & Graham, F. P. (2003). Core language predictors of behavioral functioning in early elementary school children: Concurrent and longitudinal findings. *Behavioral Disorders, 29,* 10–24.

Hughes, J., & Baker, D. B. (1990). *The clinical child interview.* New York: Guilford Press.

Illinois State Board of Education. (2000). Functional Behavior Assessment Form from http://isbe.net.

Iwata, B. A. (1995). *Functional analysis screening tool.* Gainesville, FL: The Florida Center of Self-Injury.

Jackson, C. C. (1974). An evaluation of the effect of a special reading program adapted from Aesop's Fables on reading achievement and self-concept of fifth grade students (Doctoral dissertation, Boston University, 1974). *Dissertation Abstracts International, 35,* 3575A. (University Microfilms No. 74-26, 443, 226)

Jensen, P., Roper, M., Fisher, P., Piacentini, J., Canino, G., Richters, J., Rubio-Stipec, M., Dulcan, M., Goodman, S., Davies, M., Rae, D., Shaffer, D., Bird, H., Lahey, B., & Schwab-Stone, M. (1995). Test-retest reliability of the Diagnostics Interview Schedule for Children (Ver. 2.1): Parent, child, and combined algorithms. *Archives of General Psychiatry, 56,* 61–71.

Kalff, A. C., Kroes, M., Vles, J. S. H., Hendriksen, J. G. M., Feron, F. J. M., Steyaert, J., van Zeben, T. M. C. B., Jolles, J., & van Os, J. (2001). Neighborhood level and individual level SES effects on child problem behavior: A multilevel analysis. *Journal of Epidemiology and Community Health, 55,* 246–250.

Kauffman, J. (1993). *Characteristics of emotional and behavioral disorders of children and youth.* New York: MacMillan.

Kazdin, A. E. (1982). *Single-case research designs: Methods for clinical and applied settings.* New York: Oxford University Press.

Kovacs, M. (1981). Rating scales to assess depression in school-aged children. *Acta Paedopsychiatria, 46,* 305–315.

Kovacs, M. (1992). *Children's Depression Inventory.* Los Angeles: Multi-Health Systems.

La Greca, A. M., & Stone, W. L. (1993). Social Anxiety Scale for Children—Revised: Factor structure and concurrent-validity. *Journal of Clinical Child Psychology, 22,* 17–27.

Lewis, T. J., Scott, T. M., & Sugai, G. (1994). The Problem Behavior Questionnaire: A teacher-based instrument to develop functional hypotheses of problem behavior in general education classrooms. *Diagnostique, 19,* 103–115.

Lord, C., Rutter, M., & Le Couteur, A. (1994). Autism Diagnostic Interview—Revised: A revised version of a diagnostic interview for caregivers of individuals with possible pervasive developmental disorders. *Journal of Autism and Developmental Disorders, 24,* 659–685.

March, J. S. (1997). *Multidimensional anxiety scale for children: Technical manual.* New York: Multi-Health Systems.

McCarney, S. B. (1995). *The Attention Deficit Disorders Evaluation Scale* (2nd ed.). Columbia, MO: Hawthorne Educational Services.

McCarney, S. B., & Leigh, J. E. (1990). *Behavior Evaluation Scale—2.* Columbia, MO: Hawthorne Educational Services.

McConaughy, S. H. (2003). Interviewing children, parents, and teachers. In M. Breen & C. Fiedler (Eds.), *Behavioral approach to the assessment of youth with emotional/behavioral disorders: A handbook for school based practitioners* (2nd ed., pp. 123–169). Austin, TX: PRO-ED.

McConaughy, S. H. (2005). *Clinical interviews for children and adolescents: Assessment to intervention.* New York: Guilford Press.

McConaughy, S. H. & Achenbach, T. M. (2001). Manual for the Semistructured Clinical Interview for Children and Adolescents (2nd ed.). Burlington, VT: University of Vermont, Research Center for Children, Youth, and Families.

McIntyre, T. (1993). Reflections on the impact of the proposed definition for emotional and behavioral disorders: Who will still fall through the cracks and why. *Behavioral Disorders, 18,* 148–160.

McIntyre, T. (1995). *The McIntyre assessment of culture: An instrument for evaluating the influence of culture on behavior and learning.* Columbia, MO: Hawthorne Educational Services.

Merrell, K. W. (1994). *Assessment of behavioral, social, & emotional problems: Direct & objective methods for use with children and adolescents.* New York: Longman.

Merrell, K. W., & Walker, H. M. (2004). Deconstructing a definition: Social maladjustment versus emotional disturbance and moving the EBD field forward. *Psychology in the Schools, 41,* 899–910.

Moller, L. C., & Schnurr, R. G. (1995). A comparison of self-esteem measures of attractiveness in a psychiatric population of adolescents: The Piers-Harris and the Harter scales. *Journal of Social Behavior and Personality, 10,* 743–754.

Myles, B., Bock, S., & Simpson, R. (2001). *Examiner's manual for the Asperger Syndrome Diagnostic Scale.* Circle Pines, MN: American Guidance Service.

National Center for Education Statistics. (2003). *Digest of Education Statistics, 2002* (NCES 2003-060). Washington, DC: U.S. Department of Education.

National Center for Education Statistics. http://nces.ed.gov/programs/digest/. Retrieved on November 5, 2008.

Office of Special Education Programs. (2001). *Functional behavioral assessment.* Washington, DC: Author. Retrieved March 1, 2006, from http://www.cec.sped.org/law_res/doc/resources/detail.php?id=2083

Olympia, D., Farley, M., Christiansen, E., Pettersson, H., Jenson, W., & Clark, E. (2004). Social maladjustment and students with behavioral and emotional disorders: Revisiting basic assumptions and assessment issues. *Psychology in the Schools, 41,* 835–847.

O'Neill, R. E., Horner, R. H., Albin, R. W., Sprague, J., Storey, K., & Newton, J. S. (1997). *Functional assessment and program development for problem behavior: A practical handbook.* Pacific Grove, CA: Brooks/Cole.

Orvaschel, H., Puig-Antich, J., Chambers, W., Tabrizi, M. A., & Johnson, R. (1982). Retrospective assessment of prepubertal major depression with the Kiddie-SADS-E. *Journal of the American Academy of Child Psychiatry, 21,* 392–397.

Perrin, S., & Last, C. G. (1992). Do childhood anxiety measures measure anxiety? *Journal of Abnormal Child Psychology, 20,* 567–578.

Piers, E. V. (1984). *Revised manual for the Piers-Harris Children's Self-Concept Scale.* Los Angeles: Western Psychological Services.

Puig-Antich, J., & Chambers, W. (1978). *The Schedule for Affective Disorders and Schizophrenia for School-aged Children (Kiddie-SADS)*. New York: New York State Psychiatric Institute.

Quay, H. C. (1986). Classification. In H. C. Quay & J. S. Werry (Eds.), *Psychopathological disorders of childhood* (3rd ed., pp. 1–34). New York: Wiley.

Reich, W., & Welner, Z. (1992). *DICA-R-C. DSM-III-R version. Revised version of DICA for children ages 6–12*. St. Louis, MO: Washington University, Department of Psychiatry.

Reich, W., Welner, Z., Herjanic, B., & MHS Staff. (1997). *Diagnostic Interview for Children and Adolescents-IV*. North Tonawanda, NY: Multi-Health Systems.

Reynolds, C. R., & Kamphaus, R. W. (1992). *Behavior Assessment System for Children*. Circle Pines, MN: American Guidance Service.

Reynolds, C. R., & Kamphaus, R. W. (2004). *Behavior Assessment System for Children—Second Edition—Manual*. Circle Pines, MN: American Guidance Service.

Reynolds, C. R., & Paget, K. D. (1981). Factor analysis of the Revised Children's Manifest Anxiety Scale for Blacks, Whites, males, and females with a national normative sample. *Journal of Consulting and Clinical Psychology, 49,* 352–359.

Reynolds, C. R., & Richmond, B. O. (1985). *Revised Children's Manifest Anxiety Scale*. Los Angeles: Western Psychological Services.

Reynolds, W. M. (1987). *Professional manual for the Reynolds Adolescent Depression Scale*. Los Angeles: Western Psychological Services.

Reynolds, W. M. (1989). *Professional manual for the Reynolds Child Depression Scale*. Odessa, FL: Psychological Assessment Resources.

Rogers-Adkinson, D. L., & Hooper, S. R. (2003). The relationship of language and behavior: Introduction to the special issue. *Behavioral Disorders, 29,* 5–9.

Rugino, T. A., & Copley, T. C. (2001). Effects of modafinilin on children with attention deficit/hyperactivity disorder: An open-label study. *Journal of the American Academy of Child and Adolescent Psychiatry, 40,* 230–235.

Saylor, C. F., Finch, A. J., Spirito, A., & Bennett, B. (1984). The Children's Depression Inventory: A systematic evaluation of psychometric properties. *Journal of Consulting and Clinical Psychology, 52,* 955–967.

Schopler, E., Reichler, R., & Renner, B. (1988). *The Childhood Autism Rating Scale*. Los Angeles: Western Psychological Services.

Shaffer, D. (1992). *NIMH Diagnostic Interview Schedule for Children, Version 2.3*. New York: Columbia University, Division of Child Psychiatry.

Shaffer, D., Fisher, P., Lucas, C. P., Dulcan, M., & Schwab-Stone, M. E. (2000). NIMH Diagnostic Interview Schedule for Children, Version IV (NIMH DISC-IV): Description, differences from previous versions and reliability of some common diagnoses. *Journal of the American Academy of Child and Adolescent Psychiatry, 29,* 28–38.

Sigafoos, J., Kerr, M., & Roberts, D. (1994). Interrater reliability of the Motivation Assessment Scale: Failure to replicate with aggressive behavior. *Research in Developmental Disabilities, 15,* 333–342.

Speilberger, C. D. (1973). *State-Trait Anxiety Inventory for Children*. Palo Alto, CA: Consulting Psychologists Press.

Speilberger, C. D., Gorsuch, R. L., & Lushene, R. E. (1970). *State-Trait Anxiety Inventory*. Palo Alto, CA: Consulting Psychologists Press.

Sroufe, L. A., & Rutter, M. (1984). The domain of developmental psychopathology. *Child Development, 55,* 17–29.

Stevens, W. D. (1975). The effects of didactic group therapy on the self-esteem of potential school dropouts (Doctoral dissertation, Southern Illinois University, 1974). *Dissertation Abstracts International, 36,* 1927A-1928A. (University Microfilms No. 75-21, 932, 192)

Stevenson, J., & Richman, N. (1978). Behavior, language, and development in three-year-old children. *Journal of Autism and Childhood Schizophrenia, 8,* 299–313.

Ullmann, R. K., Sleator, E. K., & Sprague, R. L. (1984). A new rating scale for diagnosis and monitoring of ADD children, *Psychopharmacology Bulletin, 20,* 160–164.

Ullmann, R. K., Sleator, E. K., & Sprague, R. L. (1985). Introduction to the use of the ACEeRS. *Psychopharmacology Bulletin, 21,* 915–920.

Ullmann, R. K., Sleator, E. K., & Sprague, R. L. (1991). *The ADD-H Comprehensive Teacher's Rating Scale* (2nd ed.). Champaign, IL: MetriTech.

Umbreit, J., Ferro, J. B., Liaupsin, C. J., & Lane, K. L. (2007). *Functional behavioral assessment and function-based intervention: An effective practical approach.* Upper Saddle River, NJ: Merrill/Pearson Education.

Walker, H. M., & McConnell, S. R. (1988). *The manual for the Walker-McConnell Scale of Social Competence and School Adjustment.* Austin, TX: PRO-ED.

Warr-Leper, G., Wright, N. A., & Mack, A. (1994). Language disabilities of antisocial boys in residential treatment. *Behavioral Disorders, 19,* 159–169.

Ysseldyke, S. (1998). *Assessment.* Boston, MA: Houghton Mifflin.

Zentall, S. S. (2006). *ADHD and education: Foundations, characteristics, methods, and collaboration.* Upper Saddle River, NJ: Merrill/Pearson Education.

Zentall, S. S., & Javorsky, J. (1995). Functional and clinical assessment of ADHD: Implications of DSM-IV in the schools. *Journal of Psychoeducational Assessment: ADHD Special Monograph,* 22–41.

Cognitive
Assessment

KEY TERMS

Intelligence: Learning ability.

Intelligence tests: Behavior (indirect measures) associated with application of knowledge.

IQ: Intelligence quotient.

Achievement: Academic growth.

Verbal tests: Tests involving verbal abilities (i.e., vocabulary).

Performance tests: Tests involving abilities that are not verbal (i.e., motor behavior).

Gross motor: Using large muscle movements (i.e., running).

Fine motor: Using small muscle movements (i.e., writing).

Nonverbal intelligence: Skills not dependent on language (i.e., drawing pictures).

Case Study: Jenny

Jenny is a student in your seventh-grade general education class. Data analysis from multiple assessments indicates she is functioning in the range of moderate cognitive difficulties. Jenny's scores were consistent in the areas of intelligence, adaptive skills, achievement, and speech and language assessment. Her scores are 3 standard deviations below the mean in the areas of intelligence, adaptive skills, achievement, and speech and language. Thus, Jenny also receives speech and language services twice a week for 30-minute sessions. Jenny recently transferred into your school from a separate facility. Other students in class mock Jenny for issues related to social skills.

Jenny does not seem to have many friends. Students complain about her hygiene. Furthermore, she interrupts discussions, changes the topic of conversation often, and stands in close proximity to the other students and teachers. She seems to stare at individuals at times. Jenny does not complete her assignments in class. She does not complete homework correctly. Sometimes it seems like Jenny is daydreaming, and at other times she appears quite frustrated. She typically speaks in two-word utterances.

How do you help Jenny succeed in class assignments?

How do you help Jenny succeed socially with peers?

What do you do about family involvement?

What do you tell Jenny?

What do you say or do regarding Jenny's peers?

By the end of this chapter, you should be able to discuss answers regarding the questions from the case study involving Jenny. You should be able to explain theories regarding the meaning of intelligence and theories regarding the testability or test items designed to measure the construct of intelligence. Also, you should be able to identify the most prevalent and technically sound intelligence instruments for various age levels (preschool, school age, and adult) and identify the main areas measured by tests. You should be able to interpret test results in terms that students, parents, and others can understand easily. In addition, you should be able to identify informal measures involved in the assessment of cognition. You should be able to identify issues related to validity in testing intelligence in individuals who are culturally and/or linguistically diverse. In addition, you should be able to discuss how assessment results are connected with planning and how planning is connected with instruction.

This chapter addresses CEC Standards 1 (foundation), 3 (individual learning differences), and 8 (assessment). Information regarding definition, identification, assessment instruments, formal and informal assessments, the influence of diversity, and assessment decision information will facilitate learning toward these standards.

DEFINING COGNITION

EARLY CHILDHOOD

The conceptualization of cognitive issues and their academic, social, and emotional effects is complex in nature. In cases where a known syndrome or condition exists, developmental milestone delays and difficulties in certain areas are sometimes expected. For example, walking may not begin until the age of 2½ years instead of 1 year of age, which may be due to certain degrees of cognitive disability. In general, the more severe the level of cognitive disability, the more of a delay in reaching developmental milestones. During these early years, generally intelligence, language, visual/motor, and social skills are assessed (Drew & Hardman, 2004).

Examples of tests used during these early years are the Bayley Scales of Infant Development 2 (2–30 months) (Bayley, 1993) and the Battelle Developmental Inventory 2 (birth to 7 years, 11 months) (Newborg, Stock, & Wnek, 2004). Items evaluated may include gross motor, fine motor, adaptive, language, personal-social, perception, memory, and problem solving. Examples of tests utilized during the preschool years include the Stanford-Binet-5 for Early Childhood (2 to 7 years, 3 months) (Roid, 2004) and the Wechsler Preschool and Primary Scale of Intelligence—Third Edition (WPPSI-III; 2 years, 6 months to 7 years, 3 months) (Wechsler, 2002).

The Stanford-Binet IV for Early Childhood investigates a parent report on a child's performance in the areas of fluid reasoning, knowledge, quantitative reasoning, visual-spatial processing, and working memory. The WPPSI-III involves a verbal scale (i.e., information, similarities, arithmetic, vocabulary, comprehension, and sentences—optional) and performance scale (i.e., picture completion, geometric design, mazes, object assembly, and animal pegs—optional). These tests generally take one to two hours to administer. More information regarding these tests and others for this age group will be provided in Chapter 10.

Breakpoint Practice

1. Name the most common standardized tests for infants and toddlers. What major areas are included in this type of testing?

2. Name the most common standardized tests for preschool-age children. What major areas are included in this type of testing?

3. What factors might complicate the issue of reliability during the testing of preschoolers?

4. What factors might complicate the issue of validity during the testing of preschoolers?

5. What can be done to reduce these complications?

SCHOOL AGE

More often, families find out about their children's cognitive disabilities when these students begin to have difficulty in school. This may be the situation for students with mild cognitive disabilities, which account for about 95 percent of all cases of cognitive disabilities. Teachers may have concerns that the student is falling behind in completing assignments, understanding concepts, and keeping up with other students, and they may share with parents these concerns as indicators of problems in school performance. Parent and student input are essential in providing educational services. When the collaboration points to further assessment, the team gathers information regarding the student's aptitude in multiple domains. They typically look at school performance across a variety of areas. If it is a problem across the board, further assessment of cognition and behavior is performed. Intelligence, achievement, and adaptive skills are at the core of this type of assessment battery.

As the students enter elementary school, transition is a key element. Many transitions occur from prekindergarten to kindergarten, primary to intermediate grades, and intermediate to middle school. Transition is also a focal point in the high school years. Employment and housing become increasingly important as the student becomes older.

When students are considered for a variety of special education services, individual intelligence test results are utilized as part of the test battery in looking at the big picture. The assessment team looks for a pattern of behavior indicated by examining the pieces of the puzzle, including the test battery. Because the examiner is focused on the individual during the testing process, he or she could provide a great deal of information regarding the reactions of the student to the assessment and learning situation. For example, during an individual evaluation, if a student performs much more poorly on achievement tests compared to cognitive performance (in combination with other forms of assessment), a learning disability is considered.

In general, measures of cognitive performance or intelligence testing can be administered to a group or an individual. Group testing is usually used in screening groups of students. Group tests are cost effective and are typically paper-and-pencil tests. Kaplan and Saccuzzo (2001) note that they require less examiner training, have more objective and reliable scoring procedures, and have a broad application. However, group tests require reading ability that may interfere with content validity, especially for students who are suspected of having disabilities such as cognitive and learning disabilities.

Salvia and Ysseldyke (2007) described behaviors assessed in individual intelligence testing, including discrimination, generalization, motor behavior, general knowledge, vocabulary, induction, comprehension, sequencing, detail recognition, analogical reasoning, pattern completion, abstract reasoning, and memory. Discrimination involves the assessor asking the student to indicate an item that is different from other items. Generalization involves requiring students to match a response to a stimulus item. Motor behavior involves the student showing an active role. For example, the student would place an object in a certain spot. General knowledge includes data about what the student has learned. Vocabulary could take the form of receptive language (i.e., student pointing) or expressive language (i.e., student stating definitions). Induction refers to looking at an item and describing a general rule. Comprehension involves understanding the meaning of a word or combination of words. Sequencing involves ordering items (i.e., numbers). Detail recognition deals with filling in missing details from pictures. Analogies involve appropriate responses to series of items that are missing one of those items. Pattern completion deals with finishing patterns with missing items. Abstract reasoning deals with solving problems. Memory involves long-term and short-term memory.

The test administrator is generally a school psychologist. The administrator looks at qualitative as well as quantitative issues of the test. That is, the examiner looks at performance in terms of how the student scores in relation to others. In addition, she or he looks at behavioral aspects such as the student's approach to problem solving, frustration level, repetition of items, response time, ease, and accuracy of test taking. Information related to qualitative aspects in addition to the quantitative details give a much more robust and practical picture of what the student is like and how he or she performs on learning tasks.

Many of these tests measure verbal abilities and math skills. Furthermore, these tests often measure abilities related to school skills rather than general skills (McLoughlin & Lewis, 2005). Intelligence tests for school-age children are divided by subtests and/or age levels. Furthermore, they progress from easier to harder, in terms of level of difficulty. Verbal, quantitative, memory, auditory processing, visual processing, comprehension, and reasoning sections are often included.

Tests of Intelligence

Some individual tests of intellectual functioning are the Kaufman Assessment Battery for Children, Second Edition (KABC-II) (Kaufman & Kaufman, 2004); Standford-Binet, Fifth Edition (Roid, 2004); Wechsler Intelligence Scale for Children—Fourth Edition Integrated (WISC-IV; Weschsler, Kaplan, Delis, Fein, Maerlender, Morris, & Kramer, 2004); Woodcock-Johnson III NU, Tests of Cognitive Abilities (WJ-NU III; Woodcock, McGrew, & Mather, 2006); and the Bateria III Woodcock-Munoz NU (for Spanish speaking children, based on the WJ III) (Woodcock, Munoz-Sandoval, McGrew, & Mather, 2006). See Table 6.1 for an overview of these tests.

Table 6.1   Examples of Intelligence Tests

Name	Company	Content	Age	Time to Administer
Kaufman Assessment Battery for Children, Second Edition	American Guidance Service	Overall cognitive ability (simultaneous, sequential, planning, learning, and knowledge)	3 years through 18 years, 11 months	25–55 minutes for the Luria model, 35–70 minutes for the CHC model
Stanford-Binet, Fifth Edition	Riverside	Fluid reasoning, knowledge, quantitative reasoning, visual-spatial processing, and working memory	2 years to 85+	Less than an hour
Wechsler Intelligence Scale for Children, Fourth Edition, Integrated	Harcourt	Global intellectual performance (verbal comprehension, perceptual reasoning, working memory, and processing speed)	6 years through 16 years, 11 months	Less than an hour and a half
Woodcock-Johnson Psycho-Educational Battery—III, Normative Update, Tests of Cognitive Abilities and the Bateria III Woodcock-Munoz, Normative Update	Riverside	Overall intellectual functioning, verbal ability, thinking ability, cognitive efficiency, cognitive factors, and clinical clusters.	2 years to 90+	Less than an hour

Table 6.2 Five Scales and Corresponding Subtests from Kaufman Assessment Battery for Children, Second Edition

Simultaneous	Sequential	Planning	Learning	Knowledge
Triangles, face recognition, pattern reasoning (age 5 and 6 years), block counting, story completion (age 5 and 6 years), conceptual thinking, rover and gestalt closure	Word order, number recall, and hand movements	Pattern reasoning (age 7–18 years) and story completion (age 7–18 years)	Atlantis, atlantis delayed, rebus, and rebus delayed	Riddles, expressive vocabulary, and verbal knowledge

For example, the Kaufman Assessment Battery for Children, Second Edition, offers information via two theoretical models for simultaneous processing, planning ability, learning ability (Luria model) and visual processing, short-term memory, fluid reasoning, long-term storage and retrieval, and crystallized ability (CHC). Five scales and their corresponding subtests are included in Table 6.2.

The norm sample appears appropriate. Construct validity is discussed in light of support from factor-analytic studies. This instrument is correlated with the WISC-IV and WJ III. Values were less than desired. Furthermore, low reliability coefficients in the areas of internal consistency (e.g., hand movements, gestalt closure subtests) and test-retest (e.g., sequential, simultaneous, learning, and planning scales) should be considered. Scores include global scales, standard scores, percentile ranks, sociocultural percentile ranks, and age equivalents. The K-ABC ASSIST program provides a score summary, graphic profile, composite comparisons, high/low analysis, shared/unique abilities, and aptitude achievement discrepancy analysis. An administration CD is available. This test allows for marking correct responses in languages other than English. Furthermore, a Spanish version is included in the responses.

The Stanford-Binet, Fifth Edition, includes one nonverbal and one verbal domain in each of five factors, yielding ten subtests. The five factors include fluid reasoning, knowledge, quantitative reasoning, visual-spatial processing, and working memory. The resulting four intelligence scores include full scale, abbreviated, nonverbal, and verbal. Norming sample was appropriate; however, limited information related to the performance of students with disabilities was available. In the area of validity, comparisons with Weschler tests and WJ revealed acceptable correlations. In terms of reliability, split-half reliability coefficients are acceptable. Composite indices scores, standard scores for full test and standard scores for subtests (mean 10, SD 3), percentile rank equivalent, and confidence intervals are also available.

WISC-IV includes subtests on the following standard subtests: block design, similarities, digit span, picture concepts, coding, vocabulary, letter-number sequence, matrix reasoning, comprehension, and symbol search. Furthermore, subtests on picture completion, cancellation, information, arithmetic, and word reasoning (supplementary subtests) are also available. Sixteen process subtests (WISC-IV-I) could be administered, depending on the referral questions. Those subtests include the verbal domain (Similarities Multiple Choice, Vocabulary Multiple Choice, Picture Vocabulary Multiple Choice, Comprehension Multiple Choice, and Information Multiple Choice), perceptual domain (Block Design Multiple Choice, Block Design Process Approach, and Elithorn Mazes), working memory domain (Visual Digit Span, Spatial Span, Letter Span, Letter-Number Sequencing Process Approach, Arithmetic Process

Approach, and Written Arithmetic), and process speed domain (Coding Recall and Coding Copy).

Sampling information appears lacking in information regarding students with disabilities. In terms of validity information, concurrent validity data exist with acceptable coefficients with the previous version of the test only. Factor analysis results are acceptable. In terms of reliability, internal consistency (split-half) method revealed acceptable coefficients. Test-retest validity results are good. IQ scores for each index, subtest scaled scores, composite scores, percentile ranks, and confidence intervals can be derived from this test. Furthermore, composite score profiles can be charted. WISC-IV Spanish is also available.

The WJ-III/NU (based on WJ III) includes standard subtests on verbal comprehension, visual-auditory learning, spatial relations, sound blending, concept formation, visual matching, numbers reversed, incomplete words, auditory working memory, and visual-auditory learning—delayed. Extended battery subtests include general information, retrieval fluency, picture recognition, auditory attention, analysis-synthesis, decision speed, memory for words, rapid picture naming, planning, and pair cancellation. Norming sample appears adequate. Concurrent validity exists with adequate results. Furthermore, a discussion about construct validity is included in the manual. However, some issues regarding reliability, and therefore validity, exist for WJ III. For example, information regarding test-retest reliability is incomplete. Furthermore, internal consistency (split-half) is adequate for most subtests except picture recognition and planning (McLoughlin & Lewis, 2005). Overall intellectual ability, age-equivalent, grade-equivalent, standard score, percentile rank, and relative proficiency index scores are available with this test. Compuscore and Profiles Program are available with this test. In addition, a brief intellectual ability score was added to options for this instrument. Extended grade norms (kindergarten through graduate school) and Canadian validation have also been added.

Tests of Nonverbal Intelligence

Tests have been developed that concentrate on nonverbal intelligence to provide fairness in the testing process in the area of intelligence. Nonverbal intelligence testing is designed for individuals who have speech, language, and/or hearing difficulties. In addition, it is aimed toward individuals who are culturally and/or linguistically diverse. Three of those nonverbal intelligence tests include the Comprehensive Test of Nonverbal Intelligence (CTONI; Hammill, Pearson, & Wiederholt, 1996); the Test of Nonverbal Intelligence, Third Edition (TONI-3; Brown, Sherbenou, and Johnsen, 1997); and the Universal Nonverbal Intelligence Test (UNIT; Bracken & McCallum, 1998). Table 6.3 presents an overview of these nonverbal intelligence tests.

The CTONI is free of speaking, reading, and writing and of object manipulation responses by the individual being assessed. This test is comprised of six subtests, which include pictures and figures. The child generally chooses one of a number of options in pictorial analogies, geometric analogies, pictorial categories, geometric categories, pictorial sequences, and geometric sequences. Individuals being assessed select a picture to solve problems (analogies, categorizations, and sequences). A computer-administered version (CTONI-CA) is available. This program gives instructions to the individual being tested and provides results to the assessor. Standard scores, percentiles, age equivalents, and composite scores are available with this test. Norming appears adequate. Content (adequate), criterion-related (limited), and construct (limited) validity are discussed. Furthermore, results about internal consistency (adequate), test-retest (limited), and interscorer reliability (limited) are provided. Results are limited due to inadequate samples, with some coefficients in the .80s.

Table 6.3 Tests of Nonverbal Intelligence

Name	Company	Content	Age	Time to Administer
Comprehensive Test of Nonverbal Intelligence	PRO-ED	Analogical reasoning, categorical classifications, and sequential reasoning	6 years through 90 and 11 months	One hour
Test of Nonverbal Intelligence, Third Edition	AGS	Nonverbal measure of abstract reasoning and problem solving	6 years through 89 and 11 months	15 minutes
Universal Nonverbal Intelligence Test	Riverside	General intelligence measured by nonverbal means	5 years through 17 and 11 months	10–15 minutes for abbreviated battery, 30 minutes for standard battery, and 45 minutes for extended battery

The TONI-3 language-free design (no reading, writing, speaking, or listening required from individual being tested) contains two parallel forms (A and B). The individual selects one of several possible options. Each form contains 50 test items yielding a total score. Data can be reported as standard scores, percentile ranks, and stanines. The norming sample appears adequate. Content validity and concurrent validity are discussed. However, limited information exists. This test is compared to nonverbal subtests of the Stanford-Binet 5, WISC-III, and WAIS-R. Internal consistency, test-retest, and alternate forms reliability appear adequate.

The UNIT requires the use of manipulatives, paper and pencil, and pointing. Gestures are used by the examiner. The UNIT includes an abbreviated battery (two subtests), a standard battery (four subtests), and an extended battery (six subtests). Subtests include symbolic memory, spatial memory, object memory, cube design, analogic reasoning, and mazes. Performance on these subtests results in five quotients, including memory (short-term recall and recognition of meaningful and abstract information), reasoning (problem solving in familiar and unfamiliar situations), symbolic (performing tasks using meaningful information), nonsymbolic (performing tasks involving abstract material), and full-scale intelligence (overall ability). UNIT Compuscore is computer software available to score data. Scores include scaled scores, subtest scores (mean of 10, SD of 3), and full-scale IQ scores. Norming information appears adequate. Content, concurrent, and discriminant validity are discussed and appear adequate. Reliability quotients are in the low .8 for the subtests, high .8 for the scaled scores, and above .9 for the full-scale scores. These coefficients appear adequate.

Breakpoint Practice

1. Define intelligence.
2. What are the major tests used for testing school-age children in the area of cognitive skills?
3. What are the major areas tested in the assessment of cognitive skills?

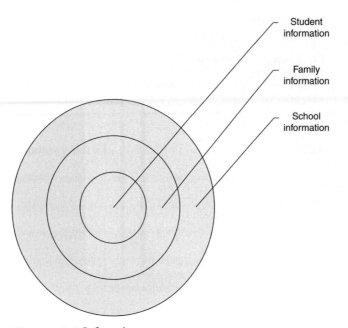

Figure 6.1 Informal assessment

INFORMAL ASSESSMENT

Informal assessments (see Figure 6.1) provide important assessment information, especially for students who may not be "testable." Informal assessment can be structured. In assessing cognitive skills, developmental milestones are examined. For example, the team asks the family about milestones such as sitting, walking, talking, and toileting. A delay in all of these milestones would indicate a possible issue. Furthermore, family history and birth or medical problems are examined. Parents, grandparents, uncles, aunts, great-uncles, or great-aunts with learning issues may indicate a genetic pattern in terms of cognitive difficulty. Furthermore, problems at birth may indicate lack of oxygen to the brain or trauma, which may affect cognitive functioning. School history may indicate problems in other classes or problems with learning.

Teacher observations are an essential element of the assessment process in the area of intelligence. The student's behavior in various settings, with different students, and at different times of the day is critical in the judgment of cognitive skills such as problem solving in a natural environment. For example, details and analysis of participation in lecture, large-group discussions, small-group activities, and unstructured activities (i.e., recess and lunch) give much valuable information. Does the student use appropriate behavior? How does he or she interact with the teacher? How does he or she deal with other students? When the student does not understand a question, how does he or she respond? In addition, student self-assessment (Allen & Cowdery, 2005) is essential in improvement, self-efficacy, and generalization.

DYNAMIC ASSESSMENT

Research studies regarding dynamic assessment and intelligence utilizing classroom activities have revealed useful information. Feedback from the assessor is built into this process in evaluating the student's functioning (new learning) (Grigorenko & Sternberg, 1998). Elliott (2003) noted that there was a disconnect between intelligence test scores and instructional practices, therefore supporting dynamic assessment. Furthermore,

Krista Greco/Merrill

support is given for a more fair assessment of individuals who are culturally and/or linguistically diverse (Hessels, 1997), have a disability (Saldana, 2004), and/or are gifted (Johnsen, 1997). However, Resing (2001) makes a case that a tool designed to measure learning potential should depend on information the assessor wishes to investigate. She maintains that traditional intelligence testing and dynamic assessment can guide assessors to measure whether the child has gaps in his or her learning development and potential. Nevertheless, she argues that the assessor could receive more information regarding the link between learning ability and school achievement through dynamic assessment.

Fabio (2005) explored the association of fixed measures of intelligence and codifying speed, codifying accuracy, and school performance. The test performance of students who were in kindergarten through high school was compared to dynamic assessment measures. Results showed that dynamic assessment measures were more accurate in the prediction of codifying speed, codifying accuracy, and school performance than were the standard measures.

Swanson and Howard (2005) explored whether dynamic assessment measures gave any additional information than that provided by traditional intelligence tests in the prediction of reading achievement scores. They studied the cognitive performance of students with reading disabilities, students with math/reading disabilities, poor readers, and skilled readers and found that dynamic assessment did add information when predicting reading and mathematics performance. The investigators noted that poor readers and skilled readers had a higher frequency of positive change and maintenance of those gains than the other two groups consisting of students with learning disabilities.

Lauchlan and Elliot (2001) investigated dynamic assessment with students who had moderate and severe learning difficulties. They found that when students who were found to have high potential via dynamic assessment were given cognitive training, they made great gains. They outperformed students who were found to have high potential and received no training. Furthermore, students who were found to have low potential and received training performed better than students who had high potential and received no training.

TECHNOLOGY

Martin (2000) proposed enforcing electronic portfolios (using Composer via Netscape's Navigator) for students in an effort to ascertain baselines and gauge development in intelligences via classroom activities. Some activities included in electronic portfolios were book review and interview, newspaper names, and people search. Formative evaluation and technology are utilized in this assessment-to-instruction connection.

Gerber, Semmel, and Semmel (1994) proposed a computer-based dynamic assessment tool for math (DynaMath). The program appraises multiplication facts and uses multidigit problems. Researchers support this type of evaluation due to controlled procedures and the capacity to store data and graphical records (Bahr & Bahr, 1997). Kalyuga and Sweller (2005) also found that utilizing e-learning with dynamic assessment increased knowledge and cognitive efficiency in the area of mathematics. In their study, working memory and cognitive load were examined in the context of decreasing knowledge retrieved from long-term memory. Online dynamic algebra learning tasks appeared to optimize cognitive performance.

On the other hand, Noyes, Garland, and Robbins (2004) discussed assessments using the computer mode as an increase of effort compared to traditional testing. They suggested that more effort is needed for students with lower comprehension levels. The researchers noted that students who perform at lower levels have more difficulty using the computer mode. Clearly more research needs to be conducted in this area.

Breakpoint Practice

1. Name five informal assessment measures.
2. How would you collect these informal assessment data?
3. What are some disadvantages to these methods?
4. Which two informal assessment measures do you think would be the most useful?
5. How would behavior, intelligence level, and other issues (i.e., context) influence results?
6. What contextual information could confuse the results?

THEORIES OF INTELLIGENCE

MAJOR THEORIES

Many researchers have influenced the depth and possibilities of the theoretical development of the concept of intelligence. Figure 6.2 lists seven contributions (and their contributors) to the study of intelligence. We will discuss each one in this section.

Binet and Simon (1905) discussed mental ability as a total package or product. They did not look at single aspects of cognition when measuring mental ability. They also used age as a measuring stick. They looked at how older children had higher capabilities than younger children and used those findings to separate tasks to calculate mental age.

Spearman (1927) further defined general mental ability by offering the factorial approach. He contributed the general ("g") factor and the specific ("s") factor. The general ("g") factor dealt with activities that could not be linked with particular situations, and the specific ("s") factor dealt with activities that could be linked with situations.

Thorndike (1927) proposed that three factors were involved in intelligence: abstract intelligence, mechanical intelligence, and social intelligence. Abstract intelligence was connected with verbal and mathematical symbols. Mechanical intelligence dealt with the ability to utilize objects in a significant way. Social intelligence involved dealing with people.

Piaget (1952) has been a major contributor in the conceptualization and assessment of cognition. He used a developmental model; that is, he posited that behavior

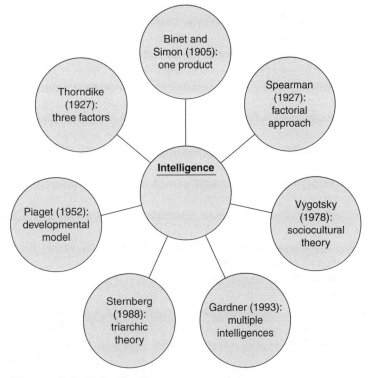

Figure 6.2 Major theorists

develops in a certain order over time. He defined developmental stages or periods: the sensorimotor period (1½ to 2 years of age), the preoperational period (1½ to 7 years of age), concrete operations period (7 to 11 years of age), and formal operations period (11 years and older). The sensorimotor period involves a child using his or her senses to understand his or her environment. The preoperational period has two stages. These include the preconceptual stage (1½ to 4 years of age) and the intuitive substage (3 to 7 years of age). The preconceptual stage deals with the child's awareness of objects and his or her relation to them. The intuitive substage deals with constancy and the recognition of other points of view. The concrete operations stage involves the child's understanding of quantity, length, and number. The formal operations period deals with reasoning/metalinguistic (thinking about language) activities.

Vygotsky's (1978) theory of cognitive development is based on a sociocultural perspective. He viewed the child as an active learner in his or her environment. Social language is the tool which he or she uses to learn from adults and more knowledgeable peers. This interactive process points to a critical focus on culture as shaping the cognitive process. Also, the idea of scaffolding, where a more knowledgeable adult or peer gives less and less support in a learning process as the child becomes more independent, is a key component in the instructional process stressed today in classrooms. Furthermore, increasing the opportunity for active learning via interaction in small groups is another strategy widely used today in classrooms. Vygotsky's work has great implication for teaching all students.

Gardner and his colleagues (1993) propose seven original intelligences. These multiple intelligences include logicomathematical (i.e., numerical and reasoning tasks), linguistic (i.e., language), musical, spatial (i.e., visual spatial), bodily kinesthetic (i.e., bodily movement), interpersonal (i.e., interactions with others), and intrapersonal (i.e., understanding of oneself). This theory involves analyzing strengths and weaknesses in various areas. Because verbal and quantitative skills are traditionally only two of the seven typi-cally examined and emphasized (Diaz-Lefebvre, 2004), this is groundbreaking informa-tion. Furthermore, it promotes an assessment-to-instruction loop. Knowing students' strengths feeds into activities in which the teacher can use strengths to support needs.

Sternberg (1988) discusses componential, contextual, and experiential elements in his triarchic theory of intelligence. The componential element involves internal cogni-tive factors, including the process, activities, and encoding involved in problem solving. Metacognitive, performance, and knowledge acquisition components are prominent in this discussion. The experiential element deals with how humans respond to new tasks or problems, as well as responses to highly familiar circumstances. The contextual ele-ment involves culture and behaviors. Adaptation, selection of a better environment, and shaping of the existing environment are key components of this element. These can be investigated further as analytic, creative, and practical intelligence (Viadero, 1995).

Furthermore, Sternberg has developed a theory of successful intelligence (Sternberg, 1999) and methods of teaching for this successful intelligence (Sternberg & Grigorenko, 2000). Individuals find ways to be successful; that is, they know their assets and make the most of those strengths, while recognizing their needs and com-pensating for them. Sternberg and Grigorenko (2004) noted that there is no single correct way of teaching or assessing students. They encouraged teachers to teach ana-lytically (analyze, critique, judge, compare and contrast, evaluate, and assess), creatively (create, invent, discover, imagine, suppose, and predict), and practically (apply, use, put into practice, implement, employ, and render practical). This is an example of the assessment-to-instruction loop regarding intelligence offered by these researchers.

Breakpoint Practice

1. Discuss five theories of intelligence.
2. Which theory of intelligence do you find most meaningful? Why?
3. Compare and contrast the theories of Vygotsky, Gardner, and Sternberg.
4. Discuss the implications of these theories in the classroom.

THEORIES INVOLVING THE TESTING OF INTELLIGENCE

Of particular interest is the intertwining of intelligence and adaptive skills in many of these definitions. The social aspect and the application of behavior in context are seen throughout the evolution of notions of cognition. The inherent interdependence of the concepts is remarkable. In fact, attempting to re-create a setting out of context for this particular type of testing is complex and difficult. Many questions regarding the mean-ing of the outcome of this type of testing arise. Three theories are more prevalent when looking at the connection between test development and theory. According to Esters and Ittenbach (1999) these theories include the fluid-crystallized theory of intelligence (Horn & Cattell, 1966); planning, attention, simultaneous, and successive theory (Das, Naglieri, & Kirby, 1994); and the three-stratum theory of intelligence (Carroll, 1993).

The nine factors involved in the fluid-crystallized theory of intelligence include (1) fluid reasoning, (2) crystallized intelligence, (3) visual processing, (4) auditory processing, (5) processing speech, (6) short-term memory, (7) long-term retrieval, (8) quantitative knowledge, and (9) correct decision speed. Li, Lindenberger, Hommel, Aschersleben, Prinz, and Baltes (2004) examined fluid and crystallized abilities in rela-tion to maturation. They found support for the dynamic development of fluid and crystallized abilities. Fluid abilities appeared to expand in earlier child development and decrease earlier during aging compared to crystallized abilities. Furthermore, they found that crystallized abilities depend on fluid abilities.

Kaufman, Kaufman, Chen, and Kaufman (1996) investigated seven subtests measuring six Horn abilities. Based on Horn and Hofer's (1992) findings, they looked at vulnerable abilities, which decline with brain damage or age (broad visualization, short-term acquisition, and retrieval), and maintained abilities (quantitative ability and long-term retrieval). Kaufman et al (1996) found that crystallized (application of knowledge) and quantitative (mathematical) abilities were maintained. Furthermore, they found that fluid and broad visualization were vulnerable. Short-term acquisition and retrieval was maintained through the sixties. Results from long-term retrieval produced conflicting results. The Weschler Series, Standford-Binet Scales, and Woodcock-Johnson Psycho-Education Battery—Revised, Tests of Cognitive Ability appear to be in accord with the fluid-crystallized theory of intelligence (Esters & Ittenbach, 1999).

In the planning, attention, simultaneous, and successive (PASS) theory, individuals process stimuli that they find relevant while tuning out stimuli that they do not find useful. The Kaufman series are tests that corroborate this theory (Esters & Ittenbach, 1999). Furthermore, the cognitive assessment system (Naglieri & Das, 1997) is based on PASS. However, research results (Kranzler & Keith, 1999) revealed that the PASS model did not provide a particularly good fit to the test (CAS).

The three-stratum theory of intelligence includes (1) general intelligence, (2) broad abilities, and (3) more specific abilities. It blends key features of Spearman's theory and Horn and Cattell's theory (Bickley, Keith, & Wolfle, 1995). Also, this theory addresses individual differences. Carroll (1997) classified the three strata into "narrow" abilities (stratum I), "broad" abilities (stratum II), and "general" ability (stratum III). Stratum I included about 70 specific abilities with each regarding a specific Stratum II factor (i.e., originality, reading comprehension). Stratum II included fluid intelligence, crystallized intelligence, broad auditory perception, broad visual perception, broad retrieval capacity, broad cognitive speed, general memory and learning, and processing speed. Stratum III was analogous to "g, or general factor mental ability" (Carroll, 1993). This factor is a single measure of intelligence.

Bickley et al (1995) tested the three-stratum theory of cognitive abilities across the life span via factor analysis. Results revealed support for the theory, but they did not support the changes in organization of cognitive abilities across a lifetime.

Facon and Facon-Bollengier (1999) studied the effect of chronological age and fluid intelligence on the crystallized intelligence of individuals with intellectual disabilities, age 6 to 20 years. They found that chronological age (experience) and fluid intelligence both accounted for a large portion of crystallized intelligence.

Breakpoint Practice

1. Discuss the similarities and differences of the three theories on the testing of intelligence.
2. Which theory do you find most meaningful?
3. What are the implications for instruction based on these theories?

CHALLENGES INVOLVING THE TESTING OF INTELLIGENCE

Challenges with intelligence testing include many aspects. Standardized tests involving intelligence have been reported to be invalid and unreliable (Czubaj, 1995). Examiners' errors, overinterpretation of the tests' data, failure to include certain age groups of students, and marketability have been reported to negatively affect this type of testing (Czubaj, 1995).

Furthermore, some important factors involving theoretical issues also negatively affect validity. For one, there is a lack of ability to define precisely the construct of intelligence. Second, intelligence tests do not cover the full realm of intelligence. Therefore, content validity is in question. Third, intelligence test results can change significantly over time. Factors can include contextual, emotional, motivational, and other issues. Therefore, reliability and validity issues are in question. Fourth, researchers have shown these tests to be culturally biased, and thus validity issues are in question. This aspect has a considerable impact on the outcome of these tests for students who are culturally and/or linguistically diverse. All of these issues have a connection involving a given student's ability to access learning opportunities and, at the very least, they have social and occupational implications. The emotional and financial implications are also called into question. Therefore, extreme caution should be taken when interpreting these test results. Ethical and legal considerations are critical in this type of decision making.

Characteristics of persons with cognitive disabilities could further complicate the assessment process. For example, individuals with cognitive disabilities are at an increased risk for also having psychiatric disorders, such as mood and anxiety disorders, schizophrenia, and conduct disorders. Furthermore, speech-language, hearing, vision, motor, epilepsy (McDermott, Moran, Platt, Wood, Isaac, & Dasari, 2005), autism, and health issues may be involved.

Some test makers have attempted to lessen problems with the verbal aspects of tests by administering nonverbal intelligence tests. However, complications have been revealed regarding these tests as well. Reid (2002) investigated a measure of nonverbal intelligence, the Evaluation of the Adapted Kohs Block Design Test (Kohs, n.d.). Results revealed sufficient reliability and initial concurrent validity. However, construct validity results were inconclusive. Further complications to testing the intelligence of individuals with visual impairments is that assessment of students with sensory disabilities in rural school districts is affected by shortages of specially trained personnel (Bowen & Ferrell, 2003).

In addition, Maller and French (2004) investigated a measure of nonverbal intelligence, the Universal Nonverbal Intelligence Test (UNIT) Factor between groups of individuals who were deaf and hearing. They found that expected subtest scores in the group of individuals who were deaf were lower than those for participants in the standardization sample. These results were in agreement with results found by Maller (1996, 1997). For more information regarding sensory disabilities, see Chapter 11.

Motivational characteristics such as locus of control, learned helplessness, expectancy of failure, outerdirectedness, and self-regulatory behavior (Beirne-Smith, Ittenbach, & Patton, 2006) may affect the assessment behavior and outcome. All of these aspects could further obscure reliability and validity issues in the assessment process.

Multicultural Considerations

Without sound construct validity for standardized intelligence tests, results should be interpreted cautiously. For example, some researchers have questioned the development of intelligence tests without an apparent definition of the theory measured. The Weschler and Binet Scales were specifically mentioned. Because Alfonso, LaRocca, Oakland, and Spanakos (2000) found that the tests most often emphasized by graduate courses dealing with individual intelligence tests were the Wechsler series and the Standord-Binet Intelligence Test—Fourth Edition, this issue is especially alarming. In addition, *Assessment of Children's*

Intelligence and Special Abilities, Third Edition, Revised (Sattler, 2002) and *Intelligent Testing with the WISC-III* (Kaufman, 1994) were the books utilized most often by the participants.

Because the concept of intelligence is culturally bound, utilizing the same concept-bound tests is inappropriate (Overton, 2006). For example, the variables considered important in the concept of intelligence may be different across cultures. So utilizing tests that emphasize only certain verbal or quantitative skills bring into question issues of construct and content validity.

Shafer (1999) notes that language and cultural factors may influence the assessment of intelligence in standardized testing. Because students respond to the testing environment in the same style they would use to function in their everyday environment, low scores may be the result of a difference between testing and the child's familiarity with the testing context. This affects reliability and, therefore, the validity of the test results.

The evidence supports these doubts (Oswald, Coutinho, Best, & Nguyen, 2001); that is, students who are culturally and linguistically diverse are overrepresented in receiving services related to cognitive disabilities. For example, Schwartz, Glass, Bolla, Stewart, Glass, Rasmussen, Bressler, Shi, and Bandeen-Roche (2004) found that even after controlling for the variables of educational status, household income, household assets, occupational status, health-related behaviors, health conditions, and levels of lead in blood when looking at neurobehavioral tests comparing race/ethnicity, large differences among the groups persisted. Beishuizen (2002) refers to sociopolitical, ethical, and test-theoretical levels in analyzing standardized psychological tests and the suitability of assessing individuals who are culturally and/or linguistically diverse.

The most widely used intelligence tests, the Wechsler scales (Esters & Ittenbach, 1999), have shown different scores among different racial groups (Naglieri & Rojahn, 2001). Research results involving the WISC-III revealed that this test classified disproportionately more individuals who were African American as having cognitive disabilities than it classified whites. Furthermore, Neely-Barnes and Marcenko (2004) studied the impact on families with a child who had developmental disabilities across race/ethnicity. They compared white, African American, and Latino families and found that family impact differed for each racial or ethnic group. The researchers reported that white families noted medical needs and therapy services external to the school. African American families noted medical needs. Hispanic families reported personal care, special education services, therapy external to the school, coordination of services, and less involvement in organized events as factors.

Alfonso, LaRocca, Oakland, and Spanakos (2000) investigated the graduate course training regarding individual cognitive assessment required of all accredited school psychology programs in the United States. Survey data revealed that many characteristics of this course remain the same as compared to data from 1986. They noted that developments in cognitive theory, test development, and professional guidelines should be integrated in courses. These results matched those of Wilson and Reschly (1996), who found that there was a lag between research and practice.

Based on this body of research dealing with intelligence testing, labeling students with disabilities, and the effects of these practices, it is clear that major moral, ethical, and legal problems (at the very least) are occurring within the fields of assessment and special education. Reliability and validity troubles plague these practices. As responsible

(*continued*)

professionals and citizens, it is our duty to reflect on these factors when assessing all students, but especially students who are culturally and/or linguistically diverse. We have a huge responsibility in shaping their school and life experiences.

In reflecting on the thoughts and data presented in this chapter, it would seem realistic to scrutinize the information regarding intelligence assessment used in an evaluation report. Items to consider would be the assessment tools used and the characteristics of the individual tested. What are his or her learning, behavioral, health, sensory, motor, speech and language, motivational, and other characteristics in relation to validity complications related to the test construction and norm group used in the test result makeup? How do informal measures fit in this puzzle?

Breakpoint Practice

1. What are some validity issues regarding intelligence testing of students who are culturally and/or linguistically diverse (including students with sensory disabilities)?
2. What are some solutions to these issues?
3. Discuss intelligence as a culturally bound concept.

REVISITING JENNY

In the chapter-opening case study involving Jenny, contextual factors played a big part in Jenny's performance and reported happiness. The academic and social success of this student should be examined. The student and the student's family should drive the decision-making process. Because contextual factors influence the success of instruction, these methods should be reexamined.

You should work on activities requiring collaboration between Jenny and the other students. You could attempt to raise class awareness of disabilities in a positive way. Providing structured group work would likely aid Jenny's success. You should provide modifications and accommodations to instruction, materials, and mode of completing projects and in-class assessments. An application of a variety of methods within the context of the classroom would help determine which adaptations would be the most effective for Jenny.

Adding a self-assessment component could keep Jenny involved and increase her self-determination skills. Self-assessment skills could also increase generalization skills for the areas of social, language, and adaptive skills and functional academics. Active involvement of the family could help with home and community performance skills.

ACTIVITIES

1. Discuss the role of formal and informal assessment in the assessment of cognition.
2. Compare cognitive assessment for early childhood and school-age children.
3. What are some issues that may arise regarding the validity of standardized intelligence testing of a person with visual impairments or hearing impairments?
4. What are some issues that may arise regarding the validity of standardized intelligence testing of a person with speech and language disorders?
5. What are some issues that may arise regarding the validity of standardized intelligence testing of a person who is culturally and/or linguistically diverse?

WEB RESOURCES

www.tash.org

www.cec.sped.org

www.aamr.org

http://www.robertexto.com/archivo13/beyond_piaget_vygotsky.htm

http://www.psychist.com/cognition.html

http://www.webaim.org/articles/cognitive

http://www.piaget.org/Journal

REFERENCES

Alfonso, V. C., LaRocca, R., Oakland, T., & Spanakos, A. (2000). The course on individual cognitive assessment. *School Psychology Review, 29*(1), 52–65.

Allen, K. E., & Cowdery, G. E. (2005). *The exceptional child: Inclusion in early childhood education* (5th ed.). New York: Delmar.

Bahr, M. W., & Bahr, C. M. (1997). Educational assessment in the next millennium: Contributions of technology. *Preventing School Failure, 41*, 90–94.

Bayley, N. (1993). *Bayley Scales of Infant Development*—2nd Edition (BSID-II). San Antonio, TX: Psychological Corporation.

Beirne-Smith, M., Ittenbach, R. F., & Patton, J. R. (2006) *Mental retardation* (7th ed.). Upper Saddle River, NJ: Merrill/Pearson Education.

Beishuizen, J. J. (2002). Psychological testing in a multicultural society: Universal or particular competencies? *Intercultural Education, 13*(2), 201–213.

Bickley, P. G., Keith, T. Z., & Wolfle, L. M. (1995). The three-stratum theory of cognitive abilities: Test of the structure of intelligence across the life span. *Intelligence, 20*, 309–328.

Binet, A., & Simon, T. (1905). Methodes nouvelles pour le diagnostic du niveau intellectual des anormaux. *Annee Psychologique,* 11, 191–244.

Bowen, S., & Ferrell, K. A. (2003). Assessment in low-incidence disabilities: The day-to-day realities. *Rural Special Education Quarterly, 22*, 4, 10–20.

Bracken, B. A., & McCallem, R. S. (1998). *Universal test of nonverbal intelligence.* Itasca, IL: Riverside.

Brown, L., Sherbow, R. J., & Johnsen, S. K. (1990). *Test of nonverbal intelligence.* Austin, TX: PRO-ED.

Brown, L., Sherbow, R. J., & Johnsen, S. K. (1997). *Test of nonverbal intelligence—3.* Itasca, IL: Riverside.

Carroll, J. B. (1993). *Human cognitive abilities: A survey of factor-analytic studies.* Cambridge, England: Oxford University Press.

Carroll, J. B. (1997). The three-stratum theory of cognitive abilities. In D. P. Flanagan, J. L. Genshaft, & P. L. Harrison (Eds.), *Contemporary intellectual assessment: Theories, tests, and issues* (pp. 122–130). New York: Guilford Press.

Czubaj, C. A. (1995). Standardized assessments used in American public schools are invalid and unreliable. *Education, 116*(2), 179–184.

Das, J. P., Naglieri, J. A., & Kirby, J. R. (1994). Assessment of cognitive processes: The PASS theory of intelligence. Boston: Allyn & Bacon.

Diaz-Lefebvre, R. (2004). Multiple intelligences, learning for understanding, and creative assessment: Some pieces to the puzzle of learning. *Teachers College Record, 106*(1), 49–57.

Drew, C. J., & Hardman, M. L. (2004). *Mental retardation: A life cycle approach* (8th ed.). Upper Saddle River, NJ: Merrill/Pearson Education.

Elliot, J. (2003). Dynamic assessment in educational settings: Realizing potential. *Educational Review, 55*(1), 15–32.

Esters, I., & Ittenbach, R. F. (1999). Contemporary theories and assessments of intelligence: A primer. *Professional School Counseling, 2*(5), 373–377.

Fabio, R. A. (2005). Dynamic assessment of intelligence is a better reply to adaptive behavior and cognitive plasticity. *Journal of General Psychology, 132*(1), 41–64.

Facon, B., & Facon-Bollengier, T. (1999). Chronological age and crystallized intelligence of people with intellectual disability. *Journal of Intellectual Disability Research, 43*(6), 489–496.

Gardner, H. (1993). *Multiple intelligences: The theory in practice.* New York: Basic Books.

Gerber, M. M., Semmel, D. S., & Semmel, M. I. (1994). Computer-based dynamic assessment of multidigit multiplication. *Exceptional Children, 61*(2), 114–125.

Grigorenko, E. L. L., & Sternberg, R. J. (1998). Dynamic testing. *Psychological Bulletin, 124,* 75–111.

Hammill, D. D., Pearson, N. A., & Wiederholt, J. L. (1996). *Comprehensive test of nonverbal intelligence.* Austin, TX: PRO-ED.

Hessels, M. G. (1997). Low IQ but high learning potential: Why Zeyneb and Moussa do not belong in special education. *Educational and Child Psychology, 14,* 121–136.

Horn, J. L., & Cattell, R. B. (1966). Refinement and test of the fluid and crystallized general intelligences. *Journal of Educational Psychology, 57,* 253–270.

Horn, J. L., & Hofer, S. M. (1992). Major abilities and development in the adult period. In R. J. Sternberg & C. A. Berg (Eds.), *Intellectual development* (pp. 44–99). Boston, MA: Cambridge University Press.

Johnsen, S. K. (1997). Assessment beyond definitions. *Peabody Journal of Education, 72*(3–4), 136–152.

Kalyuga, S., & Sweller, J. (2005). Rapid dynamic assessment of expertise to improve the efficiency of adaptive e-learning. *ETR&D, 53*(3), 83–93.

Kaplan, R. M., & Saccuzzo, D. P. (2001). *Psychological testing: Principles, applications, and issues* (5th ed.). Belmont, CA: Wadsworth/Thomson Learning.

Kaufman, A. S. (1994). *Intelligent testing with the WISC-III.* New York: Wiley.

Kaufman, A. S., & Kaufman, N. L. (2004). *Kaufman assessment battery for children* (2nd ed.). Circle Pines, MN: American Guidance Service.

Kaufman, A. S., Kaufman, J. C., Chen, T., & Kaufman, N. (1996). Differences on six Horn abilities for 14 age groups between 15–16 and 75–94 years. *Psychological Assessment, 8*(2), 161–171.

Kohs, S. C. (n.d.). Kohs block design instruction manual. Wood Dale, IL: Stoelting.

Kranzler, J. H., & Keith, T. Z. (1999). Independent confirmatory factor analysis of the Cognitive Assessment System (CAS): What does the CAS measure? *The School Psychology Review, 28*(1), 117–144.

Lauchlan, F., & Elliot, J. G. (2001). The psychological assessment of learning potential. *British Journal of Educational Psychology, 71,* 647–665.

Li, S., Lindenberger, U., Hommel, B., Aschersleben, G., Prinz, W., & Baltes, P. B. (2004). Transformations in the couplings among intellectual abilities and constituent cognitive processes across the life span. *Psychological Science, 15*(3), 155–163.

Maller, S. J. (1996). WISC-III verbal item invariance across samples of deaf and hearing children of similar measured ability. *Journal of Psychoeducational Assessment, 14,* 152–165.

Maller, S. J. (1997). Deafness and WISC-III item difficulty: Invariance and fit. *Journal of School Psychology, 35,* 299–314.

Maller, S. J., & French, B. F. (2004). Universal nonverbal intelligence test factor invariance across deaf and standardization samples. *Educational and Psychological Measurement, 64*(4), 647–660.

Martin, G. (2000). Maximizing multiple intelligences through multimedia: A real application of Gardner's theories. *Multimedia Schools, 7*(5), 28–33.

McDermott, S., Moran, R., Platt, T., Wood, H., Isaac, T., & Dasari, S. (2005). Prevalence of epilepsy in adults with mental retardation and related disabilities in primary care. *American Journal on Mental Retardation, 110*(1), 48–56.

McLoughlin, J. A., & Lewis, R. B. (2005). *Assessing students with special needs* (6th ed.). Upper Saddle River, NJ: Merrill/Pearson Education.

Naglieri, J. A., & Das, J. P. (1997). *Cognitive assessment system.* Chicago: Riverside.

Naglieri, J. A., & Rojahn, J. (2001). Intellectual classification of Black and White children in special education programs using the WISC-III and the Cognitive Assessment System. *American Journal on Mental Retardation, 106*(4), 359–367.

Neely-Barnes, S., & Marcenko, M. (2004). Predicting impact of childhood disability on families: Results from the 1995 national health interview survey disability supplement. *American Association on Mental Retardation, 42*, 284–293.

Newborg, J., Stock, J. R., and Wnek, L. (2004). *Battelle Developmental Inventory 2.* Chicago: Riverside.

Noyes, J., Garland, K., & Robbins, L. (2004). Paper-based versus computer-based assessment: Is workload another test mode effect? *British Journal of Educational Technology, 35*(1), 111–113.

Oswald, D. P., Coutinho, M. J., Best, A. M., & Nguyen, N. (2001). Impact of sociodemographic characteristics on the identification rates of minority students as having mental retardation. *American Association on Mental Retardation, 39*(5), 351–367.

Overton, T. (2006). *Assessing learners with special needs: An applied approach* (5th ed.). Upper Saddle River, NJ: Merrill/Pearson Education.

Piaget, J. (1952). The origins of intelligence in children. New York: International Universities Press.

Reid, J. (2002). Testing nonverbal intelligence of working-age visually impaired adults: Evaluation of the Adapted Kohs Block Design Test. *Journal of Visual Impairment & Blindness, 96*(8), 585–596.

Resing, W. C. M. (2001). Beyond Binet. *Issues in Education, 7*(2), 225–236.

Roid, G. (2004). The Standford-Binet intelligence scale (5th ed.). Chicago: Riverside.

Saldana, D. (2004). Interactive assessment of metacognition: Exploratory study of a procedure for persons with severe mental retardation. *European Journal of Psychology of Education, 19*(4), 349–364.

Salvia, J., & Ysseldyke, J. E. (2007). Assessment (10th ed.). Boston, MA: Houghton Mifflin.

Sattler, J. M. (2002). *Assessment of children: Behavioral and clinical applications* (4th ed.). San Diego, CA: Jerome M. Sattler, Publisher.

Schwartz, B., Glass, T., Bolla, K., Stewart, W., Glass, G., Rasmussen, M., Bressler, J., Shi, W., Bandeen-Roche, K. (2004). Disparities in cognitive functioning by race/ethnicity in the Baltimore Memory Study. *Environmental Health Perspectives, 112*(3), 314–320.

Shafer, L. (1999). What does the literature reveal on the appropriate assessment of English language learners for placement in special education programs? Retrieved January 1, 2005, from http://mason.gmu.edu/~lshafer/ELL-LDcritoflit.shtml.

Spearman, C. E. (1927). The abilities of man. New York: Macmillan.

Sternberg, R. J. (1988). *The triarchic mind: A new theory of intelligence.* New York: Viking.

Sternberg, R. J. (1999). The theory of successful intelligence. *Review of General Psychology, 3*, 292–316.

Sternberg, R. J., & Grigorenko, E. L. (2000). *Teaching for successful intelligence.* Arlington Heights, IL: Skylight.

Sternberg, R. J., & Grigorenko, E. L. (2004). Successful intelligence in the classroom. *Theory Into Practice, 43*(4), 274–281.

Swanson, H. L., & Howard, C. B. (2005). Children with reading disabilities: Does dynamic assessment help in the classroom? *Learning Disability Quarterly, 28*, 17–34.

Thorndike, E. L. (1927). The measurement of intelligence. New York: Teacher's College Press.

Viadero, D. (1995). Intelligence report. *Teacher Magazine, 6*(4), 16–18.

Vygotsky, L. S. (1978). *Mind in society.* Cambridge, MA: Harvard University Press.

Wechsler, D. (2002). The Wechsler preschool and primary scale of intelligence (3rd ed.). San Antonio, TX: Psychological Corporation.

Wechsler, D., Kaplan, E., Delis, D., Fein, D., Maerlender, A., Morris, R., & Kramer, J. (2004). *The Wechsler intelligence scale for children—Integrated* (4th ed.). San Antonio, TX: Harcourt.

Wilson, M. S., & Reschly, D. J. (1996). Assessment in school psychology training and practice. *School Psychology Review, 25*, 9–23.

Woodcock, R. W., McGrew, K. S., and Mather, N. (2006). *Woodcock-Johnson III Normative Update tests of cognitive abilities.* Itasca, IL: Riverside.

Woodcock, R. W., Munoz-Sandoval, A. F., McGrew, K., & Mather, N. (2006). *Bateria III Woodcock-Munoz Normative Update.* Chicago: Riverside.

Adaptive Skills

KEY TERMS

Vocational: Work training.

Thematic: Instruction centered around themes.

Adaptive behavior: The way individuals deal with demands and changes in their environment.

Conceptual skills: Skills involving verbal and quantitative concepts.

Social skills: Skills involving interpersonal and intrapersonal areas.

Interpersonal: Between or among two or more people.

Intrapersonal: Reflection within oneself.

Practical skills: Skills involving daily living.

Self-determination: Freedom to live as one decides without the influence of others.

Self-advocacy: Living one's own life legally and practically.

Self-direction: Following personal preferences in activities.

Supports: Strategies that help individuals with cognitive disabilities.

Intermittent supports: Support needed occasionally across the life span.

Limited supports: Support needed during part of the life span or support needed in a particular area.

Extensive supports: Support needed on a daily basis.

Pervasive supports: Continuous support needed across a number of contexts.

Functional academics: Applying academic skills to authentic useful tasks.

Pragmatic language: Social language.

Transition: Bridge between school and adulthood or independence.

Case Study: Assessing Sam

Sam is a student in your eleventh-grade class. He is in a vocational high school where students with mild to moderate cognitive disabilities take courses with a thematic unit focus. One theme involves the restaurant industry. During the math focus, students use calculators to add food charges, tax, and tip. During the reading focus, students learn food (e.g., *soup*) and restaurant (e.g., *restrooms*) sight words. During the science focus, students learn about health issues, such as the length of time chicken should be left in the refrigerator, freezer, and/or oven.

Sam does well in these areas of study. He has difficulty when the activities are applied in social settings, and he has difficulty with social language. He does not easily read social cues and has problems expressing his emotions and language intentions. His employer has serious concerns and wants to terminate him immediately. Sam does not understand why his boss is upset with him and wants to let him go.

What do you say to Sam's boss?

What do you say to Sam?

How could you have prevented this situation?

What do you do to salvage the practicum?

What do you do in terms of the assessment-to-instruction link?

By the end of the chapter, you should be able to discuss the questions posed in the case study about Sam. You should also be able to explain the process that assessors use to gather information regarding adaptive skills. You should be able to name, explain, and give an example of the American Association on Mental Retardation's (1992) ten adaptive skills. You should also be able to utilize these concepts to choose appropriate formal and informal methods for evaluation purposes.

When we think about quality of life issues, such as relationships with loved ones, holding down a job, and functioning within one's home and community, adaptive skills are critical. For example, an individual with disabilities will often lose his or her job due to responsibility issues (i.e., tardiness) rather than scoring low on an intelligence test. Furthermore, in the areas of health and home safety, these skills can mean the difference between life and death.

DEFINITION OF ADAPTIVE BEHAVIOR

The way individuals deal with demands and changes in their environment is what we think of as adaptive behavior skills. Individuals learn these skills first at home and then in preschool. The key disposition that aids individuals with disabilities begins with skill building early on, from toddler age to adulthood. These everyday actions, not "maximal" performance (Beirne-Smith, Ittenbach, & Patton, 2006), guide the way individuals function in the context of their activities.

Furthermore, the American Association on Mental Retardation (AAMR) (1992) refers to adaptive skills as conceptual, social, and practical skills (see Figure 7.1). Conceptual skills often involve verbal and quantitative concepts. Some examples of conceptual skills include receptive and expressive language, reading and writing, money concepts, and self-directions. Examples of social skills are interpersonal

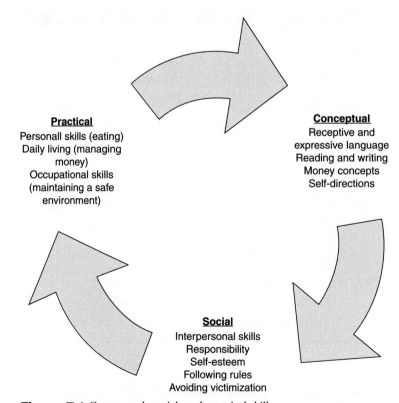

Figure 7.1 Conceptual, social, and practical skills

skills, responsibility, self-esteem, gullibility, naivete, following rules, obeying laws, and avoiding victimization. Practical skills include personal skills (i.e., eating, dressing, mobility, and toileting), instrumental activities of daily living (i.e., taking medication, preparing meals, using the phone, managing money, using transportation, and doing housekeeping activities), and occupational skills (i.e., maintaining a safe environment) (American Association on Mental Retardation [AAMR], 2005).

Many of the disabilities (i.e., learning, emotional/behavioral, autism, etc.) include behavioral, social, and emotional characteristics that can negatively affect adaptive behavior skills. For example, difficulty with understanding social cues (Learning Disabilities Association, 2005), interpersonal skills, self-determination, and general social behavior can be part of many types of disabilities. Therefore, this is an important topic for disabilities in general.

Researchers have used various terms to describe social skills when related to individuals with various disabilities. *Social competence* is a term associated with adaptation to societal demands. According to Vaughn and Hogan (1990), it includes relations with others, age-appropriate social thinking, nonappearance of maladaptive behaviors, and successful social behaviors. Another notion is social/emotional competence (Zinn, Elias, Greenberg, & Weisberg, 2000). These researchers include feelings, intentions, respect, dealing with problems, communication, goals, and self-assertion in their discussion of social/emotional competence.

Utilizing practical social aspects in light of age and cultural appropriateness is a vital part of assessing adaptive skills. Many of the tests used in the measurement of adaptive skills are called adaptive behavior tests. The focus of these tests differs based on the authors' theoretical framework regarding adaptive behavior. This explains the variability in terms of items on some of the major standardized tools. In addition, adaptive behavior is connected to intelligence, and adaptive behavior expectations vary with age (Sattler, 2002). Furthermore, many of the adaptive behavior norm-referenced tests do not have appropriate validity or reliability established. These factors, in combination with cultural bias and the different expectations from people who interact with the individual in a variety of contexts, are complex when considering the assessment of adaptive skills (Pierangelo & Giuliani, 2006).

Breakpoint Practice

1. What adaptive behavior issues arise for a child who is preschool age?
2. What adaptive behavior issues arise for a child who is in elementary school?
3. What adaptive behavior issues arise for a child who is in middle school?
4. What adaptive behavior issues arise for a child who is in high school?
5. What adaptive behavior issues arise for an adult?
6. What adaptive behavior issues arise for a person who is elderly?

DEFINITION OF MENTAL RETARDATION

Based on the previous discussion, it is easy to see why adaptive behavior skills are essential in the definition of mental retardation, cognitive disability, or intellectual disability. According to the American Association on Intellectual Developmental Disabilities (AAIDD), formerly known as the American Association on Mental Retardation (AAMR)

(2002) "intellectual disability consists of significant limitations both in intellectual functioning and adaptive behavior." Adaptive behavior skills include conceptual, social, and practical skills. At least two areas of adaptive behavior skills need to be limited for this definition to hold. Intellectual functioning, adaptive skills functioning, and an age cutoff of 18 years (symptoms must have been displayed) are stated by AAIDD as requirements for the label of mental retardation, cognitive disability, or intellectual disability.

According to the American Psychological Association (APA) (1994), the following are needed in the diagnosis of mental retardation: significant limitations in general intellectual functioning and adaptive functioning and onset before the age of 22. The age of onset difference between the two associations' definitions is of particular interest.

When looking at state guidelines, differences occur among states in the term used for mental retardation or cognitive disabilities, definition used, and cutoff for deviations in intelligence testing (Beirne-Smith, Ittenbach, & Patton, 2006). Delays, disorders, disabilities, and impairments of cognition, development, intelligence, learning, and educational ability are most commonly used in states. Furthermore, depending on whether they utilize the AAMR's or APA's definition, a guideline of 18, 21, or no age is mentioned. In terms of intelligence score deviation cutoff, typically 2 standard deviations are required. In some cases, no standard deviation cutoff is mentioned (Beirne-Smith, Ittenbach, & Patton, 2006). This lack of consistency across states leaves special educators with little structure in the areas of assessment and adaptive skills.

After the assessment of intelligence and adaptive behavior, strengths and needs are identified to indicate supports. The four dimensions of strengths and needs include intellectual and adaptive behavior skills, psychological/emotional considerations, physical/health/etiological considerations, and environmental considerations (Arc, 2005). Data in each of these areas can be gathered by formal testing, interviews, observations, and/or interactions with the individual.

Breakpoint Practice

1. Compare and contrast the adaptive skills definitions of APA and AAMR.
2. What problems can occur if a child moves from one state to another?
3. What are the pros and cons of using the age cutoffs of 18 and/or 22?

SUPPORTS

According to CEC Content Standard 8 (assessment), special educators must identify supports and adaptations that individuals need to participate in "general curriculum and to participate in school, system, and statewide assessment programs" via the assessment process. Supports are "resources and individual strategies necessary to promote the development, education, interests, and personal well-being of a person with a cognitive disability. Supports can be provided by a parent, friend, teacher, psychologist, doctor or by an appropriate person or agency" (AAMR, 1992, p. 101).

Supports are critical in discussing adaptive skills to increase personal, social, and emotional development (AAMR, 1992). They include human development activities, teaching and educational activities, home living activities, community living, employment, health and safety, behavior, social protection, and advocacy (AAMR, 2005). These supports can be provided at one of four levels of intensity: intermittent, limited, extensive, or pervasive. Intermittent is the least intensive, and pervasive is the most

Table 7.1 Levels of Intensity

	Intermittent	**Limited**	**Extensive**	**Pervasive**
Definition	Occasionally by the individual over a lifetime	Part of the life span	Daily basis	Continuous support in many contexts and life areas
Example	Community assistance	Support within the home	Support within the home	Vocation, domestic, community, leisure, and recreation

intensive (see Table 7.1). The expectation is that the student has the ability to access the same age-appropriate curriculum if she or he did not have a disability.

Technology has also been discussed in the literature regarding support with adaptive skills. For example, Mechling (2004) investigated multimedia programs in connection with use of the grocery store. Computer simulations involving sequences for completing grocery shopping (i.e., electronic video and photographs) preceded shopping at a local grocery store. Results revealed that individuals improved their grocery shopping skills.

Furthermore, Twyman and Tindal (2006) investigated the comprehension and problem-solving of students with disabilities in social studies using computer-adapted materials. Although experimental and control groups showed no difference in comprehension, the experimental group did better statistically than the control group in an extended-response essay. Results show a positive outcome of computer-adapted methodology.

Breakpoint Practice

1. Give examples of when intermittent supports would be needed.
2. Give examples of when limited supports would be needed.
3. Give examples of when extensive supports would be needed.
4. Compare and contrast extensive and pervasive supports.

TEN ADAPTIVE SKILLS

The American Association on Mental retardation's 10 (AAMR, 1992) adaptive skills (with examples) are:

Communication: expressive language, pragmatic language

Self-care: dressing

Home living: laundering clothes, cooking meals

Social skills: making friends, turn taking

Community use: using transportation, going to the store

Self-direction: using personal preferences in activities, using a calendar

Health and safety: taking medication, going to the doctor when appropriate

Functional academics: reading signs, writing a check

Leisure: participating in age-appropriate recreational activities, exercising

Work: using job skills and interviewing skills

Breakpoint Practice

1. Give an example of each of the 10 adaptive skills.

2. Give an example of the intersection of the language and social skills related to the adaptive skills you listed in question 1.

3. Give an example of the intersection of leisure and self-direction related to the adaptive skills you listed in question 1.

4. Give an example of the intersection of leisure and health and safety skills related to the adaptive skills you listed in question 1.

MEASURES OF ADAPTIVE BEHAVIOR

Some of the more common standardized adaptive behavior measurements and formal assessment instruments, presented in Table 7.2, are usually administered individually. As a teacher, you will administer and/or be expected to understand the results and

Table 7.2 Formal Adaptive Behavior Tests

Name	Company	Content	Age of Grade Level	Time to Administer
AAMR Adaptive Behavior Scales—School:2	PRO-ED	Personal independence and social maladaption	3-0 through 18-11	15–30 minutes
Adaptive Behavior Evaluation Scale—Revised	Hawthorne	Adaptive skills	K through twelfth grade	20 minutes
Adaptive Behavior Inventory	PRO-ED	Functional daily living skills	6-0 through 18-11	20–25 minutes
A Developmental Assessment for Students with Severe Disabilities—2	PRO-ED	Language, sensory-motor skills, daily living activities, basic academic skills, and social-emotional skills	Birth through 6-11 developmentally	2–3 hours
Scales of Independent Behavior—Revised	Riverside	Adaptive and maladaptive behavior	Infancy to 80 years or older	45–60 minutes for full scale, 15–20 minutes for short form or early development form
Vineland Adaptive Behavior Scales, Second Edition	American Guidance Service	Personal and social skills	Survey Interview Form, Parent/Caregiver Rating Form, Expanded Interview Form—birth through 90 years, Teacher Rating Form—3 years through 21 years, 11 months	20–60 minutes for survey form, 60–90 minutes for expanded form, 20 minutes classroom edition

implications of those results for instruction. Therefore, in this section of the chapter, the most commonly used and researched tests are noted.

FORMAL MEASURES

The AAMR Adaptive Behavior Scales—School (ABS-S:2) (Lambert, Nihira, & Leland, 1993) was developed for assessing children who are being evaluated for the possibility of cognitive disabilities. Furthermore, the authors note that this test can be used for the evaluation of adaptive behavior for children with autism and behavior difficulties. Part One assesses personal independence and responsibility. The nine domains include independent functioning (i.e., eating, cleanliness, dressing), physical development (i.e., sensory and motor), economic activity (i.e., money handling, budgeting), language development (i.e., comprehension and expression), numbers and time, prevocational/ vocational activity (i.e., work habits, job performance), self-direction (i.e., initiative), responsibility (i.e., dependability), and socialization (i.e., social maturity). See Figure 7.2.

Part Two assesses social maladaptation. The seven domains include social behavior (i.e., physical violence), conformity (i.e., absenteeism), trustworthiness (i.e., cheating and stealing), stereotyped and hyperactive behavior, self-abusive behavior, social engagement (i.e., shyness), and disturbing interpersonal behavior (i.e., reaction

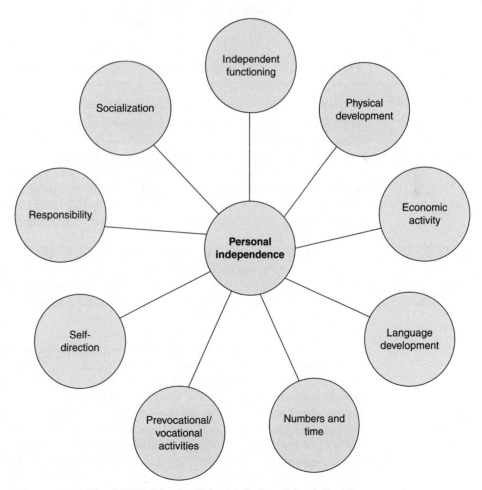

Figure 7.2 The AAMR Adaptive Behavior Scales—School: Part One

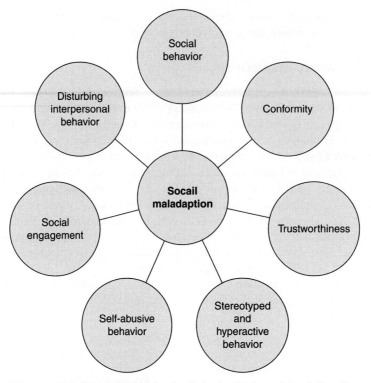

Figure 7.3 The AAMR Adaptive Behavior Scales—School: Part Two

to others). The five factors this test taps into are personal self-sufficiency, community self-sufficiency, personal-social responsibility, social adjustment, and personal adjustment. See Figure 7.3.

Results are reported as standard scores and percentiles. Content validity, criterion-related validity, and construct validity are discussed. Internal consistency and interrater reliability are also discussed. Norms and reliability appear adequate. However, validity is in question (Stinnet, 1997; Stinnett, Fuqua, & Coombs, 1999). A form of this test can be used in assessing individuals in residential placements (Nihira, Leland, & Lambert, 1993).

The Adaptive Behavior Evaluation Scale—Revised (ABES-R) (McCarney, 1995) is based on AAMR's adaptive skills. Therefore, the 10 subtests include communication skills, self-care, home living, social interactions, community use, self-direction, health and safety, functional academics, leisure, and work. Anyone familiar with the student can serve as the person completing the test. A score of 0 to 5 is given for each of the 104 items (0 "is not developmentally appropriate for age group," 1 "does not demonstrate the behavior or skill," 2 "is developing the behavior or skill," 3 "demonstrates the behavior or skill inconsistently," 4 "demonstrates the behavior or skill most of the time," or 5 "demonstrates the behavior or skill at all times"). Results are reported as standard scores and percentiles. Content validity, criterion-related validity, and construct validity are discussed in the manual. Internal consistency (coefficient alpha), test-retest reliability, and interrater reliability are noted by the authors. This test includes a school version, and English and Spanish home versions. Questions exist regarding norms, reliability, and validity. The home versions can be completed by a parent or guardian. ABES-R Quick Score, a Windows-compatible program, calculates raw scores and converts them to standard and percentile scores.

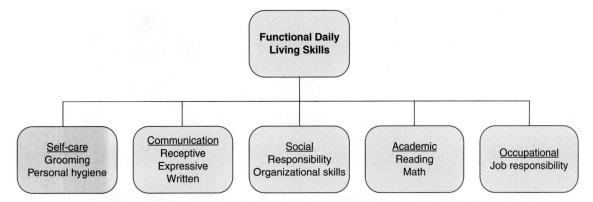

Figure 7.4 Examples of functional daily living skills in the Adaptive Behavior Inventory

The Adaptive Behavior Inventory (ABI) (Brown & Leigh, 1986) assesses functional daily living skills, including self-care (i.e., grooming and personal hygiene), communication (i.e., receptive, expressive, and written language), social (i.e., responsibility and organizational skills), academic (i.e., reading and math), and occupational (i.e., job responsibility) skills with 150 items. See Figure 7.4. This test is designed to identify students who may have cognitive disabilities or emotional difficulties. Results can be in the form of standard scores, adaptive behavior quotients, and percentile ranks. Concurrent, content, and construct validity are discussed. In addition, internal consistency (coefficient alpha) and test-retest reliability are offered. Norms seem adequate. Some validity concerns exist. A short form (with 50 items) of this test has also been developed by the authors.

The Developmental Assessment for Students with Severe Disabilities (DASH-2) (Dykes & Erin, 1980) is a criterion-referenced instrument. Performance is assessed in the areas of language, sensory-motor skills, daily living, basic academic skills, and social-emotional skills. The results take the form of indicating whether the skills are task resistive, need full assistance, need partial assistance, need minimal assistance, or are at independent performance.

The Scales of Independent Behavior—Revised (SIB-R) (Bruininks, Woodcock, Weatherman, & Hill, 1996) include 14 adaptive behavior subscales and 8 problem behavior subscales. Motor skills (gross and fine), social interaction (verbal and nonverbal), communication (receptive and expressive) skills, personal living skills (i.e., eating, dressing), and community living skills (i.e., time, money, home skills) are investigated by the adaptive subscales. Internalized (i.e., hurtful to self, unusual or repetitive habits, withdrawal or inattentive behavior), asocial (i.e., socially offensive behavior or uncooperative behavior), and externalized (i.e., hurtful to others, destructive to property, or disruptive behavior) maladaptive indices are included in the problem behavior subscales.

Support levels are categorized into pervasive, extensive, frequent, limited, intermittent, and infrequent (no support). Three forms of the test exist. Those include full scale, short form (screening), and early development (below 8 years of age). Results can be reported in the form of standard scores, percentile ranks, age equivalents, and normal curve equivalents. Criterion-related and content validity are discussed. Internal consistency (split-half), test-retest, and interrater reliability are offered. A short form of this test for individuals who are visually impaired is also available. This test has 40 adapted items. Questions regarding norms exist. Reliability and validity appear adequate.

Scott Cunningham/Merrill

The Vineland Adaptive Behavior Scales, Second Edition (VABS-II) (Sparrow, Cicchetti, & Balla, 2005), has recently been revised. A survey interview, a parent/caregiver rating, and expanded interview forms are available. Key constructs examined include communication (i.e., receptive, expressive, written), daily living skills (i.e., personal, domestic, community), socialization (i.e., interpersonal relationships, play and leisure time, and coping skills), and motor skills (i.e., gross and fine). A maladaptive behavior index (i.e., internalizing, externalizing, and other) is optional. This index can be useful if maladaptive behaviors are suspected. Standard scores, percentile ranks, adaptive levels, and age equivalents are provided. Some coefficients (i.e., internal consistency, test-retest, and interrater) are low. Vineland-II ASSIST software is available for calculating scores for the test.

INFORMAL MEASURES

In addition to formal measures, informal measures are also part of the evaluation in the area of adaptive behavior skills. Many of the formal tools rely on informants' ratings in the measurement of adaptive behavior. Questions regarding the consistency of informants' ratings when compared to other informants and self-ratings (Achenbach, 1993) add credence to the required use of more modes of information gathering.

Conducting interviews with family members and teachers, as discussed in other chapters, is important. It is very important to obtain information regarding how the student is functioning within a variety of community and school contexts from these sources. The importance of the child interview in examining behaviors cannot be overlooked (McConaughy, 1996). Information from the family and the child gives educators an insight into how the individuals perceive current situations, priorities, difficulties, and aspirations. These factors are critical for appropriate programming information.

Observation of the student in multiple contexts is ideal in the investigation of adaptive behavior. Academic, social, work, and family environments can reveal critical information regarding the various natural settings and individuals the student interacts with on a daily basis. This functional assessment helps the educator learn how the student functions in his or her natural environments. Information can be gained to explore questions such as "Does the individual use his or her communication skills to ask for assistance to access transportation, stores, and leisure activities?"

Functional behavioral analysis involves observation (Taylor, 2006) to examine aspects of environment. This could be key information in the assessment and intervention of maladaptive behavior. Here, the educator is attempting to determine what purpose the target behavior serves so that he or she can intervene (Fad, Patton, & Polloway, 1998; McConnel, Hilvitz, & Cox, 1998). According to Simpson (1998), one must define and measure a target behavior, ascertain the variables of that behavior, identify its causes, and clarify actions for intervention.

Dynamic assessment, which includes examining the process of learning, is also vital. Here, the professional has the opportunity to combine the assessment and instruction processes into one. This type of assessment lends itself easily to creating links with curriculum. Especially for students with disabilities, a functional curriculum is most favorable because focusing on the context without generalizing produces greater success in authentic tasks.

FUNCTIONAL CURRICULUM

In the case study about Sam, a thematic functional curriculum unit was noted based on the area of restaurant work. Because of some characteristics of students with cognitive disabilities (i.e., difficulties with concepts that are not concrete (Drew & Hardman, 2004), it is critical to allow students to practice the appropriate tasks in a practical and authentic setting. Therefore, it makes sense that the tasks should be real and do-able. For a high school student with mild to moderate cognitive disabilities, vocational skills are an ideal focus for infusion into the curriculum. This is an important link in the execution of the transition plan.

For example, if one were to look at the area of hospitality, the content areas of math, reading, social studies, and science/health can naturally be incorporated into the lesson plans. In a specific area of hotel work, math can be related to measuring shampoo and liquid soap. Reading the labels associated with items to be measured can be a target. The development or change in the areas of hotels or even housing can be included in the discussion in terms of the social studies component. Bathing can be infused into the health piece of the unit. What is interesting about the functional academics in this discussion is that all of these skills are adaptive skills and essential in the area of vocation.

The transition from the role of student to adult is critical. Students learn and practice skills in a meaningful way before they are expected to perform tasks independently, without support. These are skills that the students will need to survive. When providing the context in which these skills are necessary, the educators help students form a basis for these skills. Furthermore, academic goals are met because they are being addressed in the lesson plans. Personal relevance can serve as a motivation factor that increases academic success.

SOCIAL SKILLS

A critical area of focus in the functional curriculum for many students with cognitive disabilities is social skills. For example, individuals with cognitive disabilities often have difficulties recognizing emotions. Harwood, Hall, and Shinkfield (1999) found that individuals with cognitive disabilities had more difficulty identifying others' expressions of anger, fear, disgust, and surprise than individuals without cognitive disabilities. They noted that visual-perceptual limitations can contribute to this issue.

In a recent study, Walden (1997) found differences in social signals produced by children with developmental delays with differing etiologies. She also found that participants were more accurate when viewing visual looks by children with typical development, less accurate when judging looks of children with developmental delays, and least accurate when judging looks of children with Down syndrome. This finding supports the need to stress the importance of instruction in this area of social skills.

SPECIFIC ETIOLOGY

Researchers have investigated adaptive skills based on specific etiologies (i.e., attention deficit hyperactivity disorder [ADHD]) related to this area. Stein, Szumowski, and Blondis (1995) compared groups of children with ADHD or attention deficit disorder (ADD) and a comparison group comprised of children with pervasive developmental disorders or mild cognitive disabilities using the Vineland Adaptive Behavior Scales (VABS). They found that the groups with ADD and ADHD performed significantly more poorly in the areas of communication, socialization, and daily living.

In addition, strength and weakness patterns by etiology of cognitive disability are important in the connection to instruction. Dykens, Ort, Cohen, Finucane, Spiridigliozzi, Lachiewicz, Reiss, Freund, Hagerman, and O'Conner (1996) found that children with Fragile X have adaptive behavior skills that matched levels of performance more than their measured cognitive abilities. In addition, Hatton, Wheeler, Skinner, Bailey, Sullivan, Roberts, Mirrett, and Clark (2003) looked at 70 children with Fragile X syndrome. The age range of these children was 1 year to 12 years. Using the Vineland Adaptive Behavior Scales (VABS), they found that adaptive behavior skills increased over time during childhood. However, some evidence suggests that there may be a plateau, and these skills may decrease after childhood (Fisch, Simensen, & Schroer, 2002). Multiple theories exist for explaining the plateau or decrease of skills. One explanation may be test properties changing over ages. A different justification could be that IQ declines over time. Other researchers report that two types of Fragile X mutations could cause different results in IQ over time (http://www.fragilex.org/html/iq.htm).

Stone, Ousley, Hepburn, Hogan, and Brown (1999) utilized the Vineland Adaptive Behavior Scales (VABS) to explore adaptive behavior in children with autism under the age of 36 months. Participants were matched on chronological age and mental age. When compared to controls, the children with autism showed weaker socialization and communication domains. Similar results were found by Carpentieri and Morgan (1996).

Dykess, Hodapp, and Evans (1994) found that individuals with Down syndrome scored lower in the communication domain when compared to their scores in the other adaptive behavior domains. Mervis, Klein-Tasman, and Mastin (2001) found that individuals with Williams syndrome demonstrated strengths in socialization and communication domains and weaknesses in daily living skills and motor skills. Interpersonal skills were higher, not related to chronological age.

Breakpoint Practice

1. Give examples of content areas in a unit regarding real-life issues (i.e., substance abuse prevention).

2. Give an example of a functional curriculum task.

3. How can etiology affect adaptive skills?

Multicultural Considerations

According to the CEC Content Assessment Standard 10, "special educators collaborate with families and other colleagues to assure nonbiased, meaningful assessments and decision-making." Looking at the 10 adaptive skills (i.e., communication, self-care, home living, social skills, community use, self-direction, health and safety, functional academics, leisure, and work; American Association on Mental Retardation, 1992) through the lens of an individual who is part of a culture other than the American mainstream is important.

Evaluating Adaptive Skills

For example, let's say that language is affected due to a bilingual/bicultural status. Next, looking at the impact of cultural differences could be significant. Think of some of the responsibilities of home living. Perhaps one comes from another country where dishwashers, washers, and driers were not available within the home. Perhaps the individual was not responsible for doing the laundry.

Maybe different eye contact and proximity rules exist within one's family or among society members. Maybe individuals in this student's home country use facial expressions quite differently to communicate feelings and emotions. Some cultures expect individuals to use a poker face so that emotions are not revealed. Another example would be appropriateness of taking the bus. In terms of self-direction, perhaps parents were responsible for scheduling. In the area of health and safety, perhaps one's religion prohibits certain or all medications or contact with physicians. In one's home country, academics could have been viewed as purely lecture and question-and-answer instruction. Leisure activities could have been controlled according to religious rules. Work may not have been allowed for certain age groups or genders.

If the assessor were unfamiliar with the person's culture, at least two of the adaptive skill areas could be judged inappropriately. The validity of a formal or informal measure is seriously in question. The fact that in some adaptive behavior measures, a second person is involved in judging whether the behavior is or is not present and appropriate adds to the possibility of error. This validity aspect, coupled with cultural- and/or language-biased testing affecting intelligence testing, could have detrimental effects on an appropriate diagnosis of the student. The possible results are alarming.

Many parts of a culture, such as ethnic background, gender, age, and socioeconomic status, influence adaptive skills. What may be seen as appropriate in one context may not be viewed as appropriate in another context. The lens of the assessor is also important when considering the assessment of adaptive skills. Information on many adaptive skills tests relies on secondhand information from a reporter. The reporter records information based on his or her memory of events and/or observations. Errors and biases are risk factors that can affect outcomes in this type of assessment. The reporters may not have seen the student's behavior in various settings. The student may behave in a different way in front of the reporter. Furthermore, the individual reporting and/or scoring the student's adaptive skills is the filter that guides determination as to what is appropriate.

(continued)

Beliefs Regarding Adaptive Skills

Our beliefs filter these expectations. The adult administering the test may want a certain outcome, which can color the results. The test administrator may be a family member, teacher, speech-language pathologist, social worker, counselor, aide, or nurse. As an example, Tasse and Lecavalier (2000) compared parent and teacher ratings on the Nisonger Child Behavior Rating Form, a measurement of social competence and problem behaviors of individuals with developmental disabilities. They found that, even though no significant differences were evident on two social competence subscales, differences in three behavior subscales (i.e., conduct problem, insecure/anxious, and hyperactive) were noted. Because of the different expectations that individuals bring with them as reporters or raters, the reliability and validity of the results of these types of tests are in jeopardy.

The label of cognitive disability cannot be applied unless adaptive skills are affected. The issue of referral of students should not be overlooked (Hosp, 2003). O'Reilly, Northcraft, and Sabers (1989) introduced the concept of confirmation bias. That is, an evaluator draws conclusions that align with a preferred hypothesis, even though data is missing. Referral rates for individuals who are African American and Latino are higher. Therefore, it is critical that students be assessed in their natural contexts (Arc, http://www.thearc.org). The more sources of credible information and the more contexts involved when that assessment information is gathered, the more reliable and valid the assessment results will be.

The Individuals with Disabilities Education Act (P.L. 94-142) increased the role of adaptive behavior in identifying students with cognitive disabilities. The home-to-school connection is extremely important in the assessment of adaptive behavior skills. Voelker, Shore, Hakim-Larson, and Bruner (1997) found that teachers rated children more positively in global and specific domains of adaptive behavior than did caregivers. The Vineland Adaptive Behavior Scales were utilized in this study. The study involved 59 children with multiple disabilities. The mean age of the children was 6 years. Communication and collaboration among teachers and caregivers would help bridge this gap and make the assessment more valid.

Social Rules

Different values and rule systems involving social rules can certainly affect pragmatic skills (social language). In fact, when the communication interaction rules at school are different than the rules at home, social language differences can be misperceived as language disorders (Iglesias, 1985). The rules often are different in different contexts within schools (cafeteria, playground, classroom, gym, and hallway).

Damico and Damico (1993) specifically concentrated on social language in individuals who are diverse and reviewed variations that should be addressed early with school-age children. They included the areas of language code difference and its impact on intelligibility and socialization. Conversation style shifting and bias were included in the discussion of dialect and style. In addition, conversational discontinuities were discussed. Contextualization cues (verbal and nonverbal) were highlighted in this review. The impact of social language variations included misperceptions, stereotyping, miscommunication, and bias. The authors noted that professionals must be familiar with these issues and attempt to improve the situation.

Researchers have indicated that culture-driven social rules within the classroom can be barriers to the learning process (Cheng, 1996). Westby (1997) specifically targeted students who are culturally and linguistically diverse when she looked at social information regarding the context where students learn. She used data from observations and interviews of teachers of elementary school children. Those data indicated that students who are from cultures that value interdependence, obedience to authority, and passive learning may have problems with learning the academic content in a classroom where the teacher expects students to be independent. Students who do not master social content may not fully acquire academic content. Students who do not fully acquire academic content as well as social content may be viewed as having a behavioral or learning disability.

It is also important to look at how caregivers view services provided by the school system. Shapiro, Monzo, Rueda, Gomez, and Blesher (2004) found that Latina mothers noted five primary concerns related to developmental disabilities and service systems: poor communication, low effort by the provider, negative attitudes of professionals, negative treatment by professionals, and the central role of the mother to the well-being of the child. Also troubling was that the mothers appeared to separate themselves from the provider. It is important to be aware of these areas to improve professional services.

Furthermore, Kritikos and Birnbaum (2004) interviewed 12 caregivers of African American children with mild cognitive disabilities on their views and experiences regarding needs and services provided for their families. Results revealed that the most common concerns included curriculum and instructional needs. Caregivers also noted that if they could provide suggestions for teachers who provide services to students with disabilities, they would suggest increasing teacher involvement with students.

Breakpoint Practice

1. What can you do to increase the validity of your assessment of a student who is linguistically and/or culturally diverse?
2. What do you need to evaluate within your belief system regarding adaptive skills?
3. How can social rules influence the outcome of adaptive behavior skills results?

REVISITING SAM

When considering the information in this chapter and in the chapter-opening case study about Sam, several thoughts may come to mind. Discussion of the problem issues with Sam and the employer separately and then together seems appropriate. During the work practicum at the restaurant, several issues arose. Defining those issues is critical for a more successful outcome. For example, was Sam sick and did not call to say he would not work his shift? Does he give food away and/or eat and drink while on the job? Does he cough and sneeze in the food? Answers to these types of questions mean that more specific targeted remediation information could then be addressed. Intervention would vary based on the identified issues. Practicing and evaluating the follow-up of these skills on the job would be important.

Discussion with Sam's boss regarding how you will address the problem, and reassurance that you or a representative will be there to provide extensive supports for Sam, should help. Using these strategies before a problem occurs could have prevented it, or it could have reduced the severity of the problem. In addressing the assessment-to-instruction link, assessment of Sam's preferences, skills, particular job skills, needs in particular skills, and practice on the job would be key.

ACTIVITIES

1. Discuss the pros and cons of formal and informal assessment for adaptive behavior skills.

2. Discuss the significance of secondhand information in the assessment process as it relates to standardized adaptive behavior measures.

3. Give examples of multicultural issues for each of the 10 adaptive areas listed by the AAMR.

4. Discuss the connection of adaptive behavior skills and cognitive disability.

5. Discuss the significance of adaptive behavior skills assessment of individuals who are culturally and/or linguistically diverse and the consequences of errors in this assessment process.

6. Suppose a fourth-grade student was referred for an evaluation due to concerns regarding academic performance. Interviews and observations confirmed the concerns. Adaptive behavior and intelligence tests revealed scores more than 2 standard deviations below the expected norm. What could these findings indicate?

7. Suppose a fifth-grade student was referred for an evaluation due to concerns regarding behavior and academic performance. Interviews and observations confirmed the concerns. Adaptive behavior results revealed that the student scored 2 standard deviations below the mean. Intelligence tests revealed levels 1 standard deviation below the mean. Would this student be determined eligible for special education and related services under a diagnosis of having a cognitive disability?

8. Suppose a third-grade student was referred for an evaluation due to concerns regarding academic performance. The student scores within the normal range for adaptive behavior and 2 standard deviations below the mean on intelligence testing. Would this student be determined eligible for special education and related services under a diagnosis of cognitive disability?

WEB RESOURCES

http://www.aamr.org/Policies/faq_mental_retardation.shtml
http://www.nasponline.org/resources/factsheets/socialskills_fs.aspx
http://www.tash.org

http://www.ldonline.org/article/6034

http://www.aamr.allenpress.com/aamronline

REFERENCES

AAMR (2005). http://www.aamr.org.

Achenbach, T. M. (1993). Implications of multiaxial empirically based assessment for behavior therapy with children. *Behavior Therapy, 24,* 91–116.

American Association on Mental Retardation. (1992). *Mental retardation: Definition, classification, and systems of support* (9th ed.). Washington, DC: American Association on Mental Retardation.

American Psychological Association (1994). *Diagnostic and statistical manual of mental disorders* (4th ed.). Washington, DC: American Psychiatric Association.

ARC (2005). Retrieved from http://www.thearc.org on February 21, 2008.

Association for Retarded Citizens (formerly). Retrieved from www.thearc.org. on November 6, 2008.

Beirne-Smith, M., Ittenbach, R. F., & Patton, J. R. (2006). *Mental Retardation* (7th ed.). Upper Saddle River, NJ: Merrill/Pearson Education.

Brown, L., & Leigh, J. E. (1986). *Adaptive behavior inventory.* Austin, TX: PRO-ED.

Bruininks, R. H., Woodcock, R. W., Weatherman, R. F., & Hills, B. K. (1996). *Scales of independent behavior—Revised* (SIB-R). Itasca, IL: Houghton Mifflin.

Carpentieri, S., & Morgan, S. B. (1996). Adaptive and intellectual functioning in autistic and nonautistic retarded children. *Journal of Autism and Developmental Disorders, 26,* 611–620.

Cheng, L. L. (1996). Enhancing communication: Toward optimal language learning for limited English proficient students. *Language, Speech, and Hearing Services in School, 27,* 347–352.

Damico, J. S., & Damico, S. K. (1993). Language and social skills from a diversity perspective: Considerations for the speech-language pathologist. *Language, Speech, and Hearing Services in Schools, 24,* 236–243.

Drew, C. J., and Hardman, M. L. (2004). *Mental Retardation: A Life Cycle Approach* (8th ed.). Upper Saddle River, NJ: Merrill/Pearson Education.

Dykens, E., Ort, S., Cohen, I., Finucane, B., Spiridigliozzi, G., Lachiewicz, A., Reiss, A., Freund, L., Hagerman, R., & O'Conner, R. (1996). Trajectories and profiles of adaptive behavior in males with fragile X syndrome: Multicenter studies. *Journal of Autism and Developmental Disorders, 26,* 287–300.

Dykens, E. M., Hodapp, R. M., & Evans, D. W. (1994). Profiles and development of adaptive behavior in children with down syndrome. *American Journal on Mental Retardation, 98,* 580–587.

Dykes, M. K, & Erin, J. (1980). A Developmental Assessment for Students with Severe Disabilities (DASH-2). Austin, TX: PRO-ED.

Fad, K., Patton, J. R., & Polloway, E. A. (1998). *Behavioral intervention planning.* Austin, TX: PRO-ED.

Fisch, G. S., Simensen, R. J., & Schroer, R. J. (2002). Longitudinal changes in cognitive and adaptive behavior scores in children and adolescents with the fragile X mutation or autism. *Journal of Autism and Developmental Disorders, 32,* 107–114.

Harwood, N. K., Hall, L. J., & Shinkfield, A. J. (1999). Recognition of facial emotional expressions from moving and static displays by individuals with mental retardation. *American Journal on Mental Retardation, 104*(3), 270–278.

Hatton, D. D., Wheeler, A. C., Skinner, M. L., Bailey, D. B., Sullivan, K. M., Roberts, J. E., Mirrett, P., & Clark, R. D. (2003). Adaptive behavior in children with fragile X syndrome. *American Journal on Mental Retardation, 108,* 373–390.

Hosp, J. L. (2003). Referral rates for intervention or assessment: A meta-analysis of racial differences. *Journal of Special Education, 37*(2), 67–80.

Iglesias, A. (1985). Communication in the home and classroom: Match or mismatch. *Topics in Language Disorders, 5,* 29–41.

Kritikos, E. P., & Birnbaum, B. (2004). Parental perspectives of needs and services provided for families of children with mild disabilities. *Learning Disabilities: A Multidisciplinary Journal, 13*(2), 61–68.

Lambert, N. M., Nihira, K., and Leland, H. (1993). *AAMR Adaptive Behavior Scales (ABS:2): School* (2nd ed.). Austin, TX: PRO-ED.

Learning Disabilities Association (2005). Retrieved from http://www.ldanatl.org/ on February 21, 2008.

McCarney, S. B. (1995). Adaptive Behavior Evaluation Scale—Revised (ABES-R). Columbia, MO: Hawthorne Educational Services.

McConaughy, S. H. (1996). Contributions of a child interview to multimethod assessment of children with EBD and LD. *School Psychology Review, 25*(1), 24–40.

McConnell, M. E., Hilvitz, P. B., & Cox, C. J. (1998). Functional assessment: A systematic process for assessment and intervention in general and special education classrooms. *Intervention in School and Clinic, 34,* 10–20.

Mechling, L. C. (2004). Effects of multimedia, computer-based instruction on grocery shopping fluency. *Journal of Special Education Technology, 19*(1), 23–34.

Mervis, C. B., Klein-Tasman, B. P., & Mastin, M. E. (2001). Adaptive behavior of 4- through 8-year-old children with Williams syndrome. *American Journal on Mental Retardation 106*(1), 82–93.

O'Reilly, C., Northcraft, G. B., & Sabers, D. (1989). The confirmation bias in special eligibility decisions. *School Psychology Review, 18,* 126–135.

Pierangelo, R., & Giuliani, G. A. (2006) *Assessment in special education: A practical approach.* Boston, MA: Allyn & Bacon.

Sattler, J.M. (2002). *Assessment of children: Behavioral and clinical applications* (4th ed.). San Diego, CA: Jerome M. Sattler.

Shapiro, J., Monzo, L. D., Rueda, R., Gomez, J. A., & Blesher, J. (2004). Alienated advocacy: Perspectives of Latina mothers of young adults with developmental disabilities on service systems. *Mental Retardation, 42*(1), 37–54.

Simpson, R. (1998). Behavior modification for children and adolescents with exceptionalities. *Intervention in School and Clinic, 33,* 219–226.

Sparrow, S. S., Cicchetti, D. V., & Balla, D. A. (2005). *Vineland Adaptive Behavior Scales* (VABS). Circle Pines, MN: American Guidance Service.

Stein, M. A., Szumowski, E., & Blondis, T. (1995). Adaptive skills dysfunction in ADD and ADHD children. *Journal of Child Psychology and Psychiatry and Allied Disciplines, 36,* 663–670.

Stinnett, T. (1997). Review of the AAMR Adaptive Behavior Scale—School (2nd. ed.). *Journal of Pscychoeducational Assessment, 15,* 361–372.

Stinnett, T., Fuqua, D., & Coombs, W. (1999). Construct validity of the AAMR Adaptive Behavior Scales—School Editiion: 2. *School Psychology Review, 28,* 31–43.

Stone, W. L., Ousley, O. Y., Hepburn, S. L., Hogan, K. L., & Brown, C. S. (1999). Patterns of adaptive behavior in very young children with autism. *American Journal on Mental Retardation, 104,* 187–199.

Tasse, M. J., & LeCavalier, L. (2000). Comparing parent and teacher ratings of social competence and problem behaviors. *American Journal on Mental Retardation, 105*(4), 252–259.

Taylor, R. K. (2006). *Assessment of exceptional students: Educational and psychological procedures* (7th ed). Boston, MA: Allyn & Bacon.

Twyman, T., & Tindal, G. (2006). Using a computer-adapted, conceptually based history text to increase comprehension and problem-solving skills of students with disabilities. *Journal of Special Education Technology, 21*(2), 5–16.

Vaughn, S. & Hogan, A. (1990). Social competence and learning disabilities: A prospective study. In H. L. Swanson & B. K. Keough (Eds.), *Learning disabilities: Theoretical and research issues* (pp. 175–191). Hillsdale, NJ: Erlbaum.

Voelker, S., Shore, D., Hakim-Larson, J., & Bruner, D. (1997). Discrepancies in parent and teacher ratings of adaptive behavior of children with multiple disabilities. *Mental Retardation, 35*(1), 10–17.

Walden, T. A. (1997). Differences in social signals produced by children with developmental delays of differing etiologies. *American Journal on Mental Retardation, 102*(3), 292–305.

Westby, C. (1997). There's more to passing than knowing the answers. *Language, Speech, and Hearing Services in Schools, 28,* 274–287.

Zinn, J., Elias, M., Greenberg, M., & Weisberg, R. (2000). Promoting social and emotional competence in children. In K. M. Minke & G. C. Bear (Eds.), *Preventing school problems—promoting school success* (pp. 71–99). Bethesda, MD: National Association of School Psychologists.

Achievement tests: Assessment of past learning of content areas

Screening tests: Tests administered to determine whether students should be recommended for further testing

Group tests: Tests administered in groups, usually by paper and pencil

Individual tests: Tests administered to one person, usually by paper and pencil

Diagnostic tests: Individual, standardized, norm-referenced tests used to evaluate a student

Aptitude tests: Assessment of the ability to change behavior when presented with certain situations

Case Study: Assessing Nathaniel

Nathaniel is one of your ninth-grade students whose performance indicates evidence of a learning disability. Nathaniel also receives speech and language services three times a week for 20-minute sessions. Nathaniel transferred from a middle school in your district. Other students in class consider Nathaniel to be amusing because he entertains them by acting silly.

Nathaniel has a couple of good friends. During informal conversation, he often answers questions inappropriately. Nathaniel changes topics often and stumbles on his pronunciation of multisyllabic words (i.e., *refrigerator*, *meaningful*). In addition, he does not seem to follow conversations. Nathaniel sometimes mispronounces words. Nathaniel speaks to peers and teachers in the same manner. Goals and activities of the speech-language pathologist involve work in semantics, pragmatics, and phonology.

Nathaniel reads and writes several levels below grade level. He attempts to avoid completing tasks during the school day and rarely turns in homework. You collaborate with his general education teachers and provide in-class support for Nathaniel. You also collaborate with his speech-language pathologist. Your primary focus is on his reading and writing skills. You are to collect informal assessment information to satisfy his individualized education program (IEP) requirements. You have attempted to collaborate with his parents, but they have many work and family demands and are often unavailable to meet on a school day.

The assessment battery includes formal and informal measures in the areas of intelligence, adaptive skills, achievement, and speech and language assessment. When looking at Nathaniel's scores, you see that his intelligence and adaptive skills are in the low average category. You see achievement skills 1½ standard deviations below the mean, and speech and language skills 2 standard deviations below the mean. Achievement skills show strengths in performance-based measures and needs in verbal measures. Math subtest scores are significantly higher than verbal subtest scores.

Nathaniel often tells you that he wants to drop out of school. He notes that he has a lot better things to do than show up in class each day. Nathaniel also states that he does not understand how this information has anything to do with him or how it could help him in the future.

How do you respond to Nathaniel?

What do you tell his parents?

What do you tell his other teachers?

How do you infuse this information into informal assessment?

How do you infuse this information into instruction?

By the end of this chapter, you should be able to discuss answers regarding the questions posed in the chapter-opening case study involving Nathaniel. You should be able to discuss the meaning of achievement and group and individual achievement tests. You should also be able to identify the most prevalent and sound achievement instruments for multiple content-area and single content-area tests. You should be able to identify the main areas measured by tests and to interpret test results. You should be able to identify issues related to validity in testing achievement in individuals who are culturally and/or linguistically diverse. You should be able to discuss how test results are connected to planning and how planning is connected to instruction.

This chapter addresses CEC Standards 3 (individual learning differences) and 8 (assessment). These standards correspond to Interstate New Teacher Assessment and Support Consortium (INTASC) standards covering learner diversity (3) and assessment (8) (www.cec.sped). Information regarding definition, identification, assessment instruments, formal and informal assessments, the influence of diversity, and assessment decision information will facilitate learning related to these standards.

DEFINING ACHIEVEMENT

Achievement tests are intended to quantify how much a student has learned. Some tests may measure many areas of school performance without depth (screening instruments). Other tests may measure one or more areas of the curriculum (i.e., math, reading, science) in depth (diagnostic tests). See Figure 8.1. Screening tests are often given in a group format and are administered to determine areas that need additional investigation or diagnostic testing. Diagnostic tests are intended to reveal information regarding specific skills and needs and are usually administered individually.

When students have difficulty with performance in school, they are often referred for an evaluation. During those evaluations, diagnostic tests of achievement are one type of assessment utilized in the assessment battery. Many of the tests used in an assessment battery are developed to evaluate if students have needs in certain domains on the basis of how they compare to other students of the same age or grade level. Thus, these tests are norm-referenced tests and are given in a standardized format.

Informal assessment (including curriculum-based assessment) information is also necessary to give a fair, complete, and robust description of how the student is performing in the area of achievement. Informal assessment tools are important components of an assessment battery. Standards-based assessment necessitates an extensive array of assessment techniques (Kluth & Straut, 2001), including observations, interviews, portfolios, projects, etc. (See Chapter 4 for further discussion.)

LEGAL IMPLICATIONS

In connecting achievement measures and legal issues, the Individuals with Disabilities Education Act (IDEA) calls for all students to be involved in state- and districtwide assessment. Accommodations should be used where appropriate. Involvement of

Figure 8.1 Broad and narrow abilities measured by the WJ III COG and WJ III ACH

Broad CHC Factor	WJ III TESTS OF ACHIEVEMENT	
	Standard Battery Test *Primary Narrow Abilities Measured*	**Extended Battery Test** *Primary Narrow Abilities Measured*
Reading-Writing (*Grw*)	Test 1: Letter-Word Identification *Reading decoding* Test 2: Reading Fluency *Reading speed* Test 9: Passage Comprehension *Reading comprehension* *Verbal (printed) language comprehension* Test 7: Spelling *Spelling ability* Test 8: Writing Fluency *Writing speed* Test 11: Writing Samples *Writing ability*	Test 13: Word Attack *Reading decoding* *Phonetic coding: Analysis and synthesis* Test 17: Reading Vocabulary *Verbal (printed) language comprehension* *Lexical knowledge* Test 16: Editing *Language development* *English usage* Test 22: Punctuation and Capitalization *English Usage*
Mathematics (Gq)	Test 5: Calculation *Math achievement* Test 6: Math Fluency *Math achievement* *Numerical facility* Test 10: Applied Problems *Quantitative reasoning* *Math achievement* *Math knowledge*	Test 18: Quantitative Concepts *Math knowledge* *Quantitative reasoning*
Comprehension-Knowledge (Gc)	Test 3: Story Recall *Language development* *Listening ability* Test 4: Understanding Directions *Listening ability* *Language development*	Test 14: Picture Vocabulary *Language development* *Lexical knowledge* Test 15: Oral Comprehension *Listening ability* Test 19: Academic knowledge *General information* *Science information* *Cultural information* *Geography achievement*
Auditory Processing (Ga)		Test 13: Word Attack *Reading decoding* *Phonetic coding: Analysis* *Phonetic coding: Synthesis* Test 20: Spelling of Sounds *Spelling ability* *Phonetic coding: Analysis* Test 21: Sound Awareness *Phonetic coding: Analysis* *Phonetic coding: Synthesis*
Long-Term Retrieval (Glr)	Test 12: Story Recall—Delayed *Meaningful memory*	

students with severe disabilities in large-scale alternate assessment is also important in meeting new requirements. Ford, Davern, and Schnorr (2001) identified five principles to contemplate pertaining to standards and alternate assessment: (1) Each student should focus on the development of foundational skills; (2) individualization is critical to high-quality education; (3) students' membership in the learning community should be respected and reflected within schedules and locations; (4) students should have a chance at sensing mastery over tasks; and (5) the immediate value of student experiences should be given special attention.

No Child Left Behind (NCLB) (2001) stipulates that states: (1) ascertain academic standards, (2) ensure that all students be instructed and assessed on skills linked with those standards, and (3) hold educators and educational institutions accountable for all students. Assessment issues discussed in the literature have included the proper alignment of assessment programs with the standards (Hargrove, Walker, Huber, Corrigan, & Moore, 2004).

NCLB requires that all children in grades 3–8 are tested in math and reading. By 2007, all children in grades 3–8 were tested in science. The results of these tests give states data that identify poorly achieving schools. This information could aid in improving poor achievement (Fremer & Wall, 2004). The legal accountability provisions have inspired much discussion regarding standards-based assessment and the value of high-stakes group testing (Stodden, Galloway, & Stodden, 2003). For example, Hoover and Patton (2004) discuss comparing students' test results to standards instead of other students.

Cohen and Spenciner (2003) report the advantages and disadvantages of group tests involving achievement. They note that consistency of administration, scoring, and interpretation is an advantage for group tests. On the other hand, especially for students with disabilities, requirements about writing and reading and the complexity of transferring answers to answer sheets are disadvantages (Cohen & Spenciner, 2003). In addition, these tests are timed. McLoughlin and Lewis (2005) report that individual achievement tests are more ideal than group tests for students with disabilities. For example, the examiner could provide additional direction for test tasks. Therefore, the tester could supply motivation and clarification to the student and make the test results more valid.

Notwithstanding this discussion among researchers about group tests of academic achievement, group tests are required and used. Educational change has been coupled with policy change, including standards-based reform (Lawrenz, Huffman, & Lavoie, 2005). Reform changes educational practices related to student achievement outcomes and well-structured expectations (Cawthon, 2004).

Breakpoint Practice

1. What are the major implications of NCLB when it comes to achievement?
2. How will NCLB affect you as a classroom teacher?
3. How are high-stakes testing and NCLB connected?

MEASURES OF ACHIEVEMENT

The following sections include widely used formal group achievement measures, diagnostic tests investigating multiple areas of the curriculum, and single curricular area tests (reading, writing, and math).

Table 8.1 Examples of Group Achievement Tests

Name	Company	Content	Grade Level	Time to Administer
California Achievement Tests (CAT/5)	CTB McGraw-Hill	Reading, language, spelling, mathematics, study skills, science, and social studies	Grades K–12	Varies by grade level: K = 1 hour, 28 minutes; 5-12 = 5 hours, 16 minutes
Iowa Tests of Basic Skills	Riverside	Vocabulary, word analysis, listening, reading comprehension, language, math, social studies, science, and sources of information	Grades K–8	30 minutes per subtest
Iowa Tests of Educational Development	Riverside	Vocabulary, reading comprehension, language, spelling, mathematics, computation, social studies, science, sources of information	Grades 9–12	40 minutes per subtest
Stanford Achievement Test Series—Tenth Edition	Harcourt	Sounds and letters, word study skills, word reading, sentence reading, vocabulary, reading comprehension, mathematics, mathematics problem solving, mathematics procedures, spelling, language, science, environment, social science, listening	Grades K–12	Untimed
TerraNova, the Second Edition (CAT/6)	CTB McGraw-Hill	Reading/language arts, mathematics, science, and social studies	Grades K–12	4 to 5½ hours

GROUP ACHIEVEMENT TESTS

Some frequently researched and utilized group achievement tests include the California Achievement Tests (CAT/5) (CTB, Macmillan, McGraw-Hill, 1993); Iowa Tests of Basic Skills (Hoover, Dunbar, & Frisbie, 2001); Iowa Tests of Educational Development (Forsyth, Ansley, Feldt, & Alnot, 2003); Stanford Achievement Tests—Tenth Edition (Harcourt Brace Educational Measurement, 2002); and TerraNova, the Second Edition Assessment Series (CTB, McGraw-Hill, 2000). Table 8.1 provides an overview of these group achievement tests.

The California Achievement Tests (K–12) consist of two forms (A and B). Subtests include areas of reading (prereading, word analysis, vocabulary, and comprehension), spelling (vowel sounds, consonant sounds, and structural elements), language (language mechanics and language expression), and mathematics (mathematics computation and mathematics concepts and applications). Supplementary content areas are study skills, science, and social studies. See Figure 8.2.

Concerns regarding missing norming data exist. Internal consistency information is included. Missing data are reflected in test-retest reliability and alternate-forms reliability. Therefore, reliability should be approached with caution. Scores include percentile ranks, normal curve equivalents, stanines, performance index, and standard error of measurement.

The Iowa Tests of Basic Skills (K–8) consists of forms A and B. Subtests include vocabulary (listening and reading), word analysis, reading comprehension, language skills (including spelling), mathematics skills (including quantitative reasoning), science,

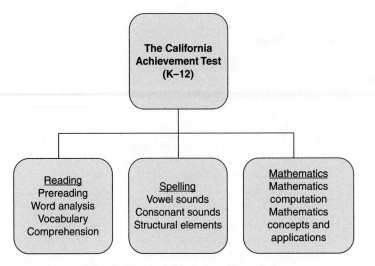

Figure 8.2 The California Achievement Tests: Subtests

social studies, maps and diagrams, and references. The Iowa Tests of Educational Development (grades 9–12) are available in a complete battery and survey battery of form M. Subtests for the complete battery include vocabulary (reading, writing, and listening), language, revising written materials, spelling, mathematics: concepts and problem solving, computation, analysis of social studies materials, analysis of science materials, and sources of information. Norming appears adequate. Limited validity measures include content validity. Some internal-consistency coefficients are low. Reliability should be approached with caution. Scores available include grade equivalents, normal curve equivalents, percentile ranks, stanines, and standard scores.

The Stanford Achievement Test (grades 1–9) includes subtests in reading (sounds and letters and reading comprehension), mathematics (mathematics problem solving and mathematics procedures), language (traditional language—form A, comprehensive language—form D), spelling, listening (vocabulary and comprehension), science (life, earth, and physical science, and the nature of science), and social science (geography, political science, and economics). Two special editions exist for individuals who are visually impaired and deaf students. This is important to remember, as there are very few tools for these two low-incidence populations. Norming appears adequate. Content validity is included and appears adequate. Reliability includes internal consistency and alternate forms. Reliability appears adequate. Scores include grade equivalents, standard scores, stanines, and national and local percentiles.

TerraNova, Second Edition (CAT/6), includes subtests in reading/language arts, mathematics, science, and social studies. Supplemental subtests in word analysis, vocabulary, language mechanics, spelling, and mathematics computation are available. Norming appears appropriate. However, all the students in the norm group were not given all subtests. Norm-referenced scores include grade equivalents, normal curve equivalents, stanines, and national percentiles.

Breakpoint Practice

1. Name five areas tested by group tests.

2. As a teacher, how will group tests affect you?

3. What are the weaknesses of group testing?

MULTIPLE-AREA DIAGNOSTIC ACHIEVEMENT TESTS

Some frequently researched and utilized individual formal tools include the Kaufman Test of Educational Achievement—II (K-TEA-II) (Kaufman & Kaufman, 2004); Peabody Individual Achievement Test—Revised/Normative Update (PIAT-R/NU) (Markwardt, 1998); Wechsler Individual Achievement Test, Second Edition (WIAT-II) (Harcourt Brace Educational Measurement, 2001); the Wide Range Achievement Test—4 (WRAT4)(Wilkinson & Robertson, 2006); the Woodcock-Johnson III NU Tests of Achievement (WJ-NU III) (Woodcock, McGrew, & Mather, 2006); and the Bateria III Woodcock-Munoz, designed for use with Spanish-speaking children and based on the WJ III (Woodcock, Munoz-Sandoval, McGrew, & Mather, 2006). See Table 8.2.

The Kaufman Test of Educational Achievement—II (KTEA-II) includes subtests in a reading standard battery (letter and word recognition, nonsense word decoding, and reading comprehension), math standard battery (math concepts and applications and math computation), written language standard battery (written expression and spelling), oral language supplemental subtests (listening comprehension and oral expression), and reading supplemental subtests (phonological awareness, rapid automatized naming, fluency—semantic and phonological, timed word recognition, and timed nonsense word decoding). See Figure 8.3.

There are two parallel forms for the comprehensive form. A brief form is also available. This test was co-normed with the Kaufman Assessment Battery for Children—II (K-ABC-II) and Kaufman Brief Intelligence Test (K-BIT). Construct and concurrent validity information is available. Validity is sufficient. Alternate-forms, interrater reliability, and internal consistency information are available. Reliability is appropriate.

Table 8.2 Examples of Individual Achievement Tests

Name	Company	Content	Age	Time to Administer
Kaufman Test of Educational Achievement, Second Edition	American Guidance Service	Reading, math, written language, and oral language	4-6 to 25 years (4-6 through 90+ for brief form)	30–80 minutes (15–45 minutes for the brief form)
Peabody Individual Achievement Test—Revised/Normative Update	American Guidance Service	Reading, mathematics, and spelling	5-0 through 22-11	60 minutes
Wechsler Individual Achievement Test, Second Edition	Psycho-logical Corp.	Reading, mathematics, written language, oral language, and academic knowledge	4-0 to 85-11	45 minutes to 2 hours
Wide Range Achievement Test, Third Edition	Psychological Assessment Resources	Reading, sentence comprehension, spelling, and arithmetic	5-0 through 75	30–45 minutes
Woodcock-Johnson III NU, Tests of Achievement	Riverside	Oral expression, listening comprehension, written expression, basic reading skills, reading comprehension, math calculation skills, and math reasoning	2-0 through 90+	About 5 minutes per test, about 1 hour total

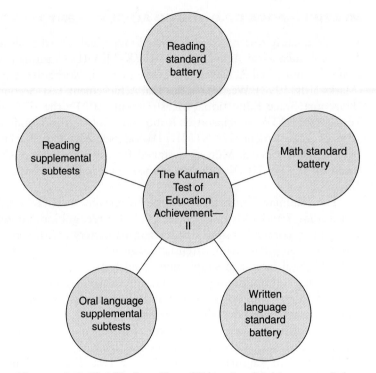

Figure 8.3 The Kaufman Test of Educational Achievement: Subtests

Results can be reported in age equivalent, grade equivalent, standard score, stanines, and percentile rank. Normal curve equivalents and confidence intervals are supplied with this test. Computer scoring with error analysis is also available with this test.

The Peabody Individual Achievement Test—Revised/Normative Update (PIAT-R/NU) includes subtests in general information (general encyclopedic knowledge), reading recognition (recognition of printed letters and oral reading of words), reading comprehension (student points to a picture connected with a sentence), written expression (prewriting and writing a story associated with a picture), mathematics (math concepts and fact knowledge and application), and spelling (recognition of word spelling). See Figure 8.4.

Response formats include multiple choice, copying, dictation, writing, oral, and free response. Norms appear appropriate. Content, construct, and concurrent validity information is noted. A more varied and recent set of assessment tools utilized in the concurrent validity information would be useful. Internal consistency, test-retest, and interrater reliability information is available. Lower coefficients are present with interrater and Kuder-Richardson reliability coefficients. Some test-retest reliability coefficients are in the high .80s. Age equivalent, grade equivalent, standard scores, normal curve equivalents, and percentile rank scores for subtests, and total reading and total test score formats, are available with this test.

The Wechsler Individual Achievement Test, Second Edition (WIAT-II), includes standard subtests in word reading, numerical operations, reading comprehension, spelling, pseudoword decoding, mathematics reasoning, written expression, listening comprehension, and oral language. Each of the subtests must be given in the order presented. Some subtests are timed. Norming appears appropriate. Validity exists with construct, content, and concurrent measures. Questions regarding validity exist due to some lowered coefficients (http://www.cps.nova.edu). Test-retest, interrater, and internal

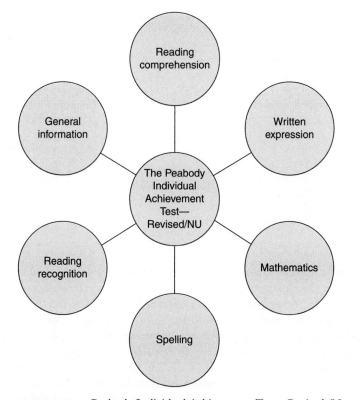

Figure 8.4 Peabody Individual Achievement Test—Revised/Normative Update: Subtests

consistency (split-half) measures are available with this test. Some scores for each of the reliability coefficients fall below a cutoff of .8. Therefore, results should be approached with caution. Age equivalents, grade equivalents, stanines, percentile ranks, and normal curve equivalents are available for this test. Computer scoring is available. An abbreviated form, which can be administered in 10 to 20 minutes, is also available. Results of this test can be compared to the age-appropriate Wechsler Tests of intelligence.

The Wide Range Achievement Test—4 (WRAT4) includes subtests in word reading (recognizing and naming letters, and pronouncing printed words), sentence comprehension (cloze techniques), spelling (writing names, writing letters and words from dictation), and math computation (counting, reading number symbols, and oral and written problem computations). One or more of these subtests could be given in any order to an individual or a group. Two alternative forms exist (green and blue). Prespelling, prearithmetic, and prereading sections are available for students age 5 years to 7 years, 11 months who are not successful in meeting the conditions required of these sections. Norming appears appropriate. Content and criterion-related validity information is available. Construct validity information and some concurrent validity information exists. Validity has increased with the current edition of the test. Test-retest, alternate-forms, and internal consistency information is available and appears adequate. Grade scores, age scores, standard scores, percentiles, normal curve equivalents, and absolute scores are available with this test.

The Woodcock-Johnson III NU Tests of Achievement (WJ-NU III) include standard subtests (forms A and B) on letter-word identification, reading fluency, story recall, understanding directions, calculation, math fluency, spelling, writing fluency, passage comprehension, applied problems, writing samples, and story recall—delayed. Extended

Table 8.3   Woodcock-Johnson III: Subtests

Standard Batteries	Extended Battery Subtests
• Letter-word identification • Reading fluency • Story recall • Understanding directions • Calculation • Math fluency • Spelling • Writing fluency • Passage comprehension • Applied problems • Writing samples • Story recall—delayed	• Word attack • Picture vocabulary • Oral comprehension • Editing • Reading vocabulary • Quantitative concepts • Academic knowledge • Spelling of sounds • Sound awareness • Punctuation and capitalization

battery subtests include word attack, picture vocabulary, oral comprehension, editing, reading vocabulary, quantitative concepts, academic knowledge, spelling of sounds, sound awareness, and punctuation and capitalization. See Table 8.3. Five clusters include reading, oral language, mathematics, written language, and academic knowledge. A supplemental curricular area exists (i.e., story recall, spelling of sounds, sound awareness, and punctuation and capitalization). Some portions of this test are timed, in the subject response booklet, and audio-recorded. Alternate forms of this test are available. Results can be compared to the WJ III Tests of Cognitive Abilities because they were co-normed.

The norming sample appears adequate. Concurrent validity exists with adequate results. Content and construct validity discussion is included. Validity appears to be adequate. Test-retest, interrater, and alternate-forms reliability (for part of the test) and internal consistency (split-half) exist. Some questions exist regarding the handwriting subtest in the areas of test-retest and interrater reliability. It is important to note, however, that this is one of the few tools that assesses handwriting. Standard error of measurement is also included. Reliability measures appear adequate. Age equivalent, grade equivalent, standard scores, percentile rank, proficiency (basic interpersonal communication skill and cognitive-academic language) scores are available with this test. Scoring software is also available.

Breakpoint Practice

1. Name three areas that an individual test may address.
2. Name one test that you would use to test Nathaniel and explain why.
3. Name one test that you would not use with Nathaniel and explain why.

READING

Widely used tests of reading include the Gray Oral Reading Tests—4 (GORT-4) (Wiederholt & Bryant, 2001), Test of Reading Comprehension—3 (TORC-3) (Brown, Hammill, & Wiederholt, 1995), and Woodcock Reading Mastery Test—Revised/Normative Update (WRMT-R/NU) (Woodcock, 1998). See Table 8.4.

The Gray Oral Reading Tests—4 (GORT-4) measures development in oral reading and identifies oral reading difficulties. Two parallel forms are available with this test. The forms contain 14 reading passages (that are read aloud), including five orally

Table 8.4 Examples of Reading Tests

Name	Company	Content	Age	Time to Administer
Gray Oral Reading Tests—4	PRO-ED	Oral reading	6-0 through 18-11	15–45 minutes
Test of Reading Comprehension—3	PRO-ED	Silent reading comprehension	7-0 through 17-11	30 minutes per subtest
Woodcock Reading Mastery Test—Revised/ Normative Update	American Guidance Service	Reading achievement	5-0 through 75+	30 minutes

presented comprehension questions for each passage. Norming appears adequate. Concurrent validity is provided mostly using the previous version of this test. Questions regarding content validity exist. Alternate forms, interrater, and test-retest validity information is noted and appears to be adequate. Age equivalents, grade equivalents, percentiles, standard scores, fluency scores, oral reading comprehension scores, and oral reading quotients are available.

The Test of Reading Comprehension—3 (TORC-3) includes eight subtests of silent reading. These subtests can also be administered to small groups of students. Four general reading comprehension subtests include general vocabulary, syntactic similarities, paragraph reading, and sentence sequencing. Four supplementary subtests include mathematics vocabulary, social studies vocabulary, science vocabulary, and reading the directions of schoolwork. See Table 8.5. Norming appears adequate. Content, construct, and criterion-related validity are included. Test-retest, internal consistency, and interrater reliability information is included and appears adequate. Age equivalents, grade equivalents, percentiles, and standard scores are available with this test.

The Woodcock Reading Mastery Test—Revised/Normative Update (WRMT-R/NU) includes two forms: forms G and HM. These forms include parallel tests of readiness (visual-auditory learning, letter identification) and tests of reading achievement (word identification, word attack, word comprehension, and passage comprehension). Form H includes the four parallel tests of reading achievement. Norming

Anthony Magnacca/Merrill

Table 8.5   The Test of Reading Comprehension—3: Subtests

General Reading Comprehension	Supplementary
General vocabulary	Mathematics vocabulary
Syntactic similarities	Social studies vocabulary
Paragraph reading	Science vocabulary
Sentence sequencing	Reading the directions of schoolwork

data appears outdated. Validity appears adequate, but content should be evaluated. Incomplete test-retest reliability is offered. Reliability information regarding internal consistency is provided. Some coefficients appear low. Scores available include age equivalents, grade equivalents, percentile ranks, standard scores, normal curve equivalents, aptitude-achievement discrepancy analysis, and confidence bands.

WRITTEN EXPRESSION

Commonly used tests of written language expression include the Test of Written Expression (TOWE) (McGhee, Bryant, Larsen, & Rivera, 1995), the Test of Written Language—3 (TOWL-3) (Hammill & Larsen, 1996), and the Test of Written Spelling—4 (TWS-4) (Larsen, Hammill, & Moats, 1999). See Table 8.6.

The Test of Written Expression is an assessment of writing achievement. It could also be administered to groups of students. Two methods of assessment are involved. The first method requires responding to 76 items linked with specific writing skills. A second method requires writing an essay after reading or hearing a story starter. Skills assessed include ideation, grammar, vocabulary, capitalization, punctuation, spelling, and general written language ability. More norming information would increase the quality of this tool. Content validity, criterion-related validity, and construct validity information is included. More information regarding validity and reliability would increase the quality of this tool. Standard scores are available with this test.

The Test of Written Language—3 (TOWL-3) measures written language skills. Two parallel forms (A and B) contain two formats, spontaneous and contrived. The test could be administered individually or in small groups. The spontaneous formats include contextual conventions (capitalization, punctuation, and spelling), contextual language (vocabulary, syntax, and grammar), and story construction (plot, character development, and general composition). Contrived formats include vocabulary (word usage), spelling (forming letters into words), style (punctuation and capitalization), logical sentences (writing conceptually sound sentences), and sentence combining (syntax). Norming appears sufficient. Concurrent validity and factor analysis data were

Table 8.6   Examples of Written Expression Tests

Name	Company	Content	Age or Grade Level	Time to Administer
Test of Written Expression	PRO-ED	Writing achievement	6-0 through 14-11	Varies
Test of Written Language—3	PRO-ED	Written language skills	7-6 through 17-11	90 minutes
Test of Written Spelling—4	PRO-ED	spelling	Grades 1 through 12	20 minutes

adequate. More information regarding content validity would be useful. Test-retest, internal consistency, and interrater reliability information appears appropriate. Some scores are in the .80s. Age equivalents, percentiles, and standard scores are available.

The Test of Written Spelling—4 (TWS-4) contains two parallel forms (A and B), which could be administered to individuals or groups of students. The assessor orally presents a word, a sentence (as the context for the word), and repeats the word. The student then writes the word target. Norming appears adequate. Content, construct, and criterion-related validity are reported in this test. Internal consistency, alternate-form, test-retest, and interrater reliability were reported and generally adequate (small samples). Age equivalents, grade equivalents, percentiles, and standard scores are available with this test.

MATH

Commonly used math tests include the Comprehensive Mathematical Abilities Test (CMAT) (Hresko, Schlieve, Herron, Swain, & Sherbenou, 2003), KeyMath—3 (Key-Math-3) (Connolly, 2007), and the Test of Mathematical Abilities—2 (TOMA-2) (Brown, Cronin, & McEntire, 1994). See Table 8.7.

The Comprehensive Mathematical Abilities Test (CMAT) contains six core subtests and six supplemental subsets. Core subtests include addition; subtraction; multiplication; division; problem solving; and charts, tables, and graphs. Supplemental subtests include algebra, geometry, rational numbers, time, money, and measurement (see Table 8.8). A minimum of 2 to 12 of these subtests can be administered to students based on need. Core composites include basic calculations, mathematical reasoning, and general mathematics. Supplemental composites include advanced calculations, practical applications, and overall mathematic abilities. Norming appears adequate. Content validity, construct validity, and criterion-prediction validity are included in this test. Internal consistency and interrater reliability information is available. Age scores, grade scores, and standard scores are available with this test, as are computer scoring and a report system.

The KeyMath—3 contains two parallel forms. The test does not necessitate reading capability, so it reduces possible confounding effects. Areas tested include basic concepts (numeration, algebra, geometry, measurement, and data analysis and probability), operations (mental computation and estimation, written computation: addition and subtraction, and written computation: multiplication and division), and applications (foundations of problem solving and applied problem solving). Norming appears

Table 8.7 Examples of Math Tests

Name	Company	Content	Age	Time to Administer
Comprehensive Mathematical Abilities Test	PRO-ED	Mathematics	7-0 to 18-11	30 minutes to 3 hours
KeyMath—3	American Guidance Service	Understanding and application of mathematics concepts and skills	4-6 to 22-11	30–90 minutes
Test of Mathematical Abilities—2	PRO-ED	Math performance for major skills and related areas	8-0 to 18-11	60–90 minutes

Table 8.8 The Comprehensive Mathematical Abilities Test: Subtests

Core Subtests	Supplemental Subtests
Addition	Algebra
Subtraction	Geometry
Multiplication	Rational numbers
Division	Time
Problem solving	Money
Charts, tables, and graphs	Measurement

appropriate. Content validity, construct validity, and concurrent validity information is included. Alternate form scores were in the .8 and .9 range. Age equivalents, grade equivalents, percentile ranks, stanines, normal curve equivalents, standard scores, and domain scores are available.

The Test of Mathematical Abilities—2 (TOMA-2) is a measure of performance (including attitude) regarding mathematics and can be administered to an individual or groups of students. Four core subtests include vocabulary, computation, general information, and story problems. Attitude toward math is a supplemental subtest. An individual's disposition can provide great insights. Norming appears adequate. Content, construct, and criterion-related validity information is provided; however, more information would be useful. Reliability information appears to be generally appropriate, with some data falling in the .80s. Age equivalents, grade equivalents, percentiles, and standard scores are available with this test.

Breakpoint Practice

1. Name three areas tested in a reading test.
2. What diagnostic information would a spelling test give the teacher?
3. How can informal assessment supplement a math test?
4. Which test do you think you would be most likely to use? Why?

Multicultural Considerations

Research data have revealed multiple factors to consider when using achievement testing for individuals who are culturally and/or linguistically diverse. Those topics include issues and strategies connected with specific tests and content areas of math, reading, socioeconomic status, related disabilities, and teachers' beliefs.

Specific Tests

Researchers have reported bias in the Scholastic Aptitude Test (SAT) (Smith & Garrison, 2005). Smith and Garrison (2005) noted that adding the factors of ethnicity, race, and gender decreases the test's power to predict future school performance.

For example, Lawlor, Richman, and Richman (1997) studied the validity of using the SAT as a predictor of college performance (grade point average and class rank at graduation) for African American and European American students. They found that, although the verbal portion of the SAT was the strongest correlate of African American and European American students, the math portion of the SAT did not predict college performance for either group. Furthermore, even though the total SAT scores for European American students was about 80 points higher than those for African American students, the grade point average and class rank at graduation for the two groups did not differ. The researchers propose that the SAT is a biased instrument. Therefore, results of this test should be regarded with caution.

Math

Tate (1997) conducted a literature review to investigate diversity issues (race/ethnicity, socioeconomic status, gender, and language proficiency) as they relate to mathematics achievement. He found that recent differences in mathematics achievement scores as related to race/ethnicity, class, gender, and language proficiency were decreasing compared to previous data. He noted the importance of focusing on standards-based reform.

Smith-Maddox (1998) investigated predictors of mathematics academic achievement for eighth-grade students who were African American, European American, and Asian American. The researcher used data from the National Education Longitudinal Survey of 1988 regarding the students' reports of experiences related to transition. Results revealed that parent's discussions with teachers, teacher-student interaction, parental expectations, parents' socioeconomic status, students' participation in extracurricular activities, positive homework habits, and students' aspirations were positively significant in students' achievement. Placement in low-ability groups, percentage of minorities in school, and cultural content had a negative effect on academic achievement. Cultural synchronization was also significant. This information indicates negative student achievement consequences for teachers' low expectations.

Lee, Silverman, and Montoya (2002) offer strategies for the understanding of mathematics for students who are culturally and or/linguistically diverse. They discuss the use of manipulative objects and diagrams, students' self-assessment, student interviews, and students' journal writing as ways to focus on areas other than extensive oral language. Similarly, Blechner, Coates, Franco, and Mayfield-Ingram (1997) focus on mathematics and offer discussion of general strategies for students. They specifically refer to female students, linguistically and/or culturally diverse students, and students who are of lower socioeconomic backgrounds. They note the following ways to increase the fairness of assessment practices: (1) making assessment goals unambiguous from the start, (2) providing appropriate materials (age and ability level), (3) methods and opportunities to learn, (4) using fair assessment tools, (5) using simple language, (6) using appropriate contexts in instruction and assessment, (7) providing teacher support, (8) providing opportunities for discussion and writing, (9) allowing students to organize materials, and (10) including student self-assessment.

Reading

Madhere (1998) used data from the National Center for Education Statistics (NCES) to investigate reading performance among cultural membership and to determine the quality of classroom pedagogy. Represented group membership

(*continued*)

breakdowns included African American, Afro-Caribbean, Afro-Latino, Continental American Whites, Anglo-Saxon Whites, and White Latinos. The quality of classroom pedagogy was based on student report regarding level and quality of instruction and teacher support. The researcher controlled for socioeconomic status, which was a significant variable. Results revealed outcomes in order of highest to lowest score means in reading achievement: White Anglo-Saxon, Afro-Caribbean, Continental American White, White Latino, African American, and Afro-Latino. Furthermore, the different groups had differences in amount of gain depending on improved instruction and/or support. For example, the Anglo-Saxon students gained much from enhanced instruction but not much from teacher support. For African American students, enhanced instruction and improved teacher support significantly improved reading performance. The Afro-Caribbean students achieved at the same level as the Anglo-Saxon group when enhanced instruction and increased teacher support were in place. This study shows the dangers of interpreting information strictly comparing White and non-White students, without investigating many more factors in the discussion.

Haager and Windmueller (2001) offered continuing additional reading instruction as a strategy to enhance literacy outcomes in urban schools for students who are linguistically and/or culturally diverse. Furthermore, they suggested teacher training grounded in authentic classroom context as a legitimate way to provide effective instruction.

Socioeconomic Status

Socioeconomic status is also a factor when interpreting test scores. According to Betts, Reuben, and Danenberg (2000), low socioeconomic status could be a factor in lower test performance. They also found an association between school resources and student achievement.

Caldwell and Ginther (1996) investigated learning styles of low and high achievers who were of low socioeconomic status. Third- and fourth-grade students were tested using the Learning Styles Inventory (Dunn, Dunn, & Price, 1989). The students' math and reading achievement was predicted with significance. Results indicate that motivation factors predicted achievement in this group. Findings indicate significant implications concerning success with regard to achievement results. This is also a key in paying attention to the importance of student input in the assessment process.

Gustafson (2002) suggests the following strategies for building knowledge in students with low socioeconomic status: reading experiences, performance-based activities, encouragement, field experiences, and integrated curricula. He stressed enrichment activities in school and in the community as a way to encourage students and provide them with a knowledge base that will help them succeed.

Related Disabilities

Studies have shown that related disorders can have negative effects on academic achievement. Williams et al. (1996) investigated the relationship between academic achievement and students with epilepsy (controlled and uncontrolled) who had not been diagnosed with a learning disability. Results revealed that students without control or with poor control over seizures had significantly lower reading scores than students with controlled seizures. Researchers suggested a closer supervision of school progress in these students.

Investigators have also examined interventions for students with emotional behavioral disorders (EBD) to increase academic achievement because this group shows an increase of academic deficits (McEnvoy & Welker, 2000; Sabornie, Culuinan, Osborne, & Brock, 2005). Pierce, Reed, and Epstein (2004) reviewed teacher-mediated interventions related to academic performance in students with EBD. Researchers found that teacher-mediated interventions showed success across subject matter content areas (reading, math, writing, oral expression, science, and listening). Interventions included token reinforcement (low to moderate improvements), student choice intervention (positive improvements), antecedent interventions (high improvements), and consequence-focused interventions (moderate to high improvements). Ryan, Reid, and Epstein (2004) reviewed peer-mediated interventions as they related to academic achievement in students with EBD. The peer-mediated interventions included peer tutoring or cooperative learning across academic subject matter (reading, math, language arts, spelling, history, and science). Results revealed successful results in academic achievement related to peer-mediated interventions.

Researchers have also proposed self-monitoring of academics and behavior as strategies for increasing academic performance (Shimabukuro, Prater, Jenkins, & Edelen-Smith, 1999). Shimabukuro et al. investigated the effects of self-monitoring (reading, mathematics, and writing) of students with learning disabilities, attention deficit disorder and attention deficit hyperactivity disorder (ADD/ADHD) and academic performance. They found that self-monitoring strategies increased academic efficiency and precision. This information highlights the importance of the student as a partner in the assessment process.

Garcia (1997) discussed strategies for decreasing the negative effects of curricular tracking in students who have not performed well. He shared techniques for students who are culturally and/or linguistically diverse. An orientation to the high school curriculum, core preparation courses in languages other than English, positive alternative lifestyle programs, and increasing academic expectations were strategies used successfully by this administrator with high school students.

Technology Strategies

Researchers have proposed utilizing technology as an approach to enhancing academic performance. Brown and Capp (2003) suggested that we embrace technology tools to facilitate a systematic approach to managing formative and summative assessment practices.

Researchers report that increasing the amount of active responding to computer-based activities increases achievement levels (Shin, Deno, Robinson, & Marston, 2000). Shin et al. (2000) used a computer-based groupware system with second-grade students to investigate active responding during the school year and performance at the beginning of the school year. They found that active responding was significantly correlated with initial and final measures (performance). Implications for improving performance in achievement are provided by these researchers. The study showed that computer-based software could predict

(continued)

achievement and help students who have a reduced time of classroom engagement.

Martindale, Pearson, Curda, and Pilcher (2005) investigated the influence of online instruction on standardized test scores in reading and mathematics. They examined the impact of technology on elementary and high school students. The researchers found that technology was connected to an increase in scores of elementary school students, but scores were not significantly different at the high school level.

Hill (2003) offers strategies for students who are culturally diverse using authentic and technological avenues for language arts learning. This researcher suggests digital tools (for example, a graphic organizer) to plan tasks focused on facts, interpret factual content, and apply that content to a more expansive situation.

Teachers' Beliefs

In their study involving culturally responsive teaching, Daunic, Correa, and Reyes-Blanes (2004) found that general and special educators differed in their awareness of students' backgrounds, fairness, and encouraging creative and/or critical thinking. These findings pinpoint areas that can be incorporated into collaboration discussion between general and special educators to better serve their students.

It is clear that diversity issues, such as ethnicity, race, gender, and socioeconomic status can be affected by the validity of the assessment process. Practitioners should be cautious in how they interpret the findings of these assessments.

REVISITING NATHANIEL

Nathaniel needed to understand how services can help him. You also needed to understand which activities and goals would motivate Nathaniel. More involvement from Nathaniel in the planning and self-monitoring process would benefit him. Discussion with parents to increase awareness and improve authentically meaningful instruction and assessment can be a positive motivator for all involved. Working around the parents' schedule to increase participation would be beneficial. Discussion with the team of professionals about infusing strategies would also be helpful. Increasing self-assessment of Nathaniel would also improve his involvement in the process. You could formulate a rubric collaboratively, and both you and Nathaniel could score the rubrics. Meaningful discussion could arise from comparing these results. Working in the area of need as a basis for the development of rubrics could serve as stimulating activities. Nathaniel could choose one of three activities to increase self-determination, motivation, and self-esteem.

ACTIVITIES

1. What is the difference between a screening test and a diagnostic test?
2. Why is it important to include formal and informal achievement measures during an evaluation?

3. What would low achievement scores indicate?

4. How is No Child Left Behind related to group achievement testing?

5. What are the positive and negative aspects of group tests?

6. Which group test do you find the strongest? Why?

7. Which diagnostic test do you find the strongest? Why?

8. Which diversity factor do you find is the most strongly connected to achievement assessment? Why?

WEB RESOURCES

http://www.studentprogress.org/default.asp

http://wrightslaw.com/advoc/articles/tests_measurements.html

http://www.ncld.org/index.php?option=content&task=view&id=314

http://www.nasponline.org/resources/principals/nassp_probsolve.aspx

http://www.ldaamerica.us/aboutld/parents/assessment/evaluation.asp

http://www.nimh.nih.gov/publicat/NIMHadhdpub.pdf

REFERENCES

Belcher, T., Coates, G. D., Franco, J., & Mayfield-Ingram, K. (1997). Assessment and equity. In J. Trentacosta & M. Kennly (Eds.) 1997. *Yearbook*, 195–200. Reston, VA: National Council of Teachers of Mathematics.

Betts, J. R., Reuben, K. S., & Danenberg, A. (2000). Equal resources, equal outcomes? *The distribution of school resources and student achievement in California.* San Francisco, CA: Public Policy Institute of California. (ERIC Document Reproduction Service No. ED 451291).

Brown, K., & Capp, R. (2003). Better data for better learning. *Leadership, 33*(2), 18–19.

Brown, V. L., Cronin, M. E., & McEntire, E. (1994). *Test of mathematical abilities* (2nd ed.). Austin, TX: PRO-ED.

Brown, V. L., Hammill, D. D., & Wiederholt, J. L. (1995). *Test of Reading Comprehension* (3rd ed.). *(TORC-3)*. Austin, TX: PRO-ED.

Caldwell, G., & Ginther, D. W. (1996). Differences in learning styles of low socioeconomic status for low and high achievers. *Education, 117*, 141–147.

Cawthon, S. W. (2004). Early elementary curricular alignment and teacher perspectives on standards-based reform. *American Annals of the Deaf, 149*(5), 428–435.

Cohen, L., & Spenciner, L. (2007). *Assessment of children and youth* (3rd ed.). New York: Longman.

Connolly, A. J. (2007). *KeyMath-III.* Circle Pines, MN: American Guidance Service.

CTB/McGraw-Hill (1993). California Achievement Tests. Monterey, CA: Author.

CTB/McGraw-Hill (2000). TerraNova, the Second Edition Assessment Series. Monterey, CA: Author.

Daunic, A. P., Correa, V. I., & Reyes-Blanes, M. E. (2004). Teacher preparation for diverse classrooms: Performance-based assessments of beginning teachers. *Teacher Education and Special Education, 27*(2), 105–118.

Dunn, R., Dunn, K., & Price, G. E. (1989). *Learning style inventory.* Lawrence, KS: Price Systems.

Ford, A., Davern, L., & Schnorr, R. (2001). Learners with significant disabilities: Curricular relevance in an era of standards-based reform. *Remedial and Special Education, 22*(4), 214–222.

Forsyth, R. A., Ansley, T. N., Feldt, L. S., & Alnot, S. D. (2003). *Guide to Research and Development: Iowa Tests of Educational Development.* Itasca, IL: Riverside.

Fremer, J., & Wall, J. (2004). "Why use tests and assessments?" In J. E. Wall & G. R. Walz (Eds.), *Measuring up: Assessment issues for teachers, counselors, and administrators* (pp. 3–19). Austin, TX: PRO-ED.

Garcia, P. A. (1997). Academic achievement through critical inquiry. *Thrust for Educational Leadership, 26*, 25–26.

Gustafson, J. P. (2002). Missing the mark for low-SES students. *Kappa Delta Pi Record, Winter*, 60–63.

Haager, D., & Windmueller, M. P. (2001). Early reading intervention for English language learners at-risk for learning disabilities: Student and teacher outcomes in an urban school. *Learning Disability Quarterly, 24*(4), 235–250.

Hammill, D. D., & Larsen, S. C. (1996). *Test of written language* (3rd ed.). *(TOWL-3)*. Austin, TX: PRO-ED.

Harcourt Brace Educational Measurement. (2002). *Stanford Achievement Tests—Tenth Edition (Stanford 10)*. Harcourt Brace.

Hargrove, T., Walker, B. L., Huber, R. A., Corrigan, S. Z., & Moore, C. (2004). No teacher left behind: Supporting teachers as they implement standards-based reform in a test-based education environment. *Education, 124*(3), 567–572.

Hill, C. (2003). Integrating digital tools into a culturally diverse curriculum: An assessment model for the Pacesetter Program. *Teachers College Record, 105*(2), 278–296.

Hoover, H. D., Dunbar, S. B., & Frisbie, D. A. (2003). *Iowa Tests of Basic Skills, Forms A and B (ITBS)*. Itasca, CA: Riverside.

Hoover, J. J., & Patton, J. R. (2004). Differentiating standards-based education for students with diverse needs. *Remedial and Special Education, 25*(2), 74–78.

Hresko, W.P., Schlieve, P.L., Herron, S.R., Swain, C., & Sherbenou, R.J. (2003). *Comprehensive mathematical abilities test.* Austin, TX: PRO-ED. http://www.cps.nova.edu

Kaufman, A. S., & Kaufman, N. L. (2004). *Kaufman Test of Educational Achievement* (2nd ed.). *(K-TEA II)*. Circle Pines, MN: American Guidance Service.

Kluth, P., & Straut, D. (2001). Standards for diverse learners. *Educational Leadership, 59*, 43–46.

Larsen, S. C., Hammill, D. D., & Moats, L. C. (1999). *Test of Written Spelling* (4th ed.). *(TWS-4)*. Austin, TX: PRO-ED.

Lawlor, S., Richman, S., & Richman, C. L. (1997). The validity of using the SAT as a criterion for black and white students' admission to college. *College Student Journal, 31*, 507–515.

Lawrenz, F., Huffman, D., & Lavoie, B. (2005). Implementing and sustaining standards-based curricular reform. *NASSP Bulletin, 89*, 2–16.

Lee, F. Y., Silverman, F. L., & Montoya, P. (2002). Assessing the math performance of young ESL students. *Principal, 81*(3), 29–31.

Madhere, S. (1998). Cultural diversity, pedagogy, and assessment strategies. *Journal of Negro Education, 67*(3), 280–295.

Markwardt, F. C. (1998). *Peabody Individual Achievement Test—Revised/Normative Update (PIAT-R/NU)*. Circle Pines, MN: American Guidance Service.

Martindale, T., Pearson, C., Curda, L. K., & Pilcher, J. (2005). Effects of an online instructional application on reading and mathematics standardized test scores. *Journal of Research on Technology in Education, 37*(4), 349–360.

McEnvoy, A., & Welker, R. (2000). Antisocial behavior, academic behavior, and school climate: A critical review. *Journal of Emotional and Behavioral Disorders, 8*, 130–140.

McGhee, R., Bryant, B. R., Larsen, S. C., & Rivera, D. M. (1995). *Test of Written Expression (TOWE)*. Austin, TX: PRO-ED.

McLoughlin, J., & Lewis, R. (2005). *Assessing students with special needs* (6th ed.). Upper Saddle River, NJ: Merrill/Pearson Education.

No Child Left Behind Act of 2001 (H.R. 1), 107 Cong., 110 (2002) (enacted).

Pierce, C. D., Reid, R., & Epstein, M. H. (2004). Teacher mediated interventions for children with EBD and their academic outcomes: A review. *Remedial and Special Education, 25*(3), 175–188.

Ryan, J. B., Reid, R., & Epstein, M. H. (2004). Peer-mediated intervention studies on academic achievement for students with EBD: A review. *Remedial and Special Education, 25*(6), 330–341.

Sabornie, E. J., Culuinan, D., Osborne, S. S., & Brock, L. B. (2005). Intellectual, academic, and behavioral functioning of students with high-incidence disabilities: A cross-categorical meta-analysis. *Exceptional Children, 72*(1), 47–63.

Shimabukuro, S. M., Prater, M. A., Jenkins, A., & Edelen-Smith, P. (1999). The effects of self-monitoring of academic performance on students with learning disabilities and ADD/ADHD. *Education and Treatment of Children, 22*(4), 397–414.

Shin, J., Deno, S. L., Robinson, S. L., & Marston, D. (2000). Predicting classroom achievement from active responding on a computer-based groupware system. *Remedial and Special Education, 21*(1), 53–60.

Smith, D. G., & Garrison, G. (2005). The impending loss of talent: An exploratory study challenging assumptions about testing and merit. *Teachers College Record, 107*(4), 629–653.

Smith-Maddox, R. (1998). Defining culture as a dimension of academic achievement: Implications for culturally responsive curriculum, instruction, and assessment. *Journal of Negro Education, 67*(3), 302–317.

Stodden, R. A., Galloway, L. M., & Stodden, N. J. (2003). Secondary school curricula\issues: Impact on postsecondary students with disabilities. *Exceptional Children, 70*, 9–25.

Tate, W. F. (1997). Race-ethnicity, SES, gender, and language proficiency trends in mathematics achievement: An update. *Journal for Research in Mathematics Education, 28*, 652–679.

Wiederholt, J. L., & Bryant, B. R. (2001). *Gray Oral Reading Tests* (4th ed.). *(GORT-4)*. Austin, TX: PRO-ED.

Wilkinson, G. S., & Robertson, G. J. (2006). *Wide Range Achievement Test-4*. Lutz, FL: Psychological Assessment Resources.

Williams, J., Sharp, G., Bates, S., Griebel, M., Lange, B., Spence, G. T., & Thomas, P. (1996). Academic achievement and behavioral ratings in children with absence and complex partial epilepsy. *Education and Treatment of Children, 19*, 143–152.

Woodcock, R. W. (1998). *Woodcock Reading Mastery Test—Revised/Normative Update*. Circle Pines, MN: American Guidance Service.

Woodcock, R. W., McGrew, K. S., & Mather, N. (2006). *Woodcock-Johnson III NU Tests of Achievement*. Itasca, IL: Riverside.

Woodcock, R. W., Munoz-Sandoval, A. F., McGrew, K. S., & Mather, N. (2006). Bateria III NU Woodcock-Munoz. Itasca, IL: Riverside.

Receptive and Expressive Language

KEY TERMS

Articulation: Using body structures to form phonemes (place, manner, and voice).

Fluency: Smoothness of speech.

Voice: Appropriate pitch, tone, and resonance (free from pathology).

Swallowing: The ease and safety of liquid, puree, and/or solid food forms passing through the esophagus.

Tongue thrust: Speaking with tongue extending past teeth, mostly evident on frontal sounds.

Receptive language: Understanding communication (form, content, and use).

Expressive language: Using communication (form, content, and use).

Form: Phonology, syntax, and morphology.

Content: Semantics or meaning of word and word combinations.

Use: Pragmatics or social language.

Phonology: Understanding and use of phonemes or sounds (single and multiple combinations).

Syntax: Using and understanding the structure of sentences.

Embedding: Inserting grammar components (i.e., placing a phrase into a sentence).

Conjoining: Combining two or more grammar components (i.e., two sentences or phrases).

Gerund: A verb-word ending in -ing that serves as a noun, such as *selling*.

Agentive forms: Includes an agent in relation to the main verb of a clause, such as *leader*.

Adverb: Modifies a verb, an example is *slowly*.

Abstract nouns: Nouns you cannot see, such as *happiness*.

Collective nouns: Nouns in groups, such as *school*.

Count nouns: Nouns where there could be more than one, such as *chair*.

Mass or noncount nouns: Nouns that cannot be counted, such as *sand*.

Morphology: Using and understanding morphemes.

Morphemes: Smallest meaningful grammatical units. See Bound morpheme; Derivational morpheme; Free morpheme; Inflectional morpheme.

Free morpheme: Can stand alone (i.e., book, chair).

Bound morpheme: Dependent on other functions (i.e., -er in *jogger*).

Derivational morpheme: Prefixes and suffixes.

Inflectional morpheme: Suffixes only.

Semantics: Understanding and using meaning of words and word combinations.

Pragmatics: Social language (i.e., turn taking, eye contact).

Auxiliary verb: Helping verb, such as *are*.

Modal verb: Verb showing possibility, such as *may*.

Copula verb: Connects subject to rest of predicate.

Code-switching: Moving from one language to another.

Co-normed tests: Tests normed on the same sample.

Contrastive features: Features unique to a dialect.

Noncontrastive features: Features not unique to a dialect.

Terminable unit: No dependent clauses left over.

Case Study: Assessing Joseph

Joseph is a new student in your fourth-grade class who recently moved into the school district. He is bilingual in Spanish and English. Joseph's former teacher referred him for an evaluation. He had concerns regarding Joseph's language performance because Joseph was having a hard time keeping up with classroom discussions.

Joseph's parents reported that Joseph's birth and delivery were unremarkable. Developmental milestones, with the exception of communication, occurred within normal limits. Parents reported motor skills development of sitting unsupported at six months, crawling at six months, and walking independently at twelve months. Joseph's health history was marked by occasional colds, which were treated with decongestants. An earache was noted to follow a cold occasionally.

Joseph lives at home with his mother, father, 10-year-old sister, 2-year-old brother, and paternal grandmother. Spanish and English are spoken within the home. Joseph's parents work outside the home.

What questions should be asked of Joseph, his family members, and his teachers?

Should formal and informal assessment measures be conducted?

If so, what informal assessment measures should be taken?

What formal tests should be administered?

What are some possible complicating factors?

By the end of the chapter, you should be able to discuss the questions posed in the case study about Joseph. You should also be able to describe the areas of receptive and expressive language (i.e., form—phonology, syntax, and morphology; content—semantics, and use—pragmatics). You should be able to give examples of screening tests and examples of language tests for different age groups and in difficult areas of language. You should also be able to list the pros and cons of these tests. You should be able to identify problems and solutions associated with language assessments when evaluating individuals who are linguistically or culturally diverse.

DEFINITIONS OF RECEPTIVE AND EXPRESSIVE LANGUAGE

As a teacher, you will work collaboratively with speech-language pathologists. Your students may participate in speech and language screenings, speech and language assessment without any other suspected disabilities, speech and language services in addition to other disabilities, or language enrichment activities. Speech and language services for speech and language disorders may involve articulation, fluency, voice, swallowing, tongue thrust, receptive language, and expressive language. Speech and language assessments address these areas.

Receptive and expressive language domains are most closely connected to special education assessment, so these domains will be the focus of this chapter. Receptive language refers to the understanding of language. Expressive language refers to the use of language (speaking, using sign language, or using assistive/augmentative communication devices). It is important to note that when concerns exist regarding receptive and expressive language, it is critical that hearing issues be ruled out via a hearing screening. An audiologist or speech-language pathologist can conduct this screening. Also, school nurses and volunteers can be involved in this process. During a screening, students hear tones in both ears via headphones and indicate that they hear the sounds. Examination of speech reception thresholds can reveal much more useful information than pure tone testing alone. Once a hearing disability has been ruled out or determined, receptive and expressive language can be examined.

In looking at both receptive and expressive language, it is useful to examine the smaller components of language: form, content, and use. Form consists of phonology, syntax, and morphology; content includes semantics; and use is comprised of pragmatics (see Figure 9.1).

FORM

In terms of form, phonology incorporates how we understand and use sounds (i.e., phonemes) and sound combinations. Forty-four of these linguistic units exist in

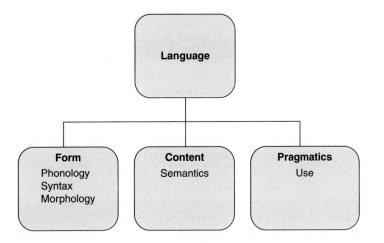

Figure 9.1 Components of language

English. There are 25 consonantal and 19 vocalic sounds. Place (i.e., alveolar ridge), manner (i.e., fricatives), and voicing (voiced or voiceless) of those sounds are ways of categorizing consonants. Height (high, middle, low) of the tongue and location of primary resonance (front, middle, or back of the mouth) are ways to categorize vowels (Schane, 1973). Timing, frequency, and duration of speech sound units are included in the area of phonology.

Individuals acquire phonemes in a developmental sequence. Graphemes embrace the written symbols associated with sounds. Speech-language pathologists assess these sounds in isolation, in consonant clusters (i.e., /gr/), in syllables, by position in single words (i.e., /p/ beginning—pan, middle—apple, and end of words—hop), phrases, sentences, combination of sentences, structured speech, and spontaneous speech.

Syntax involves the structure of sentences. The structure of sentences includes word sequences, sentence organization, word associations, word classes, and sentence components (Owens, 2004). During their language development, children expand their use of noun phrases, verb phrases, passive sentences, rule exceptions, embedding (inserting grammar components such as phrases), and conjoining (combining grammar components such as phrases) (Polloway, Miller, & Smith, 2004).

Morphology contains meaningful grammatical units or morphemes. Morphemes are the smallest units of language that have meaning. They could include sounds, syllables, or words. They can stand alone (free morphemes), or they can depend on other functions (bound morphemes). Examples of free morphemes include *car*, *woman*, and *happy*. As you can see, these are all whole words. Examples of bound morphemes include derivational morphemes (i.e., prefixes and suffixes) and inflectional morphemes (i.e., suffixes only) (Owens, 2004). Derivation morphemes (i.e., -er in *jogger*), can change the class of words. In this case, the word is transformed from verb (*jog*) to noun (*jogger*). Inflectional morphemes increase the accuracy of the morpheme. For example, -er in *smaller* signals a more precise understanding of size. During the course of language development, gerunds (a verb-word ending in -ing that serves as a noun), agentive forms (includes an agent in relation to the main verb of a clause, such as *leader*), and adverb forms (modifies a verb, for example, *slowly*) are also learned and enhanced (Hulit & Howard, 2006). In addition to standardized tests, speech-language pathologists often use language samples (which will be discussed at the end of this section) to appropriately analyze morphology.

CONTENT

In looking at content, semantics refers to the meaning of word and word combinations. According to Bloom and Lahey (1978), the most common communicative purposes that children use during the development of language include rejection, nonexistence or disappearance, cessation or prohibition of action, recurrence, existence, action on objects, locative action (where, such as "to Chicago"), attribution (describes noun, "smart girl"), naming, possession, commenting, and social interaction. Ideas and the relationship among ideas are included in semantics. The word labels for these ideas are an important factor in discussing semantics.

Children expand vocabulary by evolving nouns, including common, proper, concrete, abstract (nouns you cannot see, such as *happiness*), collective (group nouns, such as *school*), count (nouns that can be more than one, such as *chair*), and mass or noncount (nouns you cannot count such as *sand*). The addition of adjectives, adverbs, practical and content vocabulary, and verbs also expand children's vocabulary. (Polloway, Miller, & Smith, 2004). Furthermore, figurative language is a key aspect of this element of language. Examples include idioms, metaphors, similes, and proverbs.

Idioms use figurative language and cannot be comprehended literally (i.e., "has gone down the tubes"). In metaphors, a word or phrase representing one thought is used in place of another to indicate that two typically unlike ideas are similar (i.e., "couch potato"). Similes compare two items that are typically unalike. "Like" or "as" is usually used to connect the ideas (i.e., "the bed was as hard as a rock"). Proverbs are brief sayings regarding frequently held thoughts of a culture (i.e., "better late than never"). Many of these terms are difficult for individuals with hearing impairments and/or individuals who are bilingual.

USE

In understanding use, we must look at pragmatics. Pragmatics involves the intersection of language and social aspects. Communication and interaction are the focus points of this aspect of language. Those include speech acts as well as gestures and body language. In addition, loudness, pitch, intonation, and stress (emphasis) are also involved in this process. Loudness includes the volume of the sound, and pitch includes the frequency of sound. Intonation embraces the rise and fall of voice. Stress takes the variation of pitch or tone into account when placing emphasis on syllables, words, or phrases.

Intentions and presuppositions are important aspects of pragmatics. Intentions are signaled by children early in language development. They include naming, commenting, requesting objects, requesting actions, requesting information, responding, protesting or rejecting, attention seeking, and greeting (Roth & Spekman, 1984). Presupposition describes the speaker's assumptions about what the listener already knows. These assumptions help the speaker say the words required to make communication effective (Polloway, Miller, & Smith, 2004).

Breakpoint Practice

1. Compare and contrast the concepts of receptive and expressive language.
2. Define and give examples of the three components of language (form, content, and use).
3. Describe and give examples of receptive and expressive language for phonology, syntax, morphology, semantics, and pragmatics.
4. How does receptive language influence expressive language?

The context of the communication exchange is critical in the conceptualization, assessment, and interpretation of pragmatic language. Language samples in multiple contexts with multiple speaking partners are important in the assessment of pragmatic language.

During the first year of age, the following sequence of typically developing language components come into play: (1) reflexive cries and vegetative sounds, (2) cooing (vowel-like sounds), (3) babbling (vowel-consonant combinations in single syllables), (4) reduplicated babbling (same syllable repetition), (5) echolalia (imitation), (6) variegated babbling (more than one consonant-vowel combination), (7) jargon babbling (sounds like real sentences), and (8) first word (Hulit & Howard, 2006).

NONLINGUISTIC COMMUNICATORS

Not all children with severe disabilities acquire language. One of the barriers to achieving language is symbolic understanding. A number of methods have been described by researchers in assessing individuals who are nonlinguistic communicators. Van Dijk (1966) discussed child-guided assessment techniques. In this approach, students are not pushed to perform an assessment task. Instead, to increase motivation and comprehension, the assessor allows the student to take the lead in interests and explorations of his or her environment. The assessor imitates the actions of the student and adds communicative information. Turn taking facilitates identification of communication information.

A developmental scale intended for use with students who are deaf-blind and students with severe and profound disabilities, the Callier-Azusa Scale, was updated by the Stillman Edition (G Scale) to include 18 subscales. Six areas are assessed, including directions, motor development, perceptual development, daily living skills, language development, and social development. The H Scale (another updated edition) concentrated on representational and symbolic abilities, receptive communication, intentional communication, and reciprocity. Reliability and validity concerns exist. For more information, go to http://www.callier.utdallas.edu/scale.html.

In addition, when students have difficulty understanding and using language due to severe disabilities and deaf-blindness, an approach using four aspects of communication (i.e. form, function, content, and context) is often used. Five critical features of receptive and expressive language were discussed by McLean and Snyder-McLean (1978). Those features included forms (ways individuals receive and send communication information), functions and/or intents (reason for communications), content (what is communicated—people, actions), partners (who the person is interacting with), and physical environment (where the interaction is happening).

Rowland (1996) established a language assessment tool based on communicative behaviors and intents. The Communication Matrix was designed for use with students with severe or multiple disabilities who are developing early language skills. This instrument consists of observations, interviews with parents and/or teachers, and direct observation. Two elements are utilized to organize the matrix. One element is reasons to communicate (i.e., refuse, obtain, social, and information). The second element is levels of communication. Seven levels include pre-intentional behavior, intentional behavior, unconventional communication, conventional communication, concrete symbols, abstract symbols, and language. The instrument provides the assessor with a profile and a communication skills list. This tool is easy to use for both teachers and caregivers.

The Communication and Symbolic Behavior Scales Developmental Profile—First Normed Edition (Wetherby & Prizant, 2002) is a standardized, norm-referenced test that

Laima Druskis/PH College

investigates communicative, social, affective, and symbolic activities in children 6 months to 6 years. The functional communication age is 6 months to 2 years. This instrument determines seven language predictors: emotion and eye gaze, communication, gestures, sounds, words, understanding, and object use. A four-page caregiver questionnaire (5–15 minutes) and multiple-choice protocol (5–10 minutes) give information regarding the student. A profile of functioning is developed through this assessment and connects results to intervention. Validity and reliability studies (Wetherby, Allen, Cleary, Kublin, & Goldstein, 2002) support the use of this test.

Additional resources for assessing and teaching students with multiple disabilities could be found at http://www.tr.wou.edu/DBLINK/lib/comm2.htm.

LINGUISTIC COMMUNICATORS

When individuals have learning disabilities, mental retardation, and other disabilities, they often have a communication disorder (Spinelli, 2006). A number of standardized tests have been developed in an effort to facilitate the evaluation of communication. Standardized tests can include group tests or individual tests.

GROUP TESTS

Group tests are generally for the purpose of screening. Two common screening tests include the Bankson Language Screening Test—2s (Bankson, 1990) and the Boehm Test of Basic Concepts, Preschool, Third Edition (Boehm, 2000). See Table 9.1.

The Bankson Language Test was normed on 1,200 children across 19 states. The semantic knowledge category includes information regarding body parts, nouns, verbs, categories, functions, prepositions, and opposites. Morphological/syntactical rules include pronouns, verb tense, verb usage (auxiliary-helping verb such as *are*, modal—show possibility such as *may*, copula—connects subject to rest of predicate), plurals, comparatives/superlatives, negation, and questions. Pragmatics information is comprised of ritualizing, informing, controlling, and imagining. A short form (20 items)

Table 9.1 Examples of Group Tests

Name	Company	Content	Age	Time to Administer
Bankson Language Screening Test—2s	PRO-ED	Semantic understanding, morphology and syntax rules, and pragmatics	3-0 through 6-11	Varies
Boehm Test of Basic Concepts—Third Edition	Psychological Corporation	Understanding of verbal instructions (space, quantity, and time)	3-0 through 5-11	About 30 minutes

version of this test is also available. Standard scores and percentile ranks are included for this test. Internal consistency, content, concurrent, and construct validity information is included in the test manual.

Rhyner, Kelly, Brantley, and Krueger (1999) investigated the use of this instrument with African American kindergarten children with low socioeconomic status. Results revealed elevated failure rates. Therefore, probable overidentification of the participants indicates that this test should be used with caution when screening this population.

The Boehm Test of Basic Concepts, Preschool, Third Edition, was normed on more than 1,600 children. This test includes information regarding relational concepts: size (i.e., *tallest*), direction (i.e., in *front*), position (i.e., *nearest*), time (i.e., *before*), quantity (i.e., *some, but not all*), classification (i.e., *all*), and general information (i.e., *another*). Suggestions for adaptations are incorporated in the test manual. Percentile scores by 6-month age segments are included in this test. Coefficients alpha and test-retest reliability are included in the test manual. Reliability and validity are adequate. The Spanish edition of this test has adequate reliability information, but more validity information is needed.

INDIVIDUAL TESTS

Individual tests may be used during the evaluation process and involve testing the student by him- or herself. Some examples of individual tests include receptive vocabulary, expressive vocabulary, auditory comprehension and discrimination, multiple language areas, tests of pragmatic language, and criterion-referenced tests.

Receptive Vocabulary

One area of individual language testing includes the theme of receptive vocabulary. The Peabody Picture Vocabulary Test—IV (PPVT-IV) (Dunn & Dunn, 2007), the Test de Vocabulario en Imagenes Peabody (TVIP) (Dunn, Lugo, Padilla, & Dunn, 1986) and Receptive One-Word Picture Vocabulary Test (ROWPVT-2000) (Brownell, 2000b) are three commonly used receptive language tests. See Table 9.2.

The PPVT-IV has two parallel forms (IVA and IVB) with full-color pictures. This tool requires no reading or writing by the examinee. The examiner shows a plate (a page from the test booklet) with four items, and the student points to the picture matching the examiner's spoken word. Standard scores, percentiles, normal curve equivalents (NCEs), stanines, age equivalents, grade equivalents, and growth scale values are included with this testing tool. Norming appears adequate. Students with disabilities were included in the

Table 9.2   Examples of Receptive Vocabulary Tests

Name	Company	Content	Age	Time to Administer
Peabody Picture Vocabulary Test—IV	American Guidance Service	Single-word receptive vocabulary	2-6 through 90+	10–15 minutes
Test de Vocabulario en Imagenes Peabody	American Guidance Service	Single-word receptive vocabulary (Spanish)	2-6 through 17-11	10–15 minutes
Receptive One-Word Picture Vocabulary Test—2000 Edition	PRO-ED	Single-word receptive vocabulary	2-0 through 18-11	10–15 minutes

norm group. Content, construct, and criterion-related validity information is discussed. Also, internal consistency (split-half), alternate-form, and test-retest reliability results are included in the manual. Reliability and validity are adequate.

The Spanish version of the PPVT-IV, TVIP has 125 translated items and has standardized norms consisting of individuals who are Mexican and Puerto Rican. Combined and separate standardization samples exist. No reading, writing, or speaking is necessary in this test. The test has the same directions as those found in the PPVT-IV. Standard scores, percentile ranks, and age equivalents are included.

The ROWPVT-2000 consists of test pages with color drawings. The examinee shows the examiner the picture she or he chooses (from four possible choices) that matches the word spoken by the assessor, which is similar to the PPVT-IV. The ROWPVT-2000 is designed to be compared to the Expressive One-Word Picture Vocabulary Test, 2000 Edition (Brownell, 2000a), so that receptive and expressive vocabulary skills can be compared. Percentiles and standard scores are included. Norming sample data is limited.

Expressive Vocabulary

Another area of individual language testing includes expressive vocabulary. The Expressive One-Word Picture Vocabulary Test, 2000 Edition (EOWPVT-2000) (Brownell, 2000a), and the Expressive Vocabulary Test—2 (EVT-2) (Williams, 2007) measure single-word expressive vocabulary. See Table 9.3.

The EVT-2 was co-normed (normed on the same sample) with the PPVT-IV. The examinee labels and provides synonyms (one-word responses) for picture stimuli. The measure of expressive vocabulary is meant for Standard American English. The test (Form A, Form B) consists of 190 items across 20 content areas. Standard scores, percentiles, normal curve equivalents (NCEs), stanines, age equivalents, grade equivalents, and growth scale values are included. Norming appears adequate. Students with disabilities were included in the norm group. Internal consistency, split-half, alternate-form, and test-retest reliabilities are offered. Concurrent, construct, and content validity information is examined. Reliability and validity appear adequate.

The Expressive One-Word Picture Vocabulary Test, 2000 Edition (EOWPVT), was co-normed with the Receptive One-Word Picture Vocabulary Test. The examinee labels (one-word verbal/oral responses) the illustrations, which are color drawings. With this revision of the test comes the ability to cue examinees so they can focus on the pertinent features of the pictures. No reading or writing is required to complete

Table 9.3 Examples of Expressive Vocabulary Tests

Name	Company	Content	Age	Time to Administer
Expressive One-Word Picture Vocabulary Test, 2000 Edition	PRO-ED	Single-word expressive vocabulary	2-0 through 18-11	10–15 minutes
Expressive Vocabulary Test—2	American Guidance Service	Single-word expressive vocabulary	2-6 to 90+	10–20 minutes

Table 9.4 Examples of Auditory Discrimination and Comprehension Tests

Name	Company	Content	Age	Time to Administer
Test of Auditory Comprehension of Language— Third Edition	American Guidance Service	Receptive spoken vocabulary, grammar, and syntax	3-0 through 9-11	10–20 minutes
Goldman- Fristoe- Woodcock Test of Auditory Discrimination	American Guidance Service	Auditory discrimination	3-8+	20–30 minutes

tasks on either of these tests. English and Spanish forms exist. Standard scores, percentiles, and age equivalents are included. Split-half reliability (Kuder-Richardsen) and standard error of measurement information is included. Concurrent validity and content validity are discussed. Some age groups should be examined closely. The norming sample is limited.

Auditory Comprehension and Discrimination

Another area of language includes auditory comprehension and discrimination. The Test of Auditory Comprehension of Language—Third Edition (Carrow-Woolfolk, 1999), and the Goldman-Fristoe-Woodcock Test of Auditory Discrimination (Goldman, Fristoe, & Woodcock, 1970) target auditory comprehension and discrimination. See Table 9.4.

The test of Auditory Comprehension of Language—Third Edition, consists of 142 multiple-item responses. Three subtests include vocabulary, grammatical morphemes, and elaborated phrases and sentences. The vocabulary subtest consists of nouns, verbs, adjectives, adverbs, and basic concept words. The grammatical morphemes subtest is made up of prepositions, noun number, noun case, verb number, verb tense, noun-verb agreement, derivational suffixes, and pronouns. Elaborated phrases and sentence understanding is assessed via interrogative sentences, negative sentences, active and passive voice, direct and indirect object, embedded sentences, partially conjoined sentences, and completely conjoined sentences. Percentile ranks and age equivalents, z-scores, T-scores, deviation quotients, and NCEs are noted. Reliability information for total scores is adequate; however, category scores should be closely examined. Validity information is needed.

The Goldman-Fristoe-Woodcock Test of Auditory Discrimination does not require writing or speaking. The examinee points to pictures that he or she hears on

Table 9.5 Language Batteries

Name	Company	Content	Age	Time to Administer
Test of Language Development—Primary—Fourth Edition	PRO-ED	Receptive and expressive vocabulary, grammar, and phonology	4-0 through 8-11	1 hour
Test of Language Development—Intermediate—Third Edition	PRO-ED	Semantics, syntax, and phonology	8-0 through 17-11	½ hour to 1 hour
Test of Adolescent and Adult Language—Fourth Edition	American Guidance Service	Receptive language, expressive language, reading and writing	12-0 through 24-11	1–3 hours

tape. Quiet and noise backgrounds are utilized in the assessment of speech sound discrimination. Standard scores and percentile ranks are included.

Language Batteries

Some language batteries take multiple areas of language into account. The Test of Language Development—Primary—Fourth Edition (TOLD-P:4) (Newcomer & Hammill, 2008), the Test of Language Development—Intermediate—Fourth Edition (TOLD-I:4) (Hammill & Newcomer, 2008), and the Test of Adolescent and Adult Language—4 (TOAL-4) (Hammill, Brown, Larsen, & Wiederholt, 2007) are popular language batteries utilized by language experts. See Table 9.5.

The Test of Language Development—Primary—Fourth Edition was renormed in 2005 on at least 1,000 children across 30 states. The assessor presents information and the student responds in a variety of formats, including multiple choice, open-ended questions, repetition of sentences, fill in the blanks, discrimination tasks, and naming color pictures. Nine subtests include picture vocabulary, relational vocabulary, oral vocabulary, syntactic understanding, sentence imitation, morphological completion, word discrimination, word analysis, and word articulation (Newcomer & Hammill, 2008). Composites include (1) semantics and grammar; (2) listening, organizing, and speaking; and (3) overall language ability. Percentile ranks, age equivalents, and standard scores are available for core subtests. Content, construct, and criterion-related validity information is included. Content sampling, internal consistency, time sampling, and interscorer reliability results are included. Reliability and validity are adequate.

Test of Language Development—Intermediate—Fourth Edition was normed on at least 700 children across 19 states. The evaluator presents the information orally and the student answers multiple choice and open-ended questions. Subtests include sentence combining, picture vocabulary, word ordering, relational vocabulary, morphological comprehension, and multiple meanings. Composites include listening abilities, organizing abilities, and speaking abilities (Hammill & Newcomer, 2008). Percentile ranks, age equivalents, and standard scores are available for subtests. Criterion-related, construct, item, and factor analysis validity information is included. Internal consistency (coefficient alpha and content sampling) and interscorer reliability data are offered. Reliability and validity are adequate.

The Test of Adolescent and Adult Language—Fourth Edition was normed on more than 1,671 individuals across 35 states. Composites include spoken language (word opposites, word derivations, and spoken analogies), written language (word similarities, sentence combining, and orthographic usage), and general language (all six subtests) (Hammill, Brown, Larsen, & Wiederholt, 2007). Standard scores, percentiles, and composite scores are included. Content, criterion-related, and construct validity data are included. Internal consistency, test-retest, and interscorer reliability are included. Reliability and validity are adequate.

Pragmatic Language

Tests involving pragmatic language include the Test of Pragmatic Language (Phelps-Terasaki & Phelps-Gunn, 1992), Let's Talk Inventory for Children (Bray & Wiig, 1987), and the Test of Pragmatic Skills—Revised (Shulman, 1986). In general, more information regarding reliability and validity is needed for these tests. The Test of Pragmatic Language (TOPL) can be administered to children 5 to 14 years of age. Physical setting, audience, topic, purpose, visual-gestural cues, and abstraction are investigated. The assessor shows the student a picture and asks questions regarding the situation presented. The individual's responses requesting, informing, regulating, expressing, ritualizing, and organizing are examined. Percentile ranks and quotient and age equivalent scores are included.

The Let's Talk Inventory for Children involves a picture that shows a communication situation, accompanied by a short narrative that is presented by the examiner. The student responds orally, and ritualizing, informing, controlling, and feeling responses are assessed. The Let's Talk Inventory for Children can be utilized for students ages 4 to 8. In the Test of Pragmatic Skills, play interactions, which include scripts, are used to elicit responses and can be administered to children 3 to 8 years. Communicative intents, including requesting information, requesting action, rejection/denial, naming/labeling, answering/responding, informing, reasoning, summoning/calling, greeting, and closing conversation, are examined. Play-based format includes puppets, pencil and paper, telephones, and blocks. Percentile ranks are given.

Criterion-Referenced

Some criterion-referenced tests exist for evaluating language. These include the Carrow Elicited Language Inventory (Learning Concepts) (Carrow-Woolfolk, 1974) and Goldman-Fristoe Test of Articulation—Revised (GFTA-2) (Goldman & Fristoe, 2000). See Table 9.6.

Table 9.6 Criterion-Referenced Tests

Name	Company	Content	Age	Time to Administer
Carrow Elicited Language Inventory	PRO-ED	Expressive morphology and grammar	3 through 7-11	20–30 minutes
Goldman-Fristoe Test of Articulation—2	American Guidance Service	Articulation	2 through 21	15 minutes

The Carrow Elicited Language Inventory explores the areas of grammatical structures and syntax through elicited imitation. Percentile ranks and stanine results are provided. Test-retest and interrater reliability information is provided. Error scores can be unstable. Content validity and concurrent validity are discussed. Reliability and validity are adequate.

The Goldman-Fristoe Test of Articulation—Revised (GFTA-2) uses the context of imitation and spontaneous sound production. The participant names pictures that are in color, answers questions, and uses sounds correctly in sentences. The test is comprised of three subtests: sounds in words (initial, medial, and final positions), sounds in sentences, and stimulability. Thirty-nine consonant sounds and clusters are included in this test. Standard scores, percentile ranks, and test-age equivalents are included. Reliability is adequate, but validity information is lacking.

Breakpoint Practice

1. How does the evaluation of nonlinguistic and linguistic communicators differ?

2. Which area of assessment (nonlinguistic and linguistic) do you think has the most reliability and validity issues? Why?

3. What tests are recommended for students who are second-language learners?

INFORMAL MEASURES

Informal measures can include interviews with caregivers, teachers, and students. Artifacts from assignments in class and homework assignments can be valuable tools. Language samples should also be utilized. Three popular methods of interpreting language samples are spontaneous language sample, mean length of utterance (MLU), and the Developmental Sequence Analysis.

LANGUAGE SAMPLES

In a spontaneous language sample, spontaneous speech that contains 50 to 100 utterances is used to discover what language the student uses in typical spontaneous speech (Wiig & Semel, 1984). Prutting (1981) noted that context, communicative partner, and goals of the communicative interaction are three essential components in the collection of a language sample. This approach is less structured than the next two approaches discussed.

In the mean length of utterance (MLU) approach, the clinician elicits a sample by asking open-ended questions. An utterance could be a sentence, phrase, or word. The second page of transcription is used. Optimally, 100 utterances are used. Fifty utterances should be used at a minimum. Morphemes are counted and divided by 100. MLU or Brown's procedure based on Brown's (1973) stages is most useful for young children and children with serious language difficulties. Linares (1981) gave general procedures and rules involving counting bound morphemes for calculating MLU for Spanish. Some interesting points include contractions *del* and *della* having two morphemes, gender rules (counting marking as morpheme), and diminuitives (counting marking as morpheme). In the Developmental Sentence Analysis (Lee, 1974), stimulus materials are utilized by a speech-language pathologist to elicit a language sample. Fifty consecutive sentences are used to categorize words by grammatical types. Points are assigned to those words. This technique is used for children 2 years to 6 years, 11 months. Refer to Chapter 6 for more information regarding language samples with young children.

DYNAMIC ASSESSMENT

Dynamic assessment has been discussed by researchers as an effective element in the assessment-to-instruction link (Robinson-Zanartu, 1996). Lidz and Pena (1996) note that intervention is the most essential aspect of this type of assessment. They add that dynamic assessment allows the assessor to look at how the student learns, how changeable the student is, and what types of instruction are most useful for the student. A focus of dynamic assessment has been the use of this tool with students who are culturally and/or linguistically diverse.

For example, Ukrainetz, Harpell, Walsh, and Coyle (2000) investigated the relationship between dynamic assessment and language learning ability in children who are Native American (Arapahoe/Shosone) and who were in kindergarten. Children's learning strategies (i.e., attending, planning, self-regulating, and responses) were related to more effective language learning. Pinpointing these skills can help professionals better discriminate the strength of language learning. Results supported the utilization of dynamic assessment in evaluating language learning skills in this population.

In addition, Gutierrez-Clellen and Pena (2001) compared dynamic assessment methods with assessment applications for students who are culturally and/or linguistically diverse. Three methods they examined included testing the limits (feedback and/or questioning during testing), graduated prompting (hierarchical), and test-teach-retest. The researchers noted that the test-teach-retest methods matched better with the concept of differentiation of disorders and differences (language and/or cultural). They discussed modifiability (changeability) based on the research of Pena and Quinn (1997). The authors offered the protocol for assessing the student's responsiveness, assessing the child's modifiability, and examining aspects that help with alteration in language areas.

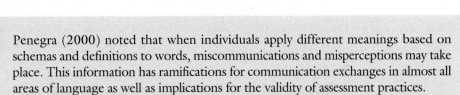

Multicultural Considerations

Penegra (2000) noted that when individuals apply different meanings based on schemas and definitions to words, miscommunications and misperceptions may take place. This information has ramifications for communication exchanges in almost all areas of language as well as implications for the validity of assessment practices.

Language loss is another factor to consider when examining language and bilingual student populations. Paucity in both languages does not automatically indicate a language disorder. As individuals increase proficiency in a second language, a loss of proficiency may occur in the first language. This is considered a normal occurrence (Schiff-Myers, 1992). Even though an individual speaks English more proficiently than another spoken language, she or he may still have less exposure to English than a typical participant in the standardization sample. Consequently, he or she may not be familiar with the tasks necessary to do well on a test (Mattes & Omark, 1991).

Task Familiarity

In an example of exposure to tasks, Pena and Quinn (1997) investigated task familiarity and test results in children who are Puerto Rican and African American. They compared performances on description (familiar) and one-word labeling (unfamiliar) items. Results revealed that the participants did better on familiar test items. This type of test was more insightful in distinguishing typical language and atypical language when compared to unfamiliar test tasks (Pena & Quinn, 1997).

(*continued*)

In addition, Campbell, Dollaghan, Needleman, and Janosky (1997) examined the effects of prior knowledge and experience on language assessment performance. They compared language measures dependent on knowledge and test measures dependent on processing in children. These participants came from the majority group (Caucasian) and from minority groups (African American, Asian, and Native American). Results revealed that the majority group participants scored higher than the minority group participants on measures that were dependent on knowledge. However, the groups did not perform differently on tasks that were processing measures.

Type of Task

The type of task may be a barrier to revealing valid assessment results. Rodekohr and Haynes (2001) performed a follow-up study comparing African American children (speaking African American English) with typical language, African American children with a language disorder (speaking African American English), Caucasian children (speaking Southern English) with typical language, and Caucasian children (speaking Southern English) with a language disorder in measures of knowledge-based and processing-based language tasks. Results revealed that the children who were African American did not do as well as the Caucasian children on knowledge-based tasks, but did the same as Caucasian children on processing-based tasks. A critical finding was that the processing-dependent measures distinguished typical and atypical language in both the children who were African American and Caucasian. Strong implications exist in using processing measures that appear to be bias-free when assessing individuals who are culturally and linguistically diverse.

Research has been conducted in the area of comprehension tasks in the assessment of African American children who were from urban middle-income households (Craig, Washington, & Thompson-Porter, 1998). Researchers investigated relationships in responses to wh- questions, performance on active/passive sentence task constructions, and chronological age/grade level. They found the data showed that the two tasks were appropriate to use in the assessment of comprehension skills of young African American children.

In a follow-up study, Craig and Washington (2000) compared the language performance of African American children identified with language impairment who received school-based language therapy and two groups of typically developing peers (all speaking African American English) on five types of language measures. Those tasks included MLU, frequencies of syntax, numbers of different words (based on a language sample from play activity), comprehension of wh- questions, and comprehension of active/passive sentence forms. Students in the group with language impairments performed lower on all five measures. The authors supported the use of these informal tasks in the assessment of young African American children.

Gutierrez-Clellen, Restrepo, Bedore, Pena, and Anderson (2000) discussed code switching (moving from one language to another) and dialect as factors regarding the use of the Development Assessment of Spanish Grammar, mean length of response in words, mean length of terminable unit (no dependent clauses left over), and mean length of utterance in morphemes in Spanish-speaking children. Clinical methods for assessing individuals who have limited English were suggested, including information regarding (1) Spanish morphosyntactic categories, (2) comparison of data from individuals of similar sociolinguistic backgrounds, (3) analysis of errors per simple or complex sentence (T-unit), (4) use of parent and teacher reports to validate observations, (5) clarification of issues of language loss, (6) investigation of second-language errors that may be associated with second-language acquisition, and (7) comparison of unexpected performance to children of similar sociolinguistic backgrounds.

Seymour, Bland-Stewart, and Green (1998) looked at shared features of African American English and Standard American English. The authors used syntax analysis from language samples of children with and without language disorders. The features that the two dialects had in common (noncontrastive—features not unique to a dialect) were compared to features the two dialects did not have in common (contrastive—features unique to a dialect). Results revealed that the noncontrastive features were different and the contrastive features were not different (except in the past tense/ed/) in the two groups. Therefore, using these concepts in assessment may lead to better differentiation of language disorders in students speaking African American English.

McGregor, Williams, Hearst, and Johnson (1997) explored contrastive analysis in the process of differentiating a language difference from a language disorder. Specifically, they targeted the scenario of a speech-language pathologist coming from a different speech community than the client. They defined this method as taking apart speech-language patterns from the individual's first language or dialect compared to true errors. They offered four procedures in this process: (1) familiarity with the dialect of the client, (2) collecting expressive language information from the assessment process, (3) comparing data to the dialect pattern to find "true errors," and (4) examining all of the pieces of the assessment process (i.e., case history).

Specific Quantitative Tests

Researchers have provided valuable information regarding specific tests and individuals who are culturally and/or linguistically diverse. Saenz and Huer (2003) looked at results from four standard and modified subtests of the Clinical Evaluation of Language Fundamentals—Third Edition (CELF-3) in bilingual Latino children. They found that scores improved with modification and repeated testing. The students had a higher performance on the second administrations of the CELF-3, perhaps due to experience in the test taking.

In researching the area of articulation, Cole and Taylor (1990) examined the performance of African American children who spoke Black English Vernacular on three tests of articulation. Specifically, they investigated test-client correspondence (context appropriateness) on these tests. The tests included the Templin-Darley Tests of Articulation—Second Edition, Arizona Ariculation Proficiency Scale—Revised (AAPS-R), and the Photo Articulation Test. The researchers not only examined test items of concern but also which tests might lead to misdiagnoses if dialect was not considered. They found that of the 10 participants, the following misdiagnoses would occur if dialect was not accounted for: AAPS-R, 7; Templin-Darley, 6; and Photo Articulation Test, 2. Dialect sensitive scores were as follows: AAPS-R, 0; Templin-Darley, 2; and Photo Articulation Test, 1. Results reveal that

(*continued*)

if dialect variation is not considered during the assessment process, the outcome could be devastating.

Roberts, Medley, Swartzfager, and Neebe (1997) examined the use of the Communication and Symbolic Behavior Scales and found that the tool was appropriate in the area of internal consistency for African American one-year-olds (Roberts, et al., (1997).

Professionals' Judgment

Culture determines behavior and also how behavior is judged (Kayser, 1995). Bebout and Arthur (1992) found differences in individuals' beliefs about the emotional health and potential for change in the speech of persons who have speech disorders based on culture (i.e., North American–born and foreign-born). Participants included individuals born in the United States, Japan, Latin America, Southeast Asia, China, and Hong Kong. More specifically, in a question involving effort to improve speech, participants from Southeast Asia, China, and Hong Kong more often reported that individuals with speech disorders could speak better if they tried harder. Chinese participants reported more frequently that a person with a speech disorder (such as cleft palate or hearing disorders) would have an emotional disturbance.

Speech-language pathologists are often asked to judge whether English language learners have language disorders associated with learning difficulties. Many of these professionals are not well equipped to perform this task (Roseberry-McKibbin & Eicholtz, 1994). Roseberry-McKibbin (1994) presents interference, fossilization, interlanguage code switching, silent period, language loss, reduced exposure to both languages, and proficiency in both languages as learning processes involved in second-language acquisition. She adds that the ethnographic interview and case history are key components of the assessment. In analyzing the literature, Roseberry-McKibbin (1994) indicates support for the following informal assessment procedures: evaluating the student's language over time, focusing on the functional components of language, utilizing observations in authentic contexts, using questionnaires for various important individuals who interact with the student, using narratives, and using spontaneous language samples. For a discussion of language sampling and multicultural issues please refer to Chapter 6.

In looking specifically at phonology, Yavas and Goldstein (1998) investigated phonological patterns in languages, sound pattern influence across languages, and guidelines for assessment practice. They indicated case history, oral-peripheral examination (visual inspection of mouth and oral cavity), hearing screening, language, voice fluency, and phonological patterns should be in the battery of tests involved in this process. The authors considered sociocultural factors, assessing phonological skills in all languages, choosing an appropriate assessment tool, and using assessment alternatives (i.e., informal samples, dynamic assessment, and contextual sampling). In addition, the authors included describing common and uncommon phonological patterns in both languages, identifying bilingual phonological patterns, outlining interference patterns, and accounting for dialect features.

The information gleaned from this multitude of studies points in the direction of extreme caution when looking at formal test results. Useful information can be extracted to improve the assessment process. Language sampling and dynamic assessment appear to have the potential of being fruitful in the assessment-to-instruction process.

> **Breakpoint Practice**
> 1. How can you decrease issues of task familiarity with your students?
> 2. What does the research reveal regarding specific quantitative tests?
> 3. How can you increase the validity of your judgment when assessing students who are culturally and/or linguistically diverse?

REASSESSING JOSEPH

When looking at the chapter-opening case study about Joseph, the earache information in his medical history raises questions regarding a possible hearing loss. A hearing screening would be the first checkpoint in the discussion of his possible language issues. Discussion or an interview with the parents with regard to their assessment of Joseph's language in the home and community setting would be the next checkpoint. Have they noticed any language issues in Spanish or English? How does his language use compare to that of his siblings? Observations of Joseph in multiple settings (i.e., with teachers, classmates, and family members) would be a window to his language functioning in Spanish and English. What percentage of the time does he use Spanish? English? With whom? In what contexts?

If the previous information points to difficulties with language, the assessment process can include language samples and classroom artifacts. Formal assessment practices could take place after a proper evaluation protocol has been completed. Possibilities for formal testing include the Peabody Picture Vocabulary Test, Expressive One-Word Picture Vocabulary Test, Goldman-Fristoe Articulation Test, Test of Language Development—Intermediate, and the Test de Vocabulario en Imagenes Peabody. In the informal testing domain, it would be appropriate to include interviews, observations, classroom artifacts, attendance data, language samples, and dynamic assessment.

SUMMARY

While investigating the areas of receptive and expressive language, the important concepts to understand are form (phonology, syntax, and morphology), content (semantics), and use (pragmatics). Formal and informal measures should be used to address these areas of language. Formal tests can include group tests (i.e., Bankson Language Screening—2 or Boehm Test of Basic Concepts) or individual tests in the areas of receptive vocabulary (i.e., PPVT-IV), expressive vocabulary (i.e., EVT-2), and auditory comprehension and discrimination (i.e., TACL-3). In addition, language batteries (i.e., TOLD-III), pragmatic language (i.e., Test of Pragmatic Language), and/or criterion-referenced tests (i.e., GFTA-2) are available. Informal measures can include interviews, observations, language samples, and dynamic assessment. Researchers have found that issues related to task familiarity, type of task, specific test, and professionals' judgment can influence the assessment of students who are culturally and/or linguistically diverse. Awareness of these issues should enhance our assessment procedures.

ACTIVITIES

1. Discuss the pros and cons of formal and informal testing in the area of receptive language.
2. Discuss the pros and cons of formal and informal testing in the area of expressive language.
3. Compare and contrast two formal measures of receptive vocabulary.
4. Compare and contrast two measures of pragmatic language.
5. Discuss the pros and cons of dynamic assessment.
6. Discuss how the issue of task familiarity can affect test performance.
7. What research information can increase the fairness of language assessment?

WEB RESOURCES

http://www. asha.org/public/speech/disorders
http://www.nidcd.nih.gov/health/voice/autism.asp
http://www.fragilex.org/html/speech.htm
http://www.apraxia-kids.org
http://www.ldonline.org/indepth/speech
http://www.hyperlexia.org
http://www.nlda.org
http://www.ndss.org

REFERENCES

Bankson, N. W. (1990). *Bankson Language Screening Test*—2s. Austin, TX: PRO-ED.

Bebout, L., & Arthur, B. (1992). Cross-cultural attitudes toward speech disorders. *Journal of Speech and Hearing Research, 25,* 45–52.

Bloom, L., & Lahey, M. (1978). Language development and language disorders. New York: Wiley.

Boehm, A. E. (2000). *Boehm Test of Basic Concepts*—3rd ed. (BTBC-3). San Antonio, TX: Psychological Corporation.

Bray, C. M. & Wiig, E. H. (1987). *Let's Talk Inventory for Children*. San Antonio, TX: Psychological Corporation.

Brown, R. (1973). *A first language: The early stages.* Cambridge, MA: Harvard University Press.

Brownell, R. (2000a). *Expressive One-Word Picture Vocabulary Test.* (2000 ed.). Novato, CA: Academic Therapy.

Brownell, R. (2000b). *Receptive One-Word Picture Vocabulary Test.* (2000 ed.). Novato, CA: Academic Therapy.

Campbell, T., Dollaghan, C., Needleman, H., & Janosky, J. (1997). Reducing bias in language assessment: Processing-dependent measures. *Journal of Speech, Language, and Hearing Research, 40,* 519–525.

Carrow-Woolfolk, E. (1974). *Carrow Elicited Language Inventory.* Chicago: Riverside.

Carrow-Woolfolk, E. C. (1999). *Test of Auditory Comprehension of Language*—III. (TACL-3). Austin, TX: PRO-ED.

Cole, P. A., & Taylor, O. L. (1990). Performance on working class African-American children on three tests of articulation. *Language, Speech, and Hearing Services in Schools, 21,* 171–176.

Craig, H. K., & Washington, J. A. (2000). An assessment battery for identifying language impairments in African American children. *Journal of Speech, Language, and Hearing Research, 43*(2), 366–380.

Craig, H. K., Washington, J. A., & Thompson-Porter, C. (1998). Performances of young African American children on two comprehension tasks. *Journal of Speech, Language, and Hearing Research, 41,* 445–457.

Dunn, L. M., & Dunn, D. M. (2007). *Peabody Picture Vocabulary Test—4.* (PPVT-IV). Circle Pines, MN: American Guidance Service.

Dunn, L. M., Lugo, D. E., Padilla, E. R., & Dunn, L. E. (1986). *TVIP: Test de Vocabulario en Imagenes Peabody.* Circle Pines, MN: American Guidance Service.

Goldman, R., & Fristoe, M. (2000). *Goldman-Fristoe Test of Articulation* (2nd ed.). Circle Pines, MN: American Guidance Service.

Goldman, R., Fristoe, M., & Woodcock, R. (1970). *Goldman-Fristoe-Woodcock Test of Auditory Discrimination.* Circle Pines, MN: American Guidance Service.

Gutierrez-Clellen, V. F., & Pena, E. (2001). Dynamic assessment of diverse children: A tutorial. *Language, Speech, and Hearing Services in Schools, 32,* 212–224.

Gutierrez-Clellen, V. F., Restrepo, M. A., Bedore, L. M., Pena, E., & Anderson, R. (2000). Language sample analysis in Spanish-speaking children: Methodological considerations. *Language, Speech, and Hearing Services in Schools, 31*(1), 88–98.

Hammill, D., Brown, V. L., Larson, S., & Wiederholt, J. L. (2007). *Test of Adolescent and Adult Language*—Fourth Edition. (TOAL-4). Circle Pines, MN: American Guidance Service.

Hammill, D. D., & Newcomer, P. L. (2008). *Test of language development*—4. (TOLD-4), *Intermediate.* Austin, TX: PRO-ED.

Hulit, L. M., & Howard, M. R. (2006). *Born to talk: An introduction to speech and language development* (4th ed.). Boston: Allyn & Bacon.

Kayser, H. (1995). *Bilingual speech-language pathology: An Hispanic focus.* San Diego, CA: Singular.

Lee, L. L. (1974). *Developmental sentence analysis.* Evanston, IL: Northwestern University Press.

Lidz, C., & Pena, E. D. (1996). Dynamic assessment: The model, its relevance as nonbiased approach, and its application to Latin American preschool children. *Language, Speech, and Hearing Services in Schools, 27,* 367–372.

Linares, T. (1981). Rules for calculating mean length of utterance in morphemes for Spanish. In J. Erickson & D. Omark (Eds.), *Communication assessment of the bilingual bicultural child* (pp. 291–295). Baltimore: University Park Press.

Mattes, L. J., & Omark, D. R. (1991). *Speech and language assessment for the bilingual handicapped* (2nd ed.). Oceanside, CA: Academic Communication Associates.

McGregor, K. K., Williams, D., Hearst, S., & Johnson, A. C. (1997). The use of contrastive analysis in distinguishing difference from disorder: A tutorial. *American Journal of Speech-Language Pathology, 6*(3), 45–56.

McLean, J., & Snyder-McLean, L. (1978). *A transactional approach to early language training.* Columbus, OH: Merrill.

Newcomer, P. L., & Hammill, D. D. (2008). *Test of Language Development—Primary:4.* (TOLD-P:4). Austin, TX: PRO-ED.

Owens, R. E. (2004). *Language development: An introduction* (7th ed.). Needham Heights, MA: Allyn & Bacon.

Pena, E. D., & Quinn, R. (1997). Task familiarity: Effects on the test performance of Puerto Rican and African American Children. *Language, Speech, and Hearing in Schools, 28,* 323–332.

Penegra, L. M. (2000). *Your values, my values: Multicultural services in developmental disabilities.* Baltimore: Brookes.

Phelps-Terasaki, D., & Phelps-Gunn, T. (1992). *Test of Pragmatic Language.* Austin, TX: PRO-ED.

Polloway, E. A., Miller, L., & Smith, T. E. C. (2004). *Language instruction for students with disabilities* (3rd ed.). Denver: Love.

Prutting, C. (1981). Assessing communicative behavior using a language sample. In J. Erickson & D. Omark (Eds.), *Communication assessment of the bilingual bicultural child* (pp. 90–93). Baltimore: University Park Press.

Rhyner, P. M., Kelly, D., Brantley, A. L., & Krueger, D. M. (1999). Screening low-income African American children using the BLT-2S and the SPELT-P. *American Journal of Speech-Language Pathology, 8,* 44–52.

Roberts, J. E., Medley, L. P., Swartzfager, J. L., & Neebe, E. C. (1997). Assessing the communication of African American one-year-olds using the Communication and Symbolic Behavior Scales. *American Journal of Speech-Language Pathology, 6*(2), 59–65.

Robinson-Zanartu, C. (1996). Serving Native American children and families: Considering cultural variables. *Language, Speech, and Hearing in Schools, 27,* 373–384.

Rodekohr, R., & Haynes, W. (2001). Differentiating dialect from disorder: A comparison of two processing tasks and a standardized language test. *Journal of Communication Disorders, 34,* 1–18.

Roseberry-McKibbin, C. (1994). Assessment and intervention for children with limited English proficiency and language disorders. *American Journal of Speech Language Pathology, September.*

Roseberry-McKibbin, C. A., & Eicholtz, G. (1994). Serving children with limited English proficiency in the schools: A national survey. *Language, Speech, and Hearing Services in Schools, 25,* 156–164.

Roth, F., & Spekman, N. (1984). Assessing the pragmatic abilities of children. Part 1: Organizational framework and assessment parameters. *Journal of Speech and Hearing Disorders, 49,* 2–11.

Rowland, C. (1996). *Communication Matrix.* Portland, OR: Oregon Health Sciences University.

Saenz, T. I., & Huer, M. B. (2003). Testing strategies involving least biased language assessment of bilingual children. *Communication Disorders Quarterly, 24*(4), 184–194.

Schane, S. (1973). *Generative phonology.* Upper Saddle River, NJ: Prentice Hall.

Schiff-Myers, N. B. (1992). Considering arrested language development and language loss in the assessment of second language learners. *Language, Speech, and Hearing Services in Schools, 23,* 28–33.

Seymour, H. N., Bland-Stewart, L., & Green, L. J. (1998). Difference versus deficit in child African American English. *Language, Speech, and Hearing Services in Schools, 29,* 96–108.

Spinelli, C. G. (2006). *Classroom assessment for students with special needs in inclusive settings* (2nd ed.). Upper Saddle River: Merrill/Pearson Education.

Ukrainetz, T. A., Harpell, S., Walsh, C., & Coyle, C. (2000). A preliminary investigation of dynamic assessment with Native American kindergarteners. *Language, Speech, and Hearing Services in Schools, 31*(2), 142–154.

Van Dijk, J. (1966). The first steps of the deaf-blind child toward language. *International Journal for the Education of the Blind, 15*(4), 112–114.

Wetherby, A. M., Allen, L., Cleary, J., Kublin, K., & Goldstein, H. (2002). Validity and reliability of the communication and symbolic behavior scales developmental profile with very young children. *Journal of Speech, Language, and Hearing Research, 45,* 1202–1218.

Wetherby, A., & Prizant, B. (2002). *Communication and Symbolic Behavior Scales Developmental Profile—First Normed Edition.* Baltimore: Paul H. Brookes.

Wiig, E. H., & Semel, E. (1984). *Language assessment and intervention for the learning disabled* (2nd ed.). New York: Merrill/Macmillan.

Williams, K. T. (2007). *Expressive Vocabulary Test-2.* Circle Pines, MN: American Guidance Service.

Yavas, M., & Goldstein, B. (1998). Phonological assessment and treatment of bilingual speakers. *American Journal of Speech-Language Pathology, 7,* 49–60.

Additional Considerations

Early Childhood

Phyllis LeDosquet

Service delivery: The way in which early intervention is provided for young children.

Infants and toddlers: Children who are between the ages of birth to 3 years.

Developmental delay: Term used to state that a child is showing development at a younger age than what is typical for the child's chronological age.

Noncategorical: Does not fit into any specific disability category.

Multidisciplinary: Term used to describe a group of professionals that evaluate a child independently and share their results with each other and the parents.

Transdisciplinary: Term used to describe a group of professionals who share roles and cross disciplines when evaluating a child.

Functional development: Skills that a child uses to interact with the environment.

Developmental domains: Categories that describe a specific group of skills.

Motor development: Skills that a child has that allow movement of the body, including gross motor (all of the larger muscle movements) and fine motor (arm, hand, and finger movement).

Language development: The communication skills of a child, including receptive (understanding what is said) and expressive (using words) language.

Cognitive development: The overall knowledge that a child has, including memory and the ability to solve everyday problems.

Self-help development: The skills that allow a child to independently take care of him- or herself, including dressing, toileting, eating, etc.

Social-emotional development: The skills that allow a child to interact with other individuals.

Sensory-motor development: The use of senses and movement to interact with the environment; sensory and motor functions.

Categorical disability: One of 13 disability areas as recognized by IDEA, including motor impairment, cognitive impairment, speech and language impairment, autism, etc.

Chronological age: The actual physical age of a child, usually described in months and/or years.

Developmental age: The age that is typical of a child for a certain set of skills. For example, a child may be 3 years old but using skills as a 1-year-old would use them, so the child's developmental age would be 1.

Emerging skill: A skill that a child may not use all of the time, or has used only once or twice (the skill of walking would be emerging for a child who has taken one or two steps).

Natural environment: Place or places that are most familiar and comfortable to a child.

Early interventionist: Professional who provides services to young children (a special educator who works with a child and family in the child's home is called an interventionist).

Case Study: Assessing Missy

Missy is an 18-month-old toddler who was screened by an outreach program. She did not pass the screening, and your early intervention program was contacted. Several professionals (speech-language pathologist, occupational therapist, physical therapist, special education teacher, and social worker) form a transdisciplinary team and are available to assess Missy as needed. Your program has scheduled a home visit. Missy's mother has concerns regarding her development. She seems to be doing things at a later and slower rate than her two siblings, and she has some difficulties with feeding. Missy is the third child. She is a twin and was born with a bluish color; the delivery was two months premature. Her mother is her primary caregiver with support from her grandmother, who babysits when Missy's mother works at her part-time job. Most children's families in her neighborhood are at poverty level. Many children are from single-parent families with multiple siblings. Like Missy's mother, many parents in this neighborhood did not finish high school.

What information would you like the team to collect from Missy's family?

What formal tests would the team use?

What informal assessment tools would the team use?

How will this information be connected to service delivery?

By the end of the chapter, you should be able to discuss the questions posed in the case study about Missy. You should be able to name and explain domains and give examples of items involved in the commonly used standardized and criterion-referenced tools. You should be able to explain the process that assessors use to gather information regarding early childhood assessment, such as play-based assessment, assessment conducted in the natural environment, family assessment, and judgment-based assessment. You should be able to identify cultural and linguistic factors that affect family-centered multidisciplinary early childhood assessment. Finally, you should be knowledgeable of the fact that Part B of IDEA refers to service delivery for children between the ages of 3 and 5, and Part C mandates program guidelines for infants and toddlers at birth and through the age of 3.

This chapter addresses CEC Standard 1 (foundations), 2 (development and characteristics of learners), 5 (learning environments and social interactions), 6 (language), 8 (assessment), and 10 (collaboration). Information regarding legal issues related to early childhood, human development and varying ability, active engagement and learning environments, communication skills, formal and informal assessment, and collaboration with families contribute to meeting these goals.

DEFINING EARLY CHILDHOOD

FEDERAL LEGISLATION

The philosophical belief that education should be provided to young children with special needs emerged from Great Society programs established by President Lyndon Johnson in the 1960s. Head Start programs were established to serve disadvantaged children who lived in poverty. Poverty was believed to be the underlying cause for developmental problems in children, and without intervention, such children were at risk for academic failure when they entered public education.

This was also the time when approximately 20,000 babies were born with disabilities due to their in-utero exposure to the rubella virus. Because there were few programs and limited services available, funding was legislated for assessment, programming, and teacher training in the area of special education (Fewell, 2000).

In 1986, amendments to the Education for All Handicapped Children Act included funding for special education programs for children from birth to age 5. The Individuals with Disabilities Act Amendments (IDEA 1997) revised program guidelines one more time. It included Part B, which outlined service delivery to young children between the ages of 3 and 5 years, and Part C, which outlined the guidelines for services for infants, toddlers, and their families.

Certain components of Part C set it apart from the other guidelines of IDEA. First, it requires all states to have a clear definition of the term *developmental delay* and allows programs to serve children without having to label them according to the 13 categorical disabilities. The second unique component is that the comprehensive assessment includes an assessment of family needs. These family needs are addressed in the individual plan called the individual family service plan (IFSP) because it is family-focused rather than only child-focused.

Part B is an extension of service guidelines for students between the ages of 5 and 21. However, it also allows eligibility under the category of developmental delay (age 3 to 9), as well as the other disability categories listed in IDEA. Educational programs that provide services to this age group are given the option of writing an individualized education program (IEP) or an individual family service plan (IFSP). However, because the majority of programs are housed in public education settings, the IEP is the plan used to design the child's program (Individuals with Disabilities Education Act Amendments, 1997). See Chapter 1 for more information regarding legal issues.

Breakpoint Practice

1. If a child was born in 1955 and was diagnosed with Down syndrome, what educational services would he or she receive?
2. If a child was born in 1966 and was diagnosed with blindness, what educational services would he or she receive?
3. If a child was born in 1975 with severe hearing loss, what educational services would he or she receive?

Screening

IDEA 2004 requires that all states have an extensive plan in place for locating and screening infants, toddlers, and young children who may be at risk for developmental delay. An all-inclusive process of identifying and referring all children who may be in need of special education services is referred to as Child Find. An integral component of Child Find is public awareness of typical and atypical development of infants, toddlers, and young children. This awareness is accomplished through a variety of media, including television, radio, local newspapers, and pamphlets. Key screening agencies include hospitals, social services, and public health agencies.

Screening is a less involved method of assessment than the comprehensive evaluation. It is an efficient method for recognition of indicators of possible developmental delay (Lerner, Lowenthal, & Egan, 2003). It is important that screening be understood as only part of the identification process; it should not be used as the sole eligibility criterion (Meisels & Provence, 1989). Screenings can be conducted en masse (large-scale programs using specifically designed screening instruments) or selectively (targeting specific groups such as children in poverty areas or all children prior to kindergarten entry).

Breakpoint Practice

1. If a 2-year-old child was not yet walking, where can the parent go to receive help or advice?
2. What kind of testing would take place for a 3-year-old who has not attended preschool and whose parent is concerned that the child prefers to play alone and doesn't yet use language?
3. Jason is 6 months old and doesn't look at toys or at faces. His parents aren't concerned because they say that he prefers to listen to sounds rather than look at things. His Aunt Jill thinks there may be more to the issue than learning style preference. What can she do to help the situation?

Comprehensive Assessment

If a child's screening indicates problem areas of development, a comprehensive multi-disciplinary evaluation takes place. IDEA does not define the specific kinds of assessment used in the comprehensive evaluation. Instead, it states, "a timely, comprehensive, multidisciplinary evaluation of the functioning of each infant or toddler with a disability in the State, and a family-directed identification of the needs of each family of such an infant or toddler, to assist appropriately in the development of the infant or toddler" must be conducted (IDEA Sec 635.3).

McConnell (2000) states that "assessment is more than testing" (p. 2). It is an all-inclusive process of gathering information that will identify the needs of the infant or toddler with a disability. The key is to find the appropriate means for gathering the data needed to determine whether the child qualifies for early intervention services (McConnell, 2000). Each state is given the freedom to decide who will conduct assessments, and what assessments and data collection methods will be used to gather the necessary information.

Infants and toddlers qualify for early intervention services if they meet the federal definition criteria for "infant or toddler with a disability" or (at the state's discretion) "at-risk infant or toddler." According to IDEA, an infant or toddler who is at risk is defined as

> an individual under 3 years of age who would be at risk of experiencing a substantial developmental delay if early intervention services were not provided to the individual (IDEA Sec. 632.1).

An infant or toddler with a disability is defined as

> (i) an individual under 3 years of age who needs early intervention services because the individual is experiencing developmental delays, as measured by appropriate diagnostic instruments and procedures in 1 or more of the areas of cognitive development, physical development, communication development, social or emotional development, and adaptive development, or
>
> (ii) has a diagnosed physical or mental condition that has a high probability of resulting in developmental delay; and
>
> (iii) may also include, at a state's discretion—
>
>> (i) at-risk infants and toddlers.

Breakpoint Practice

1. Who would be part of a multidisciplinary team for an infant who has been born with a severe physical impairment?

2. Nine-month-old Matt was born prematurely and has been in and out of the hospital for most of his short life. He was screened by a local agency and found to have problems in all areas of development. He is again in the hospital due to respiratory infection. When should his comprehensive assessment take place?

3. Four-year-old Maria has been referred for a comprehensive assessment. She speaks only Spanish. The early interventionist who was going to assess her abilities does not speak Spanish. What should the interventionist do?

IFSP Development

Once it has been determined that an infant or toddler qualifies for early intervention programming, the assessment process continues as information is collected to identify the specific strengths and needs of the infant and of the family. IDEA states that the infant or toddler and the infant or toddler's family receive

> (1) a multidisciplinary assessment of the unique strengths and needs of the infant or toddler and the identification of services appropriate to meet such needs;
> (2) a family-directed assessment of the resources, priorities, and concerns of the family and the identification of the supports and services necessary to enhance the family's capacity to meet the developmental needs of the infant or toddler (IDEA, Part C, Sec. 636.a.1-2).

This involves an even more extensive and intensive evaluation of the needs of the child and should include curriculum-referenced or criterion-referenced tools that examine the accomplishment of specific developmental skills (Lerner et al., 2003). IDEA, Part C requires that the IFSP include a statement of the infant's or toddler's present level of functioning in all developmental domains (IDEA, Part C, Sec. 636.d), including motor development (fine- and gross-motor skills), language development (receptive and expressive), cognitive development, self-help (adaptive) development, social and emotional development, and sensory skills (Lerner et al., 2003). IDEA also states that the IFSP be evaluated at least once annually and that the family receive a program review at least every six months.

Breakpoint Practice

1. What skill areas should be assessed more extensively once the child has been identified as needing services?
2. How can assessment take place informally?
3. When would it be appropriate to test a child informally rather than formally?
4. How should an early interventionist learn about the strengths and needs of the family?
5. How often should the IFSP for a 3-month-old be evaluated?
6. How often should the IFSP for an 18-month-old be evaluated?

STANDARDIZED TESTING OF YOUNG CHILDREN

When services were first mandated for young children with special needs, few assessment instruments were available for the diagnosis of a disability. Although IDEA did not specify which assessments should be used to identify the young child with disabilities, it was common to use a standardized assessment tool such as the Bayley Scales of Infant Development. Unfortunately, this assessment was not always used appropriately. It was originally designed to assess infants up to 30 months of age, but it was used inappropriately to assess older children who were suspected of functioning below 30 months of age (McLean, Wolery, & Bailey, 2004).

Standardized tools designed for screening were also used to qualify young children for enrollment in programs (McLean et al., 2004). Due to advancements in technology and statistical analysis, the development of assessment tools, including standardized assessment, has changed considerably over the past decades (Fewell, 2000). However, the question still arises about the appropriateness of using standardized tools as measurements of ability in young children. Standardized tools should "have been validated for the specific purpose for which they are used; [be] administered by trained and knowledgeable personnel; should be administered in accordance with any instructions provided by the producer of such tests" (IDEA, Part B, Sec 614.3.b.i-iii).

Standardized testing of young children has been criticized as lacking social validity (Myers, McBride, & Peterson, 1996). Social validity refers to the usefulness of an assessment for planning appropriate programs for children. Myers et al. (1996) divided 40 children under 3 years of age into two groups; they assessed one group using a multidisciplinary, standardized assessment and the other using a transdisciplinary play-based assessment. They then compared the processes through the perceptions of parents and staff, time factors, and functionality. The results indicated that the transdisciplinary play-based approach was far superior to the multidisciplinary standardized assessment process in social validity. Meyers et al. (1996) also stated that one of the reasons why the transdisciplinary play-based approach is superior to the multidisciplinary standardized method is that it is more time efficient. Sometimes it takes several weeks for the various professionals to schedule appointments and then work through typical developmental issues that affect the lives of children, including their own routines, illness, transportation issues, etc. (Meyers et al., 1996).

Neisworth and Bagnato (1992) argued that the measurement of intellectual functioning of infants is a measurement of sensorimotor development. When intelligence is measured at an older age, however, it no longer emphasizes sensorimotor ability; it is a measurement based on language. Although this incongruence is recognized by researchers, they have failed to find characteristics that remain consistent throughout the childhood years (Neisworth & Bagnato, 1992).

Standardized testing of the intelligence of children with disabilities is especially precarious because skill level varies extensively within a categorical disability and across disabilities. A child with a hearing impairment will test quite differently than a child with visual impairment or motor impairment.

Breakpoint Practice

1. Describe a situation where standardized testing should be included in the comprehensive, multidisciplinary assessment of a child under age 5.

2. Give an example of how standardized testing may not be valid for a young child who is visually impaired.

3. Twenty-month-old Emmy has just been taken from her home and placed in foster care due to severe physical abuse. Describe characteristics that would hinder accurate results in standardized testing.

Table 10.1 lists tests for assessment in early childhood. We will discuss several of them in the following chapter sections.

Standardized Tests

The Bayley Scales of Infant Development—Second Edition (BSID-II) (Bayley, 1993) is a commonly used standardized assessment tool that was originally designed to assess infants and toddlers from birth to age 30 months. The revised version has been expanded to assess infants and toddlers up to age 42 months.

The BSID-II consists of three separate scales: (1) mental scale, (2) motor scale, and (3) behavior rating scale (BRS). The mental scale assesses cognitive development, including memory, habituation, problem-solving skills, number concepts, the ability to generalize information, and the ability to classify objects. It also assesses language skills, such as sound production, and social and emotional development. The motor scale assesses skills that depend on gross- (large) and fine- (small) motor muscle groups. Examples of gross-motor items include rolling, sitting, crawling, and walking. Fine-motor items include

Table 10.1 Tests in the Area of Early Childhood

Test Name	Company	Areas Assessed	Age	Time to Administer	Type
Bayley Scales of Infant Development (2nd ed.)	The Psychological Corporation	Cognitive	0–42 months	45–60 minutes	Norm-referenced
Battelle Developmental Inventory—2	Riverside	Five developmental domains	0–7 years, 11 months	1–2 hours	Norm-referenced
Peabody Motor Scales—2	Curriculum Associates	Gross motor, fine motor	0–5 years	Varies	Norm-referenced
Brigance Inventory of Early Development—II	Curriculum Associates	Five developmental domains	0–7 years	20–55 minutes	Criterion-referenced
Developmental Activities Screening Inventory—II	PRO-ED	Cognitive, fine motor	1–60 months	8–9 minutes	Criterion-referenced
Early Learning Accomplishment Profile	Kaplan Early Learning Company	Five developmental domains	0–36 months	1½ hrs	Criterion-referenced
Learning Accomplishment Profile (3rd ed.)	Kaplan Early Learning Company	Five developmental domains	36–72 months	1½ hrs	Criterion-referenced
Learning Accomplishment Profile—Diagnostic	Kaplan Early Learning Company	Cognitive, language, fine motor, gross motor	30–72 months	1½ hrs	Norm-referenced
Transdisciplinary Play-Based Assessment	Paul H. Brookes	Cognitive, language, social-emotional, sensorimotor	Infancy–6 years	55–75 minutes	Curriculum-referenced
Carolina Curriculum for Infants and Toddlers with Special Needs (2nd ed.)	Paul H. Brookes	Five developmental domains	0–24 months	20 minutes	Curriculum-referenced
Carolina Curriculum for Preschoolers	Paul H. Brookes	Five developmental domains	24–60 months	20 minutes	Curriculum-referenced
Callier-Azusa Scale	University of Texas—Dallas	Motor, perceptual, daily living, communication, cognitive, social	0–6 years	45 minutes	Criterion-referenced
Hawaii Early Learning Profile (HELP)	VORT Corporation	Five developmental domains	0–60 months	½ to 1½ hours	Curriculum-referenced
Receptive-Expressive Emergent Language (REEL-3)	PRO-ED	Prelinguistic skills	1–36 months	20 minutes	Norm-referenced
Preschool Language Scale (PLS-3)	The Psychological Corporation	Expressive and receptive language skills	1–6 years	15–30 minutes	Standardized
Peabody Picture Vocabulary Test (PPVT-IV)	American Guidance Service	Receptive language	2½–adult	10–15 minutes	Standardized

finger usage, dexterity, prewriting skills, object manipulation, and imitation. The BRS looks specifically at the behavior of the child during testing that will assist in the ultimate interpretation of the results attained from the mental and motor scales.

The assessment starting point is determined at the discretion of the administrator and is based on the child's chronological or suspected developmental age. The tool is structured as sets of skills for age ranges (e.g., set one of the mental scale begins with item 1 and ends with item 22). Five passed items in a set constitutes a basal score. A ceiling is reached when the child does not receive credit for three or more items in a set. A raw score is obtained by adding the passed items, including the items below the basal item. The raw score can then be converted to a mental development index (MDI) score on the mental scale and a psychomotor development index (PDI) score on the motor scale. A protocol is also provided; it gives a visual display of the items passed and failed, and an overall developmental level of functioning or developmental age.

The BISD-II used a normative random sample of 1,700 infants and toddlers nationwide and included children from a variety of ethnic groups and cultural backgrounds. Test reliability, which is discussed extensively in the testing manual, was established using coefficient alpha, standard error of measurement, confidence intervals, test-retest stability, and interscorer agreement. The manual also includes comprehensive information supporting the test validity, including content, construct, predictive, and discriminant validity. The test has its own set of testing materials that are used for specific test items. It is imperative that the materials be used as specified in the test manual. It is also crucial that the items be administered as directed in the manual and the provided criteria be used for the scoring of each test item.

The test administrator should be properly trained to use this instrument and have a general knowledge base in test administration and interpretation. This person should also understand the characteristics of young children, especially those with cultural backgrounds similar to the children who are being tested. Failure to comply with standardized procedures will negatively affect validity.

The author emphasizes that the BSID-II should not be used to measure deficit in specific areas of development. The test is not designed as a tool that can be adapted or modified to accommodate the needs of a child with a physical or sensory impairment. Therefore, the author states that it is not appropriate for assessment of children with these disabilities.

The Battelle Developmental Inventory—2 (BDI-2) (Newborg, 2005) is a standardized tool that was developed in 1984 and revised in 2005 and was the cooperative effort of persons from several disciplines. It consists of 450 test items (100 screening items) that assess skill development in the five developmental domains, labeled as: (1) personal social (adult interaction, peer interaction, self-concept, and social role), (2) adaptive (self-care and personal responsibility), (3) motor (gross, fine, and perceptual), (4) communication (receptive and expressive), and (5) cognitive (attention and memory, reasoning and academic skills, and perception and concepts).

The BDI-2 is a uniquely designed standardized assessment tool because it uses a 3-point (0-1-2) scoring system and allows some credit to be given if a skill appears to be emerging (1). Information is collected through test administration, parent interview, teacher interview, and teacher observations within the natural environment. It also allows for a variety of test administration modifications for children who have sensory or physical disability.

This assessment also includes a screening tool that can be administered in 10 to 30 minutes, depending on the age of the child. The comprehensive exam takes 1 to 2 hours. The BDI-2 can be administered by educational staff and is used primarily for identifying children with developmental delays and outlining their specific strengths and needs. Scoring of the BDI-2 is less structured than the BSID-II because, although instructions are given for administration, adaptations and modifications are allowed based on the child's disability. A script for administration is provided, and a Spanish translation is available.

Test administration begins at the suspected age of development of the child. If the screening was used to determine a need for further assessment, it is used to find a starting point for the full BDI-2 assessment. A basal score is established when a child receives a score of 2 on three consecutive items. A ceiling is attained when the child receives a score of 0 on three consecutive items.

The BDI-2 describes normative information that appears appropriate. Students with disabilities were included in the norm sample. Reliability was determined with internal consistency, standard error of measurement, test-retest reliability, and interrater reliability. The instrument includes content, construct, and concurrent validity.

The Peabody Developmental Motor Scales—2 (PDMS-2) (Folio & Fewell, 2000) is a standardized tool that was developed to assess the gross- and fine-motor development of children from birth to age 5. Results indicate gaps in motor development and can provide justification for intervention in the areas of concern. Initially, the authors tested children who were deaf-blind and, as a result, incorporated adaptations into test administration. The specific gross-motor skills tested with the PDMS include reflexes, stationary locomotion, and object manipulation. The fine-motor portion tests the use of small muscles, such as in the subtests of grasping and visual-motor integration.

A kit is provided with the assessment that contains most of the materials needed to administer the items. However, the remaining materials are typically found in homes and educational environments. Test administrators of the PDMS-2 should be familiar with general assessment process. Possible assessment administrators include professionals from a variety of disciplines and instructional aides or volunteers. The person who administers the test should be very familiar with it so that it is administered with ease.

Items are scored with a success (+2), resemblance of the skill (+1), or a fail (0). A basal score is established when the child successfully scores 2 on all of the items at one level. A ceiling is attained when the child scores a 0 or 1 on all items at a given level or scores a 2 on only one item in the given level. A raw score is converted to a percentile rank, a standard score, or an overall age equivalence in gross-motor and fine-motor development separately, or to a mean motor age equivalent score, which is an average of gross- and fine-motor development.

The updated test appears to have adequate norming. Content validity and construct validity are provided. Reliability was established through standard error of measurement, test-retest reliability, and interrater reliability. Wang, Liao, and Hsieh (2006) reported high test-retest reliability for students with cerebral palsy, ages 2 to 5.

Peabody Picture Vocabulary Test—Fourth Edition (PPVT-IV) is a standardized instrument used to measure the receptive language skills of children starting at age 2, and can be used appropriately through adulthood. The PPVT was first published in 1959 and was one of the first assessments used to assess language development specifically.

The PPVT-IV is organized into 20 categories, including verbs, adjectives, and nouns. Each item is in a multiple-choice format, with the child listening to the examiner's request and choosing the correct response from a display of four pictures. The items are organized into sets, with all of the items within a set being administered to the child. Basal and ceiling information is established according to sets; the basal level is the set with one or no errors, and the ceiling is the set with eight or more errors. Each correct response is worth 1 point. (See Chapter 9 for technical information regarding this test.)

The unique characteristic of this assessment is that it does not require the child to use reading skills or expressive language skills to complete the test. Also, because of the size and contrast of the pictures (black outline of color pictures), many children with visual impairment can be assessed accurately (Dunn & Dunn, 2007).

Preschool Language Scale—3 (PLS-3) is a standardized assessment that evaluates language development in children between 2 weeks and 6 years of age. The complete assessment consists of two subscales, auditory and expressive communication, and it includes three additional measures: the articulation screener, language sample checklist (LSC), and family information and suggestions form (FISF). The LSC assesses conversational speech; the FISF, which is completed by the parents, examines communication in the home environment. It also gives the parents an opportunity to share their concerns and needs regarding the child's communication.

The PLS-3 is scored easily, with a check for a successful response and a minus for an item to which the child responds incorrectly. If the child does not respond, NR is used. The information is transferred to a supplied graph protocol that allows the speech-language clinician to compare the child's scores visually. The assessment provides standardized scores, percentile ranks, age equivalents in the areas of auditory and expressive communication, and an overall total language score. The PLS-3 manual includes scoring instructions and guidelines regarding the severity of the child's language disability.

The PLS-3 manual shares information about internal test-retest and interrater reliability. It also addresses concurrent and predictive validity (Zimmerman, Steiner, & Pond, 1997).

A unique characteristic of this assessment is that the manual includes guidelines for assessing young children with disabilities such as hearing impairments, physical impairments, and severe developmental delay. It also provides a worksheet that allows the clinician to use the PLS-3 results to develop IFSP goals and objectives.

The Receptive-Expressive Language Test (REEL-3) is a standardized assessment of receptive and expressive language development in infants and toddlers through age 3. The results are provided as an expressive language age, receptive language age, or a combined language age. Standard scores, percentile ranks, and age equivalents are also provided. The REEL-3 was normed with a sample size of 1,112 infants and toddlers across the nation. This sample was stratified according to age, gender, race, ethnicity, and geographic location (Bzoch & League, 2003).

Breakpoint Practice

1. Which standardized assessment can be used with a newborn who was diagnosed with Down syndrome?

2. Which standardized assessment can best measure the abilities of an infant who was born 3 months premature?

3. When would you use the Peabody Developmental Motor Scales instead of the Battelle Developmental Inventory to assess the development of a young child?

4. When would you use the Battelle Developmental Inventory instead of the Bayley Scales of Infant Development to assess the development of a young child?

CRITERION- AND CURRICULUM-REFERENCED ASSESSMENT

Educators are most concerned with how assessment information will assist them in planning the program for a child. Criterion-referenced assessment does not compare the child to other children of the same age, as does norm-referenced assessment. Instead, it focuses on individual strengths and weaknesses in skill development.

Although the curriculum-referenced assessment is actually a criterion-referenced instrument, it differs because it is designed specifically in accordance with the classroom curriculum.

The Brigance Inventory of Early Development II (Brigance IED-II) (Brigance, 1985) was developed in 1978 as a criterion-referenced tool that assesses the developmental skills of children birth through 7 years of age. It is unique because it can be used as a standardized option with certain identified skills. The developmental sections are labeled as pre-ambulatory motor skills and behaviors, gross-motor skills and behaviors, fine-motor skills and behaviors, self-help skills, speech and language skills, general knowledge and comprehension, and social-emotional development; and the early academic sections include readiness, basic reading, manuscript, and basic math.

The Callier-Azusa Scale is a developmental assessment tool that was intended specifically to evaluate the skills of children between the ages of birth and 8 years who were deaf-blind and those who had a severe and profound disability. It is categorized into six areas of development, including directions, motor, perceptual, daily living, communication, and social development. There are 18 subscales within these skill areas. The scale is criterion-referenced and is in developmental sequence. It is designed to assess a child's developmental skills primarily through observation. However, direct instruction with modifications applied, such as communication systems, can assist in attaining assessment results (Stillman, 1978). For more information on this tool, see Chapter 9.

Developmental Activities Screening Inventory—(DASI-II) is a criterion-referenced screening tool that has been used to look at specific cognitive and fine-motor skills of preschool children. It assesses development between the ages of 1 and 60 months of age and can be administered easily to children who are nonverbal. The specific areas of focus are fine-motor skills and cognitive skills, including cause-effect, means-end, association, number concepts, size discrimination, memory, spatial relationships, object function, and seriation. An advantage of this assessment is that testing modifications are provided for various disabilities.

The package includes a materials kit that contains all of the materials needed to complete this assessment. The manual also includes instructional strategies in the specific cognitive skill areas. Though this assessment is criterion-referenced, it uses a raw score that is converted into a developmental age and a developmental quotient (DQ). It is important that the DQ not be interpreted as being equivalent to IQ (Fewell & Langley, 1984).

The Early Learning Accomplishment Profile—3 (E-LAP-3) (Hardin & Peisner-Feinberg, 2002) and the Learning Accomplishment Profile—3 (LAP-3) (Hardin & Peisner-Feinberg, 2004) are criterion-referenced assessments that give a holistic picture of a child's level of development. The E-LAP-3 assesses the skills of infants and toddlers between the ages of 0 and 36 months. The LAP-R assesses children between 36 and 72 months of age.

The E-LAP-3 investigates the areas of gross motor (e.g., holds head up), fine motor (e.g., picks up spoon), cognitive (e.g., scribbles spontaneously), language (e.g., follows directions), self-help (e.g., takes off clothing), and social emotional (e.g., stops crying when picked up). The LAP-3 consists of the domains of gross motor, fine motor, prewriting, cognitive, language, self-help, and social emotional.

The Carolina Curriculum for Infants and Toddlers with Special Needs and the Carolina Curriculum for Preschoolers with Special Needs are curriculum-referenced assessments that assess the developmental skills in infants and toddlers who have severe to moderate disabilities from birth to 24 months and preschoolers through 5 years of age. All five developmental domains are assessed primarily through observation (Johnson-Martin, Jens, Attermeier, & Hacker, 1991).

David Mager/Pearson Learning Photo Studio

The Transdisciplinary Play-Based Assessment (TPBA) was first developed by Tony Linder in 1990. It is a curriculum-referenced assessment that assesses four developmental domains, including cognitive, language, social-emotional, and sensorimotor development, of young children between infancy and 6 years of age. This assessment is structured so that the evaluators can obtain information about the growth and development of a child at five levels of play. The person or persons who are assessing the child through this structure first arrange the toys and objects. The items for this setting are preselected to represent all domains of development. Linder (1993) organized the assessment process in five consecutive phases. In stage 1, the child initiates all of the play activities. In stage 2, the assessor initiates some, but not all, of the play activities. Stage 3 brings a peer into the play environment and is an optimal time to observe the social skills of the child. Stage 4 is play between the parents and the child, and Stage 5 concludes the play setting with a snack being served to the child and the peer.

The Hawaii Early Learning Profile (HELP) is a curriculum-referenced tool that measures the development of children from birth to 36 months of age. It covers six developmental domains, including cognitive, language, gross-motor, fine-motor, social-emotional, and self-help skills. All of the skills are age-sequenced. The HELP is designed as a play-based assessment, with the environment being prearranged by the evaluator.

The items on the HELP are scored as present, not present, emerging, atypical/dysfunctional, or not applicable. This information is then used to measure outcomes and to track progress over a period of time. A chart is available on which the evaluator can record the results of the assessment and then update the information as the child learns and develops new skills. An activities guide is also offered; it gives several ideas and activities for working on each of the skill items assessed on the HELP (Furuno, O'Reilly, Inatsuka, Hosaka, Allman, & Zeisloft-Falbey, 1987). Thus, there is a link to instruction.

The Play Assessment Scale (Fifth Revision) (Fewell, 1986) was developed to investigate play that indicated perceptual or conceptual skills. Condition I uses toys selected (four of eight are toys). The assessor facilitates the child's playing with the toys by using statements and then scores the child's interaction with the toys. Condition II involves the assessor's use of more detail in the instructions used.

> **Breakpoint Practice**
>
> 1. When is it appropriate to use a criterion-referenced assessment rather than a curriculum-referenced assessment to measure the progress of children in a self-contained early intervention classroom?
>
> 2. Which assessment would give the most comprehensive developmental information for a 2-year-old who has cerebral atrophy and hydrocephalus and who is blind?
>
> 3. Which assessment would provide the most comprehensive information for a young infant?
>
> 4. Which assessment would provide the most comprehensive information for a 3-year-old?
>
> 5. Which assessment would provide the most comprehensive information for a 5-year-old?

ASSESSMENT PROCEDURAL ISSUES

Authentic assessment of young children depends on several factors. First, the environment in which the assessment takes place is crucial in gathering accurate information about the child's abilities. Second, several data collection methods have been identified as best practice in understanding the true developmental levels of infants and toddlers. Third, federal law has mandated that families be involved in the assessment process and be allowed to provide pertinent information about the skills and abilities of their young children. Finally, federal law has mandated that assessment be sensitive to cultural differences among families and children with special needs.

Environment

Federal legislation amended IDEA to include specific guidelines that assure that services, including assessment, are provided to infants and toddlers with special needs in their natural environments. Frequently, the term *natural environment* has been misconstrued as meaning only in the child's home. However, natural environment includes any setting that is most used and preferred by families and their children with disabilities. (Turnbull, Turnbull, Erwin, & Soodak, 2006). It is the place where the child and family carry out everyday routines and activities. This may be a childcare center, a community center, or a grandparent's home. The key to the situation being natural is that it is very familiar and comfortable for the child.

Dunst, Hambry, Trivette, Raab, and Bruder (2000) concluded that in the natural environment, young children are more likely to engage in activities that are familiar and motivating to them. In natural environments, children connect with activities that have meaning, and optimal learning is the ultimate outcome. Dunst et al. (2000) also found that involvement and interest in activities increases in natural environments because learning is supported in various ways when carried out in everyday life and routines. Finally, the study concluded that children are more likely to refine the methods they presently use to connect with people and objects when they are in that natural environment, an environment that provides ample opportunities to employ those connections that enhance children's existing skills and support the evolution of new skills.

Campbell and Halbert (2002) completed a study in which 241 early intervention practitioners were asked to name their three wishes in creating changes in early intervention programs. Most reported that they would like service delivery to return to a center-based model, despite the ongoing research that supports home-based service delivery. From the group, practitioners with more than 10 years of experience were most vocal about returning to the center-based approach. Campbell and Halbert (2002) also reported that those with this amount of experience had originally worked in center-based programs. One could interpret this finding as providers who have difficulty changing or possibly feeling that there is a need to provide services more effectively.

Providing early intervention programming, including assessment in rural areas, is especially challenging if the family's home is several hours from the community that houses the early intervention program (Jung, McCormick, & Jolivette, 2004). It may take a full day to travel to and from a natural environment such as the family farm, and factors such as distance and weather conditions effect the timeliness of assessment completion (Jung et al., 2004) However, the key is to consider once again the semantics of the term *natural environment* and to be open to this setting as defined by what is ordinary and comfortable for the child. While home-based is not exclusively the natural environment, it continues to be considered the most likely option for what is best for the child.

Methods of Data Collection

As early as the 1960s, researchers advocated for the naturalistic approach to the intervention of young children. The naturalistic approach differs slightly from the philosophy of natural environment because it emphasizes the importance of examining the natural interactions and contacts between the young child and those with whom the child has an attachment or relationship (Bandura, 1969). Included in these contacts are teachers, and a close look at building programs around the natural routines within the educational setting and the embedded routines in the home environments with families (Barnett, Ehrhardt, Stollar, & Bauer, 1994) were warranted. In the 1990s, some referred to this collection of information as ecobehavioral analysis, an approach that carefully examined the multitude of factors within the child's social structure that affect the growth and development of the child (McConnell, 2000). Though the process label has changed and continues to change, the point that stays the same is that the place where children spend most of their time is the environment where educators can acquire the most accurate information about each child.

Play-Based Assessment

As educators and researchers began to realize the value of assessing the skills of young children in their natural environments, they also realized the value of assessing them as they participated in activities that were naturally engaging (Fewell, 1997). A child who is engaged is interacting with the environment in a way that is developmentally appropriate and appropriately connected to the given context of the environment (McWilliam & Bailey, 1995). Children learn as they maneuver and manipulate their environments according to their interests and curiosities; therefore, a child's work is play. Lerner et al. (2003) stated that "play is developmental, transdisciplinary, holistic and dynamic" (p. 86). The outcome of play is learning. It is the most genuine way in which a child interacts with the world. Play is inclusive of all areas of development, at all levels of development.

The play-based assessment concept is used in what programs have referred to as arena assessment (Myers et al., 1996). The arena assessment is a transdisciplinary approach that involves professionals from several backgrounds. With this method, professionals who are observing and evaluating the child come together as a team. One team member becomes the assessor; the other team members look on and record data as they see the child perform various skills. The assessor is cognizant of the developmental domains and attempts to facilitate play that elicits specific domain skills. The play-based method is time efficient as well as relaxed and natural for children. It allows parents and professionals to interact and share their judgment-based observations and perceptions and to validate or challenge each other's perspectives (Myers et al., 1996).

> ### Breakpoint Practice
>
> 1. How would you find out what the most natural environment is for a 3-year-old who has been referred for comprehensive assessment?
> 2. Would play-based assessment be appropriate for a child who has a severe cognitive disability?
> 3. How do natural environment and play-based assessment compliment each other?

INCLUDING FAMILIES IN THE ASSESSMENT PROCESS

IDEA 1997 and IDEA 2004 have been instrumental in recognizing parents as important participants in the assessment process. Informing parents of their rights as the guardians and primary caretakers of children was an instrumental step in understanding the positive effect that parent involvement can have on true understanding of the needs of the child. Legislators took this concept one step further when they revised the service delivery criteria and stated that parents had pertinent input that would assist in determining if the child indeed had a disability and, if so, the program needs.

Though the mandates have been in place for several years, the inclusion of parents has been a slow and many times difficult process. States have provided endless training on collaborating with parents of children who have special needs. Several textbooks have been written on the topic, and early childhood special education training programs require that at least one class be taken that looks at the specific needs of parents. Yet it continues to be a major barrier in the implementation of early intervention and an uncomfortable experience for both parents and educators. Bruder (2000) suggested that family-centered early intervention may fail because of the attitude among educators that they are the experts and the family and child are the clients (p. 110). While the expertise of interventionists in specific disability areas is appreciated, the wealth of family knowledge regarding the child's specific learning characteristics, routines, schedules, likes, and dislikes can have a powerful impact on the overall understanding and assessment of a child's strengths and needs (Bruder, 2000). Interventionists need to work through their own issues regarding the protection of their expertise. Once this is accomplished, their involvement in the assessment process as team players will be enhanced.

Frequently, parents are most comfortable when assessment takes place in their home, which is most likely the natural environment. Also, for many families who do not have transportation or who have other young children in the home, the home setting is the most accessible environment. Parents are in their own areas of comfort when in their homes, and this allows them to share their knowledge about the child (Bryant, Lyons, & Wasik, 1990). Also, the transdisciplinary, arena assessment process ideally includes the parent as a significant team member. A family member may be chosen to interact with the child during the assessment process, which would enhance the spontaneity of the child's responses (Guillory, Woll, & Nielson, 1994).

Turnbull et al. (2006) stated that the outcome of inclusion of families in service delivery, including evaluation, is the key to educators having an optimal perspective of the student and the student's needs. To understand the complete picture of the child's abilities and needs, one has to include the information of parents, who know the child in a variety of environments and situations. However, to include parents' information successfully as valid insight into the child's abilities, one has to be open to parents' viewpoints, needs, ideas, and perspectives. Only then will the result be authentic communication, mutual respect, and a balance of power among team members, including parents (Turnbull et. al., 2006).

The INSITE model was developed to provide appropriate at-home services to children who have multiple disabilities with sensory involvement. The major goals of this model were identifying individuals as soon as possible in order to interact with individuals and objects, using residual senses, and building communication skills (http://www.ed.gov/pubs/EPTW/eptw12/eptw12b.html, Morgan, 1992).

EMPOWERING PARENTS

Parents become an equal part of the assessment team when all parties involved clearly understand the intent of the communicated information. Clear communication is free of professional jargon that may be common language to an educator yet foreign ground for many parents. Acronyms such as IEP (individualized education program), IFSP (individual family service plan), SLP (speech-language pathologist), OT (occupational therapist), PT (physical therapist), and a multitude of others may be used casually by those in the special education community. Even after hearing them several times, however, parents may find them confusing and sometimes frightening. Jargon-free conversations are less intimidating and allow parents to feel mutually empowered in understanding the needs of their children.

Nonverbal communication greatly influences the empowerment of parents. Body language includes facial expressions; body positioning, including a relaxed or tense position; eye contact; and respect of others' personal space.

CREATING A RELATIONSHIP OF TRUST

Mutual trust is established between parents and educators when they find a common ground in understanding the needs of the child (Turnbull et al., 2006). Educators need to believe that the parents are telling them the truth about the child's abilities in everyday life situations. The differences are typically not in the reporting but in the interpretation of what a skill may be. What independent eating is to a parent may be quite different from the way in which the educator qualifies independent eating.

Minke and Scott (1995) studied three parent meetings in depth, looking for major issues that resulted in a positive relationship between parents and teachers. Early in their study and analysis, they found that a recurring theme was the positive bond between the parent and the staff. The bond is an outcome of the mutual trust that occurs when both parties see that the common goal is the good of the child with special needs.

Breakpoint Practice

1. How would you describe to a parent that the IFSP team will include an OT, PT, and SLP, and that the BSID-II, as was the PDMS, was used to complete the comprehensive evaluation?

2. What professional jargon was used in question 1 that you don't understand?

3. Why would a parent choose not to have a comprehensive evaluation of his or her child completed in the home?

4. If parents told you that their 3-year-old child, who is deaf, could talk, what would you say?

INDIVIDUAL FAMILY SERVICE PLAN (IFSP)

In Part C of IDEA, the parents and the child are recognized as being interdependent, and family needs are an integral part of the child's needs. The family environment is where the young child typically develops and learns optimally. The family is ultimately responsible for the primary care of the child and has a great deal of influence on the child's growth and development. It is inherent that the needs of child and family are intricately entwined (Bruder & Dunst, 2005).

Beckman (1991) describes four kinds of outcomes that are included in the IFSP: (1) child outcomes, (2) family-related child outcomes, (3) child-related family outcomes, and (4) general family outcomes. Child outcomes are goals that are traditionally seen on IEPs. They include interventions that will develop, increase, improve, decrease, or eliminate specific child behaviors or skills (Beckman, & Bristol, 1991).

Family-related child outcomes reflect family needs for child changes that will make family life safer, easier, more pleasant, and more secure over time and are directly related to the improvement of family life. They include assistance with issues such as feeding or sleeping schedules, the child's behavior with the family in public places, and toilet training (Beckman, 1991).

Child-related family outcomes relate to the family needs. Intervention is focused on the family rather than on specific child behaviors. Such outcomes include the need for respite care, parent or sibling support, financial support for families of infants who are medically fragile, or genetic counseling (Beckman, 1991).

General family outcomes are goals that provide support for the family and can be related or not related to the child with disability. Some of these outcomes may center on marital difficulties; interfamily communication problems; alcoholism; and finding food, clothing, shelter, or regular income (Beckman, 1991).

When assessing the needs of the family, it is crucial that professionals be sensitive to the family's comfort level in discussing issues that may be personal and considered private family concerns. Just because a child has a disability or is at risk for disability does not automatically give the professionals in educational programs the right to know all of the personal family business (Beckman, 1991). Families are most willing to share their needs and concerns once trust has been established with the professional, and the development of that trust is sometimes an ongoing, lengthy process.

Breakpoint Practice

1. What would you do if you have observed that the parents of a child who has been referred to your program argue openly in front of their child and also at educational meetings?

2. How long do you think it would take to build a trusting relationship with a family of a child with special needs?

3. What are some techniques that you would use to build a relationship with a family?

4. What would be barriers in building a relationship between an early interventionist and a family?

5. What are ways in which a professional would violate a relationship that has already been established or is in the process of being established?

Multicultural Considerations

Creating a Relationship of Respect

One of the primary aspects of showing respect to another person or another family is to show sensitivity to cultural diversity. To show sensitivity to differences, educators must take a close look at their own belief systems and traditional and cultural influences. When they understand themselves, they can begin to see through the eyes of others.

We all work from paradigms that influence what we do and how we do it. Our attitudes greatly affect the trust relationship that is needed for parents of a child with a disability to feel part of the process. These belief systems or paradigms include attitudes toward family characteristics. Family characteristics include culture and microcultures, ethnicity, socioeconomic status, family makeup, and geographical placement (Turnbull et al., 2006).

Because most educators are born into middle-class, European American families, they may bring the thinking styles of this culture into their work (Beckman, 1991). Also, our educational system is based on the influences of European American culture. Those who have grown up in these cultures typically have an individualistic perspective. In the individualist society, children learn to have autonomy and be independent in all aspects of life. The paradox is that most other cultures value collectivism, and the families teach interdependence rather than independence (Turnbull et al., 2006).

The individualistic influence is evident in several approaches used by early intervention programs. Goals for young children center around helping them become independent and self-sufficient. We work toward developmental milestones such as walking, talking, dressing, and eating independently. We expect parent participation in all entities of service delivery. The interventionist who is culturally sensitive realizes that some cultures do not value this level of independence, which may actually clash with the basic beliefs of the culture (Hanson & Lynch, 1990).

Cultural sensitivity is also evident when the professional realizes how personal biases can unintentionally influence assessment methods and ultimately the outcome. This can result in overidentification of disability in some cultures (Skiba, Knesting, & Bush, 2002).

Parenting styles are culturally influenced, and respect is evident when the unique child-rearing methods are recognized. Some cultures raise their children in a world of physical affection and closeness; other cultures may not value affection as part of the safe, secure home environment. Some cultures believe in authoritarian discipline methods; others prefer that children grow and develop optimally with an authoritative upbringing. Some cultures believe that the mother is most responsible for raising the child, and others see this as the family's role, frequently giving older siblings parenting responsibilities (Hanson & Lynch, 1990).

The reality may be that the family finds a close relationship with a professional or involvement in the assessment and ongoing educational process as being inappropriate. If this occurs, this preference must also be respected. Also, the parent who is working through grief or emotional adjustment to a new diagnosis, especially if the child is an infant, may have difficulty establishing a relationship with someone who is a continual reminder of the child's disability (Minke & Scott, 1995).

When the large number of individual differences among cultures, learning styles, and perspectives on child rearing and childcare are respected, the assessment becomes socially validated, which will have a great effect on the outcomes of the program that will ultimately be created for the child (Beckman, 1991). Observations of children during evaluations should address the social context of the children and their families.

Increasing Validity

Researchers have discussed formal and informal assessment procedures that are related to individuals who are culturally and/or linguistically diverse. Language samples, dynamic assessment, and specific standardized tests have been examined in the literature.

Informal Assessment. Researchers have emphasized that incorporating a language sample from the individual's natural context is a critical component of the language assessment (Kayser, 1989; Mattes & Omark, 1991). Stockman (1996) discussed the advantages and disadvantages in using language sample analysis while assessing individuals who are culturally and linguistically diverse. Advantages include the increase of cultural sensitivity, validity, accessibility, and flexibility in the use of this technique. Challenges include managing context variation, observing and transcribing a large amount of conversation, deciding on the criteria to use in appraising the language sample, and the time demands of a language sample analysis.

Gutierrez-Clellen and Quinn (1993) discussed using oral narratives with children from diverse backgrounds. The authors' discussion involved the issues of narrative experience (i.e., familiarity with setting), exposure to narrative tasks, notions regarding audience involvement, paralinguistic strategies (i.e., prosody, repetition, and fluency), and the use of dynamic assessment as essential ingredients in the assessment and instruction of this aspect of language. They noted that familiarization with different contexts and verbal mediation is used to provide examples and practice. Therefore, the child's language can be expanded.

In addition, Washington, Craig, and Kushmaul (1998) investigated the effect of language sampling context (free play and picture description) on variability in the utilization of African American English. Participants were from low socioeconomic status. Results revealed significant differences in the production of language based on context. The picture description context showed more usage of African American English. It took less time to gather a language sample during picture description than it did in the free play context. In addition, boys used more tokens than girls in the context of free play.

Laing and Kamhi (2003) also focused on the use of process-dependent and dynamic assessment methods in the language assessment of individuals who are culturally and/or linguistically diverse. These methods were discussed as solutions to problems that could occur using standardized testing, such as content bias, linguistic bias, and disproportionate representation in norm samples.

Standardized Tests. In looking at test-related measurement issues for preschool children, Fagundes, Haynes, Haak, and Moran (1998) compared 12 African American and 12 Caucasian preschool participants (both groups from a lower

(continued)

socioeconomic class in the South) on the Preschool Language Assessment Instrument in two formats. They compared standard format and thematic interactions in examining test scores. Results revealed that the African American children scored higher when the thematic mode was used, compared to the standard format. The researchers noted that, because the participants were assessed in authentic classroom activities, they were able to show their abilities. Therefore, dynamic assessment is a more useful measure in the evaluation of children's language abilities.

In looking at measurement issues related to tests in general, Hambleton, Merenda, and Spielberger (2005) reported that construct equivalence, communication problems in test administration, test format familiarity, speed tests, technical factors within the test, translators, the process of translation, adaptation designs, and data collection and analysis could be cultural/language factor differences affecting test scores. In addition, Van de Vijver and Tanzer (1997) noted construct bias, method bias, and item bias as possible sources of bias in cross-cultural assessment.

REVISITING MISSY

As we revisit Missy's situation, there are several factors to consider as the initial home visit is planned. First, her birth history qualifies her for services according to the criteria of "high risk" as defined in Part C of IDEA. Therefore, evaluation at this point would be needed to develop program goals and objectives. Because standardized assessment does not typically provide this type of information, it would be most conducive to use a criterion-referenced or curriculum-referenced assessment tool. Next, it will be important to assess the family needs. You already have some basic information that would direct your initial conversation with Missy's mother. She has expressed her concerns for her daughter's development, but you want to find out specifically what concerns her. This information would assist in developing family-generated goals. Because of the existing family characteristics, you want to know what support systems are presently in place for Missy's family. You would also need to reflect on your own bias toward single-parent families, poverty, and limited education and how these factors affect her ability to parent and communicate with others.

ACTIVITIES

1. Discuss your awareness of Child Find efforts in your area.
2. Develop your own definition of the term *developmentally delayed*. Are there situations where this description would not be appropriate when referring to the disability of an infant, toddler, or young child?
3. Discuss the pros and cons of not using standardized assessment for the comprehensive evaluation of an infant, toddler, and young child.
4. Brainstorm all of the possible descriptions of *family* and the unique characteristics of each. How would these characteristics influence your assessment of the needs of a family?

5. List three disabilities that could be diagnosed in an infant. How would your assessment differ for each disability area?

6. How would your assessment of an infant who is deaf differ from your assessment of a 3-year-old who is deaf?

WEB RESOURCES

http://www.naeyc.org

http://www.dec-sped.org

http://www.nabe.org

http://www.ncate.org

http://www.zerotothree.org

http://www.isbe.state.il.us/earlychi

http://www.cec.sped.org/AM/Template.cfm?Section=Early_Childhood&Template=/TaggedPage/TaggedPageDisplay.cfm&TPLID=36&ContentID=5543

REFERENCES

Bandura, A. (1969). *Principles of behavior modification*. New York: Holt, Rinehart & Winston.

Barnett, D. W., Ehrhardt, K. E., Stollar, S. A., & Bauer, A. M. (1994). PASSKey: A model for naturallistic assessment and intervention design. *Topics in Early Childhood Special Education, 14,* 350–373.

Bayley, N. (1993). *Bayley scales of infant development* (2nd ed.). San Antonio, TX: Psychological Corporation.

Beckman, P. (1991). Issues in developing the IFSP: A framework for establishing family outcomes. *Topics in Early Childhood Special Education, 11*(3), 19–31.

Brigance, A. H. (1985) *Brigance diagnostic inventory of early development*. North Billerica, MA: Curriculum Associates.

Bruder, M. B. (2000). Family-centered early intervention: Clarifying our values for the new millennium. *Topics in Early Childhood Special Education, 20*(2), 105–115, 122.

Bruder, M., & Dunst, C. (2005). Personnel preparation in recommended early intervention practices: Degree of emphasis across disciplines. *Topics in Early Childhood Special Education, 25*(1), 25–33.

Bryant, D., Lyons, C., & Wasik, B. H. (1991). Ethical issues involved in home visiting. *Topics in Early Childhood Special Education, 10*(4), 92–107.

Bzock, K., & League, R. (2003). *Receptive-Expressive Emergent Language Test—3*. Los Angeles: Western Psychological Services.

Campbell, P., & Halbert, J. (2002). Between research and practice: Provider perspectives on early intervention. *Topics in Early Childhood Special Education, 22*(4), 213–226.

Carpenter, B. (1997). Early intervention and identification: Finding the family. *Children & Society, 11,* 173–182.

Dunn L., & Dunn, L., (2007). *Peabody Picture Vocabulary Test—Fourth Edition*. Circle Pines, MN: American Guidance Service.

Dunst, C. J., Hamby, D., Trivette, C. M., Raab, M., & Bruder, M. B. (2000). Everyday family and community life and children's naturally occuring learning opportunities. *Journal of Early Intervention, 23,* 151–164.

Fagundes, D. D., Haynes, W. O., Haak, N. J., & Moran, M. J. (1998). Task variability effects on the language test performance of southern lower socioeconomic class African American five-year-olds. *Language, Speech, and Hearing Services in Schools, 29,* 148–157.

Fewell, R. (1986). *Play Assessment Scale* (5th revision). Seattle, WA: University of Washington.

Fewell, R. (1997). The relationship between play and communication skills in young children with Down syndrome. *Topics in Early Childhood Special Education, 7,* 103–118.

Fewell, R. (2000). Assessment of young children with special needs: Foundations for tomorrow. *Topics in Early Childhood Special Education, 20*(1), 38–42.

Fewell, R., & Langley, M. B. (1984). *Developmental Activities Screening Inventory—2.* Austin, TX: PRO-ED.

Folio, R., & Fewell, R. F. (2000). *Peabody Developmental Motor Scales* (2nd ed.). Allen, TX: Developmental Learning Materials Teaching Resources.

Furuno, S., O'Reilly, K., Inatsuka, T., Hosaka, C., Allman, T., & Zeisloft-Falbey, B. (1987). *Hawaii Early Learning Profile.* Palo Alto, CA: VORT Corp.

Guillory, A. W., Woll, J., & Nielson, S. (1994). How professionals can work with families to assess children's disabilities. *Education Digest, 60*(3), 58–60.

Gutierrez-Clellen, V. F., & Quinn, R. (1993). Assessing narratives of children from diverse cultural/linguistic groups. *Language, Speech, and Hearing Services in Schools, 24,* 2–9.

Hambleton, R. K., Merenda, P. F., & Spielberger, C. D. (2005). *Adapting educational and psychological tests for cross-cultural assessment.* Mahwah, NJ: Lawrence Erlbaum Associates.

Hanson, M. J., & Lynch, E. W. (1990). Honoring the cultural diversity of families when gathering data. *Topics in Early Childhood Special Education, 10*(1), 112–131.

Hardin, B. J., & Peisner-Feinberg, E. S. (2002). *The Early Learning Accomplishment Profile—3rd ed.* New York: Kaplan.

Hardin, B. J., & Peisner-Feinberg, E. S. (2004). *The Learning Accomplishment Profile—3rd ed.* New York: Kaplan.

Hooper, S. R., & Umansky, W. (2004). *Young children with special needs* (4th ed.). Upper Saddle River, NJ: Pearson Prentice Hall.

Johnson-Martin, N., Jens, K. G., & Attermeier, S. M. (1991). *The Caroline curriculum for handicapped/infants and infants at risk.* Baltimore: Paul H. Brookes.

Jung, L., McCormick, K., & Jolivette, K. (2004). Early intervention in rural natural environments: Making the most of your time. *Rural Special Education Quarterly, 23*(3), 30–35.

Kayser, H. (1989). Speech and language assessment of Spanish-English speaking children. *Language, Speech, and Hearing Services in Schools, 20,* 226–241.

Laing, S. P., & Kamhi, A. (2003). Alternative assessment of language and literacy in culturally and linguistically diverse populations. *Language, Speech, and Hearing Services in Schools, 34,* 44–55.

Lerner, J. W., Lowenthal, B., & Egan, R. (2003). *Preschool children with special needs: Children at risk and children with disabilities* (2nd ed.). Boston: Allyn & Bacon Pearson Education.

Linder, T. (1993). *Transdisciplinary play-based assessment: A functional approach to working with young children.* Baltimore: Paul H. Brookes.

Mattes, L. J., & Omark, D. R. (1991). *Speech and language assessment for the bilingual handicapped* (2nd ed.). Oceanside, CA: Academic Communication Associates.

McConnel, S. R. (2000). Assessment in early intervention and early childhood special education: Building on the past to project into our future. *Topics in Early Childhood Special Education, 20,* 143–48.

McLean, M., Wolery, M., & Bailey Jr., D. B. (2004). *Assessing infants and preschoolers with special needs* (3rd ed.). Upper Saddle River, NJ: Merrill/Pearson Education.

McWilliam, R. A., & Bailey, D.B. (1995). Effects of classroom social structure and disability on engagement. *Topics in Early Childhood Education, 15*(2), 124–150.

Meisels, S. J., & Provence, S. (1989). *Screening and assessment: Guidelines for identifying young disabled and developmentally vulnerable children and their families.* Washington, DC: National Center for Clinical Infant Programs.

Minke, K., & Scott, M. (1995). Parent-professional relationships in early intervention: A qualitative investigation. *Topics in Early Childhood Special Education, 15*(3), 335–352.

Morgan, E. C. (1992). *The INSITE Model: Resources for family-centered intervention for infants, toddlers, and preschoolers who are visually impaired.* Logan, VT: SK HI Institute, Department of Communicative Disorders, Utah State University.

Myers, C. L., McBride, S. L., & Peterson, C. A. (1996). Transdisciplinary, play-based assessment in early childhood special education: An examination of social validity. *Topics in Early Childhood Special Education, 16*(1), 102–126.

Neisworth, J., & Bagnato, S. (1992). The case against intelligence testing in early intervention. *Topics in Early Childhood Special Education, 12*(1), 1–20.

Newborg, J. (2005). *Battelle Developmental Inventory*—2. Chicago, IL: Riverside.

Parks, S., Furuno, S., O'Reilly, K. A., Inatsuka, T. T., Hoska, C. M., & Zesloft-Falbey, B. (1994). *Hawaii Early Learning Profile (HELP)*. Palo Alto, CA: VORT.

Skiba, R. J., Knesting, K., & Bush, L. D. (2002). Culturally competent assessment: More than non-biased tests. *Journal of Child and Family Studies, 11*(1), 61–78.

Stillman, R., & Battle, C. (1978–1985). *The Callier-Azuza Scale*. Dallas, TX: South Central Regional Center for Services to Deaf-Blind Children and Callier Center for Communication Disorders, University of Texas at Dallas.

Stockman, I. J. (1996). The promises and pitfalls of language sample analysis as an assessment tool for linguistic minority children. *Language, Speech, and Hearing Services in Schools, 27*, 355–366.

Turnbull, A., Turnbull, R., Erwin, W., & Soodak, L. (2006). *Families, professionals, and exceptionality positive outcomes through partnerships and trust* (5th ed.). Upper Saddle River, NJ: Prentice Hall/Pearson Education.

Van de Vijver, F. J. R., & Tanzer, N. K. (1997). Bias and equivalence in cross-cultural assessment: An overview. *European Review of Applied Psychology, 47*, 263–280.

Wang, H., Liao, H, & Hsieh, C. (2006). Reliability, sensitivity to change, and responsiveness of the Peabody Developmental Motor Scales—Second Edition for children with cerebral palsy. *Physical Therapy, 86*(10), 1351–1359.

Washington, J. A., Craig, H. K., & Kushmaul, A. (1998). Variable use of African American English across two language sampling contexts. *Journal of Speech, Language, and Hearing Research, 41*, 1115–1124.

Zimmerman, I., Steiner, V., & Pond, R. (1997). *Preschool Language Scale*—3. San Antonio, TX: Psychological Corp.

Assessing Students with Visual, Motor, and/or Hearing Disabilities

With Phyllis LeDosquet

KEY TERMS

Occupational therapy: Working on improving performance, learning skills to adapt to life changes, promoting health, and functioning independently (primarily upper body movement and eye/hand coordination).

Physical therapy: Working on lower body locomotion.

Gross motor: Large muscle activity (i.e., walking).

Fine motor: Small muscle activity (i.e., writing).

Visual-motor integration: Coordinating motor skills from visual input.

Auditory motor processing: Perceptual processing of auditory information in the central nervous system.

Visual acuity: Clarity of a person's vision.

Hyperopia: Farsightedness.

Myopia: Nearsightedness.

Astigmatism: Variation in refraction is due to irregularities in the shape of the cornea, resulting in blurred vision.

Albinism: Lack of pigment.

Aniridia: Underdevelopment of the iris of the eye.

Congenital cataract: Cloudy opacity in one or both lenses of the eyes.

Congenital glaucoma: Damage of eye tissue due to increased eye pressure.

Coloboma: Hole in various parts of the eye.

Nystagmus: Involuntary movement in one or both eyes.

Optic atrophy: Deteriorated optic nerve.

Retinitis pigmentosa: Inherited disorder resulting in slow, progressive loss of visual ability.

Retinopathy of prematurity: Retinas of eyes underdeveloped, causing blood vessels that rupture easily, often due to high level of oxygen.

Assistive technology: Permits individuals with disabilities to increase independence and quality of life.

Low-level technology: Technologies requiring little training.

High-level technology: Technologies requiring user training.

Labial: Pertaining to the lips.

Lingual: Pertaining to the tongue.

Augmentative communication: Addition to natural spoken, written, or gestural speech.

Alternative communication: Substitute to natural spoken, written, or gestural speech.

Digitized speech: Individual records speech that is artificially compiled from recordings of human speech.

Synthesized speech: Electronically constructed speech.

Adaptation: Changes to instruction or assessment.

Case Study: Assessing Dale

Dale is in the sixth grade at a middle school and has a physical impairment. His last testing report from three years ago indicates that his mobility is very limited, but his cognitive skills are within normal limits. He receives speech and language services as well as occupational therapy (OT). In speech therapy, the focus includes clarity of articulation in single words and phrases. His OT services include work in fine-motor skills, specifically in learning to use his wheelchair more independently. The activity and therapy sessions focus on skills that help Dale with integration into the community. As his classroom teacher, you are actively involved in the evaluation process and would like to concentrate on the assessment-to-instruction link within his academic studies. Furthermore, you express an interest that Dale and his family members become actively involved in the process to facilitate carryover of activities in the home setting. In addition, you would like the school activities to reflect authentic assessment. You need to become more familiar with the various technologies available to him and would like an assessment within this domain.

Which formal and informal assessment strategies would you use?

Which specific speech, language, motor, and other skills would you investigate?

Where would you go to receive information regarding the technologies that you would like to see Dale use?

Which low- and high-level technologies would you explore?

What other adaptations would you explore?

How would you infuse the assessment information and outcomes within your classroom?

What recommendations would you make to the parents? How could you get more involved with the process?

You will be able to answer all of these questions after reading this chapter. Furthermore, you will be able to identify what technologies and other adaptations might benefit Dale in the long term. You will also be able to understand the aspects of your legal responsibility to utilize low- and high-technology devices in the classroom. You will be able to give examples of the different types of technologies and adaptations. You will also be able to discuss how the different types of technologies can be used for vision, hearing, motor, and language disabilities. In addition, you will be able to apply adaptations to the areas of reading and language arts, writing, mathematics, science, social studies, and daily living skills.

This chapter addresses standards 4 (instructional strategies), 5 (learning environments and social interaction), 8 (assessment), 9 (professional and ethical practice), and 10 (collaboration). Information regarding individualizing assessment and the instruction loop; learning environments and active engagement; legal; diversity; evidence-based strategies; and working with other professionals will facilitate learning toward these standards.

DEFINING ASSESSMENT OF VISUAL, MOTOR, AND/OR HEARING DISABILITIES

In several chapters, we have discussed various formal and informal instruments in the areas of development (i.e., tests sequenced by developmental scales), intelligence (i.e., nonverbal), adaptive behavior, achievement, and natural environment. Areas of sensory skills are often explored in diagnostic evaluations due to the co-occurrence of sensory and other disabilities that affect learning and the classroom (Maples, 2003). This chapter will focus on the assessment of sensory areas, including vision, motor, and hearing.

ASSESSMENT OF STUDENTS WITH VISUAL IMPAIRMENT

According the American Foundation for the Blind (AFB), approximately 93,600 students are visually impaired or blind, 10,800 of whom are deaf-blind, and receive special education programming in the United States. These students vary widely in cause of disability and ability levels, including the severity of the visual impairment itself (Zaba, 2003). With this in mind, it is obvious that assessment of a person with visual impairment should take a comprehensive approach, including medical information, family input, and the educational input of special education and regular education personnel who are part of the educational team. The discussion of vision will comprise partial sight and blindness.

There continues to be discrepancies in the definition of low vision, with no "universal definition" (Barraga, 2004, p. 581). American Printing House for the Blind (APH) uses a very specific definition: legal blindness refers to a person with a central visual acuity of 20/200 or less in the better eye after correction (glasses) or a peripheral field so reduced that the widest diameter of such field is no greater than 20 degrees.

IDEA, however, uses a less restrictive and more functional definition of visual impairment, defining the disability as vision that, even with correction, adversely affects a child's educational performance. The definition includes both partial sight and blindness.

A misconception is that a decrease in visual acuity (clarity of vision) constitutes a visual impairment. To understand this concept, you must first become familiar with basic eye anatomy and function. Visual images are received in the form of light rays that enter the eye through the pupil and are projected on the fovea, the center of the macula that is the place on the retina that is the clearest point of central vision (Levack, 1994). It is then transmitted to the optic nerve and eventually to the visual cortex (Jose, 1999). In normal vision, the light rays enter the eyes and focus perfectly on the retina to provide a crisp, clear image (The Pediatric Eye Disease Investigator Group, 2002).

The American Optometric Association (AOA) defines 20/20 vision as the clearness of vision from a measured distance of 20 feet. A person who has 20/20 vision can see clearly at 20 feet. If you have 20/70 vision, it means that what a person with normal vision can see at 70 feet, you must be 20 feet from in order to see with the same clarity. Commonly, the light does not refract perfectly due to conditions known as hyperopia (farsightedness), myopia (nearsightedness), or astigmatism (Fredrick, 2002). Nearsightedness occurs when the eye is larger than normal or its focusing ability is stronger than the normal eye. Farsightedness occurs when the eye is smaller than normal or the focusing ability is weaker than the normal eye. Astigmatism results when there is a variation in refraction due to irregularities in the shape of the cornea (Jose, 1999). A refractive error can be corrected by a concave lens when a person is nearsighted and a convex lens if the person is farsighted. By wearing glasses with the prescribed lens, the person will see with normal vision.

VISUAL DISORDERS

Many disorders result in visual impairment (American Academy of Pediatrics et al., 2003). Most of the national and federal organizations such as APH, AFB and AOA have comprehensive lists with definitions of visual disorders. Some, however, are more commonly observed than others in the educational setting. The definitions of visual disorders described in the following paragraphs have been retrieved from the American Foundation for the Blind website (http://www.afb.org).

Albinism is a congenital hereditary disorder. It is due to the lack of or inability to produce pigment. It is characterized by a fair complexion; very blond to white body hair, including eyebrows and eyelashes; and very light-colored, often red-appearing irises. Visual characteristics include severe sensitivity to light, nystagmus, and decreased vision due to a poorly developed macula (area on the retina responsible for central vision) (American Foundation for the Blind [AFB], 2006).

Aniridia refers to the underdevelopment of the iris of the eye. The iris is instrumental in controlling the amount of light that enters the eye and also the focusing of the light rays on the retina. As a result, the student experiences blurred vision and light sensitivity. Students with aniridia are at risk for the development of secondary visual conditions including nystagmus, cataracts, and glaucoma (AFB, 2006).

Congenital cataract(s) refers to opacity in one or both lenses of the eyes. This affects the internal structure needed for focusing. The lens is surgically removed, but visual blurriness can remain due to the inability to focus. Also, many students who have been diagnosed with congenital cataracts experience light sensitivity, especially with glare. With new surgical procedures, including the insertion of a lens into the eye and glasses, vision can return to the normal range. However, some individuals continue to have difficulty with clarity, focus, and light sensitivity (AFB, 2006).

Congenital glaucoma damages the eye tissue due to increased eye pressure. This condition is serious because, if left untreated, the student may lose all vision. Glaucoma causes a decrease in visual acuity and a loss of vision starting in the peripheral (outer) fields. Students experience light sensitivity and can develop cataracts (AFB, 2006).

Coloboma is a cleft or hole in various parts of the eye. The effects on vision depend on the severity of the coloboma and its location(s) in the eye. The effects on visual performance include decreased acuity, nystagmus, and possible loss of certain visual fields or parts of fields. Possible secondary visual conditions include cataracts and microphthalmia (an abnormally small eye) (AFB, 2006).

Cortical visual impairment happens when there is damage to the visual cortex, the area of the brain that processes visual information. It is most often present with another disability such as cerebral palsy or with multiple disabilities. With this disorder, the eye actually sees, but what is transmitted to the brain cannot be processed. These students appear as if they are looking at items and people; however, they are unable to process the visual information. It is characterized by fluctuating visual performance, lack of attention to visual information, and frequent light gazing (AFB, 2006.)

Nystagmus is a condition that is secondary to many other visual disorders. However, it can be a condition by itself and is typically referred to as congenital nystagmus. It is defined as an involuntary movement in one or both eyes. In some cases, it is hardly visible to the observer, but in other cases, there is very obvious uncontrolled movement of the eyes. Nystagmus causes a decrease in visual acuity. Many students with nystagmus locate a null point, or a positioning of the eyes that slows the eye movement, allowing for a clearer focus (AFB, 2006).

Optic atrophy is a visual disorder in which the optic nerve has deteriorated or shows atrophy. The optic nerve is instrumental in the transmission of visual information to the visual cortex in the occipital lobe and damage to it results in a loss in visual acuity and loss of all or parts of the visual fields. Its effects on visual functioning range from mild visual loss to visual field cuts, or blindness. Secondary conditions usually include nystagmus, which affects the ability for the eyes to focus clearly (AFB, 2006).

Retinitis pigmentosa is an inherited disorder resulting in a slow, progressive loss of visual ability. With this condition, there is a degeneration or loss of rods (light receptors) in the retina and atrophy to the rest of the retina, including the pigment of the eye (Jose, 1999). The first symptom is usually night blindness, following by light sensitivity, visual field loss, and decrease in acuity (AFB, 2006).

Retinopathy of prematurity develops in premature infants, primarily those born at less than 32 weeks gestation. Because the retinas of the eyes of these infants are underdeveloped, exposure to the environment outside the uterus (including oxygen levels in the normal environment) causes a rapid growth of blood vessels that are fragile and rupture easily. This causes bleeding on the retina, resulting in the development of scar tissue. The scar tissue causes stress to the retina, which results in tearing or detachment. The outcome is mild to severe visual loss, with the possibility of blindness if the condition is left untreated (AFB, 2006).

Breakpoint Practice

1. How would the visual disorders noted be manifested in the classroom?
2. How would the visual disorders noted affect formal assessment?
3. How would the visual disorders noted affect informal assessment?

COMPREHENSIVE ASSESSMENT

For the past several decades, students who are visually impaired have learned through a curriculum that was developed for students without visual impairment. While the importance of students with visual impairment continuing to master the core curriculum has been recognized, unique needs should be addressed in the educational setting. Therefore, the National Agenda for Blind and Visually Impaired Students, Including Those with Additional Disabilities, set forth guidelines for an expanded core curriculum (Hatlen, 1996). This expanded curriculum includes compensatory or functional academic skills, including communication modes, orientation and mobility, social interaction skills, independent living skills, recreation and leisure skills, career education, technology, and visual efficiency skills (Hatlen, 1996). Assessment in the core curriculum and expanded core curriculum is essential for identification of each student's areas of need and for optimal individual educational program planning (AFB, 2006).

Compensatory or Functional Academic Skills

Compensatory skills refer to skills that a student with visual impairment would need for equal access to the core curriculum. Functional skills refer to those skills needed by students with multiple disabilities to allow them the optimal options for work, play, socialization, and personal care (Beirne-Smith, Patton, & Kim, 2006; Hatlen, 1996).

Assessment of compensatory skills includes careful evaluation of the learning media used by the student and whether the student would learn through reading and writing print or by using braille. Koenig and Holbrook (1993) identified various characteristics that should be observed to classify a student as a print reader:

✔ Uses vision efficiently to complete tasks at near distances.
✔ Shows interest in pictures and demonstrates the ability to identify pictures and/or elements within pictures.
✔ Identifies name in print and/or understands that print has meaning.
✔ Uses print to accomplish other prerequisite reading skills.
✔ Has a stable eye condition.
✔ Has an intact central visual field.
✔ Shows steady progress in learning to use his or her vision as necessary to assure efficient print reading.
✔ Is free of additional disabilities that would interfere with progress in a conventional reading program in print (p. 43).

Orientation and Mobility

These skills are needed by a student with visual impairment to move about and travel environments as independently as possible (Hatlen, 1996). Orientation is defined as the perception of one's position in space, and mobility is defined as the ability to move throughout the environment based on the accurate perception of one's location (Gense & Gense, 2000; Hill & Ponder, 1976). IDEA specifically states that students with visual impairment must receive training from a qualified person, an orientation and mobility instructor. These skills are a fundamental part of a student's independence; therefore, strategies for monitoring and teaching these skills must be shared with educators who are working with the student on a daily basis.

Social Interaction Skills

While students with sight learn their social skills by observing others and developing socially appropriate behaviors based on this information, students who are visually impaired do not have this opportunity and must be purposefully taught. These skills are so important that, without them, students experience social isolation rather than a satisfying and fulfilled life (D'Allura, 2002; Hatlen, 1996).

An individual who has appropriate social skills has an understanding of interactions with family, friends, and others as well as an awareness of self-concept, nonverbal communication, and emotional responses. They also include an understanding of social politeness, awareness of morals and values, and personal and civic responsibility (Loumiet & Levack, 1993).

As a component of the expanded curriculum, the teacher with training in working with students with visual impairment would most likely implement this instruction. However, the team should work closely to embed social skills training into all aspects of the school program. A multitude of checklists, curriculums, and books on this topic are available. They can be accessed through any state or federal organization that supports services for the blind and visually impaired (see the Internet links at the end of this chapter).

Independent Living Skills

Independent living encompasses the acquisition and use of all the skills needed to live without assistance from others. It incorporates skills such as personal body care, shopping, food preparation, cleaning and laundry, sewing, and money management (Beirne-Smith, Patton, & Kim, 2006; Stenquist & Robins, 1978). It also includes the application of skills that allow a person to interact with others personally, professionally, and socially, including appropriate dressing, sexuality, social grace, and etiquette (Loumiet & Levack, 1993).

Although these skills are addressed in many content areas within the core curriculum, it is not in-depth enough for students who are visually impaired. Like social skills, most independent living skills are learned through visual modeling of others in our personal and social world and therefore must be taught through a prescribed, purposeful approach by a person proficient in teaching them (Hatlen, 1996). Many activities happen during the school day for which success depends on the understanding of these independent living skills. The collaboration among team members would ensure that training would be incorporated into all aspects of the student's life.

Recreation and Leisure Skills

Recreation and leisure is an important part of the physical and emotional well-being of all human beings (Letcher, 2006). Many of the activities taught through physical education programs are appropriate and enjoyed by students with visual impairment. However, without intentional teaching of the variety of lifelong leisure activities, a student with visual impairment would not be able to take part in and enjoy the activities into his or her adult life (Hatlen, 1996).

Assessment of the student's functional vision gives the information needed to provide modifications and adaptations required to enjoy a wide variety of games and activities (Letcher, 2006). Board games and activities such as Uno, Dominoes, Chess,

Checkers, Monopoly, and many others have been adapted with either braille or large print, allowing those with visual impairment access to this kind of enjoyment and leisurely fun (American Printing House for the Blind [APH], 2006). As part of the expanded core curriculum, the educational team would be responsible for assessing the interest areas and ensuring access to a variety of activities, thus allowing the student to expand and build a repertoire of healthy recreational and leisure skills.

Career Education

Employment is an ongoing concern for people with visual impairment. Although career planning is part of the core curriculum, most career opportunities are learned throughout life through visual observation and experience. Once again, this opportunity is not available or is quite limited for students with visual impairment. It must be addressed, starting in the early grades, to give the students hands-on exposure to a variety of fields and career options (Converse, Oswald, Gillespie, Field, & Bizot, 2004; Hatlen, 1996).

A variety of curriculums, assessments, and books address this topic. The goal is that students with visual impairment be given sufficient introduction to a variety of career options (see the Web Resources at the end of the chapter).

Visual Efficiency

Students who have residual vision need to learn to use this vision as efficiently as possible (Hatlen, 1996). Functional vision assessment has long been considered a best practice in education (Massof & Rubin, 2001; Pugh & Erin, 1999). Assessment of the functional use of vision allows the educational team to decide what adjustments are needed to create the optimal learning environment for the student (Lueck, 2004). Once functional vision has been evaluated, weaknesses in the student's use of residual vision can be identified, and strategies for improving visual performance can be implemented.

Assessment is complex because functional vision will change according to places such as indoors versus outdoors; rooms, including hallways and stairways; time of day; and time of year. Also, factors such as colors and contrast, lighting, space, size of visual information, distance from visual information, affects of low-vision devices, and technology needs must be considered an integral part of the assessment process (Massof & Rubin, 2001; Levack, 1994). Several commercially produced books, manuals, and assessments provide an organized, thorough evaluation of functional vision and visual efficiency (see the Web Resources at the end of this chapter).

STANDARDIZED ASSESSMENT

Sometimes it is necessary to administer standardized assessment to a student with visual impairment. We know that visual impairment does not cause learning problems; however, learning problems may exist along with the visual impairment (Layton & Lock, 2000). It has been difficult in the past to accept the possibility of dual diagnosis; however, by not identifying the problem, the student may not receive the services needed to create the optimal learning environment (Turnbull & Turnbull, 1998). In many states, standardized tests are used to identify a discrepancy between ability and potential. However, there is concern for the validity of test results when the test has not included students who are visually impaired or blind in the norm sample (Layton & Lock, 2000; Hall, Scholl, & Swallow, 1986). Also, there are concerns about using accommodations, adaptations, and modifications that are not in alignment with the standardized administration procedure. Because of the uniqueness of each visual disorder and the functional visual abilities of each student, few instruments have been normed for students with visual impairment (Allman, 2004; Layton & Lock, 2000). Therefore, a comprehensive

Table 11.1 Examples of Test Adaptations

Assessment	Age or Grade Level	Type	Availability	What Is Measured
Key Math—Revised/NU: A Diagnostic Inventory of Essential Mathematics—Normative Update	Grades K–12	Standardized	Braille	Mathematical concepts and skills
Oregon Project for Preschool Children Who Are Blind or Visually Impaired, 6th Edition	Ages 0–6	Standardized for students with visual impairment	(Not applicable)	All developmental domains
Stanford Achievement Test Series, 10th Edition	Grades K–12	Standardized	Braille and large print	Overall achievement
Kaufman—Functional Academic Skills Test (K-Fast)	Ages 15–85	Standardized	Braille	Reading and math functional skills
Brigance Comprehensive Inventory of Basic Skills—Revised	Birth–grade 9	Curriculum-based	Available in braille with tactile representations of diagrams	All developmental domains and academic areas
GED Basics General Education Development Test	For students who have not finished high school	Standardized	Braille and large print	Language arts/writing, social studies, science, language arts/reading, mathematics, constitution text
Cullier-Azuza Scale	0–9 years; children who are deaf-blind and/or have severe disabilities	Curriculum-based		Motor skills, daily living skills, language skills

approach using both qualitative and quantitative information is most appropriate for the assessment of learning problems with students who are visually impaired (Allman, 2004; Layton & Lock, 2000).

Many assessments are presently available in braille or large print with diagrams, pictures, and so on, that are re-created with tactual modification if needed. These assessments include Key Math: A Diagnostic Inventory of Essential Mathematics/NU, Stanford Achievement Test-19, and Kaufman—Functional Academic Skills Test (K-Fast) (APH, 2006). See Table 11.1.

FINAL CONSIDERATIONS

The National Agenda for the Education of Children and Youths with Visual Impairment, Including Those with Multiple Disabilities (2006) has recommended that a person with expertise in visual impairments be available to all students, including those in early intervention programs. Also, the expanded core curriculum states that

Table 11.2 Sources for Materials and Adaptations for the Blind and Visually Impaired

All About Vision
http://www.allaboutvision.com/lowvision/reading.htm

American Printing House for the Blind
http://www.aph.org/

American Foundation for the Blind
http://www.afb.org/

Independent Living
http://www.independentliving.com/

Enablemart: Technology for everyone
http://enablemart.com/default.aspx?store=10&dept=12

Enabling Technologies
http://www.Brailler.com/

Sight Connection
http://www.sightconnection.com/

TheLowVisionStore.com
http://www.thelowvisionstore.com/catalog/

assessments in these areas should be conducted by someone with expertise in visual impairment. It is your responsibility, as a special educator, to work with this person or persons so that you have the information needed to provide the educational setting that best meets the needs of your student(s). Your input will be an integral part of the comprehensive assessment process and will be of utmost value in deciding what is needed to make the core curriculum equally accessible to students who are blind or visually impaired. See Table 11.2.

Breakpoint Practice

1. Discuss the relationship among the various aspects of a comprehensive assessment.
2. Discuss validity issues that can arise in relation to standardized assessment and the area of visual impairments.

MOTOR ASSESSMENT

Another important focus in the area of sensory assessment is motor assessment. Motor assessment often involves investigation of motor, visual-motor, and auditory-motor processing skills.

DEFINITION OF MOTOR SKILLS

Motor assessment and visual-motor integration are commonly assessed areas in the motor realm. Motor assessment involves the consideration of efficacy (effectiveness) of muscle movements and entails gross and fine motor. Gross-motor activity describes the use of large muscles, whereas fine motor refers to the use of small muscles. Locomotion refers to getting from point A to point B. Examples of gross-motor activity consist of walking

Table 11.3 Tests of Motor Abilities

Test	Company	Content	Age	Time to Administer
Bruininks-Oseretsky Test of Motor Proficiency, 2nd Edition	American Guidance Service	Gross and fine motor	4-0 to 21	45–60 minutes for the complete battery; 15–20 minutes for the short form
Movement Assessment Battery for Children	Psychological Corporation	Movement skills	4-0 to 12 years	About 30 minutes
Peabody Developmental Motor Scales, 2nd Edition	PRO-ED	Motor abilities	Birth through 5 years	60 minutes
Test of Gross Motor Development— 2nd Edition	PRO-ED	Gross motor skills	3-0 through 10–11	15–20 minutes

and kicking. Examples of fine-motor activity are hand and finger agility, such as gripping, writing, or using eating utensils.

Visual-motor integration consists of coordinating visual movements (following and tracking objects) and hand coordination and control. Individuals who have motor, vision, or hearing difficulties may demonstrate a variety of difficulties when completing tasks in these types of tests (i.e., spelling) (Pierangelo & Giuliani, 2006).

MOTOR TESTS

Commonly used tests of motor abilities include the Bruininks-Oseretsky Test of Motor Proficiency, Second Edition (BOT-2) (Bruininks & Bruininks, 2005); Movement Assessment Battery for Children (Movement ABC) (Henderson & Sugden, 1992); the Peabody Developmental Motor Scales (Folio & Fewell, 2000); and the Test of Gross Motor Development—2nd Edition (TGMD-2) (Ulrich, 2000). See Table 11.3.

BOT-2

The Bruininks-Oseretsky Test of Motor Proficiency (BOT-2) (Bruininks & Bruininks, 2005) measures gross- and fine-motor skills. This instrument consists of eight subtests in the areas of fine motor precision (e.g., connecting dots), fine motor integration (e.g., copying shapes), manual dexterity (e.g., stringing blocks), bilateral coordination (e.g., tapping foot and finger), balance (e.g., walking on a line), running speed and agility (e.g., one-legged side hop), upper-limb coordination (e.g., catching a ball), and strength (e.g., sit-ups). Composite scores include fine manual control, manual coordination, body coordination, strength and agility, and a total motor composite. Separate measures of gross- and fine-motor skills are available with this tool. A complete battery (46 items) and a short form (14 items) are available. Standard scores, age equivalents, percentiles, and stanines are available.

Movement ABC

The Movement Assessment Battery for Children (Movement ABC) (Henderson & Sugden, 1992) measures children's movement skills. This instrument consists of eight items across three subtests (with a 0–5 score). Those subtests include manual dexterity (i.e., putting a coin in a slot in a box), ball skills (i.e., beaning a bag in a bin), and static/dynamic balance (i.e., standing on one foot on a block). Studies have used this tool for the measurement of motor skills when looking at individuals who had cerebral palsy (Evensen, Vik, Helbostad, Indredavik, Kulseng, & Brubakk, 2004). This tool is often used as a criterion-referenced instrument (Venn, 2007) due to limited technical information.

The Peabody Development Motor Scales, Second Edition

The Peabody Developmental Motor Scales, Second Edition (PDMS-2) (Folio & Fewell, 2000) includes six subtests around the areas of gross- and fine-motor skills. Subtests include reflexes, stationary (retaining equilibrium), locomotion (movement), object manipulation, grasping, and visual-motor integration and are combined to form composites of fine motor quotient, gross motor quotient, and total motor quotient. Norm group, reliability, and validity appear to be appropriate. Concurrent validity studies and construct validity appears adequate. Test-retest reliability, interrater reliability, and internal consistency appeared appropriate, but reliability was examined in individuals without disabilities (Want, Liao, & Hsieh, 2006). However, Wang et al. (2006) found appropriate test-retest reliability for children with cerebral palsy. Standard scores, age equivalents, and percentiles are available with this tool.

The Test of Gross Motor Development—2nd Edition

The Test of Gross Motor Development—2nd Edition (TGMD-2) (Ulrich, 2000) is comprised of two subtests with six skills in each subtest around the area of gross-motor skills. The locomotor subtest consists of the locomotor movements of running, galloping, hopping, leaping, horizontal jumping, and sliding. The object control subtest includes striking a stationary ball, controlling a stationary dribble, kicking, catching, overhand throwing, and underhand rolling. Norms appear appropriate. Content validity, construct validity, and predictive validity are provided for this tool. Some reliability coefficients are somewhat low.

Breakpoint Practice

1. Compare and contrast the four motor tests.
2. Which test would you be most likely to use? Why?
3. Which test would you be least likely to use? Why?

VISUAL-MOTOR TASKS

Visual-motor tasks typically involve reproducing representations by the use of motor skills after receiving visually presented material. Specific assessments regarding visual-motor activity will be discussed in the next section.

VISUAL-MOTOR TESTS

Visual-motor tests are often used to look at the connection among visual-motor, performance, and academic aspects. More specifically, the visual-motor domain is investigated to ascertain whether these skills are indicating problems that affect learning performance (Salvia & Ysseldyke, 1998). Tests often used in this type of assessment include the Beery-VMI (Beery, Buktenica, & Beery, 2004), the fifth edition of the VMI (VMI-5), the Bender Visual-Motor Gestalt Test (Bender-Gestalt II) (Bender, 1938; Brannigan & Decker, 2003), Detroit Tests of Learning Aptitude—4 (DTLA-4) (Hammill, 1998), Test of Visual Motor Integration (Hammill, 1996), and Wide Range Assessment of Visual Motor

Table 11.4 Tests of Visual-Motor Integration

Test	Company	Content	Age	Time to Administer
Beery-VMI, 5th Edition	PRO-ED	Visual-motor integration	2-0 through 18 for long form; 2 through 8 for short form	15 minutes
Bender Visual-Motor Gestalt Test—2nd Edition	Riverside	Visual-motor skills	3-0 years and older	5–10 minutes
Detroit Tests of Learning Aptitude—4	PRO-ED	General abilities, with a subtest on design reproduction	6-0 through 17 years	1–2 hours
Test of Visual Motor Integration	PRO-ED	Visual-motor ability	4-0 to 17 years	20 minutes
Wide Range Assessment of Visual Motor Abilities	Psychological Assessment Resources	Visual-motor skills	3-0 to 17 years	15–30 minutes

Abilities (WRAVMA) (Adams & Sheslow, 1995). While these tests are often administered one on one, many can also be administered in a group format. See Table 11.4.

Beery-VMI-5
The Beery-Buktenica Developmental Test of Visual Motor Integration—Fifth Edition (Beery, Buktenica, & Beery, 2004) measures visual-motor skills. This tool includes geometric figures that are copied by the student (paper and pencil). This test has a long form and a short form. Supplemental subtests (visual perception and motor coordination) are available. Teaching materials have been developed in connection with this assessment tool, linking assessment to instruction. Reliability and validity data appear appropriate. Standard scores and percentiles are available.

Bender Visual-Motor Gestalt Test II
The Bender Visual-Motor Gestalt Test II (BVMGT-2) (Bender, 1938; Brannigan & Decker, 2003) measures visual-motor integration and has gone through several revisions. The original Bender-Gestalt was comprised of nine geometric shapes, each placed on 4- by 6-inch white card. The administrator asks the examinee to copy the shapes, one by one, onto blank sheets of paper using a number 2 pencil.

Bender initially developed the test for use with children and adults. After several decades, Koppitz (1964) devised a scoring system for use with children (5 to 11 years of age). Scores are recorded based on four types of errors. Those include distortion of shape (configuration lost), perseveration (student does not stop), integration (student does not arrange pieces of the design properly), and rotation (more that 45 degrees). Koppitz (1975) updated the norms and technical data. Due to the time that has passed and some skewed norm data (geographic and no socioeconomic information reported) (Sattler, 2002), normative data is somewhat weak. Some validity correlation coefficients (i.e., concurrent validity) are low. Furthermore, some questionable coefficients exist in the test retest, interrater reliability areas. Results should be used with caution.

The Detroit Tests of Learning Aptitude—4

The Detroit Tests of Learning Aptitude—4 (DTLA-4) (Hammill, 1998) measure psychological aptitudes and perceptual processing. The test assesses 4 domains with 10 subtests and results in 16 composite scores. Three domains include linguistic, attentional, and motoric. Of the motoric domain, a motor-enhanced composite (design reproduction, design sequences, reversed letters, and story sequences) and a motor-reduced composite (basic information, picture fragments, sentence imitation, story construction, word opposites, and word sequences) exist.

The design reproduction requires students to draw geometric designs from memory, which is of particular interest in the visual-motor area. Norms appear appropriate. Content validity, construct validity, and criterion-related validity are included in the manual. Reliability data exist in the areas of test-retest, interrater, and internal consistency. Some lower coefficients exist. Standard scores, age equivalents, and percentiles are available with this tool. For younger children (age 3 through 9), the Detroit Tests of Learning Aptitude—Primary, Third Edition (Hammill & Bryant, 2005) is available. Furthermore, software regarding scoring and reporting is available.

Test of Visual Motor Integration

The Test of Visual Motor Integration (TVMI) (Hammill, 1996) includes copying geometrical figures. Children copy 12 to 30 figures, depending on their age. Norming appears appropriate. Construct- and criterion-related validity data are provided. This test correlates highly with the VMI. Test retest, interrater, and internal consistency reliability data are available. Some reliability coefficients are low. Standard scores, percentiles, and age equivalents are available with this tool.

Wide Range Assessment of Visual Motor Abilities

The Wide Range Assessment of Visual Motor Abilities (WRAVMA) (Adams & Sheslow, 1995) investigates visual-motor skills via three subtests of visual-motor integration (drawing), visual-spatial relations (matching), and fine motor (pegboard). These subtests can be administered together, separately, or in combination. Construct validity data are available. Test-retest coefficients and internal consistency coefficients are also available. Some test-retest coefficients were low. Standard scores, scaled scores, age equivalents, and percentiles are available with this tool.

Breakpoint Practice

1. Compare and contrast visual-motor tests.
2. Which test would you be most likely to use? Why?
3. Which test would you be least likely to use? Why?

HEARING ASSESSMENT

Hearing is also an essential component of any school assessment. Areas of communication, academic, behavior, and motor skills can be negatively affected if the hearing loss is not identified (Sattler, 2002). According to a report (National Institute on Deafness and Other Communication Disorders, 2006), each year about 12,000 children experience hearing loss. Approximately 28 million individuals in the United States have hearing difficulties. Identification of hearing loss as early as possible is critical, especially in the area of speech and language. It is important to conduct a hearing screening and any possible follow-up assessments to rule out or pinpoint difficulties. In either case, identifying issues related to responding to expressive language can lead to providing appropriate services to the student.

Often, when students have frequent colds, allergies, upper respiratory infections, ear-aches, and other health issues, hearing can be negatively affected. Furthermore, receptive language issues can also be misinterpreted as hearing problems. Some pragmatic language difficulties can also be confused with hearing issues (i.e., responding to social cues).

IDEA 2004 includes distinctions between a diagnosis of deafness and a hearing impairment. Deafness involves a hearing impairment that does not allow an individual to understand language through the hearing mode. Hearing impairment or hard of hearing involves difficulty hearing, but the individual can understand language through the hearing mode with or without hearing amplification (IDEA, 2004).

PHYSIOLOGY OF HEARING

Hearing is associated with the auditory system, which is comprised of the peripheral and central auditory systems. The peripheral auditory system consists of the three segments of the ear: (1) outer ear (pinna and the ear canal), (2) middle ear (tympanic membrane, malleus, incus, stapes, and the Eustachian tube), and (3) inner ear (acoustic nerve and cochlea containing outer and inner hair cells, for chemical electrical transmission). The outer ear serves as a resonator and conductor (it funnels sound). The middle ear receives sound from the ossicles (malleus, incus, and stapes) beating against the tympanic membrane or eardrum. The inner ear receives sound through the hair cells via the cochlear fluid. The central auditory system contains the brainstem and temporal lobe. Neural signals go from the brainstem to the temporal lobe for understanding.

HEARING TESTS

Types of hearing tests include pure-tone screening, pure-tone threshold (air conduction and bone conduction), tympanometry, speech recognition, and word recognition. See Figure 11.1.

Pure-tone screening involves the use of an audiometer. This instrument (in air conduction) produces signals at distinct frequencies, ranging in hertz (Hz) (high versus low pitch). The higher the number, the higher the pitch. Loudness is also included in decibels

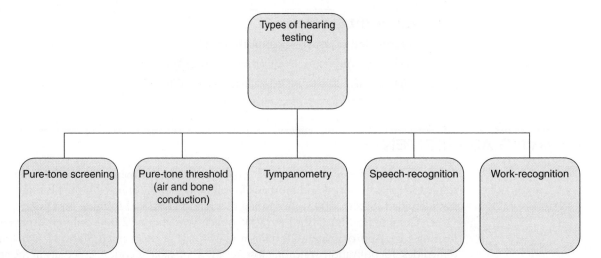

Figure 11.1 Types of hearing testing

(dB). The higher the number, the louder the sound. For school-age students, the range of normal hearing is 1000 to 4000 Hz for pure tones (20 db). Each ear is tested separately using headphones. The student raises his or her hand when the sound is heard (http://www.asha.org/hearing/testing). Figure 11.2 shows how hearing loss varies. Figure 11.3 shows an example of an audiogram.

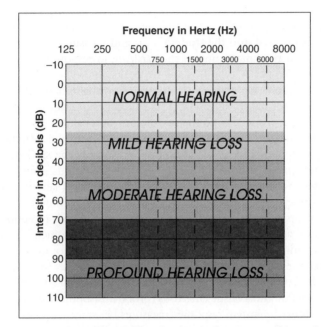

Figure 11.2 Types of hearing loss in frequency and intensity
Source: From http://www.pacificaudiology.com/audiogram/uya.html

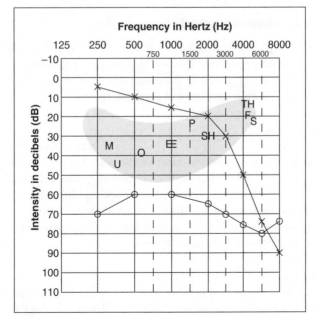

Figure 11.3 Example of an audiogram
Source: From http://www.pacificaudiology.com/audiogram/uya.html

During testing to establish pure-tone threshold (the point at which an individual indicates awareness of the presence of sound), air conduction and bone conduction results are assessed. Bone conduction involves placing a vibrator at the back of the ear, on the mastoid bone. The vibrations bypass the ossicular chain of bones in the middle ear and use the mastoid bone to stimulate the cochlea. Therefore, the functioning of the inner ear can be assessed without engaging the ear canal. This allows the examiner to diagnose the presence or absence of conductive hearing loss.

Tympanometry is utilized for the measurement of middle ear function. This hand-held tool is inserted into the student's ear and measures the movement of the middle ear. It looks at the functioning of the eardrum in response to the vibration of ossicles. Type A (normal peak), type B (flat—no peak), and type C (peak falls on the negative part of the graph) are possible outcomes of tympanometry (Onusko, 2004). A peak appears for a normal reading. Flat peak outcomes indicate possible middle-ear fluid, a stiff middle ear, tissue around the middle ear, or a tumor (Fowler & Shanks, 2002). A deep peak could indicate disarticulation of middle-ear bones (Onusko, 2004).

In speech audiometry, the evaluator investigates the student's ability to hear and understand speech at different loudness points. In language audiometry, the evaluator investigates the student's ability to hear and understand language at different loudness levels. Because very few tasks in real life involve decoding only pure tones, routine screening of students should also include determination of speech reception thresholds (SRT).

Sound field audiometry or visual reinforcement audiometry is used with young children who find it difficult to wear headphones or who are unable to show manual responses. The child looks toward the source of the sound. In conditioned play audiometry, the child performs an activity (i.e., placing a manipulative in a box) when he or she hears the sound. Otoacoustic emissions (probe measuring vibration echoed to the middle ear) or auditory brainstem response (measures brain-wave activity) can also be utilized to test infants for deafness (http://www.asha.org/hearing/testing). Many states, such as Indiana, require that all infants born in medical facilities undergo a hearing screening before being released (like a PKU heel stick is required).

TYPES OF HEARING LOSS

Results of these testing tools can indicate different types of hearing losses. Types of hearing losses include conductive hearing loss (outer or middle ear issues), sensorineural hearing loss (inner ear), mixed (combination of conductive and sensorineural hearing loss), or central auditory hearing loss (processing issues).

Conductive

Causes of conductive hearing loss include excess wax, torn eardrum, otosclerosis (bony growth around the stapes), or fluid in the middle ear. In this case, air-conduction results will not be normal, but bone-conduction results will be normal. This is because the inner ear is functioning normally (i.e., bone conduction), but overall hearing function is affected by outer or middle ear issues. Surgery or hearing aids may be helpful. Common hearing aid problems include low or dead battery, technical issues with the instrument, and blocked earmold (www.asha.org).

Sensorineural

In the case of sensorineural hearing loss, air-conduction and bone-conduction testing will reveal results that are not within normal limits. Etiology could include repeated exposure to high noise, head trauma, ototoxic drugs (drugs that cause damage in the ear, for example, drugs that treat meningitis), viral diseases (e.g., mumps, cytomegalovirus), hereditary factors, Rh incompatibility, or head trauma. Hearing aids are not generally helpful with students affected by sensorineural hearing loss. Cochlear implants are now recommended more often at all ages.

Mixed

Mixed hearing loss is revealed by air- and bone-conduction results that are out of range. Air-conduction hearing is usually more out of range. Mixed hearing loss results from a combination of causes, all of which were mentioned for the other types of hearing loss. Hearing aids can be useful for students affected by mixed hearing loss. Auditory loops and transmitters are important tools in addressing the needs of a student in and outside the classroom. Auditory loops are used in rooms where there are many people. An auditory loop enhances the use of hearing aids. In the case of a transmitter, an individual receives amplified sound using an auditory device: an adult (parent or teacher) wears a microphone transmitter and the child wears a receiver. Background noise is not amplified, whereas the sound of the speaker *is* amplified.

ETIOLOGY

The etiology of about 33 percent of hearing loss in children is due to a genetic cause, 33 percent is due to a nongenetic cause, and 33 percent is due to an unknown cause (http://babyhearing.org/HearingAmpification/Causes.index.asp; http://www.boystownhospital.org/parents/info/genetics/ten.asp). About 400 different genetic origins of hearing loss exist. These genetic origins can be part of a syndrome (i.e., Usher's syndrome, which involves progressive loss of hearing and vision). Also, most nongenetic hearing loss has an origin of illness or trauma before or during birth (www.cdc.gov/ncbddd/ehdi/researchcompleted.htm).

SEVERITY

The American Speech-Language-Hearing Association (ASHA) recognizes measurement of hearing loss levels in decibels (dB): normal range (−10 to 15 dB), slight hearing loss (16 to 25 dB), mild hearing loss (26 to 40 dB), moderate hearing loss (41 to 55 dB), moderate/severe hearing loss (56 to 70 dB), severe hearing loss (70 to 90 dB), and profound hearing loss (91+ dB) (http://www.asha.org/public/hearing/disorders/types.htm). The American Academy of Otolaryngology uses four levels of hearing loss defined in dB. Those include mild (15 to 40), moderate (40 to 60), severe (60 to 90), and profound (90+) (http://www.entnet.org/KidsENT/upload/KidsENT_HearingScreening.pdf). Furthermore, research indicates that estimates of unilateral hearing loss involve 30 per 1,000 individuals (31.1 percent—mild, 31.8 percent—moderate, 15.3 percent—severe, and 12.0 percent—profound) and bilateral hearing loss involve 60 per 1,000 individuals (26.1 percent—mild, 28.3 percent—moderate, 16.0 percent—severe, and 18.0 percent—profound) (www.cdc.gov/ncbddd/ehdi/FAQ/questionsgeneralHL.htm).

MODES OF COMMUNICATION

Different modes of communication exist for individuals who are hard of hearing or deaf. American Sign Language (ASL) is one language option. ASL has its own grammar and syntax and should not be viewed as a substandard version of standard English. Other sign systems include several versions of Signed English. This sign system utilizes the structure (grammar and syntax) of Standard American English. Cued Speech uses hand cues to supplement auditory and visual decoding of speech. Signs and speech reading is used in Standard American English language structure. Total Communication uses all communication modalities (speech reading, auditory training, signing, cues, and gestures). Assessment practices should take communication modality into consideration when making educational decisions (http://www.asha.org/about/legislation-advocacy/ federal/idea/nat-env-child-facts.htm).

Furthermore, professionals who are culturally competent, who have the technological knowledge, who are collaborative with parents, who are fluent in the student's communication modality, and who can compare the student to peers who share the student's language modality are necessary in providing appropriate assessment services to students with hearing impairments (http://www.asha.org/about/legislation-advocacy/federal/ idea/nat-env-child-facts.htm). It should be noted that professionals who provide services to students who are deaf or hard of hearing are in short supply (Bowen & Ferrell, 2003).

EDUCATIONAL TESTS IN THE AREA OF HEARING DIFFICULTIES

If hearing difficulties are found, some educational test options are available specifically for this population. A test for phoneme decoding can include the Auditory Perception Test for the Hearing Impaired (Allen & Serwatka, 1994). The Carolina Picture Vocabulary Test for Deaf and Hearing Impaired examines receptive sign vocabulary (Layton & Holmes, 1985). The Test of Early Reading Ability—2: Deaf or Hard of Hearing (Reid, Jiresko, Hammill, & Wiltshire, 1991) addresses the ability to extract meaning from printed symbols. It should be noted that when assessing intelligence, a nonverbal intelligence test (see Chapter 6) is a more appropriate test as compared to conventional intelligence testing.

Breakpoint Practice

1. What types of results are connected with sensorineural loss versus middle ear hearing loss?
2. What are some causes of hearing disorders?
3. What is the difference between deaf and hard of hearing?

CENTRAL AUDITORY HEARING LOSS

In central auditory hearing loss, students usually pass air- and bone-conduction tests, and tympanometry appears normal. However, the students have difficulty understanding speech and language in noisy environments. Furthermore, students have difficulty with learning. Types of central auditory hearing loss include auditory comprehension and discrimination difficulties. Language and learning difficulties can exist.

According to the American Speech-Language-Hearing Association (American Speech-Language-Hearing Association Working Group on Auditory Processing Disorders, 2005, p. 2), auditory processing means "the perceptual processing of auditory information in the CNS [central nervous system] and the neurobiological activity that underlies that processing and gives rise to electrophysiologic auditory potentials." That is, hearing uses electrical signals to carry information from the ear to the brain.

According to ASHA, skills such as "sound localization and lateralization, auditory discrimination, auditory pattern recognition, temporal ordering and masking, auditory performance in competing acoustic signals, and auditory performance with degraded acoustic signals" make up auditory processing (American Speech-Language Hearing Association [ASHA], 1996). ASHA (2005) lists seven types of central auditory processing disorder tests. Those include auditory discrimination, auditory temporal processing and patterning, dichotic speech, monaural low-redundancy speech, binaural interaction, electroacoustic, and electrophysiologic assessments" (ASHA, 2005, p. 9). Schow, Seikel, Chermak, and Berent (2000) noted that auditory assessment measures should be simplified in an effort to connect classifications and test measures. They discussed four behavioral areas, including "auditory pattern/temporal ordering, monaural separation/ closure, binaural separation, and binaural integration" (p. 5).

Auditory processing issues can sometimes be misdiagnosed as attention deficit disorder, behavior disabilities, motivation problems, or other issues (Minnesota Department of Children Families & Learning, 2003; Schminky & Baran, 1999). Therefore, it is important that an audiologist participate in the testing and interpretation of auditory processing (Bellis, 2004). Auditory processing issues are associated with but are not due to other disorders, such as learning disabilities and language disorders (ASHA, 2005). Difficulties can include following conversations; following directions; challenges with reading, spelling and/or writing; and ability to hear in noisy environments (Learning Disabilities Association of America, 2006).

Subtypes of auditory processing disorders include difficulties with auditory decoding (e.g., analyzing sounds), auditory integration (i.e., word recognition), auditory associative issues (i.e., receptive language), and auditory output-organization (i.e., directions) (http://www.acenta.com/audiology.auditoryprocessing.asp). Researchers have identified intervention strategies in the area of auditory processing (Bellis, 2002, 2003; Chermak, 1998; Chermak & Musiek, 1997; Crandell & Smaldino, 2000; Musiek, 1999). Strategies have included, but are not limited to, perceptual (practicing limited stimuli, which is changed slowly), compensatory (increasing language, memory, and attention) and cognitive training (can include phoneme manipulation), and modification of the environment (Keith, 1999).

Auditory processing includes auditory discrimination, which is commonly assessed. In auditory discrimination, the ability to differentiate phonemes is compromised. Some examples of high-frequency sounds include /f/, /s/, and /sh/, /th/. Words are comprised of phonemes or sounds. Therefore, when the ability to differentiate or discriminate speech sounds is negatively affected, this in turn affects one's ability to understand the speech of others. When thinking about the classroom context, issues with auditory discrimination can significantly affect classroom performance. In auditory discrimination tests, individuals are assessed on the ability to understand or use phonemes within spoken words. Some examples include identifying phonemes in the context of words, comparing phonemes, separating phonemes, and combining phonemes. For more information regarding auditory processing issues, see Chapter 9.

Breakpoint Practice

1. How does an auditory processing disorder differ from a conductive hearing loss?
2. What types of difficulties would an individual with a central auditory disorder experience?
3. What are two examples of a central auditory disorder?

Table 11.5   Tests of Auditory Processing

Test	Company	Content	Age	Time to Administer
Goldman-Fristoe-Woodcock Test of Auditory Discrimination	American Guidance Service	Auditory discrimination	3-8 through 70+ years	20–30 minutes
Wepman Test of Auditory Discrimination, 2nd Edition	Western Psychological Services	Auditory discrimination	4 through 8 years	5 minutes
Lindamood Auditory Conceptualization Test, 3rd Edition	PRO-ED	Perception through vision	5 to 19 years	20–30 minutes
Test of Auditory Processing Skills—3rd Edition	PRO-ED	Auditory perception	4 through 18-11 years	1 hour

AUDITORY PROCESSING TESTS

Some common auditory processing tests include the areas of auditory discrimination, perception through the area of vision, and auditory perception. See Table 11.5.

In the area of auditory discrimination, the Goldman-Fristoe-Woodcock Test of Auditory Discrimination (G-F-WTAD) and the Wepman Test of Auditory Discrimination, 2nd Edition (ADT-2), are commonly used. In the area of perception via vision, the Lindamood Auditory Conceptualization, Third Edition (LAC-3), is often utilized. In investigating auditory perception, the Test of Auditory Processing—3rd Edition (TAPS-3), is commonly used.

Golman-Fristoe-Woodcock Test of Auditory Discrimination

The Goldman-Fristoe-Woodcock Test of Auditory Discrimination (G-F-WTAD) (Goldman, Fristoe, & Woodcock, 1970) requires that students point to the specified pictures on plates (each plate consists of four drawings) by responding to directions that are presented via audiocassette. No speaking or writing skills are required of the examinee for this test.

Wepman Test of Auditory Discrimination—2

The Wepman Test of Auditory Discrimination, 2nd Edition (ADT-2) (Wepman & Reynolds, 1986), involves 40 pairs of words read aloud to the student by the examiner. The student judges each pair presented as being the same or different. The examiner reads the words to the student.

Lindamood Auditory Conceptualization Test—3

The Lindamood Auditory Conceptualization Test—3 (LAC-3) is separated into four portions. The precheck includes five items utilized to get an understanding of the student's general knowledge. Category I, Part A includes items with isolated sounds with a discrimination task (same/different). Category I, Part B includes sounds in isolation and examines same/different and order. Category II includes 18 items and investigates addition, omission, substitution, rearranged, or repeated sound patterns.

Test of Auditory Perceptual Skills—3

The Test of Auditory Perceptual Skills—3rd Edition (TAPS-3) consists of the following subtests: word discrimination, phonological segmentation, phonological blending, numbers forward, numbers reversed, word memory, sentence memory, auditory comprehension and auditory reasoning. Three cluster scores include basic auditory skills, auditory memory, and auditory cohesion. Standard scores, scaled scores, stanines, percentile ranks, and age equivalents are available with this test.

Breakpoint Practice

1. Compare and contrast auditory processing tests.
2. Which test would you be most likely to use? Why?
3. Which test would you be least likely to use? Why?
4. How are results linked to classroom instruction?

ASSISTIVE TECHNOLOGIES

In assessment, instruction, and daily living, technology is a crucial tool. It is important to keep in mind that technologies can be used as adaptations in many and multiple areas. For example, language issues related to cognition or learning disabilities can mean that technologies (i.e., adaptation of reading materials, communication devices) are necessary for the student to obtain optimal performance. Therefore, many of the technologies that will be mentioned in the following sections can be used for a variety of students with disabilities. See Chapter 6 about cognition, Chapter 8 about achievement, Chapter 7 about adaptive skills, and Chapter 9 about language for more discussion of these areas.

Technologies are particularly significant in the area of sensory skills. *Assistive technology* is a term used in IDEA as an item utilized to "increase, maintain, or improve functional capabilities of a child with a disability" (20USC Sec. 602(1)), and these items are the focus of the Assistive Technology Act of 1998 (105-394, S.2432). Assistive technology devices can be used and/or developed for the student during an evaluation. When the evaluation supports the use of assistive technologies, and the information is included in the student's IEP, students can be provided training in the use of and access (utilization or lease) to equipment for use at school or outside school. It is important for the team to train families, teachers, students, peers, and related service providers.

CEC Content Standard 8 specifically addresses the use of "appropriate technologies to support their assessments" (http://www.cec.sped.org/ps/perf_bases_stds/standards.html). These standards are addressed by the National Council for Accreditation of Teacher Education (NCATE) (http://www.ncate.org). Teachers should have knowledge about, use, assess, and locate assistive technology devices (Edyburn, 2003). However, special education educators report feeling unprepared to use assistive technology (AT) with their students (Wahl, 2004). It is important for team members to request training when the team makes decisions to include technology in IEPs, ITPs, and statewide assessments.

MODELS OF ASSISTIVE TECHNOLOGY

Researchers have investigated models for assistive technology approaches (Lenker & Paquet, 2003, 2004; Watts, O'Brian, & Wojcik, 2004). Two popular approaches include

Students, Environment, Tasks, and Tools (SETT) (Zabala, 1995, 2005) and Matching Person & Technology (MPT) (Scherer & Craddock, 2002).

SETT involves a dynamic process of collaboration among team members and revolves around the student's needs, the type of AT needed, and strategies needed to optimize AT (Brady, Long, Richards, & Vallin, 2004). MPT is an approach that takes environment and individuality into consideration when the team chooses assistive technologies. Functionality of the technology is also addressed in this model.

ASSISTIVE TECHNOLOGY AREAS

Assistive technology has many different applications in and outside the classroom. It can be used for mobility, communication (augmentative and alternative), hearing, orthotics, vision, and other daily living skills (Wehman & Kregel, 2004). Low-level technologies require little training, whereas high-level technologies generally require user training (Birnbaum, 1999). Examples of low-level technologies for the classroom include raised line paper, highlighters, correction pens, book holders, page turner aids, grips for writing tools, and calculators. Examples of high-level technologies include voice output devices, computer software, braille embossers, and wheelchairs.

Vision

The misconception has been that if a child has decreased visual acuity, then the modification would simply be to enlarge the print. However, many students with decreased vision actually read standard print more quickly and easily than large print (Wilkinson, Trantham, & Koenig, 2001). Also, students who read print may benefit from using optical or low-vision devices. A low-vision device is defined as any optical device made up of one or more lenses that are placed between the student's eyes and the information or object being viewed (Gardner & Corn, 2006). Optical devices can be as simple as a tinted lens in a pair of glasses and as complex as a closed-circuit television system (Gardner & Corn, 2006). In many situations, the optical device allows the student to read a standard-size print (12 point), which alleviates the expense and the inconvenience of using large-print books (Gardner & Corn, 2006).

When an individual is blind or visually impaired, output devices such as scanning/reading devices, books on tape, large-print display, braille display, braille embossers, screen reading software, and screen magnification (low- and high-level technologies) are available options.

The Perkins Brailler continues to be used by students who are blind to create braille documents. The brailler has changed little since it was originally designed in 1951. It uses a braille paper, which is heavier than print paper, and thus allows braille to be embossed on both sides of the paper (Perkins School for the Blind, 2006).

All textbooks and pleasure reading materials, including magazines, are available in braille. Most states have laws that require publishers to provide an electronic copy of their texts so they can be easily transcribed for the braille reader (AFB, 2006).

Braille technology has been one of the greatest advancements in making the sighted world more readily available to those who are blind. A braille display (placement of six raised dots in specific patterns) is a tactile device that provides braille navigation of computer systems such as Windows.

Braille translation programs translate print into a braille document and then, with the use of a braille embosser, also print the document in braille. One exciting advancement in technology has been the development of a device that prints a document in both print and braille, making it easily accessible for the classroom teachers because it bypasses the middle translator, who is usually the teacher of the visually impaired (APH, 2006).

A popular computer software option is JAWS (http://www.freedomscientific.com). JAWS allows the student to receive written data in the form of braille and synthesized speech output. Other screen readers include Hal Screen Reader (http://www.dolphinusa.com) and OutSPOKEN (http://www.aagi.com).

Screen readers are software programs that read what is projected on the computer screen, including complete access to the Internet. Many of the programs also support braille displays, giving students the choice of either or both modes of computer navigation (APH, 2006).

The third reading option is that of using audiotaped textbooks and materials. However, the exclusive use of these materials jeopardizes the student's acquisition of the structure of written language, including grammar, spelling, and overall syntax of written expression (Wilkinson, Trantham, & Koenig, 2001).

Other adaptations include books on tape, someone reading the material for the student, appropriate lighting, and arranging furniture and room for more space (reducing obstacles). Depending on vision and other sensory and cognitive skills, the appropriate technologies can be chosen during an evaluation.

Exposure to and use of technological support is a priority for students with visual impairment. Hatlen (1996) stated that the ongoing development of technology has been instrumental in providing equal opportunities for those with visual impairment in the academic world. Assistive technology is the component that closes the gap and gives total access to students who are visually impaired. It includes any product that is used to improve the abilities of a student: computer screen readers, screen magnification, scanners, adaptive keyboards, closed-circuit televisions, braille translation software, braille embossers, and braillers (AFB, 2006).

The availability of the continually expanding repertoire of assistive technology brings a wealth of information to students who can use it proficiently. The trained educator of students with visual impairment should conduct a comprehensive assessment of the unique needs of the student to find the appropriate match between technology and the student (AFB, 2006).

Valerie Schultz/Merrill

Motor

When an individual needs adaptations in the area of motor skills, a touch window, alternate keyboards, joysticks, trackballs, switches, and alternative mice are possible input options (Wisconsin Assistive Technology Initiative, 2006). During an evaluation, and depending on the person's motor skills, one or more of these options will be examined. A touch window is positioned over a monitor screen. The individual can then touch the screen to choose items. Alternate keyboards can have larger or smaller keyboards and can have a wider set of options, including keyboard labels, slant boards, and on-screen keyboards (Circle of Inclusion, 2006). The keys can be color-coded or arranged in ABC order.

Joysticks and trackballs are sold by a variety of companies. They come in many different sizes and shapes. Some joysticks have more angles of motion than others. The choice depends on the amount of control a student has. Trackballs allow the individual to maneuver a mouse more easily by using the tips of the fingers or the hand. An alternative mouse comes in a variety of sizes and colors, depending on the size of the student's hand and motor skills.

Switches can be used when motor skills are more severely impaired. Switches can be operated by muscle movements (head, eye, mouth-puffing, and sipping) and sound. During an evaluation, it is important to think about which part of the body the student would use, the amount of strength the individual has, how much aim and range of motion the individual has, and other sensory issues (TASH, 2006). Switches can also control an individual's environment, including appliances, televisions, alarms, and telephones. Low-level technologies around the environment can include mounts (to hold items in place), ramps, lifts, elevators, larger doorways, adapted furniture, adapted doorknobs, and specially designed kitchens and bathrooms (RehabTool, 2006).

Adaptations for students who have motor disabilities can also involve positioning. Proper positioning aids in the support of the body. Seating is one important aspect of positioning. According to Best, Heller, and Bigge (2005), pelvic position, foot support, and shoulder and trunk support are important elements of appropriate seating. They add that transferring students, location, and mobility of students are other areas of importance.

Assistive walking devices, lifts, canes, crutches, and wheelchairs are items open to discussion in the area of mobility (Lindsey, 2000). Depending on a person's motor skills in their arms, legs, and trunk, different options are appropriate. In the area of assistive walking devices, walkers (reverse and nonfolding) and crutches (forearm and aluminum crutches) are options (Best et al., 2005).

An individual who has use of one or both arms can use a manual wheelchair. Electric or motorized wheelchairs assist individuals who have more severe motor impairment. Wheelchair options include conventional, power base, and scooters (Best et al., 2005). Adjustable wheelchairs allow individuals to raise themselves vertically (to a standing position). Some of the assistive technologies (i.e., joystick) aid individuals with utilizing this device. Adaptive eating utensils, drinking utensils, and specialized clocks are examples of technologies for daily living skills.

Assistive Communication Devices

In many instances when the motor domain is affected, labial (lip) and lingual (tongue) muscles are affected. Augmentative communication devices represent an addition to natural spoken, written, or gestural speech. Alternative communication devices represent a substitute for natural spoken, written, or gestural communication (Lloyd & Blischak, 1992). These assistive communication devices are assistive technologies. They can be low-level technologies, such as picture books, or high-level technologies, such as synthesized speech.

Low-level communication devices can include communication boards made from cardboard or thick paper. Boards can incorporate photographs, pictures, markers, colored paper, and even real objects. Place one or more items on a blackboard with word labels using Velcro or Dycem (a sticky substance) to attach the items. Medium-level technologies are sometimes referred to as talking devices and are not computer based. Simple switches are used. The student presses a switch and a recorded message of one or more words (i.e., "I need help" or "apple") is heard. In this case, a person records his or her speech on a device that has a microphone (digitized speech).

Assistive communication high-level technologies include electronically constructed speech, which is referred to as synthesized speech. It is important to match an individual's voice with a general age category and gender category. In other words, it is important to match the voice as much as possible to the person. For more information, see http://www.cini.org/glossary.html. Personalization is an important piece of the process. The student should be an active participant in choosing the voice that will "speak" for him or her. The individual can then access the constructed or recorded words by pressing a key or a button; pointing to a picture; using his or her own voice; using a joystick or lever; using eye, head, and tongue movements; and sipping and/or puffing (Gragnani, 2006).

Synthesized speech products containing picture boards typically range from 4- to 32-key picture displays. Picture boards contain pictures, symbols, and/or letters. Based on the student's cognitive and language levels, key vocabulary can be programmed to match what is often used by the student and/or what the student is learning. Expansion occurs by tapping on a picture and going into a new screen of symbols and/or pictures. For example, a student can access a collection of pictures for food, home, and vacation words (low-tech). Another option would be typing words into an assistive technology device for voice synthesized output (text-to-speech) (high-tech). Word prediction software is also available for some of these devices.

Hearing

Interpreters and note takers are adaptations that can be used in assessment practices and in the classroom. Amplification systems, video relay services, seating close to the teacher (but not closer than 2 to 3 feet), tape recorders, limited background noises, and visual aids are other adaptation tools (http://www.deafweb.org/assist.htm; http://nclid.unco.edu). Other adaptations can include alternate forms of standardized tests, modified scheduling, modified response mode, and extended time (Bowen & Ferrell, 2003). Braden (1992) reported that only nonverbal tests should be used in the assessment of a deaf student's intelligence (see Chapter 6).

Some other general adaptations include peer support, student groupings, sign language, repeating content, giving a study guide, highlighting important content, using manipulatives, allowing calculators, using raised or graph paper, graphic organizers, reducing the number of items or length of words, increasing the amount of breaks and/or break time, increasing prompts, using words of lower vocabulary level, inserting pictures, presenting material in bold type, and/or color-coding material.

Other assistive technology devices can include speech recognition software, live captioning, telephone devices, environmental alert devices, cochlear implants, and listening devices (i.e., FM systems and hearing aids) (http://www.nclid.unco.edu). In a study conducted by the Office of Vocational Rehabilitation Services in Oregon (www.oregon.gov), 73 percent of the participants who were deaf or hard of hearing noted that they used instant messenger programs (e.g., America Online Instant Messenger), 60 percent noted that they use video remote interpreting, 61 percent noted that the use of Web cameras was a good idea, and 80 percent reported support

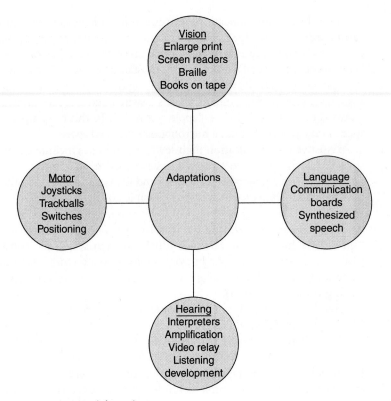

Figure 11.4 Adaptations

of video relay service. In terms of communication preferences, e-mail (92 percent), instant messenger (44 percent), and TTY calling (type text messages) (31 percent) were the top three preferences. See Figure 11.4.

General Adaptations

When conducting assessments, establishing the strengths and needs of the students is a vital part of the beginning of the assessment process to establish which supports a student needs (Downing, 2002). The supports will allow the student to display his or her skills (Wehmeyer & Agran, 2005). Only 1 percent of all students at local school districts could be considered eligible to use alternate tests for the statewide assessments (Committee on Education and the Workforce, 2006). So a widespread assessment mechanism for students who are low functioning focuses on standardized tests (Pratt & Stewart, 2006).

In this case, adaptations are used in the evaluation process. On an even wider scale, adaptations can include changes in the content and/or manner in which instructional methods, assignments, assessments, environment, and/or scheduling are delivered and/or responded to. This is meant to make tasks in instruction and assessment doable, meaningful, and fair to individuals. *Adaptations* is an umbrella term that can include providing additional or alternative methods for delivery or responses. Adaptations include modifications and accommodations. Modifications refer to significant changes in the instruction that changes the amount and/or level of material. Accommodations refer to providing materials to help level the playing field. Those typically affect the form of the instruction or response mode. They can also involve alternate goals and/or completing a portion of a program.

Wehmeyer (2002) defines curricular adaptations as any changes in the curriculum, curriculum augmentation as any enhancements to the curriculum, and curriculum alteration as infusing aspects such as vocation or life skills into the curriculum. The Council for Exceptional Children lists examples of adaptations of lesson format and teaching style (Council for Exceptional Children, 1997). These are important considerations when connecting instruction to assessment. Rubrics, checklists, and other assessment tools would be adapted based on one or more of the listed adaptations. For more information regarding literature on adaptations and accommodations and about students with disabilities, please see Williams (2001).

Breakpoint Practice

1. In terms of responsibility for training in assistive technology, who do you think is the most critical person? Why?

2. Describe how the Internet can be used specifically in the area of assessment of students with motor disabilities?

3. Which device would be most useful in the home environment for a person with a motor impairment (i.e., a person who is using a wheelchair with little use of her motor skills)? Why?

4. Which device would be most useful in the community environment for a person with a severe language impairment (i.e., to accomplish a grocery store task)? Why?

5. Which device would be most useful in the community for a person with a visual impairment (a person who has very little sight)? Why?

Multicultural Considerations

An area of significant interest when discussing multicultural considerations and sensory disabilities is research on the deaf as related to special education assessment. Several recent studies have revealed results with significant implications for teachers and parents.

In a longitudinal study, Yoshinaga-Itano (2003) investigated the language, speech, and social-emotional development of children who had hearing disabilities over the processes of screening, early identification, and intervention. This researcher found that language skills were positively related to the age of identification of hearing impairment. Speech and social-emotional development were highly linked to language development. Therefore, early identification was noted as a predictor to successful outcomes for students with hearing disabilities. These findings have significant applications for assessment practices.

Loots and Devise (2003) examined visual-tactile communication strategies of deaf and hearing parents of deaf toddlers between 18 and 24 months of age. Four groups of parents (deaf mothers, deaf fathers, hearing mothers, and hearing fathers) had significant differences. Deaf mothers and fathers adapted visual communication style to match the needs of the developmental period of their child more than did the hearing parents. These findings have implications for increasing communication strategies with deaf children. Swisher (2000) noted similar results. Parents can become trainers for teachers and related service professionals.

(continued)

In addition, Webster and Heineman-Gosschalk (2000) compared hearing teachers and deaf adults in supporting reading in deaf children. Results revealed that hearing teachers use discourse that is high in management (i.e., behavior), whereas deaf adults focus on responding to the child's intentions (i.e., communication and attention). Therefore, the students were receiving significantly different language input from adults. These findings provide significant information that can be applied in the assessment and instruction settings. In a study by Calderon (2000), the researcher studied factors such as student's hearing loss, mother's educational level, mother's communication skills related to her child, and additional services used by the mother. Results revealed that poor communication skills in the mother were related to higher externalizing behavior issues (visible behaviors). Results reveal important information regarding the impact of a child's environment on his or her behavior.

Technology

Technology is another important area in the discussion of sensory disabilities and multicultural issues. In the area of multicultural issues and technology, one can examine the linguistic and cultural aspects. In looking at the linguistic aspect, a great deal of software is written in different languages. In some cases, these programs can be used interchangeably between two or more languages, which make them a valuable tool for teaching children who are English language learners. The level of difficulty also varies so teachers can meet the individual needs of the students. Multiple dialects and levels in other languages add complexity to this process.

Many software programs record student progress and provide the teacher with detailed feedback about the errors the student made. Not only does this option reduce the paperwork for the teacher, but the program provides valuable formative diagnostic information concerning the student's ability levels.

Parette and colleagues (Hourcade, Parette, & Huer, 1997; Judge & Parette, 1998; Kemp & Parette, 2000; Parette, 1997; Parette & Anderson, 2001; Parette & Brotherson, 2004; Parette, Brotherson, & Huer, 2000; Parette, Huer, & Brotherson, 2001; Parette & Petch-Hogan, 2000) have conducted significant research in the interactions of professionals and families in the area of technology and diversity and services to children who have disabilities. Discussion of families' beliefs regarding technology (Parette & Anderson, 2001) and professionals' beliefs regarding their roles and families' roles in the assessment practice (Parette, Huer, & Brotherson, 2001) is available by exploring the works of these researchers. In addition, information regarding the role of culture and family dynamics in the assessment process involving the utilization of assistive technologies for students who have disabilities (Hourcade, Parette, & Huer, 1997) and the selection of these devices by young children (Judge & Parette, 1998) are important areas of study available in the literature. Barriers involved in the access of assistive technology by minority families (Kemp & Parette, 2000), as well as suggestions to increase family participation of students who are culturally and/or linguistically diverse (Parette & McMahan, 2002; Parette & Petch-Hogan, 2000) are areas that have been researched.

Discussion regarding a family-centered approach (Parette, 1997; Parette & Brotherson, 2004) was offered by these investigators. Specifically, information regarding family strengths, needs, and priorities in the decision-making process concerning assistive technology as influenced by the family's culture was revealed. A key is respect for family decisions rather than forming judgments.

Breakpoint Practice

1. How can you use technology to better address linguistic variation in the assessment process?

2. How can you use technology to better address cultural factors in the assessment process?

3. How can you infuse technology into the assessment process to involve family members?

REASSESSING DALE

Go back to the information in the chapter-opening case study. Some formal tests that can be administered to Dale include the Beery-Buktenica Developmental Test of Visual-Motor Integration, Fifth Edition, for fine motor skills (Beery, Buktenica, & Beery, 2004); the Universal Nonverbal Intelligence Test (UNIT) (Bracken & McCallem, 1998); the Woodcock Johnson II Test of Achievement (Woodcock, McGrew, & Mather, 2001); and the Goldman-Fristoe Test of Articulation, Second Edition (Goldman & Fristoe, 2000), for articulation skills.

Adaptations to testing can be incorporated as needed and would most affect the response mode (how the student responds) due to motor and speech/language difficulties. Assistive technologies would address these areas. Augmentative communication devices (synthesized speech) as well as alternate keyboards can be used.

In the informal assessment realm, observations and anecdotal behavioral data can be collected. Family interviews and discussion can be incorporated. A technology specialist from the district can be contacted and the family can be referred to a pediatrician. Dale's strengths can then be used in the classroom. The teacher can communicate with the technology specialist for support. Any new high technology requires much training and support for all individuals involved with the student.

In addition, the teacher can collaborate with the SLP and OT in terms of day-to-day assessments and instruction. Furthermore, the teacher can maintain communication with Dale's family to provide positive carryover activities in the home setting and to discuss Dale's progress.

ACTIVITIES

1. Name, explain, and give an example of four components of a comprehensive visual assessment.

2. Compare and contrast motor and visual-motor skills. Give an example of each.

3. Compare and contrast conductive, sensory-neural, mixed hearing loss, and central auditory processing.

4. List five adaptations for students with motor disabilities.

5. List five adaptations for students with visual disabilities.

6. List five adaptations for students with language disabilities.

7. List five adaptations for students with hearing impairments.

WEB RESOURCES

http://www.webaim.org/articles/motor/motordisabilities

http://www.mda.org

http://www.ucp.org

http://www.sbail.org

http://www.sbaa.org

http://www.nlm.nih.gov/medlineplus/hearingdisordersanddeafness. html

http://www. medicinenet.com/hearing/focus.htm

http://www. asha.org/public/hearing/disorders/

http://health.nih.gov/result.asp/309

http://www.nidcd.nih.gov/health/voice/auditory.asp

http://www.ldonline.org/article/6390

http://www.medicinenet.com/auditory_processing_disorder_in_children/article.htm

http://www.nichcy.org/pubs/factshe/fs13txt.htm

http://www.cdc.gov/ncbddd/dd/ddvi.htm

http://www.aadb.org/

REFERENCES

Adams, W., & Sheslow, D. (1995). *Wide range assessment of visual motor abilities.* Wilmington, DE: Wide Range.

Allen, S. G., & Serwatka, T. S. (1994). *Auditory perception test for the hearing impaired.* East Aurora, NY: Slosson Educational Publications.

Allman, C. (2004). *Making tests accessible for students with visual impairments: A guide for test publishers, test developers, and state assessment personnel* (2nd ed.). Louisville, KY: American Printing House for the Blind. Available from http://www.aph.org

American Academy of Pediatrics et al. (2003). Policy statement: Eye examinations in infants, children, and young adults by pediatricians. *Pediatrics, 111*(4), 902–907.

American Foundation for the Blind. Retrieved February 14, 2006, from http://www.afb.org/Section.asp?SectionID=4

American Printing House for the Blind. (2006). Retrieved April 1, 2006, from http://www.aph.org/index.htm

American Speech-Language-Hearing Association. (1996). Central auditory processing: Current status of research and implications for clinical practice. *American Journal of Audiology, 5*, 41–54.

American Speech-Language-Hearing Association. Hearing screening. Retrieved October 15, 2006, from http://www.asha.org/hearing/testing

American Speech-Language-Hearing Association. The prevalence and incidence of hearing loss in children. Retrieved October 15, 2006, from http://www. asha.org/public/hearing/disorders/types.htm

American Speech-Language-Hearing Association. Guidelines for the roles and responsibilities of the school-based speech-language pathologist. Retrieved October 10, 2006, from http://www.asha.org/about/legistlation-advocacy/federal/idea/nat-env-child-facts.htm

American Speech-Language-Hearing Association Working Group on Auditory Processing Disorders. (2005). (Central) auditory processing disorders. *Technical Report*, 1–20.

Barraga, N. C. (2004). A half century later. Where are we? Where do we need to go? *Journal of Visual Impairment & Blindness, 98*(10), 581–583.

Beery, K. E., Buktenica, N. A., & Beery, N. A. (2004). *Beery visual-motor integration*, (5th ed.). Austin, TX: PRO-ED.

Beirne-Smith, M., Patton, J. R., & Kim, S. H. (2006). *Mental retardation: An introduction to intellectual disabilities* (7th ed.). Upper Saddle River, NJ: Merrill/Pearson Education.

Bellis, T. J. (2002). Developing deficit-specific intervention plans for individuals with auditory processing disorders. *Seminars in Hearing, 23*(4), 287–295.

Bellis, T. J. (2003). *Assessment and management of central auditory processing disorders in the educational setting: From science to practice* (2nd ed.). Clifton Park, NY: Delmar Learning.

Bellis, T. J. (2004). Redifining auditory processing disorder: An audiologist's perspective. *The ASHA Leader,* March, 22–23.

Bender, L. (1938). *Bender Visual-Motor Gestalt Test.* New York: Grune & Stratton.

Best, S. J., Heller, K. W., & Bigge, J. L. (2005). *Teaching individuals with physical or multiple disabilities* (5th ed.). Upper Saddle River, NJ: Merrill/Pearson Education.

Birnbaum, B. (1999). *Connecting special education and technology for the 21st century.* Lewiston, NY: Edwin Mellen Press.

Bowen, S. K., & Ferrell, K. A. (2003). Assessment in low-incidence disabilities: The day-to-day realities. *Rural Special Education Quarterly, 22*(4), 10–19.

Bracken, B. A., & McCallem, R. S. (1998). *Universal test of nonverbal intelligence.* Itasca, IL: Riverside.

Braden, J. (1992). The Differential Ability Scales in special education. *Journal of Psychoeducational Assessment, 30,* 92–98.

Brady, R. T., Long, T. M., Richards, J., & Vallin T. (2008). Assistive technology curriculum structure and content in professional preparation service provider training programs. *Journal of Allied Health, 36*(4), 183–192.

Brannigan, G. G., & Decker, S. C. (2003). *Bender Visual-Motor Gestalt Test—II.* Itasca, IL: Riverside.

Bruininks, R. H., & Bruininks, B. D. (2005). *Bruininks-Oseresky Test of Motor Proficiency* (2nd ed.). Circle Pines, MN: American Guidance Service.

Calderon, R. (2000). Parental involvement in deaf children's education programs as a predictor of child's language, early reading, and social-emotional development. *Journal of Deaf Studies and Deaf Educaiton, 5*(2), 140–155.

Chermak, G. D. (1998). Managing central auditory processing disorders: Metalinguistic and metacognitive approaches. *Seminars in Hearing, 19*(4), 379–392.

Chermak, G. D., & Musiek, F. E. (1997). *Central auditory processing disorders: New perspectives.* San Diego, CA: Singular.

Circle of Inclusion. Retrieved on October 18, 2006, from http://www.circleofinclusion.org

Committee on Education and the Workforce. (2006). Flexibility on testing students with disabilities. Retrieved October 20, 2006 from http://www. house.gov/ed_workforce

Converse, P. D., Oswald, F. L., Gillespie, M. A., Field, K. A., & Bizot, E. B. (2004). Matching individuals to occupations using abilities and the O*NET: Issues and an application in career guidance. *Personnel Psychology, 51,* 451–487.

Council for Exceptional Children. (1997). Effective accommodations for students with exceptionalities. *CEC Today, 4*(3) 1–15.

Crandell, C., & Smaldino, J. (2000). Room acoustics for listeners with normal-hearing and hearing impairment. In M. Valente, H. Hosford-Dunn, & R. Roeser (Eds.), *Audiology: Treatment* (pp. 601–623). New York: Thieme Medical.

D'Allura, T. (2002). Enhancing the social interaction skills of preschoolers with visual impairments. *Journal of Visual Impairment & Blindness, 96,* 576–584.

Downing, J. E. (2002). *Including students with severe and multiple disabilities in typical classrooms.* Baltimore: Brookes.

Edyburn, D. L. (2003). *What every teacher should know about assistive technology.* Boston, MA: Allyn & Bacon.

Folio, R. M., & Fewell, R. R. (2000). *Peabody Developmental Motor Scales* (2nd ed.). Austin, TX: PRO-ED.

Fowler, C. G., & Shanks, J. E. (2002). Tympanometry. In J. Katz, R. F. Burkard, & L. Medwetsky (Eds.), *Handbook of clinical audiology* (5th ed., pp. 175–204). Philadelphia: Lippincott Williams & Wilkins.

Fredrick D. R. (2002). Myopia. *BMJ, 324*(7347), 1195–1199.

Gardner, L., & Corn, A. (2006). Low Vision: Access to Print. Retrieved November 23, 2008, from http://www.cecdvi.org/positionpapers.html

Gense, D. J., & Gense, M. (2000). The importance of orientation and mobility skills for students who are deafblind. DB-Link. Retrieved October 5, 2006, from http://www.tr.wou.edu/dblink/

Goldman, R., Fristoe, M., & Woodcock, R. (1970). *Goldman-Fristoe-Woodcock Test of Auditory Discrimination.* Circle Pines, MN: American Guidance Service.

Gragiani, J. (2006). *Assistive communication devices by Dynavox.* Lecture for alternative curriculum course. Chicago, IL: Pynovox.

Hall, A., Scholl, G. T., & Swallow, R. M. (1986). Psychoeducational assessment. In G. Scholl (Ed.), *Foundations of education for blind and visually handicapped children and youth* (pp. 187–214). New York: American Foundation for the Blind.

Hammill, D. D. (1996). *Test of visual motor integration.* Austin, TX: PRO-ED.

Hammill, D. D. (1998). *Detroit Tests of Learning Aptitude—4* (DTLA-4). Austin, TX: PRO-ED.

Hammill, D. D., & Bryant, B. R. (2005). *Detroit Tests of Learning Aptitude—Primary,* Third Edition (DTLA-P:3). Austin, TX: PRO-ED.

Hatlen, P. (Spring, 1996). The core curriculum for blind and visually impaired students, including those with additional disabilities. *Re:View, 28*(1), 25–32.

Henderson, S. H., & Sugden, D. A. (1992). *Movement Assessment Battery for Children.* San Antonio, TX: Psychological Corporation.

Hill, E. & Ponder, P. (1976). *Orientation and mobility techniques.* New York: American Foundation for the Blind.

Hourcade, J. J., Parette, H. P., & Huer, M. B. (1997). Family and cultural alert! Considerations in assistive technology assessment. *Exceptional Children, 30*(1), 40–44.

Jose, R. (Ed.). (1999). *Understanding low vision.* New York: American Foundation for the Blind.

Judge, S. L., & Parette, H. P. (1998). Family-centered assistive technology decision making. *Infant-Toddler Intervention: The Transdisciplinary Journal, 8*(2), 185–206.

Keith, R. W. (1999). Clinical issues in central auditory processing disorders. *Language, Speech, and Hearing Services in Schools, 30,* 339–344.

Kemp, D. E., & Parette, H. P. (2000). Barriers to minority family involvement in assistive technology decision-making processes. *Education and Training in Mental Retardation and Developmental Disabilities, 35*(4), 384–92.

Koenig, A. J., & Holbrook, M. C. (1993). *Learning media assessment of students with visual impairment: A resource guide for teachers.* Austin: TX: Texas School for the Blind and Visually Impaired.

Koppitz, E. M. (1964). *The Bender gestalt test for young children.* New York: Grune & Stratton.

Koppitz, E. M. (1975). *The Bender gestalt test for young children: Vol. 2. Research and application, 1963–1973.* New York: Grune & Stratton.

Layton, C. A., & Lock, R. H. (2000). Determining learning disabilities in students with low vision. *Journal of Visual Impairment and Blindness, 95*(5), 288–299.

Layton, T. L., & Holmes, D. W. (1985). *Carolina Picture Vocabulary Test for Deaf and Hearing Impaired.* Austin, TX: PRO-ED.

Learning Disabilities Association of America. (2006). Definition of learning disabilities. Retrieved October 1, 2006, from http://www.ldaamerica.us/aboutld/parents/help/parents.asp

Lenker, J. A., & Paquet, V. L. (2004). A new conceptual model for assistive technology outcomes research and practice. *Assistive Technology, 16*(1), 1–10.

Letcher, K. *Overbrook School for the Blind website*. Retrieved June 5, 2006, from http://www.s118134197.onlinehome.us/page.php?ITEM=39

Levack, N. (1994). *Low vision: a resource guide with adaptations for students with visual impairments* (2nd ed.). Austin, TX: Texas School for the Blind and Visually Impaired.

Lindsey, J. D. (2000). *Technology & exceptional individuals*. Austin, TX: PRO-ED.

Lloyd, L. L., & Blischak, D. M. (1992). AAC terminology policy and issues update. *Augmentative and Alternative Communication, 8*, 104–109.

Loots, G., & Devise, I. (2003). The use of visual-tactile communication strategies by deaf and hearing fathers and mothers of deaf infants. *Journal of Deaf Studies and Deaf Education, 8*(1), 31–42.

Loumiet, R., & Levack, N. (1993). *Independent living: A curriculum with adaptation for students with visual impairments* (2nd ed.). Austin: Texas School for the Blind and Visually Impaired.

Lueck, A. (2004). Functional vision: A practitioner's guide to evaluation and intervention. American Foundation for the Blind: New York.

Maples, W. C. (2003). Visual factors that significantly impact academic performance. *Optometry, 74*, 35–43.

Massof, R. W., & Rubin, G. S. (2001). Visual functional assessment questionnaires. *Survey of Ophthalmology, 456*, 531–548.

Minnesota Department of Children Families & Learning. (2003). Introduction to auditory processing disorders. www.nesc.k12.mn.us

Musiek, F. E. (1999). Habilitation and management of auditory processing disorders: Overview of selected procedures. *Journal of the American Academy of Audiology, 10*, 329–342.

National Agenda for the Education of Children and Youths with Visual Impairment, Including Those with Multiple Disabilities. (2006). Are all your students with visual impairments receiving appropriate services? Retrieved on October 25, 2006, from http://www.tsbvi.edu/agenda/index.htm

National Institute on Deafness and Other Communication Disorders. (2006). Retrieved on October 3, 2006, from http://www.nidcd.nih.gov/health/statistics/hearing.asp

Onusko, E. (2004). Rerieved on September 20, 2006, from http://www.aafp.org/afp/20041101/1713.html

Pacific Audiology. (n.d.). Example of audiogram from http://www.pacificaudiology.com/audiogram/uya.html. Retrieved September 15, 2006.

Pacific Audiology. (n.d.). Types of hearing loss in frequency and intensity from http://www.pacificaudiology.com/audiogram/uya.html. Retrieved September 15, 2006.

Parette, H. P. (1997). Family-centered practice and computers for children with disabilities. *Early Childhood Education Journal, 25*(1), 53–55.

Parette, H. P., & Anderson, C. L. (2001). Family and related service partnerships in home computer decision-making. *Special Services in the Schools, 17*(1–2), 97–113.

Parette, H. P., & Brotherson, M. J. (2004). Family-centered and culturally responsive assistive technology decision making. *Infants & Young Children, 17*(4), 355–367.

Parette, H. P, Brotherson, M. J., & Huer, M. B. (2000). Giving families a voice in augmentative and alternative communication decision-making. *Education and Training in Mental Retardation and Developmental Disabilities, 35*(2), 77–90.

Parette, H. P., Huer, M. B., & Brotherson, M. J. (2001). Related service personnel perceptions of team AAC decision-making across cultures. *Education and Training in Mental Retardation and Developmental Disabilities, 36*(1), 69–82.

Parette, H. P., & McMahan, G. A. (2002). What should we expect of assistant technology: Being sensitive to family goals. *Teaching Exceptional Children, 23*(1), 56–61.

Parette, H. P., & Petch-Hogan, B. (2000). Approaching families: Facilitating culturally/linguistically diverse family involvement. *Exceptional Children, 33*(2), 4–10.

Pediatric Eye Disease Investigator Group (2002). Retrieved November 24, 2008, from http://public.pedig.jaeb.org/Currebt_Studies.htm

Perkins School for the Blind (2006). Information Clearinghouse on Blindness and Visual Impairment. Retrieved on February 3, 2006, from http://www.perkins.org/

Pierangelo, R. & Giuliani, G. (2006). *Assessment in special education: A practical approach* (2nd edition). Boston: Allyn and Bacon.

Pugh, G. S., & Erin, J. (Eds.) (1999). *Blind and visually impaired students: Educational service guidelines.* Watertown, MA: Perkins School for the Blind.

Pratt, C., & Stewart, R. (2006). Teaching students who are low-functioning: Who are they and what should we teach? http://www.iidc.indiana.edu/irca

RehabTool. (2006). http://www.rehabtool.com

Reid, K. D., Jiresko, W. P., Hammill, D. D., & Wiltshire, S. (1991). *Test of Early Reading Ability—2: Deaf or hard of hearing.* Austin, TX: PRO-ED.

Salvia, J., & Ysseldyke, J. E. (1998). *Assessment* (7th ed.). Boston: Houghlin Mifflin.

Sattler, J. M. (2002). *Assessment of children: Behavioral and clinical applications* (4th ed.). San Diego: Sattler.

Scherer, M., & Craddock, G. (2002). Matching person & technology (MPT) assessment process. *Technology and Disability, 14,* 125–131.

Schow, R. L., Seikel, J. A., Chermak, G. D., & Berent, M. (2000). *American Journal of Audiology, 9,* 1–6.

Schminky, M. M., & Baran, J. A. (1999). Deaf-blind perspectives. From http://www.tsbvi.edu.

Stenquist, G. & Robbins, N. (1978). *Curriculum for Daily Living.* Watertown, MA: Perkins School for the Blind. Retrieved on October 15, 2006, from http://www.perkins.org

Swisher, M. (2000). Learning to converse: How deaf mothers support the development of attention and conversation skills in their young deaf children. In P. Spencer, C. Erting, and M. Marschark (Eds.), *The deaf child in the family and at school: Essays in honor of Kathryn P. Meadow-Orlans* (pp. 21–39). Mahwah, NJ: Lawrence Erlbaum Associates.

TASH. Communication rights. Retrieved on October 10, 2006, from http://www.tash.org/

Turnbull, H. R., III, & Turnbull, A. P. (1998). *Free appropriate public education* (5th ed.). Denver, CO: Love Publishing.

Ulrich, D.A. (2000). *Test of Gross Motor Development—2nd Edition (TGMD-2).* Austin, TX: PRO-ED.

Venn, J. J. (2007). *Assessing students with special needs* (4th ed.). Upper Saddle River, NJ: Merrill/Pearson Education.

Wahl, L. (2004). Surveying special education staff on AT awareness, use and training. *Journal of Special Education Technology, 19*(2), 57–59.

Wang, H., Liao, H., & Hsieh, C. (2006). Reliability, sensitivity to change, and responsiveness of the Peabody Developmental Motor Scales—Second Edition for children with cerebral palsy. *Physical Therapy, 86*(10), 1351–1359.

Watts, E. H., O'Brian, M., & Wojcik, B. W. (2004). Four models of assistive technology consideration: How do they compare to recommended educational assessment practices? *Journal of Special Education Technology 19,* 43–56.

Webster. A., & Heineman-Gosschalk, R. (2000). Deaf children's encounters with written texts: Contrasts between hearing teachers and deaf adults in supporting reading. *Deafness and Education International, 2*(1), 26–44.

Wehman, P., & Kregel, J. (2004). *Functional curriculum for elementary, middle, & secondary age students with special needs* (2nd ed.). Austin, TX: PRO-ED.

Wehmeyer, M. (2002). *Providing access to the general curriculum: Teaching students with mental retardation.* Baltimore: Brookes.

Wehmeyer, M. L., & Agran, M. (2005). *Mental retardation and intellectual disabilities.* Upper Saddle River, NJ: Merrill/Pearson Education.

Wepman, J. M., & Reynolds, W. M. (1997). *Wepman Test of Auditory Discrimination,* 2nd Edition (ADT-2). Los Angeles, CA: Western Psychological Services.

Wilkinson, M. E., Trantham, C. S., & Koenig, A. J. (2001). Achieving functional literacy for children with visual impairments. *Visual Impairment Research, 3*(2), 85–95.

Williams, J. (2001). Adaptations & accommodations for students with disabilities. Retrieved October 25, 2006, from http://www.nichcy.org

Wisconsin Assistive Technology Initiative. Retrieved October 21, 2006, from http://www.wati.org

Woodcock, R. W., McGrew, K. S., & Mather, N. (2001). Examiner's manual. Woodcock-Johnson III Tests of Achievement. Itasca, IL. Riverside Publishing.

Yoshinaga-Itano, C. (2003). From screening to early identification and intervention: Discovering predictors to successful outcomes for children with significant hearing loss. *Journal of Deaf Studies and Deaf Education, 8*(1), 11–30.

Zaba, J. N. (2003). Vision examinations for all children entering public school—the new Kentucky law. *Optometry, 74*(3), 149–158.

Zabala, J. (1995). The SETT framework. Closing the Gap Conference on the Use of Assistive Technology in Special Education and Rehabilitation. Minneapolis, MN.

Zabala, J. (2005). SETT and ReSett: Concepts for AT implementation. *Closing the Gap, 23*(5), 1–11.

Transition

KEY TERMS

Transition: Connection between being a student and becoming an adult.

ITP: Individual transition plan; by age 16, a required component of the individualized education program (IEP).

Self-determination: Managing one's life, self-direction.

Age of majority: Able to make legal choices; no longer a minor.

Functional curriculum: Addressing areas of academics and skills needed to operate within one's environment.

Case Study: Assessing Tony

Tony is a student in your eighth-grade class. He is turning 14 in May. He has an IEP and receives services for reading, mathematics, speech/language, and social skills. Tony has moderate learning disabilities. He reads at a fifth-grade instructional reading level, and he has difficulty with most types of math calculations. He receives speech/language services for phonology and morphology. Tony also receives assistance with language involved in social skills (pragmatic language). He has limited communication with teachers and peers. When he does communicate, it is often in ways that are socially inappropriate. Tony enjoys activities involving technology. He uses assistive technology for writing and information-gathering tasks. He also uses computers for leisure activities. His parents report similar behaviors in the home and community settings. By law, you are required to provide a statement of needs this year, and this statement must involve planning for coursework in high school.

How do you begin your investigation and assessment of which courses would be most appropriate for Tony?

Which formal and informal assessments do you use?

Which areas of assessment are you most interested in?

By the end of the chapter, you should be able to discuss the questions posed in the case study about Tony. You should also be able to explain the legal foundations of transition and the requirements related to those laws. You should be able to name, explain, and give an example of the areas assessed in transition. You should be able to explain the process that assessors use to gather information regarding transition. You should be able to name the tests appropriate for each area of transition assessment. You should also be able to utilize these concepts to choose appropriate formal and informal methods for evaluation purposes.

Standards involved with this chapter include CEC Standard 4, which includes knowledge involving life skills related to independence, community, personal living, and employment. Furthermore, vocational skills and transitions are included in this standard. PRAXIS, legal, and assessment issues regarding transition (formal and informal) are addressed in this chapter. Cultural diversity affecting families and communities is discussed in this chapter.

DEFINING TRANSITION

Laws require the educational system to be accountable for appropriate transition services. Public Law 99-457 (Parts C and B) includes the course transition should follow, from early intervention to preschool. Transition within the context of secondary education is the connection between being a student and being an adult. This chapter addresses transition to adulthood. The Americans with Disabilities Act of 1990 (P.L. 101-336), Secondary Education and Transitional Services for Handicapped Youth Act, the Rehabilitation Act Amendments of 1992, the Carl D. Perkins Vocational and Applied Technology Act of 1990 (and amendments of 1998), the School to Work Opportunities Act of 1994, and the No Child Left Behind Act of 2001 specifically tap into postsecondary vocational transition programs.

IDEA (1990, 1997) further mandates transition for individuals with disabilities in the school setting. Transitional planning involving course work in the secondary setting begins at age 14 within the individualized education program (IEP) and is then called the individual transition plan (ITP). Each year subsequently, a statement on needs is a required piece of the IEP. By 16 years of age, a statement focusing on needs, services required, and subjects of study must be included. Agencies involved and responsibilities of those agencies must be included. These agencies could include state and community agencies. In addition, the student must be informed about his or her rights a year before reaching the age of majority (called the transfer of rights). At the age of majority (18 in most states), the student is responsible for educational decisions, changes, and the program. Age of majority is a major event in the individual's life in the area of independence (Bremer, Kachgal, & Schoeller, 2003). If the student is deemed incompetent by the procedures in place by the state, an individual is assigned to speak for the student (NCSET & PACER Center, 2005).

Transition is an especially important aspect of the education of students with disabilities because studies have shown that students with disabilities drop out of school at higher rates than students without disabilities (Blackorby & Wagner, 1996). Students who have emotional disorders have the highest dropout rate (Bullis & Gaylord-Ross, 1991). When students with disabilities stay in school and receive assessment and instructional vocational services, they have higher employment results (U.S. Department of Education, 2001).

In one study Wagner, Newman, Cameto, Garza, and Levine (2005) found that individuals with disabilities who had dropped out of school tended to work longer hours than individuals with disabilities who had completed high school. They also found that these individuals were more likely to support children, more likely to do jail time, and less likely to have support than individuals with disabilities who had completed high school.

Research data regarding global transition issues reveal disappointing results from a study comparing individuals who have a disability to individuals who do not. Those included significantly lowered levels in individuals with disabilities in the areas of life satisfaction, work, leisure, and transportation activities (National Organization on Disability & Harris & Associates, 2000).

Transition services involving vocation have been shown to be more helpful to students in general, but even more so for individuals with disabilities (Mooney & School, 2004). Luecking and Fabian (2000) found that work experience in integrated environments extends the likelihood for competitive employment. This is especially powerful because individuals with disabilities are nearly 50 percent less likely to be employed than individuals without disabilities (National Council on Disability, 2003). Studies have revealed that students with disabilities often do not receive the complete curriculum (Shaw, 2005). Content areas such as math and science appear to be areas of weakness.

Breakpoint Practice

1. Name three laws related to transition.

2. What is required by law for students with disabilities, starting at 14 years of age, as related to transition?

3. What is required by law for students with disabilities, starting at 16 years of age, as related to transition?

4. What are some important findings related to students with disabilities and dropout rates?

5. What are some important findings related to students with disabilities and transition training?

ASSESSMENT OF TRANSITION

Assessment is a necessary component of transition. According to Bruder and Chandler (1996), three elements of transition include assessment, planning (individualized transition plan [ITP]), and follow-through. Therefore, assessment is what begins and guides the process.

Individual Transition Plan (ITP)

The information gathered from the assessment process goes into the ITP. Preferably, the ITP and IEP meetings should be held separately, with the ITP meeting preceding the IEP meeting. More time for the ITP meeting allows the student to express his or her inclinations. If this is not feasible, the ITP meeting should be conducted first to guide the IEP goals (CASE & PAI, 1992).

Information required includes present levels of performance, interests, aptitude, needs, goals, activities, and participants involved in this process. Goals generally include instructional and linkage goals (Clark, Patton, & Moulton, 2000). Storms, O'Leary, and Williams (2000) also stress the importance of linkages in the transition planning process in their three step model: goal-setting, programming, and linkages.

Spinelli (2006) reports that cognitive ability, communication skills, social-emotional development, physical functioning, and adaptive skills are all pieces of the transition process related to early childhood. These are generally the areas assessed by developmental testing.

In the secondary setting, transitional assessment can include the areas of academics, life skills, language skills (receptive, expressive, reading, and writing), vocational skills, interests, self-determination, and social skills. The student should have a considerable role in the discussion (understanding and contribution) and decision-making. Also, the student's strengths should be essential elements in determining appropriate matches for future study, employment opportunities, community living (including living arrangements and transportation), financial, medical, and leisure activities.

Determination of adaptations and needed supports is important for optimizing training and the success of a student. Adaptations follow successful tools that were used in student's education. Those tools can include adaptations to the way material is presented or responded to, changes to test presentation or response mode, and/or support programs. Modifications (change in the standard) are usually not an option for postsecondary educational settings (Scott, Shaw, & McGuire, 2003). Day and Edwards (1996) report that assistive technology is an important tool in postsecondary education settings for students with disabilities. See Chapter 11 for further discussion of adaptations.

Anderson and Asselin (1992) found that schools in Virginia were providing appropriate opportunities for inclusion, adequate support services, and positive collaboration between special education and vocational personnel. However, administrative support was reported to be low by participants. More support in this area could increase the success of transition services for students with disabilities.

Wagner et al. (2005) found that individuals with disabilities who had been out of high school for up to two years reported social skills as the most challenging. Maximizing experience in several settings should be an important aspect to planning.

Choice

Also, the incorporation of choice is a positive and necessary component of this training and experience. In fact, students with disabilities will attend more, participate more, and be more productive when choice is allowed and exercised (Flexer, Simmons, Luft, & Baer, 2005). Preparation begins in early childhood and should continue at all levels.

Participation

Cameto, Levine, and Wagner (2004) found that 6 percent of students with disabilities and 15 percent of their parents did not attend IEP/ITP meetings. In addition, data revealed that 58 percent of the students who did participate provided input, and 12 percent took a leadership role. Similarly, Hagner, Helm, and Butterworth (1996) reported that the individuals' ideas were often ignored during IEP/ITP meetings.

Thomas, Rogan, and Baker (2001) found that students were usually not prepared to be involved in the ITP process. In addition, student goals were often based on teacher and parent recommendations. Data have revealed that parents of students with hearing disabilities, visual disabilities, or traumatic brain injuries were more likely to be satisfied with the amount of involvement during the ITP meeting, and parents of students who had mental retardation or emotional disabilities were least likely to be satisfied with involvement in the ITP meeting (Cameto et al., 2004). However, parents of students with mental retardation or students with speech and hearing disorders were most satisfied with preparation for postschool transition, while parents of students with autism, health impairments, or emotional disabilities were the least satisfied with this preparation. Therefore, there is a need to focus on providing the appropriate opportunities for students and their families to provide input regarding their future.

Student and family member involvement increases person-centered planning (Gallivan-Fenlon, 1994). Person-centered planning can increase student successes by making training more applicable, allowing students to be more in charge of their lives, and assisting students by working on valued goals (Flexer, Simmons, Luft, & Baer, 2005). Miner and Bates (1997) found that parents reported more participation and overall satisfaction with a person-centered approach compared to traditional approaches. Furney and Salembier (2000) conducted a literature review and found that increasing the participation of families increases postschool outcomes. It is important to increase levels of activity in self-determination and self-advocacy.

Self-Determination Assessment Tools

Researchers have found that higher self-determination skills are associated with higher employment rates (Wehmeyer & Schwartz, 1997) and elevated outcomes after students left school (Wehmeyer & Palmer, 2003). Wehmeyer (2002) provided examples of transition planning and assessment tools that aim to assist students to self-direct their program. Those included The ChoiceMaker Self-Determination Transition Curriculum (Martin & Marshall, 1995), Whose Future Is It Anyway? (Wehmeyer & Lawrence, 1995), Next S.T.E.P. (Halpern, Herr, Wolf, Lawson, Doren, & Johnson, 1997), Self-Advocacy Strategy for Education and Transition Planning (Van Reusen, Bos, Schumaker, & Deshler, 1994), and Goal Action Planning (Turnbull, Blue-Banning, Anderson, Turnbull, Seaton, & Dinas, 1996). These tools include lessons and/or sessions to teach students about aspects of transition and how they can be more active in the process.

Collaboration Planning Assessment Tools

Flexer et al. (2005) noted three examples of transition planning tools that were comprehensive and stressed collaboration. Those included Personal Futures Planning (Mount, 1989), McGill Action Planning System (Pearpoint, 1990), and Circles of Support (Forest, Pearpoint, & Snow, 1993).

Personal Futures Planning is an important planning tool because it can be used with individuals who have sensory and/or severe disabilities. The individual and his or her family guide the decision-making process (Everson, Rachal & Michael, 1992). Participants of the meetings form a "circle" and decide what the goals are and where and when to meet. These participants are usually the individual who has the plan (directs plan), caregivers, friends, family, community members, agency provider, and school representative (Amado & McBride, 2001; Moss & Wiley, 2003). Meetings can take place wherever the group members would like. Therefore, the setting is informal. Color-coded maps (i.e., red for negative factors) are used to generate a personal profile based on input from each group member. Examples of these maps are background, people, choices, and what works and does not work (http://challengingbehavior.fmhi.usf.edu/personcentered.htm). A plan with steps can then be constructed for the individual.

Another tool that can be used with students who have severe disabilities is the Functional Skills Screening Inventory (FSSI) (Becker, Schur, & Hammer, 1986). This instrument is based on observer ratings of the individual in authentic contexts over an extended period of time (http://www.winfssi.com/howtofssipf.html). The FSSI involves an observation checklist with comments. From this information, a summary can be included in the battery of assessments used with the individual.

TRANSITION ASSESSMENT TOOLS

In addition to these self-determination and collaboration driven transition planning tools, several transition instruments with different foci can be used. In the early childhood setting, such assessments are discussed in Chapter 10 of this book. Informal as well as formal methods are offered as possibilities in this area. Therefore, transition assessment practices for secondary settings will be the focus in this chapter. Assessment tools include instruments for comprehensive transition, vocational adjustment, vocational aptitude, vocational aptitude and interest, vocational interest, and Curriculum-Based Vocational Assessment.

COMPREHENSIVE TRANSITION ASSESSMENT

Widely used comprehensive transition instruments include the Transition Planning Inventory—Updated Version (TPI-UV) (Clark & Patton, 1997), the Enderle-Severson Transition Rating Scale—Form J—Revised (ESTR-J-R) (Enderle & Severson, 2003b), the Enderle-Severson Transition Rating Scale III (ESTR-III) (Enderle & Severson, 2003a), and The Life Centered Career Education (LCCE) Knowledge Battery (Brolin, 1992). See Figure 12.1.

The Transition Planning Inventory—Updated Version (TPI-UV) is an individual comprehensive measurement of transitional needs, preferences, and interests of students, age 14 through 22 years. Supports and services needed are also meant to be outcomes based on the results of this instrument. School, home, and student forms, as well as the further assessment recommendations forms allow for the gathering of information from multiple sources. Areas of measurement and planning include rating scales of employment, further education/training, daily living, leisure activities, community participation, health, self-determination, communication, and interpersonal relationships. This tool is not a norm-referenced test.

The Enderle-Severson Transition Rating Scale—Form J—Revised (ESTR-J-R) assesses transition of students with mild disabilities. The areas of employment, recreation and leisure, home living, community participation, and postsecondary education are rated by an individual who knows the student well or by the student, using yes/no responses. The ESTR-III is utilized for transition of students with moderate to severe

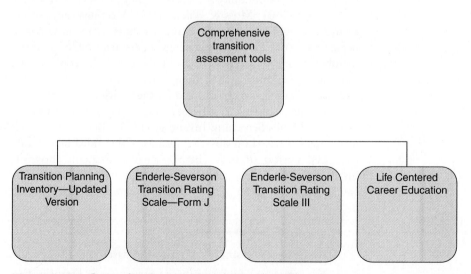

Figure 12.1 Comprehensive transition assessment tools

disabilities. The same five transition areas are evaluated. However, an individual who knows the student well rates the items on a three-point scale.

The Life Centered Career Education (LCCE) consists of parallel forms made up of multiple-choice questions. The LCCE curriculum is based on a functional life skills approach. Areas of daily living skills, personal social skills, and occupational skills are connected to the LCCE curriculum programs (mild and moderate) (Brolin, 1978). There is a link from assessment to instruction. Studies Competencies an used to develop IEP goals and guide planning and systematic instruction.

The Life Centered Career Education (LCCE)—Mild Approach consists of 22 competencies and 97 subcompetencies. Examples of daily living skills competencies include managing personal finances (i.e., counting money) and moving around in the community (i.e., understanding traffic rules). Personal social skills competencies include achieving independence (i.e., self-organization) and communication with others (i.e., responding to emergencies). Occupational skills include seeking, securing, and maintaining a job (i.e., applying for a job) (Brolin, 1993). The LCCE Moderate Curriculum includes 20 competencies and 75 subcompetencies (Brolin, 1997).

The Life Centered Career Education (LCCE) curriculum brings together skills that are academic and skills that are essential in functioning within one's environment (Brolin & Loyd, 2004). Functional skills within this tool are connected with the functional life skills approach of the Council for Exceptional Children (CEC). This tool is meant for the assessment of vocational knowledge and skills of students in grades 7 through 12 with mild disabilities, and it is norm-referenced. Lesson plans and performance assessments are components of this assessment program.

VOCATIONAL/ADJUSTMENT TOOLS

Vocational/adjustment tools involve the Brigance Life Skills Inventory, the Social and Prevocational Information Battery—Revised (SIPB-R) (Halpern, Irvin, & Munkres, 1986), the Transition Behavior Scale—Second Edition (TBS-2) (McCarney & Anderson, 2000), and the Work Adjustment Inventory (WAI) (Gilliam, 1994). See Figure 12.2.

The Brigance Life Skills Inventory (Brigance, 1995b) is a screening tool that investigates skills related to listening, speaking, reading, writing, comprehending, and computing skills in everyday contexts. This is a criterion-referenced tool. Areas addressed

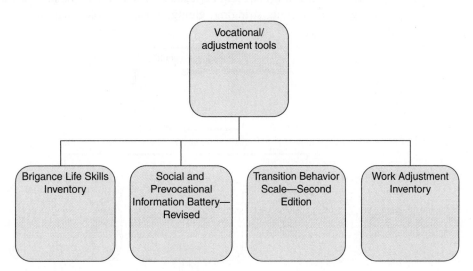

Figure 12.2 Vocational/adjustment tools

include speaking and listening skills, functional writing skills, words on common signs and warning labels, telephone skills, money and finance, food, clothing, health, travel and transportation, and rating scales.

The Social and Prevocational Information Battery—Revised (SIPB-R) involves five long-range goal areas: employability, economic self-sufficiency, family living, personal habits, and communications. Orally read true/false and some picture items are included in this test. Subtests include banking, budgeting, purchasing skills, job search skills, job-related behavior, home management, health care, hygiene and grooming, and ability to read functional signs. The norm group of this test is narrow.

The Transition Behavior Scale—Second Edition (TBS-2) includes subscales that measure behavior in work related, interpersonal relations, and social/community expectations. School and self-report versions are available. Goals, objectives, and interventions are provided for each scale item. Norm information appears adequate.

The Work Adjustment Inventory (WAI) is a group or individually administered test that measures temperament traits, including activity, empathy, sociability, assertiveness, adaptability, and emotionality. This group-administered test is for individuals 12 to 22 years of age and has a third-grade reading level.

VOCATIONAL APTITUDE TOOLS

The Brigance Employment Skills (Brigance, 1995a), the Wide Range Employability Sample Test (WREST) (Jastak & Jastak, 1980), and the Singer Vocational Evaluation System (VES) (Singer Company Career Systems, 1982) provide an avenue for addressing specific vocational aptitude. See Figure 12.3.

The Brigance Employment Skills is a screening tool involving six subtests: career awareness and understanding, job-seeking and knowledge, reading skills, speaking and listening skills, pre-employment writing, and math skills and concepts. In this informal test, students must read or understand material at the high school level. Supplemental rating scales (by students, teachers, and/or parents) include themes of self-concept and attitudes, responsibility and self-discipline, motor coordination and job requirements, thinking skills/abilities and job requirements, job interview preparation, job interview skills, and work experience.

The Wide Range Employability Sample Test (WREST) uses performance of concrete tasks that do not require reading or writing. Those include folding, stapling, packaging, measuring, stringing, gluing, collating, color matching, pattern matching, and

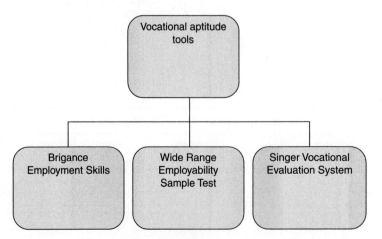

Figure 12.3 Vocational aptitude tools

assembling. The Vocational Evaluation System (VES) also includes performance of skills with work samples. Skills include areas such as plumbing, cooking and baking, filing, electronics assembly, and more.

VOCATIONAL APTITUDE AND INTEREST TOOLS

The Occupational Aptitude Survey and Interest Schedule—Third Edition (OASIS-3: IS) (Parker, 2002) and Apticom (VRI, 1995) tools address vocational aptitude and interest.

The OASIS-3: IS is comprised of the OASIS-3 Aptitude Survey and the OASIS-3 Interest Schedule for students in grades 8–12 given individually or in groups. Six aptitude scores consist of general ability, verbal aptitude, numerical aptitude, spatial aptitude, perceptual aptitude, and manual dexterity. The Interest Schedule includes factors in artistic, scientific, nature, protective, mechanical, industrial, business detail, selling, accommodating, humanitarian, leading-influencing, and physical performing. Results reveal if the student likes, dislikes, or feels neutral about 240 items. It is important to get student input.

Apticom also had a number of tests, including the Aptitude Test Battery, Occupational Interest Inventory, and the Educational Skills Development. Eleven subsets included object identification, abstract shape matching, clerical matching, eye-hand-foot coordination, pattern visualization, computation, finger dexterity, numerical reasoning, manual dexterity, word meanings, and eye-hand coordination. The new addition to this area of testing is CareerScope (VRI Career Planning Solutions, 1995). CareerScope includes an interest inventory with areas in artistic, plants/animals, mechanical, business detail, accommodating, lead/influence, scientific, protective, industrial, selling, humanitarian, and physical performing. Aptitudes include general learning ability, verbal aptitude, numerical aptitude, spatial aptitude, form perception, and clerical perception (http://vri.org/careerscope/index.html). These tools promote self-assessment and self-determination.

VOCATIONAL INTEREST TOOLS

Vocational interest tools have a long history, so the subject is worthy of discussion. In some of the initial work in the area of vocational interest assessment, Strong attempted to match the interests of individuals with interests of individuals who were happy with their careers. The test that was developed and revised from this endeavor was called the Strong Vocational Interest Blank (SVIB) (Strong & Campbell, 1966). Campbell and Strong removed gender bias and included females in a 1974 version (followed by a 1985 revision) called the Strong-Campbell Interest Inventory (SCII) Likert-type instrument. Items regarding a responder's likes are the essence of this test. The Campbell Interest and Skill Survey (CISS) (Campbell, Hyne, & Nilsen, 1992) is a follow-up to these scales and includes skills as well as interests of the individual being assessed. Criticisms of these tools include a weight on professions that involve college preparation.

The Reading-Free Vocational Interest Inventory: 2 (R-FVII:2) (Becker, 2000) and Wide Range Interest-Opinion Test—Second Edition (WRIOT2) (Glutting & Wilkinson, 2003) are two commonly used vocational interest tools. The Reading-Free Vocational Interest Inventory: 2 (R-FVII: 2) measures vocational interests of individuals with disabilities age 13 years and older. It is given to groups or it is administered individually. More specifically, the instrument measures the likes and dislikes of individuals and requires no reading or writing. Drawings of individuals performing various job activities facilitate measurement of vocational interests. The individual circles of preferred work pictures. Eleven areas of vocations include automotive, building trades, clerical, animal care, food service, patient care, horticulture, housekeeping, personal service, laundry service, and materials handling.

Separate norms exist for individuals who have mental retardation, who have learning disabilities, and who are described as being "adult disadvantaged/work sheltered." However, some results are missing for individuals who have moderate retardation. Reliability and validity information is narrow.

Wide Range Interest-Opinion Test—Second Edition (WRIOT2) measures vocational preference patterns for students age 9 through 80 years. It can be administered to individuals or in groups. Two administration options are available with no reading or writing skills needed from the individual being assessed. One option includes a manual administration utilizing a picture book, while the other option is computer administration by CD. Individuals choose whether they like, dislike, or are undecided about jobs based on pictures. Strengths related to job choice is facilitated by 17 occupational, 16 interest, and 6 Holland type scales. Norms appear appropriate.

CURRICULUM-BASED VOCATIONAL ASSESSMENT

Curriculum-Based Vocational Assessment (CBVA) is an extension of curriculum-based assessment (CBA) discussed in Chapter 4. Researchers have discussed steps and models associated with CBVA (Albright & Cobb, 1988; Lombard, Larsen, & Westphal, 1993). It is a dynamic process that links assessment and instruction of the vocational realm. Identifying particular curriculum material via the assessment provides a direct connection with skills to be developed during instruction. Albright and Cobb (1988) discuss three stages of a vocational program: pre-assessment, ongoing assessment, and postassessment. Lombard et al. (1993) discuss the MAGIC program. *M*aking a prediction, *A*ssessing skills as a baseline, *G*uiding skill attainment, *I*nstructing for generalization, and *C*onducting continuance verification are steps in the MAGIC program.

CBVA covers career development needs, with a focus on the mastery of skills and a link with the curriculum and content instruction. A constant assessment of skills takes place to guide instruction. The continuous assessment of skills related to vocational training steers the IEP and ITP to reflect meaningful goals with authentic instruction and assessment.

OTHER INFORMAL TOOLS

Informal techniques discussed in Chapter 4 can be applied to the field of transition. Work samples, interviews, rubrics, checklists, questionnaires, and teacher-made tests could be included in the assessment process. For example, an important aspect of vocational assessment is a job analysis (Kaplan & Saccuzzo, 2001). Kaplan and Saccuzzo noted that checklists are good tools to guide a job analysis. Activities necessary for the job can be included, as well as how often these responsibilities occur. They also discussed observations, interviews, and questionnaires as other components that can give students information regarding the requirements of certain vocations.

The more professional and varied artifacts that are included in the informal assessment process, the more robust the description. The formative nature of informal assessment suits the goals of transition assessment. A widely used informal measure applied in the transition process is work samples. Many work sample products are organized according to the Dictionary of Occupational Titles (DOT) occupational classifications (U.S. Department of Labor, 1991; Cohen & Spenciner, 2007).

Work samples allow the teacher and the student to see how the student performs tasks that are real. In addition, this informal tool assists teachers in evaluating the

Laura Bolesta/Merrill

student in a real-life context. Because of the many contextual variables involved in work activities (i.e., distractions and stressors), it is a critical aspect of measurement and instruction. Portfolios, checklists, questionnaires, interviews, and teacher-made tests can contribute significant quantitative and qualitative information to the transition process.

Clark, Patton, and Moulton (2000) provide a collection of informal assessment tools that can be used in the transition process. The assessments cover the areas of employment (i.e., strengths, skills, interests, job awareness, self-assessment, and supports), environment, daily living (i.e., hygiene, home living, transportation, functional academics), leisure (i.e., indoor and outdoor activities), community participation (i.e., transportation and adult services), health (i.e., preventive health and emergency), self-determination (i.e., self-advocacy and professional goals), and communication (i.e., receptive language, expressive language, reading, and writing). Formats include checklists, questionnaires, interviews, and short-essay responses.

Breakpoint Practice

1. Describe and give examples of instruments for measuring each of the following: comprehensive transition, vocational adjustment, vocational aptitude, and vocational interest.

2. Describe Curriculum-Based Vocational Assessment.

3. Give three examples of other types of informal assessments involved in transition.

POSTSECONDARY PREPARATION

Based on federal law, the assessment of transition should include all areas because school should be linked with goals in preparation for the time when school is completed. Therefore, transition is ongoing and covers any areas of focus within the schools and community.

POSTSECONDARY EDUCATION

Postsecondary education is one option examined when considering transition. A first step includes discussing whether a student wants postsecondary education. Postsecondary education options consist of training at two-year colleges, four-year colleges or universities, and vocational and/or technical training.

Wagner et al. (2005) report that more individuals with disabilities enrolled in the two-year colleges than any other postsecondary education options. In addition, they found individuals with hearing, visual, speech, or orthopedic disabilities are more likely to attend postsecondary education than individuals with mental retardation or multiple disabilities. However, Sitlingon and Frank (1990) found that many students with disabilities who enroll in postsecondary education do not stay in school. Peers without disabilities were more than four and a half times more likely to be enrolled in four-year colleges.

Cameto et al. (2004) found that approximately half of students with disabilities planned to go to college. The percentages ranged with disability types. For example, 10 percent of students with mental retardation and about 70 percent of students with visual disabilities reported planning to go to college.

Orientation programs, adapted instruction, assessment, and environment (i.e., physical barriers), individualized assistance, and technology are services that Gajar (1998) reported were found most useful in particular for students with disabilities in higher education. However, the National Center for Education Statistics (NCES) (1999) noted that services varied across postsecondary settings.

LIVING ARRANGEMENTS

In terms of living arrangements, data reveal that 75 percent of individuals with disabilities live up to two years postschool with their parents (Wagner et al., 2005). About 12 percent of the individuals lived with a spouse or roommate or on their own.

EMPLOYMENT

Researchers discuss obstacles and strategies to successful employment. Obstacles include coping, physical capability, communication, and life skills (Bowe, 2000). In effect, these are areas of adaptive skills. Implications for including time in the curriculum for directly teaching adaptive skills regarding employment are supported. Best et al. (2005) include physical self-reliance, well-founded self-assessment, and self-determination as barriers to employment. Students also do not know themselves and their disability well enough to self-advocate. The findings provide a rationale for stressing these areas in teacher training programs and providing curriculum options at the high school level.

Shafer, Banks, and Kregel (1991) found that individuals with disabilities usually lose their jobs due to inadequate attendance and limited social skills rather than job skills. These findings support direct assessment and teaching of adaptive skills.

Data have revealed that individuals with disabilities who have graduated from college have higher employment rates than individuals with disabilities who have not graduated from college (Harris & Associates, 2001). Subject matter, adaptations, and needed supports should be included in this discussion (Sitlington, Neubert, Begun, Lombard, & Leconte, 1996).

Wehmeyer and Agran (2005) noted areas of technology that are essential in the area of transition: word processing programs used for personal information (i.e., phone numbers), budgeting software programs, and utilizing ATM machines. Computers may be needed in the work setting. In addition, they noted that the use of personal digital assistants for calendar applications and prompts can be useful.

Breakpoint Practice

1. Describe a barrier and a strategy involved in postsecondary education.

2. Describe an important aspect of living arrangements as related to transition.

3. Describe a barrier and a strategy involved in successful employment.

Multicultural Considerations

Researchers have reported barriers and strategies involved with transition and students who are linguistically and/or culturally diverse (Greene & Nefsky, 1999). The data include information regarding employment, living arrangements, and collaboration.

Barriers

Individuals who have disabilities and are culturally and/or linguistically diverse are more likely to face a double stigma (Cartledge & Loe, 2001; Fine & Asch, 1988). Researchers have revealed inequities in transition results of students who are culturally and/or linguistically diverse (Geenen, Powers, Vasquez, & Bersani, 2003). For example, Blackorby and Wagner (1996) reported that students who were culturally and/or linguistically diverse (specifically Latino and African American) found work less often and earned less than European American individuals with disabilities.

Ramasamy, Duffy, and Camp (2000) examined transition effects on students with learning disabilities who were Native American and had dropped out of school. They found higher rates of unemployment, substance abuse, and living with parents when compared to their nondisabled peers.

Geenen et al. (2003) investigated families' perceptions (specifically Native American, African American, and Latino) of barriers to transition. They followed up with a quantitative study comparing groups (in addition to a European American group) in the amount of barriers encountered. Results revealed that the individuals who were culturally and/or linguistically diverse reported more barriers to transition than the European American group. Themes reported by the minority groups in the qualitative study included bias, need for accommodations, lack of supports, adolescent issues, contextual problems, and family values.

Leake and Black (2005) reported about the most considerable challenges faced by students with disabilities who are culturally and/or linguistically diverse. They listed challenges such as inclusion, self-determination, self-sponsorship, academic attainment, completion of high school, English proficiency, access to technology, and the ability to fund postsecondary education.

Blackorby and Wagner (1996) also reported that students who are culturally and/or linguistically diverse and have a disability are less likely to participate in post secondary education than individuals who have a disability and are European

(*continued*)

American. Language barriers, social barriers, and poverty may contribute to difficulties in participation in postsecondary education (Leake & Cholymay, 2002).

Strategies

Person-centered planning is a procedure that can be used with families of students who are culturally and/or linguistically diverse (Callicott, 2003; Leake & Black, 2005; Stodden, Stodden, Kim-Rupnow, Thai, & Galloway, 2002). Callicott (2003) included important aspects of person-centered planning as related to individuals who are culturally and/or linguistically diverse. Those aspects included cultural sensitivity, a team approach, a facilitator, and a process that is individual outcomes–driven. In addition, she noted that meetings, building a personal profile, developing a vision, and ongoing support and assessment must take place.

Greene (1996) offered questions to tap into the beliefs and priorities of students and families from linguistically and/or culturally diverse backgrounds. Those questions include beliefs regarding independence, work, disabilities, family structure, decision-making practices, and family advocacy.

Bruns and Fowler (2001) reported that five aspects are important in addressing the transitional needs of children with disabilities who are culturally and/or linguistically diverse: cultural context, collaboration, communication, family questions and comments, and bridging home and school. Specifically focusing on individuals who are Asian and Asian American, Chung (1992) discussed cultural competence in light of understanding one's culture, the client's culture, and cross-cultural dynamics. Benz, Doren, and Yovanoff (1998) found that three features improved the employment and educational outcomes for females with disabilities: family responsibilities, family incomes, and family agreement on student goals. These findings have implications for supports provided to students during the assessment and instruction process.

Breakpoint Practice

1. Name two barriers to successful transition for students with disabilities who are culturally and/or linguistically diverse.
2. Name two strategies for successful transition for students with disabilities who are culturally and/or linguistically diverse.

REVISITING TONY

When considering the information in this chapter in light of the chapter-opening case study about Tony, several thoughts may come to mind. Separating the IEP and ITP components, with the ITP preceding the IEP, would be a good organizational strategy. This way, the ITP discussion can drive the IEP. It is important to have the information you need before the date of the IEP meeting because skills targeted should have direct links to desired postsecondary outcomes.

Interviews with Tony and his parents regarding desires and needs for the future is an important starting point. Vocational interests and aptitudes would be assessed by tools mentioned in the chapter. For example, the OASIS-3: IS can be used. Because social skills have been difficulties for Tony, the Brigance Life Skills can guide instruction. A portfolio, work samples, and teacher-made tests can be used to collect information regarding transitional needs. It is important for Tony to work on self-determination skills and to explore the possibilities in terms of employment options in order to guide the transition process.

ACTIVITIES

1. What is the most important law that drives transition in the school setting? Why?
2. What are two important implications for transition assessment for students with disabilities?
3. What does the research tell us in regard to self-determination and transition?
4. What does the research tell us in regard to postsecondary education and students with disabilities?
5. What areas are measured by transition assessment?
6. Name three measures of transition assessment.
7. What is the Life Centered Career Education (LCCE) Knowledge Battery?
8. What is the curriculum-based vocational assessment (CBVA)?

WEB RESOURCES

http://www.ndss.org/index.php?option=com_content&task=view&id=1942&I
http://www.autism-society.org/site/PageServer?pagename=about_lwa_highschool
http://www.nsttac.org
http://www.isbe.state.il.us/spec-ed/html/transition.htm
http:::/www.ldonline.org/indepth/transition/college_tips.html
http://www.dcdt.org
http://www.ncset.org

REFERENCES

Albright, L., & Cobb, R. B. (1988). Curriculum-based vocational assessment: A concept whose time has come. *Journal for Vocational Special Needs Education, 10*(2), 13–16.

Amado, A. N., & McBride, M. (2001). Increasing person-centered thinking; improving the quality of person-centered planning: A manual for person-centered planning facilitators. Minneapolis: University of Minnesota, Institute on Community Integration. Retrieved on June 25, 2007, from http://rtc.umn.edu/staff/person.asp?personid=1

Anderson, A. G., & Asselin, S. B. (1992). *The status of transition services for secondary students with disabilities in Virginia and factors affecting service delivery.* Paper presented at American Vocational Association: Special Needs Division. St. Louis, MO.

Becker, H., Schur, S., & Hammer, E. (1986). *The Functional Skills Screening Inventory User's Guide.* Austin, TX: Functional Resources.

Becker, R. L. (2000). *Reading-Free Vocational Interest, Inventory—2* (R-FVII: 2). Lutz, FL: Psychological Assessment Resources.

Benz, M., Doren, B., & Yovanoff, P. (1998). Crossing the great divide: Predicting productive engagement for young women with disabilities. *Career Development for Exceptional Individuals, 21*(1), 3–16.

Best, S. J., Heller, K. W., & Bigge, J. L. (2005). *Teaching individuals with physical or multiple disabilities* (5th ed.). Upper Saddle River, NJ: Merrill/Pearson Education.

Blackorby, J., & Wagner, M. (1996). Longitudinal postschool outcomes of youth with disabilities: Findings from the National Longitudinal Transition Study. *Exceptional Children, 62*(5), 399–414.

Bowe, F. (2000). *Physical, sensory, and health disabilities: An introduction.* Upper Saddle River, NJ: Merrill/Pearson Education.

Bremer, C., Kachgal, M., & Schoeller, K. (2003). Self-determination: Supporting successful transition. *Research to Practice Brief: Improving Secondary Education and Transition Services through Research, 2,* 91.

Brigance, A. H. (1995a). *The BRIGANCE Employability Skills Inventory.* North Billerica, MA: Curriculum Associates.

Brigance, A. H. (1995b). *The BRIGANCE Life Skills Inventory.* North Billerica, MA: Curriculum Associates.

Brolin, D. E. (1978). *Life centered career education: A competency-based approach.* Arlington, VA: The Council for Exceptional Children.

Brolin, D. E. (1992). *Life centered career education: Competency assessment knowledge battery.* Arlington, VA: The Council for Exceptional Children.

Brolin, D.E. (1993). *Life centered career education: Professional development activity book.* Arlington, VA: The Council for Exceptional Children.

Brolin, D. E. (1997). *Life centered career education: A competency-based approach* (5th ed.). Arlington, VA: The Council for Exceptional Children.

Brolin, D. E., & Loyd, R. J. (2004). *Career development and transition services: A functional life skills approach* (4th ed.). Upper Saddle River, NJ: Merrill/Pearson Education.

Bruder, M., & Chandler, L. (1996). Transition. In S. Odom & M. McLean (Eds.). Early intervention/early childhood special education. *Recommended Practices* (pp. 287–307). Austin, TX: PRO-ED.

Bruns, D., & Fowler, S. (2001). *Transition Is More Than a Change in Services: The Need for a Multicultural Perspective* (CLAS Technical Report #4). Champaign, IL, University of Illinois at Urbana-Champaign, Early Childhood Research Institute on Culturally and Linguistically Appropriate Services. Retrieved on March 5, 2006, from http://clas.uiuc.edu/techreport/tech4 .html

Bullis, M., & Gaylord-Ross, R. (1991). *Moving on: Transitions for youth with behavior disorders.* Arlington, VA: The Council for Exceptional Children.

Callicott, K. J. (2003). Culturally sensitive collaboration within person-centered planning. *Focus on Autism and Other Developmental Disabilities, 18*(1), 60–68.

Cameto, R., Levine, P., & Wagner, M. (2004). *Transition planning for students with disabilities. A Special Topic Report from the National Longitudinal Transition Study—2 (NLTS2).* Menlo Park, CA: SRI International.

Campbell, D. P., Hyne, S. A., & Nilsen, D. (1992). *Manual for the Campbell Interest and Skill Survey.* Minneapolis, MN: National Computer Systems.

Cartledge, G., & Loe, S. A. (2001). Cultural diversity and social skill instruction. *Exceptionality, 9*(1), 33–46.

CASE (Community Alliance for Special Education) & PAI (Protection and Advocacy, Inc.). (1992). Information on transition services, including vocational education. From *Special education rights and responsibilities: A 13-chapter manual.* Center for Evidence-Based Practice: Young Children with Challenging Behavior. (n.d.). Retrieved on June 25, 2007, from http:// challengingbehavior.fmhi.usf.edu/personcentered.htm

Chung, D. K. (1992). Asian cultural commonalities: A comparison with mainstream American culture. In S. M. Furuto, R. Biswas, D. K Chung, M. Kenji, & F. Ross-Sheriff. *Social Work with Asian Americans.* Thousand Oaks, CA: Sage.

Clark, G., & Patton, J. (1997). *Transition Planning Inventory—Updated Version (TPI-UV).* Austin, TX: PRO-ED.

Clark, G. M., Patton, J. R., & Moulton, L. R. (2000). Informal assessments for transition planning. Austin, TX: PRO-ED.

Cohen, L. G., & Spenciner, L. J. (2007). *Assessment of children & youth with special needs* (3rd ed.). Boston, MA: Allyn & Bacon.

Day, S. L., & Edwards, B. J. (1996). Assistive technology for postsecondary students with learning disabilities. *Journal of Learning Disabilities, 29*(5), 486–492.

Enderle, J., & Severson, S. (2003). *Enderle-Severson Transition Rating Scales III* (ESTR-J-R). Moorhead, MN: ESTR Publications.

Everson, J. M., Rachal, P., & Michael, M. C. (1992). *Interagency collaboration for young adults with deaf-blindness: Toward a common transition goal.* Sands Point, NY: Helen Keller National Center—Technical Assistance Center.

Fine, M., & Asch, A. (1988). Beyond pedestals. *Women with Disabilities: Essays in Psychology, Culture, and Politics,* pp. 1–37. Philadelphia: Temple University Press.

Flexer, R., Simmons, T., Luft, P., & Baer, R. (2005). *Transition planning for secondary students with disabilities* (2nd ed.). Upper Saddle River, NJ: Merrill/Pearson Education.

Forest, M., Pearpoint, J., & Snow, J. (1993). Natural support systems: Families, friends, and circles. In J. Pearpoint, M. Forest, & J. Snow (Eds.), *The inclusion papers: Strategies to make inclusion work* (pp. 116–132). Toronto: Inclusion Press.

Furney, K., & Salembier, G. (2000). *Rhetoric and reality: A review of the literature on parent and student participation in the IEP and transition planning process. Issues influencing the future of transition programs and services for students with disabilities.* Minneapolis, MN: University of Minnesota, Institute on Community Integration.

Gajar, A. H. (1998). Postsecondary education. In F. R. Rusch & J. G. Chadsey (Eds.), *Beyond high school: Transition from school to work* (pp. 383–405). Belmont, CA: Wadsworth.

Gallivan-Fenlon, A. (1994). "Their senior year": Family and service provider perspectives on the transition from school to adult life for young adults with disabilities. *Journal of the Association for Persons with Severe Handicaps, 19*, 11–23.

Geenen, S., Powers, L., Vasquez, A. L., & Bersani, H. (2003). *CDEI, 26*(1), 1–2.

Gilliam, J. (1994). *Work Adjustment Inventory (WAI).* Austin, TX: PRO-ED.

Glutting, J. J., & Wilkinson, G. S. (2003). *Wide Range Interest and Occupation Test, Second edition* (WRIOT-2). Lutz, FL: Psychological Assessment Resources, Inc.

Greene, G. (1996). Empowering culturally and linguistically diverse families in the transition planning process. *Journal for Vocational Special Needs Education, 19*(1), 26–30.

Greene, G., & Nefsky, P. (1999). Transition for culturally and linguistically diverse youth with disabilities: Closing the gaps. *Multiple Voices for Ethnically Diverse Exceptional Learners, 3*(1), 15–24.

Hagner, D., Helm, D. T., & Butterworth, J. (1996). "This is your meeting": A qualitative study of person-centered planning. *Mental Retardation, 34*(3), 159–171.

Halpern, A. S., Herr, C. M., Wolf, N. K., Lawson, J. D., Doren, B., & Johnson, M. D. (1997). *Next S.T.E.P.: Student transition and educational planning. Teacher manual.* Eugene: University of Oregon.

Halpern, A. S., Irvin, L. K., & Munkeres, A. W. (1986). *Social and Prevocational Information Battery—Revised.* Monterey, CA: CTB McGraw-Hill.

Harris, L., & Associates, Inc. (2001). *N.O.D./Harris survey of Americans with disabilities.* New York: Author.

Jastak, J. F., & Jastak, S. R. (1980). *Wide range employability sample test.* Wilmington, DE: Jastak Associates.

Kaplan, R. M., & Saccuzzo, D. P. (2001). Psychological testing: Principles, applications, and issues (5th ed.). Stamford, CT: Wadsworth.

Leake, D., & Black, R. (2005). *Essential tools: Cultural and linguistic diversity: Implications for transition personnel.* Minneapolis, MN: University of Minnesota, Institute on Community Integration, National Center on Secondary Education and Transition.

Leake, D., & Cholymay, M. (2002). *Addressing the needs of linguistically diverse students with disabilities in postsecondary education.* Retrieved on October 14, 2006, from http://www.cld.hawaii.edu/final_products/PostsecBrief0503.htm

Lombard, R. C., Larsen, K. A., & Westphal, S. E. (1993). Validation of vocational assessment services for special populations in tech-prep: A model for translating the Perkins assurances into practice. *Journal for Vocational Special Needs Education, 16*(1), 14–22.

Luecking, R., & Fabian, E. S. (2000). Paid internships and employment success for youth in transition. *Career Development for Exceptional Individuals, 23*(2), 205–221.

Martin, J. E., & Marshall, L. H. (1995). ChoiceMaker: A comprehensive self-determination transition program. *Intervention in School and Clinic, 30,* 147–156.

McCarney, S. B., & Anderson, P. D. (2000). *Transition Behavior Scale—Second Edition* (TBS-2). Columbia, MO: Hawthorne.

Miner, C., & Bates, P. (1997). The effect of person-centered planning activities on the IEP/transition planning process. *Education and Training in Mental Retardation and Developmental Disabilities, 32,* 105–112.

Mooney, M., & School, L. (2004). Students with disabilities in Wisconsin youth apprenticeship programs: Supports and accommodations. *Career Development for Exceptional Individuals, 27,* 7–26.

Moss, K., & Wiley, D. (2003). A brief guide to personal futures planning: Organizing your community to envision and build a desirable future with you. Retrieved on June 25, 2007, from http://www.tsbvi.edu/outreach/deafblind/pcp-manual.pdf

Mount, B. (1989). *Making futures happen: A manual for facilitators of personal futures planning.* St. Paul, MN: Governor's Council on Developmental Disabilities.

National Center for Education Statistics. (1999). *An institutional perspective on students with disabilities in postsecondary education.* NCES 199-046. Washington, DC: U.S. Department of Education.

National Council on Disability. (2003). *People with disabilities and post-secondary education.* Position Paper. Washington, DC: National Council on Disability.

National Organization on Disability & Harris, L., & Associates. (2000). National Organization on Disability/Harris survey of American with disabilities. New York: Author.

NCSET (National Center of Secondary Education and Transition) & PACER Center. (2005). *Parent Brief: Age of majority: Preparing your child for making good choices. Promoting effective parent involvement in secondary education and transition.* Retrieved on October 1, 2005, from http://www.ncset.org/publications/viewdesc.asp?id=318

Parker, R. M. (2002). *Occupational aptitude survey and interest schedule* (3rd ed.). Austin, TX: PRO-ED.

Pearpoint, J. (1990). *From behind the piano: The building of Judith Snow's unique circle of friends.* Toronto, ON: Inclusion Press.

Ramasamy, R., Duffy, M., & Camp, J. (2000). Transition from school to adult life: Critical issues for Native American youth with and without learning disabilities. *CDEI, 23*(2), 157–171.

Scott, S., Shaw, S., & McGuire, J. (2003). Universal design for instruction: A new paradigm for adult instruction in postsecondary education. *Remedial and Special Education, 24*(6), 369–379.

Shafer, M. S., Banks, P. D., & Kregel, J. (1991). Employment retention and career movement among individuals with mental retardation working in supported employment. *Mental Retardation, 29,* 103–110.

Shaw, S. F. (2005). IDEA will change the face of postsecondary disability documentation. *Disability Compliance for Higher Education, 11*(1), 7.

Singer Company Career Systems. (1982). *Singer vocational evaluation system.* Rochester, NY: Singer.

Sitlington, P. L., & Frank, A. R. (1990). Are adolescents with learning disabilities successfully crossing the bridge into adult life? *Learning Disability Quarterly, 13,* 97–111.

Sitlington, P. L., Neubert, D. A., Begun, W., Lombard, R. C., & Leconte, P. J. (1996). *Assess for success.* Reston, VA: Council for Exceptional Children.

Spinelli, C. G. (2006). *Classroom assessment for students with special needs in inclusive settings* (2nd ed.). Upper Saddle River, NJ: Merrill/Pearson Education.

Stodden, R. A., Stodden, N. J., Kim-Rupnow, W. S., Thai, N. D., & Galloway, M. (2002). Providing effective support services for culturally and linguistically diverse persons with disabilities: Challenges and recommendations. *Journal of Vocational Rehabilitation, 17,* 1–13.

Storms, J., O'Leary, E., & Williams, J. (2000). *Transition requirements: A guide for states, districts, schools, universities and families.* The National Transition Network. Retrieved on November 5, 2005, from http://interact.uoregon.edu/wrrc/trnfiles

Strong, E. K., Jr., & Campbell, D. P. (1966). *Manual for Strong Vocational Interest Blank.* Stanford, CA: Stanford University Press.

Thomas, C., Rogan, P., & Baker, S. (2001). Student involvement in transition planning: Unheard voices. *Education and Training in Mental Retardation and Developmental Disabilities, 36*, 16–29.

Turnbull, A. P., Blue-Banning, M. J., Anderson, E. L., Turbull, H. R., Seaton, K. A., & Dinas, P. A. (1996). Enhancing self-determination through group action planning: A holistic emphasis. In D. J. Sands & M. L. Wehmeyer (Eds.), *Self-determination across the life span: Independence and choice for people with disabilities* (pp. 237–256). Baltimore: Paul H. Brookes.

U.S. Department of Education. (2001). *To assure the free appropriate education of all children with disabilities: Twenty-third annual report to Congress on the implementation of the Individuals with Disabilities Education Act.* Washington, DC: Author.

U.S. Department of Labor. (1991). *Dictionary of occupational titles* (4th ed.) Washington, DC: U.S. Government Printing Office.

Van Reusen, A. K., Bos, C. S., Schumaker, J. B., & Deshler, D. D. (1994). *The Self-Advocacy Strategy for Education and Transition Planning.* Lawrence, KS: Edge Enterprises.

VRI Career Planning Solutions. (1995). Career Scope. Retrieved on October 21, 2006, from http://vri.org/careerscope/index.html

Wagner, M., Newman, L., Cameto, R., Garza, N., & Levine, P. (2005). *After high school: A first look at the postschool experiences of youth with disabilities. A report from the National Longitudinal Transition Study—2* (NLTS2). Menlo Park, CA: SRI International.

Wehmeyer, M. L. (2002). Self-determined assessment: Critical components for transition planning. In C. L. Sax & C. A. Thoma (Eds.) *Transition assessment: Wise practices for quality lives* (pp. 25–38). Baltimore: Paul H. Brookes.

Wehmeyer, M. L., & Agran, M. (2005). Mental retardation and intellectual disabilities: Teaching students using innovative and research-based strategies. Boston, MA: Merrill/Prentice Hall.

Wehmeyer, M., & Lawrence, M. (1995). Whose future is it anyway?: Promoting student involvement in transition planning. *Career Development for Exceptional Individuals, 18*, 69–83.

Wehmeyer, M. L., & Palmer, S. B. (2003). Adult outcomes for sudents with cognitive disabilities three years after high school: The impact of self-determination. *Education and Training in Developmental Disabilities, 38*(2), 131–144.

Wehmeyer, M., & Schwartz, M. (1997). Self-determination and positive adult outcomes: follow-up of youth with mental retardation or learning disabilities. *Exceptional Children, 63*(2), 245–255.

Interpreting and Linking Assessment to Instruction

CHAPTER 13

Interpreting Tests and Reports

Interpreting Tests and Reports

Prereferral strategies: Strategies that are attempted before a referral is made.

Gross motor movements: Motor movements involving large muscles.

Fine motor movements: Motor movements involving small muscles.

Language: Phonology, morphology, semantics, syntax, and pragmatics.

Adaptive behavior skills: Language, social, health and safety, home living, self-care, leisure, work, functional academics, community use, and other areas.

Age score equivalents: The age level at which the student is performing.

Grade score equivalents: The grade level at which the student is performing.

Standard scores: Involve the use of standard deviation.

Standard deviation: Allows the interpreter to place the student's performance on the normal curve to see how he or she has performed compared to other students.

Percentile ranks: The percentage of students who scored above or below the level of the student.

Stanines: Separate the normal curve into nine pieces (1–9).

Individualized education program (IEP): A written record that guides instruction and measurable progress of a student's intervention program.

Least restrictive environment: Students should be participating in the general curriculum to the highest degree possible.

Case Study: Assessing Nicholas

Nicholas is a third-grade student in your class. He often gets up from his chair, talks to students, giggles, and needs several reminders to focus on assignments. When he does focus on assignments in class, he does so with more than 90 percent accuracy (based on observations). Sometimes, however he does not make much progress on the assignments at hand. Teachers in social studies and physical education report problematic behavior. In addition, after-school park district staff reports that Nicholas has a difficult time following directions. His parents are very involved in the educational process, and he completes his homework almost all of the time. They report that it takes him a long time to begin homework, but he completes it very quickly (15 minutes) once he starts. Depending on his or her work schedule, each parent assists Nicholas.

Nicholas is referred for an evaluation after some attempts at prereferral strategies were unsuccessful. Those attempts included prompts, behavior charts, and outlines. Nicholas is given visual, motor, and auditory screenings. He also participates in formal and informal speech and language, achievement, intelligence, adaptive skills, behavior, and visual-motor integration assessment.

Results reveal scores within limits in the visual, motor, auditory, adaptive skills, and visual-motor areas. Results reveal scores about 2 standard deviations above the mean in intelligence and achievement domains. However, informal behavior skills in some settings appear problematic, as mentioned above (i.e., excessive talking, movement, and distractibility). A functional behavior analysis reveals that when Nicholas is bored with work, he acts inappropriately. When Nicholas is presented with appropriate levels of challenge in his academic work, he is more focused. When activities include some movement, Nicholas is also more focused.

What do you make of these results?

How do you explain the results to parents in terms of individual domains and an overall picture?

Is the child eligible for special education services? Why or why not?

Are there follow-up evaluations you can suggest?

What do you propose as solutions to any issues?

By the end of the chapter, you should be able to discuss the questions posed in the chapter-opening case study of Nicholas. You should also be able to explain the process by which assessors report information in the evaluation process. You should be able to name and give examples of components of a report. You should also be able to utilize these concepts to discuss results of formal assessment methods in terms of the meaning of comparisons of students to others of the same age or grade level. You should be able to discuss not only these formal assessment results but also informal assessment results with parents. You should be able to take overall evaluation information, subtest information, and informal assessment information to determine the strengths and needs of the student, and then be able to link this information with instruction via individualized education program (IEP) or individual transition plan (ITP) planning.

Standards corresponding to the information in this chapter include CEC Standard 3 (individual learning differences), Standard 7 (instructional planning), Standard 8 (assessment), and Standard 9 (professional and ethical practice) (Council for Exceptional Children, 2003). Information regarding definition, identification, assessment instruments, formal and informal assessments, influence of diversity, and assessment decision information will facilitate learning toward these standards. Cultural diversity affecting families and communities is also discussed in this chapter.

COMPONENTS OF THE EVALUATION REPORT

Students who have participated in an evaluation by a multidisciplinary team receive a written report regarding the types of formal and informal assessment procedures used, as well as the results of those assessment tools. Interpretations of those outcomes are discussed within the report. The core of this interpretation involves the question of eligibility. If the student is found to be eligible for services, information used in the report leads to the formation of educational goals and objectives for the student. See Figure 13.1.

BACKGROUND INFORMATION

Typically, student information, such as age, grade level, address, and dates and times the information was gathered, are included in the beginning of the report. Referral source and concerns are defined in the next portion of the report. Birth and developmental history are then discussed. Any remarkable information is included. For example, if the birth process was long or difficult, the umbilical cord was wrapped around the neck, or any bluish coloring appeared, it would be reported in this section. Developmental milestones are listed; for example, the age when sitting, walking, and first words occurred are included in this section.

MEDICAL, ACADEMIC, AND SOCIAL INFORMATION

Medical, academic, and social information follow background information. Any hospitalizations, surgeries, allergies, and/or ear infections are included in this section. Any family

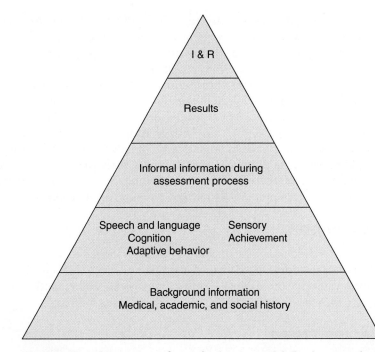

Figure 13.1 Components of an evaluation report. I & R = interpretations and recommendations.

history of disabilities is reported. Teacher reports, artifacts from class activities, parental or student report regarding response to homework, changing schools, and attendance records would be discussed in this portion of the report. An important aspect of this section includes any prereferral strategies that were attempted. Student response to those methods is an important aspect of informal assessment. Settings involved in student behaviors include vital information for the team to consider. Social history from parent, student, and teacher interviews follows. Examples of how the student responds to peers, teachers, and other adults are discussed.

SPEECH AND LANGUAGE

Speech and language assessment tools and results are presented next. Information regarding speech and language, phonology, morphology, semantics, syntax, pragmatics, and voice can be included. Receptive and expressive language components are discussed. Informal as well as formal assessment information is included in this section. Examples of informal assessment include observations, language samples, and interviews. Examples of formal assessments include the Peabody Picture Vocabulary Test IV (PPVT-IV) (Dunn & Dunn, 2007) and the Test of Language Development—Primary (3rd ed.) (TOLD-P:3) (Newcomer & Hammill, 1997).

SENSORY

Sensory information can include hearing, motor, and visual assessment data. In terms of hearing issues, conductive hearing loss, sensory-neural hearing loss, mixed hearing loss, otitis media, surplus ear wax, and/or central auditory disorders can be examined in this portion. Pure-tone audiometry and speech and word recognition tasks can be used to determine hearing ability. Air-conduction and bone-conduction hearing testing and tympanometry assessment can be used in this portion of the evaluation report.

In the areas of gross- (large muscles) and fine- (small muscles) motor skills, muscle strength, muscle control, range of motion, balance, posture, and assistive or technology needs are discussed. The Bruininks-Oseretsky Test of Motor Proficiency—2 (Bruininks & Bruininks, 2005) is an example of a formal test in the areas of gross- and fine-motor skills. A physical therapist (gross motor) and/or an occupational therapist (fine motor) can be involved in this section of the evaluation.

Areas of visual assessments can include visual discrimination (differentiate), coordination (track), memory (recall), and/or association (relate). Assessment of visual acuity, color vision, functional vision, influence of lighting and background, and use of braille can be included in this portion of the report. A vision specialist can be part of the testing and interpretation process. Areas of cognition, achievement, and adaptive behavior skills then follow. Descriptions of tools and results are included in the discussion.

COGNITION

Examples of cognition can include, but are not limited to, perceptual organization, spatial abilities, memory, speed, knowledge, and abstract thinking. Formal test possibilities include the Standford-Binet—Fifth Edition (Roid, 2003) and Wechsler Intelligence Scale for Children—Fourth Edition (WISC-IV) (Wechsler, 2003).

ACHIEVEMENT

Areas of achievement can include reading, writing, and mathematics information. Examples of formal test options include Kaufman Test of Educational Achievement (K-TEA-II) (Kaufman & Kaufman, 2004) and the Woodcock-Johnson III NU Tests of Achievement (WJ-NU III) (Woodcock, McGrew, & Mather, 2006).

ADAPTIVE BEHAVIOR SKILLS

Adaptive behavior skills can include language, social, health and safety, home living, self-care, leisure, work, functional academics, community use, and other areas. Examples of formal tests are the Adaptive Behavior Evaluation Scale—Revised (ABES-R) (McCarney, 1995) and the Scales of Independent Behavior—Revised (SIB-R) (Bruininks, Woodcock, Weatherman, & Hill, 1996).

INFORMAL INFORMATION AND ASSESSMENT PROCESS

General assessment information regarding student response during the evaluation are provided (Sattler, 2001). For example, which modality did the student prefer? Did the student repeat questions or answers? Did the student need and ask for repetitions? Did the student appear tired, distracted, frustrated? How did the student respond to testing, successes, failures, and the examiner? Did the student use any repetitive or stereotypical responses or movements? Did the student use appropriate eye contact, language, and behaviors? Were there items that provided reinforcements? Did the student prefer certain activities or tools? In diagnostic use of equipment, what worked best for the student? Do you have any concerns that require a follow-up evaluation or involvement of other professionals? Another section would follow to discuss results, interpretations, and recommendations.

RESULTS

First, some core questions need to be addressed. Are there any factors such as cultural and/or linguistic diversity issues that might affect the validity of the test? Were any of the tests used qualitatively instead of quantitatively due to these issues? That is, the norms were not used, but items were used for descriptive nature. Was a translator or interpreter utilized? How did that affect the evaluation and results?

The evaluator notes which formal and informal assessments were administered. Descriptions of the assessment domains, subtests, examples of tasks, and examples of items are noted. The professional then reports formal test results of each test in terms of standard score, standard deviation, age equivalent, and percentile rank score. Examples of items missed are supplied. The evaluator groups tests assessing similar domains. A description of informal results follows the corresponding formal tests.

INTERPRETATION AND RECOMMENDATION

When you look at all of the pieces of informal and formal testing, what services are indicated? Are the results consistent? How does the student perform on overall performance? How does the student score on subtests? What are the strengths and needs of the student? Are there significant areas of weakness, or is there poor performance globally across the areas of assessment? Are professionals and family members in agreement regarding areas of difficulties?

What are these difficulties? Give examples of items you would have expected the student to have correct answers to that he or she did not. What is the pattern? For example, is it phonology? What are the sounds? In what context are the difficulties expressed? Are the difficulties expressed across the board? For example, is the student scoring more than 2 standard deviations below level across all areas?

Based on these strengths, needs, and legal requirements, what services do you recommend? What supports and services does the student need? What setting do you recommend that the student be placed in based on least restrictive environment? Why? What ongoing monitoring will be needed to lead to the best program for this student?

Breakpoint Practice

1. What are the main components of an evaluation report?
2. Which section do you think has the most risk of subjectivity? Why?
3. What types of information go in the family history portion of the report? How could this be a delicate situation?
4. Why is it important to keep information realistic yet positive?
5. How can you demonstrate cultural sensitivity in writing and interpreting an evaluation report?

COMPARISONS WITH OTHER STUDENTS

A holistic interpretation of various formal and informal assessment results goes into a collaborative decision-making process. One aspect of this interpretive process is analyzing formal test results. As mentioned in Chapter 3, the main purpose of norm-referenced testing is to compare students to other students of the same age or grade level to get a deeper understanding of where the student stands in terms of his or her skills. Raw scores (number of items correct) are converted to standardized scores. Standardized scores include and are not limited to age scores, grade scores, standard scores, percentile ranks, and stanines.

AGE AND GRADE SCORES

Age scores indicate the age level at which the student is performing. The importance of this term is whether the student is at age level. If a student is 8 years old and scores an age score of 5, he or she has scored 3 years below age level.

Grade scores indicate the grade level at which the student is performing. Like the age score, the evaluator is interested to see whether the student is scoring at grade level. If a student is in the fifth-grade and scores at the fifth-grade level, he or she is scoring at grade level. The American Psychological Association (1999) discourages the use of age and grade scores due to generalization and possible misinterpretation. There is a range of accepted performance, usually ± one grade (for example, fifth graders range from fourth grade to sixth grade).

STANDARD SCORES

Standard scores involve the use of standard deviation. Means are determined based on student scores on age and grade levels from the norm group results. Use of standard deviations (SD) allows the interpreter to place the student's performance on the curve to see how he or she has performed compared to other students. Typically the means are 100 and standard deviations are 15. Cutoffs for scores within the mean (average scores) are 85 for the lower point in the continuum and 115 for the higher point in the continuum. Therefore, a score of 120 is more than 1 standard deviation above the mean. In addition, a score of 80 is more than 1 standard deviation below the mean. Scores beyond these cutoff points are considered significant except in the case of intelligence, where 2 standard deviations are considered significant. In the case of intelligence, 70 and 130 serve as the cutoff points for significance.

For example, when utilizing a test of cognition, a score of 60 would fall into the significant range, but a score of 80 would not (2 SD cutoff). In the case of language, scores of both 80 and 60 fall into the significant range (1 SD cutoff).

PERCENTILE RANKS AND STANINES

Percentile ranks describe the percentage of students who scored below the level of the student. If Suzie scored a 50 percent, she scored the same as or better than 50 percent of the individuals who took the test. She has scored in the average range. Percentile ranks are generally easy to comprehend. However, the percentile units are not of equal length. Both ends of the curve are accentuated (Venn, 2007). Stanines separate the normal curve into nine pieces (1–9). Stanines have a mean of 5 and a standard deviation of 2. Significance points are 3 (lower point) and 7 (higher point).

Tests measuring a variety of areas can be compared in terms of student performance by using these standardized scores. One or two areas that indicate poorer performance as compared to other areas can signify learning, language, motor, or other difficulties. Weak performance in multiple areas can indicate global difficulties, which gives the interpreter a different picture (i.e., the possibility of mental retardation).

Breakpoint Practice

1. What are the pros and cons to providing information based on an age or grade score?
2. What are the pros and cons to providing information based on a percentile rank?
3. What are the pros and cons to providing information based on standard deviations?

COMMUNICATING RESULTS

Presenting information regarding the results of multiple assessments and overall impressions of those results to the student and his or her family members is an important part of the educational process. Family members and the student can be understandably anxious regarding the results of the evaluation. However, meaningful interpretations can provide knowledge and motivation (Borich & Tombari, 2004) to the student.

ELIGIBILITY

As reported in IDEA 2004, an individual with a disability is one who has mental retardation, hearing difficulties, speech and/or language difficulties, visual difficulties, serious emotional difficulties, orthopedic difficulties, autism, traumatic brain injury, other health difficulties, or specific learning impairments and needs special education and related services (see Chapters 1 and 5 through 11).

CONNECTING ELIGIBILITY WITH AN ACTION PLAN

It is important to strike a balance between encouragement and realistic expectations for the student. A better understanding of the smaller pieces of each domain can help the student target the area needed to succeed. A structured plan aiming at appropriate goals can provide a clearer path in terms of where to focus energies and experience success. More knowledge and success can initiate the student's higher levels of self-evaluation and involvement in the assessment and instruction process.

More understanding of the domains and plan of action is not limited to the student and his or her family members. Educators can also improve their motivation and success levels based on this information. This working plan can help them focus their energies in the most useful aspects of the educational process. Teachers who provide students with instruction that has appropriate levels of difficulty and who actively involve students in learning produce higher academic achievement (Mastropieri, Scruggs, Mantizicopoulos, Sturgeon, Goodwin, & Chung, 1998). It is important that the process of communication and collaboration be continued during ongoing assessment and instruction to optimize learning outcomes. This is the ultimate link of assessment to instruction.

Breakpoint Practice

1. In teams of two, practice giving and receiving information that a child has scored 2 standard deviations below level in several areas of achievement testing. One student takes the role of a parent and the other the role of the evaluator. Give each other constructive feedback.
2. What if a parent tells you he or she disagrees with your results? What do you say?
3. What if a parent starts sobbing during the information session? What do you do?

LINKING ASSESSMENT AND INSTRUCTION

Information explored and gathered through the evaluation process is critical in providing teachers with the student's strengths and needs. This essential individual assessment information is meant to form a framework that best guides instruction of the student. Information regarding levels and types of materials used, modality of presentation, instructional and assessment adaptations, and assistive and/or adaptive technology is meant to be used by the student and teacher in the classroom, as well as at home with the family.

Not only is it important to have a good understanding of the student's strengths and needs, it is also critical to know the classroom environment in which the student is participating (Janney & Snell, 2004). This dynamic process is an essential area of knowledge that the instructional team must possess to help the student be successful.

INDIVIDUALIZED EDUCATION PROGRAM

An individualized education program (IEP) is a written record that guides instruction and measurable progress of a student's intervention program. Parental approval and input direct the design of the IEP, which takes place within 30 school days of disability determination. Assessment team members, individuals who see the student every day (i.e., parents, general education teacher, special education teacher, administrator) and professionals who provide itinerant services (i.e., assessment expert, social worker, medical professional, occupational therapist, physical therapist, and others) are also IEP members (Statewide Parent Advocacy Network, Inc., 2000). By law, one or both parents, the student's teacher, a special educator, the student, and others invited by the parent or local education agency are present for the IEP meeting. The IEP ensures that all parties involved are aware of the educational program for the student (Wright & Wright, 2003).

The IEP is driven by standards and age-appropriate activities. In addition, the student's and parents' choice must be incorporated into the IEP. The appropriate, functional, and authentic nature of instruction should be considered in the formation of these goals and activities.

According to IDEA, the student's current levels of performance guide development of annual goals, short-term objectives, services (special education, related, and transition), settings, adaptations, assessments, and a plan for evaluation of a student's program. A placement decision is also made by the participants of the meeting. Also, the possibility of extending the school year is decided. The IEP team can include additional training for the student's teacher (Autism Society of America, n.d.).

Related Services

According to IDEA, services include psychological, social work, occupational therapy, speech/language pathology, recreation, physical therapy, health, counseling, vision, audiology, and transportation services. The IEP can also direct curriculum adaptations, assistive technology, resource center use, behavior and social skills services, and use of aides and itinerate teachers.

Placement

A placement choice is made reflecting assessment results and teacher, student, and parents' input. The IEP goals should be able to be accomplished in the setting chosen (Bridges4Kids, 2007). Least restrictive environment (LRE) is an important factor in the placement of the student. LRE was defined by Congress and dictates that students should be participating in the general curriculum to the highest degree possible. Even with adaptations and/or an aide, the student may or may not be optimally served in the general classroom setting. Therefore, there is a continuum of services listed within LRE. Those options include a general education classroom; general education classroom with adaptations and/or services; resource room; separate classroom in a general education setting; separate school; or home, institution, or hospital.

Extended School Year

Extended school year (ESY) is examined and determined during the IEP process. This free and appropriate public education (FAPE) program is available through the school district. The team discusses the possibility that regression of life skills could take place during a length of time that the student would not be attending school (e.g., summer). Differences regarding eligibility for ESY services exist.

Every student with a disability is not required to participate in ESY. There is no distinct criterion in determining whether a student will receive ESY. The team reflects on the regression and failure to recover skills, progress toward goals, emerging skills, behaviors, and the nature of the student's disability (e.g., alternative resources, vocational needs, interaction with nondisabled peers) (www.wrightslaw.com/info/esy.index.htm) contributing to mastery of IEP goals. Maintenance skill services (i.e., math) in individual or group instruction, home instruction, consultation, and recreation and community services (Pinkerton, 1990) are options for ESY. The ESY services may be different from the school year program.

Progress Monitoring

Monitoring of student progress means continuous assessment of the student's progress using formal and informal tools. Information regarding the student's performance related to the instructional program is shared with the family at least several times during the year. Students are also involved in the process because they are the number 1 consumers of assessment data. Students using data entry to self-monitor can assist in setting aim/goal line. This process requires conferencing with the teacher if three points on the graph are below the goal line.

Stecker (n.d.) reported that curriculum-based measurement (CBM) is a useful tool in developing goals, benchmarks, and/or short-term objectives for the IEP process. She noted that baseline CBM scores (three to six consecutive scores of the student) can be used as present levels of performance. The goal line from the CBM graph can be used to predict a long-term goal. From this graph, short-term objectives can be determined. CBM can be used to monitor progress during the year of implementation. By monitoring on a monthly basis, instruction can be changed to meet the student's needs. Stecker added that software can help educators with the assessment process. CBM is a tool grounded in research and has the promise of providing educators assistance in constructing and monitoring meaningful IEPs (Yell & Stecker, 2003).

As the ongoing assessment and decision making are taking place, the program is shaped to best meet the student's needs. This includes changes to short-term objectives (after an additional meeting) and instruction and/or assessment procedures. An annual review of the IEP is a legal requirement that serves as a periodic evaluation and guide to special education services. Reevaluation is also an important aspect of determining whether special education services are appropriate for a student.

Breakpoint Practice

1. What do you do if a student is having great difficulty meeting his or her goal?

2. What do you do if the goal is too easy for the student you are attempting to serve?

3. What do you do if the parents disagree with the placement or number of minutes of service per week indicated by the rest of the team?

Multicultural Considerations

When developing IEPs for individuals who are culturally and/or linguistically diverse, additional requirements may apply in some states. For example, Illinois requires that when a student has limited English proficiency, an additional IEP team member should be added (Brusca-Vega, 2002). This additional team member can be a qualified bilingual teacher or specialist. If a student has limited English proficiency, those language needs, as well as any cultural and linguistic adaptations, should be included. The language or mode of communication is also specified (Brusca-Vega, 2002).

Researchers have also looked at placement and materials and addressed possible solutions to challenges in the area of culture and IEP meetings. For example, Baca and Payon (1989) included a number of variables in determining placement decisions for students who were bilingual and eligible for special education services. Some of those include the level of language difficulties, adaptive behavior, and time spent in the United States.

In addition, Baca and Cervantes (1989) noted considerations for assessing, choosing, or utilizing materials for individuals who were English language learners. Some of those examples include cultural experiences, investigating many options for students until successful, and being aware of student language abilities. Hoover and Collier (1989) include considerations for teacher-made tools used for bilingual special education. Some were adaptations to reading level and response mode and the use of study guides.

Burnette (2000) noted four principles in guiding more successful IEP meetings with families who are culturally and/or linguistically diverse. She discussed integrating interpreters, bilingual professionals, and individuals with cultural knowledge of the student. Burnette also included gaining knowledge regarding whether a student's culture or experiences are contributing to difficulties with strategies. She added that appropriate language during testing and individualized assessment practices in multiple contexts were important.

Breakpoint Practice

1. What are some challenges that can arise in the IEP planning of a student who is both bilingual and qualified for special education services?

2. What are some solutions to each of the areas you noted in question 1?

REVISITING NICHOLAS

Nicholas is testing well within normal limits on most areas of assessment. In some cases, he is testing above normal limits. Therefore, Nicholas does not qualify for services. Connected to this case study is the level of work as associated with Nicholas's behavior. It appears that when the work is appropriately challenging to Nicholas, his behavior improves. Changing the learning environment to better suit Nicholas's needs would thus help him with behavior issues. That is, Nicholas needs appropriately challenging instruction (i.e., learning materials and tasks).

ACTIVITIES

Read the following assessment results and respond to the questions below.

Case Study

Joseph is a new student in your class who recently moved into your school district. He is bilingual in Spanish and English. You notice in his evaluation report that a number of items are missing, but you try to understand the results the best you can.

> Date of Birth: 12/02/01
> Date of Evaluation: 04/02/08

REFERRAL INFORMATION

Joseph's former teacher referred him for an evaluation. He had concerns regarding Joseph's school performance. Joseph was having a hard time keeping up with reading and writing tasks. He also appeared frustrated. Joseph threw several assignments in the trash.

HISTORY

Joseph's parents reported that Joseph's birth and delivery were unremarkable. Developmental milestones, with the exception of communication, occurred within normal limits, with the following reported: sitting unsupported at six months, crawling at six months, and walking independently at twelve months. Joseph's health history was marked by occasional colds, which were treated with decongestants. An earache was noted to follow a cold occasionally.

FAMILY-SOCIAL INFORMATION

Joseph lives at home with his mother, father, 10-year old sister, 2-year-old brother, and paternal grandmother. Spanish and English are spoken within the home. Joseph's parents work outside the home.

EVALUATION

The following tests were administered to Joseph:

> Wechsler Intelligence Scale for Children—Fourth Edition (WISC-IV)
> Woodcock Johnson III NU Tests of Achievement (WJ/NU-III)
> Vineland Adaptive Behavior Scales (Survey Form)
> Peabody Picture Vocabulary Test-IV (PPVT-IV)

Informal assessments included observations, interviews, language samples, and artifacts from classroom work.

Cognition

WISC-IV

Verbal Subtests		Performance	
Information	8	Picture completion	10
Similarities	6	Picture arrangement	10
Arithmetic	10	Block design	9
Vocabulary	6	Object assembly	9
Digit span	9	Comprehension	5
		Coding	9

Observations   Joseph was observed for three 30-minute time intervals (total of three hours) in the classroom, at lunch, and during recess over a two-week period by two different observers. Observations of Joseph in the classroom, at lunch, and during recess revealed mixed results. Joseph appeared frustrated with written work and class activities involving language arts. He made some comments and facial expressions during those tasks. During lunch and recess, no such instances were noted.

Adaptive Behavior Skills

Vineland Adaptive Behavior Scales
Communication Domain
Daily Living Skills Domain
Motor Skills Domain
Standard Score = 100

Language

PPVT-IV
Stanine = 2

Observations of Joseph revealed instances where he asked the speaker to repeat words. Interviews with his parents indicated that he did not have difficulties in understanding Spanish. Interviews with teachers indicated that he sometimes was not able to answer questions in conversation in English only.

A language sample revealed a mean language utterance (MLU) of 5.2. This reveals results two years below age level in the area of expressive language.

Achievement

Woodcock Johnson III/NU Tests of Achievement

Cluster	Percentile
Verbal ability	10
Oral expression	5
Listening comprehension	10
Broad reading	5
Broad written language	5
Broad math	20
Math calculation skills	30
Math reasoning	30
Basic writing skills	5
Written expression	5

Artifacts in the areas of math, reading, science, and social studies were inconsistent. Joseph had incomplete classroom assignments. When a writing task was involved, it decreased the level of completion of the assignment. Joseph sometimes did not follow the directions noted.

Charted performance-based measurements of math, reading, science, and social studies were inconsistent. Math performance appeared appropriate. However, reading, science, and social studies slopes indicated weak performance.

Answer the following questions in your discussion of the previous information.

1. Prereferral

   a. Which two prereferral intervention strategies would you have attempted?

   b. Which two prereferral assessment strategies would you have considered?

   c. What input from the teacher and other staff members would have helped with this assessment? Name at least two types.

   d. What two types of information in the medical/developmental history do you find significant in terms of the student's issues?

   e. What two questions would you ask the parents to increase your understanding about the student?

2. Interpretation:

   a. What do the results of the cognitive test given to Joseph mean?

   b. What do the results of the achievement test given to Joseph mean?

   c. What do the results of the adaptive behavior test given to Joseph mean?

   d. What do the results of the language test given to Joseph mean?

   e. What five informal performance measures would you have performed?

3. What are three of Joseph's strengths?

4. What are three of Joseph's needs?

5. Identify and discuss at least five other factors that may influence the interpretation of Joseph's performance.

WEB RESOURCES

http://www.pacer.org/Parent/iep.htm

http://ncset.org/topics/ieptransition/default.asp?topic=28

http://www.naset.org/2224.0.html

http://www.ed.gov/parents/needs/speced/iepguide/index.html

http://www.bridges4kids.org/IEP/Goals.html

http://www.teach-nology.com/teachers/special_ed/iep

http://www.ldonline.org/indepth/iep

http://www.wrightslaw.com/info/iep.index.htm

REFERENCES

American Psychological Association. (1999). *Standards for educational and psychological testing.* Washington, DC: Author.

Autism Society of America. (n.d.). Improving educational opportunities. Retrieved on June 26, 2007, from http://www.autism-society.org/site/PageServer?pagename=govt_education

Baca, L. M., & Cervantes, H. T. (Eds.). (1989). *The bilingual special education interface* (2nd ed.). Upper Saddle River, NJ: Merrill/Pearson Education.

Baca, L. M., & Payon, R. M. (1989). Development of the bilingual special education interface. In L. M. Baca & H. T. Cervantes (Eds.), *The bilingual special education interface* (pp. 79–99). Upper Saddle River, NJ: Merrill/Pearson Education.

Borich, G. D., & Tombari, M. L. (2004). *Educational assessment for the elementary and middle school classroom* (2nd ed.). Upper Saddle River, NJ: Merrill/Pearson Education.

Bridges4Kids. (2007). IEP issues—Placement issues. Retrieved on June 26, 2007, from http://www
.bridges4kids.org/IEP/Placement.html

Bruininks, R. H., & Bruininks, B. D. (2005). *Bruininks-Oresky Test of Motor Proficiency* (2nd ed.).
Circle Pines, MN: American Guidance Service.

Bruininks, R. H., Woodcock, R. W., Weatherman, R. F., & Hills, B. K. (1996). *Scales of Independent
Behavior—Revised* (SIB-R). Itasca, IL: Houghton Mifflin.

Brusca-Vega, R. (2002). *Developing IEPs for English Language Learners.* Retrieved on June 26,
2007, from http://www.isbe.state.il/us/spec-ed/bilingualnamed2002.html

Burnette, J. (2000). Assessment of culturally and linguistically diverse students for special education eligibility. Retrieved on June 26, 2007, from http://ericec.org/digests/e604.html

Council for Exceptional Children. (2003). Retrieved on June 26, 2007, from http://www.cec
.sped.org/Content/NavigationMenu/Professional/Development/ProfessionalStandards/
Red_book_5th_edition.pdf

Dunn, L. M., & Dunn, D. M. (2007). *Peabody Picture Vocabulary Test-4 (PPVT-IV).* Circle Pines,
MN: American Guidance Service.

Hoover, J. J., & Collier, C. (1989). Methods and materials for bilingual special education. In L.
M. Baca & H. T. Cervantes (Eds.), *The bilingual special education interface* (pp. 231–255).
Columbus, OH: Merrill.

Janney, R., & Snell, M. E. (2004). *Modifying schoolwork* (2nd ed.). Brookes: Baltimore.

Kaufman, A. S., & Kaufman, N. L. (2004). *Kaufman Test of Educational Achievement—Second
Edition* (K-TEA II). Circle Pines, MN: American Guidance Service.

Mastropieri, M. A., Scruggs, T. E., Mantzicopoulos, P. Y., Sturgeon, A., Goodwin, L., & Chung, S.
(1998). A place where living things affect and depend upon each other: Qualitative and quantitative outcomes associated with inclusive science teaching. *Science Education, 82,* 163–179.

McCarney, S. B. (1995). *Adaptive Behavior Evaluation Scale—Revised* (ABES-R). Columbia,
MO: Hawthorne Educational Services.

Newcomer, P. L., & Hammill, D. D. (1997). *Test of Language Development—Primary:3* (TOLD-
P:3). Austin, TX: PRO-ED.

Pinkerton, D. (1990). Extended School Year. Retrieved on June 26, 2007, from http://kidsource
.com/kidsource/content3/extended.school.k12.2.html

Roid, G. (2004). *The Standford-Binet Intelligence Scale* (5th ed.). Chicago: Riverside.

Sattler, J. M. (2001). *Assessment of children: Behavioral and clinical applications* (4th ed.). San
Diego, CA: Author.

Statewide Parent Advocacy Network, Inc. (2000). Retrieved on June 26, 2007, from http://www
.spannj.org/BasicRights/index.html

Stecker, P. M. (n.d.). Monitoring student progress in individualized educational programs
using curriculum-based measurement. http://www.nichcy.org/parentkit/monitoring_student_
progress_in_ieps_using_cbm.pdf

Venn, J. J. (2007). *Assessing students with special needs* (4th ed.). Upper Saddle, NJ: Merrill/
Pearson Education.

Wechsler, D. (2003). *The Wechsler Intelligence Scale for Children* (4th ed.). San Antonio, TX: The
Psychological Corporation.

Woodcock, R. W., McGrew, K. S., & Mather, N. (2006). *Woodcock-Johnson III NU Tests of
Achievement.* Itasca, IL: Riverside.

Wright, P. W., & Wright, P. D. (2003). Your child's IEP: Practical and legal guidance for parents.
Retrieved on June 26, 2007, from http://www.ldonline.org/article/6078

Wrightslaw. (Unknown author). Extended School Year. Retrieved on May 4, 2006, from
http://www.wrightslaw.com/info/esy.index.htm

Yell, M. L., & Stecker, P. M. (2003). Developing legally correct and educationally meaningful
IEPs using curriculum-based measurement. *Assessment for Effective Intervention, 28,* 73–88.

SUBJECT INDEX

AAIDD. *See* American Association on Intellectual Developmental Disabilities

AAMR. *See* American Association on Mental Retardation

ABC procedure of direct observation, 89

Abstract nouns, 185, 188

Academic information, in evaluation report, 290–291

Accommodations in assessment, 19, 52–53, 164, 256–257. *See also* Assistive technology

Achenbach System of Empirically Based Assessment (ASEBA), 98

Achenbach System of Empirically Based Assessment (ASEBA), 102, 104

Achievement, in evaluation report, 292

Achievement assessment, 162–183
  accommodations in testing, 164
  achievement defined, 123, 164
  achievement tests, 163
  aptitude tests, 163
  diagnostic tests, 163, 164
  and disabilities, 178–179
  group achievement tests, 167–168
  group tests, 163, 164, 166
  high-stakes group testing, 166
  individual tests, 163, 164, 166
  Individuals with Disabilities Education Act (IDEA), 164, 166
  informal assessment, 164
  interviews, 164
  legal implications, 164–166
  math tests, 175–176, 177
  measures of achievement, 166–176
  multicultural considerations, 176–180
  multiple-area diagnostic achievement tests, 169–172
  No Child Left Behind (NCLB), 166
  norm-referenced tests, 164
  observations, 164
  portfolios, 164
  projects, 164

reading tests, 172–174, 177
screening tests, 163, 164
and socioeconomic status, 178
standardized tests, 164
standards-based assessment, 164, 166
and technology strategies, 179–180
WJ III Achievement Test, 165
written expression tests, 174–175

Achievement tests, 163

Acting-out behaviors, 85

Action plan, 295

ADA. *See* Americans with Disabilities Act (ADA) of 1990

Adaptation, and visual impairment assessment, 231

Adapted Kohs Block Design Test, 136

Adaptive behavior, 143, 144–145

Adaptive Behavior Evaluation Scale-Revised (ABES-R), 148, 150, 292

Adaptive Behavior Inventory (ABI), 148, 151

Adaptive Behavior Scales School (ABS-S:2), 148, 149

Adaptive skills, 142–161, 143, 153
  adaptive behavior, 143, 144–145
  American Association on Mental Retardation's (AAMR) ten adaptive skills, 144, 147
  beliefs regarding, 156
  conceptual skills, 143, 144
  cultural bias, 145
  in evaluation report, 292
  extensive supports, 143, 147
  functional academics, 143
  functional curriculum, 153–154
  health, 144
  home safety, 144
  and the home-to-school connection, 156
  intermittent supports, 143, 146–147
  interpersonal skills, 143
  interpretation of, 289
  intrapersonal skills, 143
  limited supports, 143, 147
  measures of adaptive behavior, 148–153, 155. *See also* Measures of adaptive behavior

mental retardation defined, 145–146
multicultural considerations, 155–157
norm-referenced tests, 145
pervasive supports, 143, 147
practical skills, 143, 144, 145
pragmatic language, 143
quality of life issues, 144
self-advocacy, 143
self-determination, 143
self-direction, 143
social competence, 145
and social rules, 156–157
social skills, 143, 144, 145, 153–154
and specific etiologies, 154
supports, 143, 146–147
and technology, 147
thematic instruction, 143
transition, 143, 153
vocational training, 143

ADD-H: Comprehensive Teacher Rating Scale (ACTeRS), 105–106, 107

ADHD. *See* Attention-deficit hyperactivity disorder

ADHD Rating Scale (ADHD-IV), 106, 107

Adverbs, 185, 187, 188

Advocacy groups, for due process and civil rights to children with disabilities, 6

AFB. *See* American Foundation for the Blind

African Americans
  and achievement tests, 176–180
  and adaptive skills, 156
  African American English, 198, 199–200, 225
  behavioral assessment of, 113–114
  Brown v. Board of Education of Topeka, Kansas, 405
  and caregivers, 157
  curriculum-based measurement (CBM) for, 74
  Fourteenth Amendment, 4
  Hobson v. Hansen, 5
  and intelligence tests, 137
  and language assessment, 197–198, 200

311